MAY SWENSON

MAY SWENSON

COLLECTED POEMS

Langdon Hammer, *editor*

THE LIBRARY OF AMERICA

Volume compilation, notes, and chronology copyright © 2013 by
Literary Classics of the United States, Inc., New York, N.Y.
All rights reserved.
No part of the book may be reproduced commercially
by offset-lithographic or equivalent copying devices without
the permission of the publisher.

Poems from *The Complete Love Poems of May Swenson* copyright © 1991, 2003
by The Literary Estate of May Swenson. Reprinted by permission of
Houghton Mifflin Harcourt Publishing Company. All rights reserved.

Poems from *Another Animal* copyright © 1954, 1982; *A Cage of Spines*
copyright © 1958, 1986; *To Mix with Time* copyright © 1963, 1991; *Half Sun
Half Sleep* copyright © 1967; *Iconographs* copyright © 1970; *New & Selected
Things Taking Place* copyright © 1978; *In Other Words* copyright © 1987 by
The Literary Estate of May Swenson. Other uncollected poems, posthumously
published poems, and selected writings are reprinted with permission of The
Literary Estate of May Swenson. All rights reserved.

The paper used in this publication meets the
minimum requirements of the American National Standard for
Information Sciences—Permanence of Paper for Printed
Library Materials, ANSI z39.48—1984.

Distributed to the trade in the United States
by Penguin Group (USA) Inc.
and in Canada by Penguin Books Canada Ltd.

Contents

ICONOGRAPHS (1970)

ANOTHER ANIMAL
(1954)

ONE

Feel Like a Bird

feel like A Bird
understand
he has no hand

instead A Wing
close-lapped
mysterious thing

in sleeveless coat
he halves The Air
skipping there
like water-licked boat

lands on star-toes
finger-beak in
feather-pocket
finds no Coin

in neat head like
seed in A Quartered
Apple eyes join
sniping at opposites
stereoscope The Scene
Before

close to floor giddy
no arms to fling
A Third Sail
spreads for calm
his tail

hand better
than A Wing?
to gather A Heap
to count
to clasp A Mate?

or leap
lone-free and mount
on muffled shoulders
to span A Fate?

Horse and Swan Feeding

Half a swan a horse is
how he slants his muzzle to the clover
forehead dips in a leaf-lake
as she the sweet worm sips
spading the velvet mud-moss with her beak
His chin like another hoof he plants
to preen the feathered green
Up now is tossed her brow from the water-mask
With airy muscles black and sleek
his neck is raised curried with dew
He shudders to the tail delicately
sways his mane wind-hurried
Shall he sail or stay?
Her kingly neck on her male
imperturbable white steed-like body
rides stately away

Lion

In the bend of your mouth soft murder
in the flints of your eyes
the sun-stained openings of caves
Your nostrils breathe the ordained air
of chosen loneliness

Magnificently maned as the lustrous savannah
your head heavy with heraldic curls
wears a regal frown between the brows

The wide bundle of your chest
    your loose-skinned belly frilled with fur
    you carry easily sinuously pacing on suede paws

Between tight thighs
    under the thick root of your tufted tail
    situated like a full-stoned fruit beneath a bough
    the quiver of your never-used malehood is slung

You pace in dung on cement
    the bars flick past your eyeballs
    fixed beyond the awestruck stares of children
Watching you they remember their fathers
    the frightening hairs in their fathers' ears

Young girls remember lovers too timid and white
    and I remember how I played lion with my brothers
    under the round yellow-grained table
    the shadow our cave in the lamplight

Your beauty burns the brain
    though your paws slue on foul cement
    the fetor of captivity you do right to ignore
    the bars too an illusion

Your heroic paranoia plants you in the African jungle
    pacing by the cool water-hole as dawn streaks the sky
    and the foretaste of the all-day hunt
    is sweet as yearling's blood
    in the corners of your lips

Sun

With your masculine stride
    you tread insidious clouds and glide
    to the unobstructed parapet of noon-blue

ruthless rip through cumulous veils of sloth
spurn their sly caresses and erect
an immediate stairway to passion's splendid throne

From yourself you fling your own earth-seed
and orbits organize in the wombless infinite
for your discipled planets

radiant boys
that imitate your stamping feet
in the elliptic dance of fire

You are not moon-dependent on desire
in rotund rhythm leashed to a mineral despot
like that satellite in female furrow sown

that white rib plucked from Adam-earth
but appended still
eclipsed beneath his dark chest
writhing to his will

one-sided shield turned to the urgent tide
compelled to yield to the night-sky slime
she that marble-smiling sinks in moss
At dawn rubbed thin a mutilate
she melts and faints in the cold cloud curd

while you are up afork the first ringing word
of potent joy the sharp-tined golden shout
divine and glistering your beard with dewy flames
sprinting to the pantheon and your godlike games

Stony Beach

The sea like Demosthenes' mouth
champs upon these stones
whose many stumblings make him suave
The argument molded monotonously by all his lips

    in a parliament of overlappings
    is vocal but incomprehensible because never finished

    Listen listen there is nothing to learn from the sea
    Listen he is lucid in sound only
    convinces with broken phrases that wizardly
    the waves round out a rune over riddling stones

   Beginning again and again with a great *A*
   a garbled alphabet he lisps and groans
 The insistent eloquence of echoes
has no omega

Sketch for a Landscape

a clearing her forehead Brisk
wilderness of hair
retreats from the smooth dancing ground
now savage drums are silent In caves
of shade twin jaguars couch
flicking their tails in restless dream Awake
they leap in unison Asleep they sink
like embers Sloping swards her cheekbones
graduate to a natural throne Two lambs
her nostrils curled back to back Follow
the shallow hollow to her lip-points
stung blossoms or bruised fruits Her
lower lip an opulent orchard Her spiral smile
a sweet oasis both hot and cool

soft in center swollen a bole of moss
hiding white stones and moist spring
where lives a snake so beautiful and shy His
undulant hole is kept a slippery secret A cleft
between the cliff-edge and her mouth we drop
to the shouldered foothills down the neck's
obelisk and rest In the valley's scoop
velvet meadowland

Cafe Tableau

Hand of the copper boy
pours tea   deft wrist square fist
salmon-satin-lined

Dark-muscled dancers among porcelain
twined   his fingers and long thumb

He stands dumb in crisp white coat
his blood in heavy neck-vein
eloquent   its flood plunges
to each purple nail   emanates
male electrons

His pupils conscienceless as midnight skies
between the moon-whites of his eyes   avoid
tea-sipper's naked shoulder
diamond-cold her throat

That she is female his broad nostrils
have denied   like figs dried when green
her breasts shrivel in the refusal
of his stare

His thigh athletic slender   retreats
behind her chair   in his hips
nothing tender   ancestral savagery
has left him lion-clean

Furtive beneath mental hedges
she sees   feels his bare wrist square fist
her boneless hand creeps up the crisp sleeve
higher   she squeals and finds the nipples
of his hairless chest

The copper boy's white coat
become a loincloth she unwinds   he wades
into the pool of her stagnant desire

The Drunkard's Brow

The drunkard's brow delicately veined
 gleams against the pavement
 stained with dog-piss

The siren in his skull run down
 his hot eyes shut
 as if the pure shade laved his face
 he is immersed in bliss
 forgotten rage a rim of spittle
 round his lips like lace

A while ago he cursed the sunny street
 the passersby striding to offices
 the thins and fats
 in suits and hats alike correct and pressed
 raw chunks of meat their jowls new-shaved
 newspapers stuck in pockets jingling change

Lights click red and green
 the bitter whistles blow
 wheels streak by
 the thousand pairs of feet
 slap at his ear

Knees drawn up shoes kicked off
 bare heels in the gutter's litter
 snag-nailed hands curled queerly
 on his chest
 the drunkard does not hear

He is at rest and cradled out of range
 beneath the breast of sleep
 the rim of spittle on his lips like milk

His smile is silk is mystery is deep

Spring in the Square

Tree trunks intercept the eye
that swoops like a bird through zigzags of green
At far end of the pupil's tunnel
beads of tiny taxis roll
People move like scissored marionettes

Beneath the eyelid's awning
benches slump Sunday sitters
A yawn goes mouth to mouth
Old necks slacken in the sun
Tranced fingers fold black headlines
that shrink like giddy bugs
in the great goblet of light

Shadow-and-sun-interbraided
children in pendulous swings
rise loose-kneed and fall
and rise loose-kneed and fall
flashing like watchfobs

The stateman's statue all
winter unmoved by snow
listens in ponderous surprise to summer's bugle

This the moment of released leaves
Innumerable green hands uncurl their puckered palms
Irrepressible grass bristles
from the city's horny hide

Boy in Canoe

In pod-shaped canoe
on the spanking lake
he propels his cradle
through uterine blue
his arms tattooed with

Grace & Force
the scoop of his long chest
Light & Strong
as the shell

Yellow his head
as if pollen-dusted
Stern-innocent his eyes
are turned to the fierce
sun's shield
unmindful of Medusas he must
pierce or yield to
voyage done

Between his thighs
like a young frog
in a loose fist
precious lies his genital
and pulsing in their
pouches wait
the little gold grains
of giant's teeth
to burrow into Dark & Wet
at summer's end
at the lake's bend

The Garden at St. John's

Behind the wall of St. John's in the city
  in the shade of the garden the Rector's wife
    walks with her baby a girl and the first
      its mouth at her neck seeking and sucking
        in one hand holding its buttocks its skull
          cupped by the other her arms like a basket
            of tenderest fruit and thinks as she fondles
              the nape of the infant its sweat is like dew
                like dew and its hair is as soft as soft
                  as down as the down in the wingpits of angels

The little white dog with the harlequin eye
　　his tail like a thumb feet nimble as casters
　　　　scoots in the paths of the garden's meander
　　　　　　behind the wall of St. John's in the city
　　　　　　　　a toy deposed from his place in her arms
　　　　　　　　　　by this doll of the porcelain bone
　　　　　　　　　　　　this pale living fruit without stone

She walks where the wrinkling tinkling fountain
　　laps at the granite head of a monk
　　　　where dip the slippery noses of goldfish
　　　　　　and tadpoles flip from his cuspid mouth
　　　　　　　　A miracle surely the young wife thinks
　　　　　　　　　　from such a hard husband a tender child
　　　　　　　　　　　　and thinks of his black sleeves on the hymnbook
　　　　　　　　　　　　　　inside the wall of St. John's in the city
　　　　　　　　　　　　　　　　the Ah of his stiff mouth intoning Amen
　　　　　　　　　　　　　　　　　　while the organ prolongs its harmonious snore

Two trees like swans' necks twine in the garden
　　beside the wall of St. John's in the city
　　　　Brooding and cool in the shade of the garden
　　　　　　the scrolled beds of ivy glitter like vipers
　　　　　　　　A miracle surely this child and this garden
　　　　　　　　　　of succulent green in the broil of the city
　　　　　　　　　　　　she thinks as setting the bird-cries apart
　　　　　　　　　　　　　　she hears from beneath the dark spirals of ivy
　　　　　　　　　　　　　　　　under the wall of St. John's in the city
　　　　　　　　　　　　　　　　　　the rectal rush and belch of the subway
　　　　　　　　　　　　　　　　　　　　roiling the corrugate bowels of the city
　　　　　　　　　　　　　　　　　　　　　　and sees in the sky the surgical gleam
　　　　　　　　　　　　　　　　　　　　　　　　of an airplane stitching its way to the West
　　　　　　　　　　　　　　　　　　　　　　　　　　above the wall of St. John's in the city
　　　　　　　　　　　　　　　　　　　　　　　　　　　　ripping its way through the denim air

Horses in Central Park

Colors of horses like leaves or stones
or wealthy textures
liquors of light

The skin of a plum that's more than ripe
sheathes a robust
cloven rump

Frosty plush of lilies
for another's head
ears and nostrils funneled are their cones

Of sere October leaves
this gaunt roan's hide
freckled dun and red

Here's a mole-gray back
and darker dappled haunch
tail and forelock mauve like smoke

This coal-colored stallion
flake of white on his brow
is slippery silk in the sun

Fox-red bay
and buckskin blond as wheat
Burgundy mare with tasseled mane of jet

Sober chestnut burnished
by his sweat
to veined and glowing oak

Seal-brown mustang
with stocking-feet
Pinto in patched and hooded domino

Naked palomino
is smooth peeled willow
or marble under water or clean morning snow

Three Jet Planes

Three jet planes skip above the roofs
    through a tri-square of blue
    tatooed by TV crossbars
    that lean in cryptic concert in their wake

Like skaters on a lake
    combined to a perfect arrowhead up there
    they sever space with bloodless speed
    and are gone without a clue
    but a tiny bead the eye can scarcely find
    leaving behind
    where they first burst into blue
    the invisible boiling wind of sound

As horsemen used to do
As horsemen used to gallop through
    a hamlet on hunting morn
    and heads and arms were thrust
    through windows
    leaving behind them the torn
    shriek of the hound
    and their wrestling dust

Above the roofs three jet planes
    leave their hoofs of violence on naïve ground

TWO

Evolution

the stone
would like to be
Alive like me

the rooted tree
longs to be Free

the mute beast
envies my fate
Articulate

on this ball
half dark
half light
i walk Upright
i lie prone
within the night

beautiful each Shape
to see
wonderful each Thing
to name
here a stone
there a tree
here a river
there a Flame

marvelous to Stroke
the patient beasts
within their yoke

how i Yearn
for the lion
in his den
though he spurn
the touch of men

the longing
that i know
is in the Stone also
it must be

the same that rises
in the Tree

the longing
in the Lion's call
speaks for all

oh to Endure
like the stone
sufficient
to itself alone

or Reincarnate
like the tree
be born each spring
to greenery

or like the lion
without law
to roam the Wild
on velvet paw

but if walking
i meet
a Creature like me
on the street
two-legged
with human face
to recognize
is to Embrace

wonders pale
beauties dim

19

during my delight
with Him

exchange
a Feast unknown
to stone

an Evolution strange
two Tongues touch

or tree or beast

Beast

my Brown self
goes on four paws
supple-twining in the
lewd Gloom

arching against the
shaggy hedges
with a relishing Purr
tasting among his
spurted fur

the Ripeness
brisk and willing
of his brown body

yawning Obscurely
glittered-glancing
couching himself
in the sunny places

beating his tail
where traces
of She-odor make
a pattern for
his unbrained thought

feeling the Budding
thorns in his
feet of felt

planning to Stab them
into the wincing pelt
of a creature smaller

my Brown self
a thing gleam-jawed
goes downright
Four-pawed

Organelle

Emerge on the farthest plane
where the rails of the senses end
their glittering parallels destroyed by light
A water-wilderness ensnarls the touch
Colors burn a spectrum too rich for sight
Sweet corporeal weight sharp-whittled bone
are drained away
The mind-tree million-leafed is overthrown
by wands of lightning

Find the angelic fold where bathes the beast
in the pure froth of his wrath
his hide unspoiled by sores of conscience
where scarce tongues taste delicious gall
as if an acid numbed their buds
This only does not pass
that moves within toward upon into itself
an ocean secretive and small
spinning its own foam

Probe beyond the final wall the place of
anti-peace the nerve-fire's nucleus
the wheel's ferocious motion the waterfall's
white pride
Untorn by spoke or stone the whirl is fed
on the fugue of stillness at its core
The spurt perpetuates its shape

in a fluid cliff of glass
Purpled in Isis' womb another king enshrines
in the phallic garden the serpent's ear
the nostrils of the hound
Swallowed in pagan ground the whines of
gravid women the fetid smell of the Christian

Yield to the wizard's piercing kiss
    Bare his breast suck up his power
    Within his vivid nimbus is erased
    the cruel diameter of night
    The rigid hour and death's dark law
    are overwhelmed
    The flaw of a nameless sin effaced
    the square's cornered barrier spills apart

Dare with him the frameless air

Love Is

    a rain of diamonds
    in the mind

    the soul's fruit
    sliced in two

    a dark spring
    loosed at the lips of light

    under-earth waters
    unlocked from their lurking
    to sparkle in a crevice
    parted by the sun

    a temple
    not of stone but cloud
    beyond the heart's roar
    and all violence

outside the anvil-stunned domain
unfrenzied space

between the grains of change
blue permanence

one short step
to the good ground

the bite into bread again

Mornings Innocent

I wear your smile upon my lips
arising on mornings innocent
Your laughter overflows my throat
Your skin is a fleece about me
With your princely walk I salute the sun
People say I am handsome

Arising on mornings innocent
birds make the sound of kisses
Leaves flicker light and dark like eyes

I melt beneath the magnet of your gaze
Your husky breath insinuates my ear
Alert and fresh as grass I wake

and rise on mornings innocent
The strands of the wrestler
run golden through my limbs
I cleave the air with insolent ease
With your princely walk I salute the sun
People say I am handsome

He That None Can Capture
comes of own accord to me

The acrobat astride his swing in space
the pole rolled under his instep
catches the pits of his knees
is lipped by his triangled groin
fits the fold of his hard-carved buttocks

Long-thighed tight-hipped he drops
head-down and writhes erect
glazed smooth by speed a twirled top
sits immobile in the void

Gravity outwhipped squeezed like dough
is kneaded to his own design
a balance-egg at the plexus of his bowels
counteracting vertigo

Empty of fear and therefore without weight
he walks a wedge of steeper air
indifferent to the enormous stare
of onlookers in rims of awe below

Drums are solid blocks beneath him
Strong brass horn-tones prolong him
on glittering stilts

Self-hurled he swims the color-stippled height
where nothing but whisks of light
can reach him

At night he is my lover

Each Day of Summer

In the unassembled puzzle of the city
a lava forest ragged crags of roofs
to a ledge hung in rare green
and a narrow garden
in immutable rock a fissure
of living grass
the sun came like a king
each day of summer
with great golden hands
caressed our skin to jasper

Miraculous as if a mounted knight
crowned caparisoned crossed a soot-grim moat
to a round tower ribbon-tipped
each day of summer
love came bearing love
a chalice of light
We bathed in love and drank it
Then our flesh
seemed like the leaves
enameled bright forever

Now the roofs are white with winter's order
the city's million gashes bandaged clean
earth and sinuous tree
stern brick and cobble
by ethereal snow composed to unity
The ledge where the sun
a coat of mail lay on us
now a coffer loaded with pearls of frost
the opulent plume in warm blue
that waved above us
now stark as ivory canopied in gray

But the honey in our veins burned deep
We are stored with sweetness
Our breasts are golden hives
In interior bone

the scepter's knob hoards ruby like a coal
In the eternal sky of mind
each day of summer
paints a lozenge in the prism of our love

August Night

Shadow like a liquid lies
    in your body's hollows
In your eyes garnet stars
    shift their facets with your breath
The August night is Nubian
    something green mixed with the dark
a powder for your skin that tints
    the implications of your bones
with copper light
    and aura round your knees your navel
a little pool with pulsing tide

Is there beauty deeper than your cool
    form drawn by the occult stylus
of this night
    slanting to autumn
the long dawn soon bringing wrappings
    for your breast?
Has any other watchman stiller stayed
    to the smiting of this gong
half in glory half afraid to look
    at what obscure in light
is now explained by shade?

Another Animal

Another animal imagine moving
 in his rippling hide
  down the track of the centaur
   Robust inside him his heart siphons unction to his muscles
    proving
     this columnar landscape lives
      Last night's dream
       flinches at the mind's lattice
        transformed into a seam of sunlight on his trunk
       that like a tree
      shimmers in ribbons of shadow
     His mystery the invert cloud engulfs me with the grass

  Imagine another moving
 even as I pass
among the trees that need not shift their feet
 to pierce the sky's academy
  and let go their leaves
   let go
    their leaves
     bright desperate as cries
      and do not cry
       Even as I he breathes
        and shall be breathless
       for the mind-connected pulse
      heaves hurries halts for but two reasons
     Loveless then deathless
    but if loved
   surrendered to the season's summit
  the ice-hood the volcano's hiccough
 the empty-orbéd zero of eclipse

The lean track dips together where our feet have pounced
 The rugs the pine boughs gave us glisten clean
  We meet like two whelps at their mother's dugs
   Does the earth trounced here recall
    the hipmarks of another fall
     when dappled animals with hooves and human knees
      coupled in the face of the convulsive spurning

of other cities and societies?
We are wizards mete for burning
and rush forward to our fate
neighing as when centaurs mate

Unable to imagine until late
in the September wood
that another stood out of God's pocket
straddled between beast and human
now each the other's first stern teacher
learns the A and B against the bitten lips
Our coiled tongues strike the first word
Turned heels our star-crossed hands
kick the mind to its ditch in leaf-mold
Open to joy to punishment in equal part
closed to the next mutation
we lie locked at the forking of the heart

To Confirm a Thing

To confirm a Thing and give thanks
                    to the stars that named me
and fixed me in the Wheel of heaven
            my fate pricked out in the Boxer's chest
in the hips curled over the Horse
                Though girled in an apple-pink month
and the moon hornless
                the Brothers glitter in my wristbones
At ankle and knee I am set astride
                    and made stubborn in love

In the equal Night where oracular beasts
                        the planets depose
and our Selves assume their orbits
        I am flung where the Girdle's double studs
grant my destiny
                    I am the Athletes in that zone

My thighs made marble-hard
                              uncouple only to the Archer
with his diametrical bow
                              who prances in the South
himself a part of his horse
              His gemmed arrow splits the hugging twins

The moon was gelded on that other night as well
                    O his feeble kingdom we will tip over
If our feet traverse the milky way
     the earth's eccentric bead on which we balance
is small enough to hide between our toes
                         its moon a mote that the Long Eye
is hardly conscious of
                              nor need we be

The tough the sensuous Body our belief
                         and fitting the pranks of Zeus
to this our universe
           we are Swans or Bulls as the music turns us
We are Children incorrigible and perverse
                         who hold our obstinate seats
on heaven's carousel
                         refusing our earth's assignment
refusing to descend
                    to beget such trifles of ourselves
as the gibbous Mothers do
                    We play in the Den of the Gods
and snort at death

Then let me by these signs
                         maintain my magnitude
as the candid Centaur his dynasty upholds
                         And in the Ecliptic Year
our sweet rebellions
                    shall not be occulted but remain
coronals in heaven's Wheel

A History of Love

Other than self
O inconceivable
How touched how kissed?
There was a lodestone
made the stars rush down
like pins that fastened us together
under the same dark cloak
We were stroked
by some magician's fur

Each became a doll
Our pure amazement
bestowed us perfect gifts
Our cravings were surpassed
by the porcelain eyes
alluring lips caressable hair
Undressed we handled ivory idols

Summer winter fall and still delighted
unmarred in the dangerous game of change
Replaced by the wonder of the found
the so long kept
The dear endurable surprised us more
than the ecstasies of ritual spring
Like Nature her transfers we adored our everydays
the never knowing what
next the sprites within us would disclose

At last acquainted smoothed by contiguity
sharpened each by opposite tempers we devined
about our nacreous effigies outlined
the soft and mortal other
Under the body's plush a density
awkward ambiguous as bone
Real as our own

O other than self
and O believable
The dream tent fallen
daylight come
we wake to a nakedness so actual
our magnet a common innocent stone

Else than beauty
else than passion then?
Their amalgam mingled mounted up to this
How sweet the plain
how warm the true
We by this mystery charmed anew
begin again to love

THREE

Secure

Let us deceive ourselves a little
while   Let us pretend that air
is earth   and falling lie resting
within each other's gaze   Let us

deny that flame consumes   that
fruit ripens   that the wave must
break   Let us forget the circle's
fixed beginning marks to the
instant its ordained end   Let us

lean upon the moment and expect
time to enfold us   space sustain
our weight   Let us be still   and
falling lie face to face and drink
each other's breath   Be still
Let us be still   We lie secure

within the careful mind of death

The Key to Everything

Is there anything I can do
or has everything been done
or do
you prefer somebody else to do
it or don't
you trust me to do
it right or is it hopeless and no one can do
a thing or do
you suppose I don't
really want to do
it and am just saying that or don't
you hear me at all or what?

You're
waiting for

35

the right person the doctor or
the nurse the father or
the mother or
the person with the name you keep
mumbling in your sleep
that no one ever heard of there's no one
named that really
except yourself maybe

If I knew what your name was I'd
prove it's your
own name spelled backwards or
twisted in some way the one you
keep mumbling but you
won't tell me your
name or
don't you know it
yourself that's it
of course you've
forgotten or
never quite knew it or
weren't willing to believe it

Then there *is* something I
can do I
can find your name for you
that's the key to everything once you'd
repeat it clearly you'd
come awake you'd
get up and walk knowing where you're
going where you
came from

And you'd
love me
after that or would you
hate me?
no once you'd
get there you'd
remember and love me

of course I'd
be gone by then I'd
be far away

The Tiger's Ghost

The tiger
and the tiger's passion
haunt this cell
in their own fashion

These cool walls
this empty place
remember well
the tiger's face
remember well
the tiger's yawn
as candle-eyed
he grinned upon
a stain of moonlight
on the floor
cleft by bars

The tiger's roar
consumed this silence
roused this stone
to raucous echo

O alone
the tiger stretched
on velvet flank
lapped by night

This room is rank
with carnal rage
and jungle smell
The tiger's ghost
lurks in this cell

An Unknown Island

No way to turn but in
No where to go but back
The earth is round and man has come full circle
Faster he flies
farther flings himself
sooner arrives at starting point
closer comes to Beginning

From foetal snail blind in a fold of the womb
to the discus thrower
uncoiling in the light of morning
his thighs' and biceps' powered juice

from earth-knuckling ape in mountain socket
to the aviator in unploughed air
scaling virgin alps of cloud

a flicker of evolution's lens
a squeeze of biology's trigger

The frontiers are internal now

Brain like the meat of a nut
but also like twin continents
is all the space
Heart like a clock
but also like a pulsing universe
is all the time we have

And this is enough and more than enough
There shall be there have been no other gods before Me

The earth our bulb from which we spring
our green body a vaster thing
an unknown island to be sought
volute discovery
the oceanic span of thought
the soul's geography

Mortal Surge

We are eager
We pant
We whine like whips cutting the air
The frothing sea
the roaring furnace
the jeweled eyes of animals call to us
and we stand frozen
moving neither forward nor back

In the breathless wedge between night and dawn
when the rill of blood pauses at the sluice of the heart
either to advance or retreat
the stars stare at us face to face
penetrating even the disguise of our nakedness
daring us to make the upward leap
effortless as falling
if only we relax the bowstring of our will

We seek the slippery flesh of other men
expecting to be comforted
or to be punished
or to be delighted beyond imagined delights
to be made clean
or to be baptized in the cool font of evil

We believe in the meeting of lips
in the converging of glances
that a talisman is given
that we shall arise anew
be healed and made whole
or be torn at last from our terrible womb-twin
our very self

We are loved in the image of the dead
We love in the image of the never-born
We shudder to beget with child
We shudder not to beget with child
We scream in the doorway of our beginning
We weep at the exit gate

We are alone and never alone
bound and never secured
let go and never freed
We would dance and are hurled
would build and are consumed
We are dragged backward by the past
jerked forward by the future

Our earth a bloody clot of the sun's cataclysm
sun a severed limb of a shattered universe
In fission
explosion
In separation
congealment

Satanic Form

Numerals forkmarks of Satan
Triangles circles squares
hieroglyphs of death
Things invented
abortions smelling of the forge
licked to gruesome smoothness by the lathe
Things metallic or glass
frozen twisted flattened
stretched to agonized bubbles
Bricks beams receptacles vehicles
forced through fire hatched to unwilling form
O blasphemies
Time caught in a metal box
Incongruous the rigid clucking tongue
the needled hands the 12-eyed face
against the open window past which drops the night
like a dark lake on end or flowing hair
Night unanimous over all the city
The knuckled fist of the heart opening and closing
Flower and stone not cursed with symmetry
Cloud and shadow not doomed to shape and fixity
The intricate body of man without rivet or nail

or the terrible skirl of the screw
  O these are blessed
 Satanic form geometry of death
  The lariat around the neck of space
   The particles of chaos in the clock
    The bottle of the yellow liquor light
     that circumvents the sifting down of night
      O love the juice in the green stem growing
      you cannot synthesize
       It corrodes in phials and beakers
        evaporates in the hot breath of industry
        escapes to the air and the dew
         returns to the root of the unborn flower
          O Satan cheated of your power

A Loaf of Time

A loaf of time
round and thick
So many layers
ledges to climb
to lie on our
bellies lolling
licking our lips
The long gaze a
gull falling
down the cliff's
table   to coast
the constant
waves   The reach-
ing wave-tongues
lick the table
But slowly grayly
slow as the ocean
is gray beyond
the green   slow
as the sky is high
and out of sight
higher than blue

is white   Around
the table's wheel
unbounded   for
each a meal the
centered mound to
be divided   A
wedge for each
and leisure on
each ledge   The
round loaf thick
we lick our lips
Our eyes gull
down the layered
cliff and ride
the reaching waves
that lick but   slowly
the table's
edge   Then slowly
our loaf   Slowly
our ledge

Why We Die

Saw a grave
upon a hill
and thought
of bones
as still
as sticks
and stones

and thought
that mouldering flesh
is worth
as much as earth

and wondered why
we die

and said
because we want to die
and be as dead
as things that
lacking thought beget
no hope and no regret

No man yet
has dared to stay
within himself
till death
dissolved away

Hunger makes him break the fast
and take a taste of death at last
Who'll forgo
the craving
who will be
discoverer of
eternity?

Question

Body my house
my horse my hound
what will I do
when you are fallen

Where will I sleep
How will I ride
What will I hunt

Where can I go
without my mount
all eager and quick
How will I know
in thicket ahead
is danger or treasure

when Body my good
bright dog is dead

How will it be
to lie in the sky
without roof or door
and wind for an eye

With cloud for shift
how will I hide?

I Will Lie Down

I will lie down in autumn
let birds be flying

Swept into a hollow
by the wind
I'll wait for dying

I will lie inert unseen
my hair same-colored
with grass and leaves

Gather me
for the autumn fires
with the withered sheaves

I will sleep face down
in the burnt meadow
not hearing the sound of water
over stones

Trail over me cloud
and shadow
Let snow
hide the whiteness of my bones

The Greater Whiteness

On winter white
  the dead are gray
    In summer night
      the dead were oh so white
        Upon their grief-wet burial day
          the dead were black against the clay
Oh soiled with grief
  when newly dead
    at foot and head
      in summer's moon-black leaf
        the dead were white
          And in the noon-green
            ghost and stone
              rose clean as light
              and fair as bone
Oh they were black the heavy dead
  that now are light
    and nothing lack
      But even they
        cannot stay
          Oh cannot be
            white as that winter purity
On winter white
  the dead are gray

A Wish

Out of an hour I built a hut
    and like a Hindu sat
        immune in the wind of time

From a hair I made a path
    and walked and both
      rock and wilderness became

my space and thoroughfare
    With sorrow for a skin
      I felt no wound

Pleasant   power   like   a   nut
      ripened   and   split   within   me
            Where   there   had   been   wrath

it   loosened   all   the   world
 to   quiet   noonday
   My   face   in   the   rock   my   name

on   the   wildest   tree
  My   flesh   the   heath
    of   a   peaceful   clime

FOUR

Any Object

any Object before the Eye
can fill the space can occupy
the supple frame of eternity

my Hand before me such
tangents reaches into Much
root and twig extremes can touch

and Hour can be the all
expanding like a cunning Ball
to a Vast from very small

skull and loin the twin-shaped Cup
store the glittering grainery up
for all the sandy stars to sup

any Single becomes the More
multiples sprout from alpha's core
from Vase of legend vessels of lore

to this pupil dark and wild
where lives the portrait of a Child
let me then be reconciled

germ of the first Intent to be
i am and must be seen to see
then every New descends from me

uncoiling into Motion i
start a massive panoply
the anamolecular atoms fly

and spread through ether like a foam
appropriating all the Dome
of absoluteness for my home

Organs

hidden in the hair
the spiral Ear
waits to Suck sound

and sly beneath its
ledge the Eye to Spear
the fish of light

the Mouth's a hole
and yet a Cry for
love for loot

with every stolen
breath the Snoot
Supposes roses

nose tongue fishing
eye's Crouched
in the same hutch

nibbling lips and
funnel's there
in the legs' lair
carnivora of Touch

Big-Hipped Nature

Big-hipped nature bursts forth the head of god
from jungle clots of green
from pelvic heave of mountains
On swollen-breasted clouds he fattens and feeds
He is rocked in the crib of the sea

Stairways of the inner earth he crawls
and coos to us from the caves
The secret worms miracle his veins

Myriads of fish embellish his iridescent bowels
In multiple syllables the birds
inscribe on air his fledgling words

Swift and winding beasts with coats of flame
serpents in their languor black and blind
in the night of his dark mind express
his awe and anger his terror and magicness

Wherever we look his eye lies bottomless
fringed by fields and woods
and tragic moons
magnify his pupils with their tears

In fire he strides
Within the waterfall
he twines his limbs of light
Clothed in the wind and tall
he walks the roofs and towers
Rocks are all his faces
flowers the flesh of his flanks
His hair is tossed with the grasses everywhere
Stained by the rainbow every shell
roars his whispered spell

When sleep the enormous shadow of his hand descends
our tongues uncoil a prayer
to hush our ticking hearts our sparrow-like fear
and we lie naked within his lair
His cabalistic lightnings play upon us there

The Playhouse

Here is the playhouse of weather-faded white
Trees like legs of elephants stamp 'round it
in the mossy light after rain
It sits on a knoll   Its chimney is red
Troll-headed weeds press against the pane

A rabbit could hop the tidy picket fence
but the gate is locked beneath the little wicket
Stooping you can peer like a marionette master
into a room with a table and chair   a sofa in the corner
with antimacassar   a hearth a scuttle and broom

The child is at the table bent above her game
The fire stretches in the grate
With doll-round eyes intent and oranged by the flame
she plays a little black machine
with clever buttons that she taps

spelling out her name perhaps   And now the plaything
is a square of cloth upon a rack   the child a boy
in one hand a plate where colored knobs are stuck
in the other something like a wand
with which he gambles   It's a game of luck

or magic   Like a stage the playhouse
or like a fairy book improbable and charming
Each time you look inside you see a different play
Is that a toy piano he's diddling on today?
Odd how they never see you watching

Now she's making up a dance
He's buffeting a lump of mud into a fancied shape
Out in the giant wood birds with beaks agape
listen   In gauzy trance the deer stand still
They sense there's something queer

Is the playhouse really here you wonder
and what's it to do with you?
There's a spatter of rain   there's thunder
In a flick of lightning will you see what it means
or will it disappear?

Are the children real if the forest is?
On the path that leads to the playhouse on its knoll
next time you come will there be a hole
matted with weeds?   What if it's you who's missing
or at least invisible   too large a beast for the landscape?

Your feet do not impress the moss
or make a sound among the plodding trees
impassive in the rain   Turn 'round
Can you see the playhouse?   No it's gone
Now do you feel the loss and the puzzling pain?

Shadow-Maker

After a season
apparently sterile he
displays his achievements
    Scale upon layered scale
    frieze upon frieze of animate
    pointed perfect spine-bright

        notes are they?
        gestures for a dance?
        glyphs of a daring alphabet?
            Innumerable intimations
            on one theme
            A primal color haunts the whole design

Shadows aping the shapes
of all his strokes
with inbetweens of dark concavity imply
    an elaboration other than the seen
    flashing intervals of quills of light
    that multiply these forms to a luxury

        These finished feathers
        or pennants
        comblike along their staffs
            hide what they depend on
            like profuse transparent surf
            the basic waves

So his body
stiff and occult
twisted by rocks and years

patient and awkward
there beneath
is hardly noticed

Bars of solid black
his acrobatic arms
peer through as pauses
In chunks of deeper greener silence
the denser language of roots
is voluble by very absence

By Morning

Some for everyone
plenty

and more coming

Fresh   dainty   airily arriving
everywhere at once

Transparent at first
each faint slice
slow   soundlessly tumbling

then quickly thickly a gracious fleece
will spread like youth   like wheat
over the city

Each building will be   a hill
all sharps made round

dark worn noisy narrows made still
wide   flat   clean   spaces

Streets will be   fields
cars be   fumbling sheep

A deep bright harvest will be seeded
   in a night

By morning we'll be   children
   feeding on manna

   a new loaf on every doorsill

Sunset

The yawn grandiose and transient
of a pink-throated whale
drowning on the pale sky tide
The prairie and our eyes are dyed
the color of longing

The train on its compulsive rail
tools forward spinning the slow
roulette wheel of the land
In miniature its windows thread the stain
The gray sand drinks it red
Our pupils spread to hold it in vain

We plow through monstrous light
approach the narrowing throat of darkness
the tragic height of scarlet passed
before we mark it
Our senses hurriedly bared like knives
to meet the pure shriek
flinch as dusk dilutes the tide
smudges the whale's cheek
to an ashen whimper

Wide
lavish his savagery
so strawberry-full of promise
spewn out so profligate
then retracted reeled-in stingied soon gone

The land turning in sorrow
where the fiery yawn has faded
the train tools on

Cumuli

Is it St. Peter's or St. Paul's this dome
reminds you of?
This blue enameled basin upside down
is it of London Luxembourg or Rome?

Would Blake know how to call it pure
yet grand
Would Shakespeare standing where I stand
compare these clouds to Michelangelo?

I have never traveled never seen
those treasure piles of history hewn
to the golden mean
art more ravishing than nature
fabled yield
gemmed sediment of centuries

This Western field under the summer noon
with sibilant lucerne sown
columned with poplars is my Parthenon
On immense blue
around its vaulted walls
alabaster shapes inhabit beauty's pedestals

A Day Is Laid By

A day is laid by
It came to pass
Wind is drained
from the willow

Dusk interlaces
the grass
Out of the husk
of twilight
emerges the moon

This the aftermath
of jaded sunset
of noon
and the sirens of bees

Day and wrath
are faded
Now above the bars
of lonely pastures
loom the sacred stars

Rusty Autumn

Rusty autumn to your breast again I come   Memorial tears
I leave in tarnished spoons of grass
Hold me Mother though I am grown and you are old
and burning only for death

Sky my childhood   Oh familiar blue cobbled with clouds
and misting now as with a cataract
where has Father gone   the abundant laughter
our tent and shelter   broad shoulders of the sun?
My dad my tall my yellow-bright ladder of delight

Rusty autumn on your flat breast I lie
and rocks and ragweed my ribs feel in the shaggy field
A blemish on each beam of stubble
and its slanting lash of shadow   These are spears
that were your milk-soft breast I trod in the upright green
Summer's flesh lay all the years between
and hid the bloom of hate

seeded that other time the horizontal world heaved
with my tears   Now too late for planting

Oh mummied breast Oh brown Mother hold me
though you are cold   and I am grown   grown old

A Dream

I was a god and self-enchanted
I stood in a cabinet in the living wood
The doors were carved with the sign of the lizard
whose eye unblinks on emptiness
whose head turns slower than a tooth grows

I wore a mask of skin-thin silver
My hair was frenzied foam stiffened to ice
My feet gloved in petals of imperishable flowers
were hooves and colder than hammers

I lived by magic
A little bag in my chest held a whirling stone
so hot it was past burning
so radiant it was blinding

When the moon rose worn and broken
her face like a coin endlessly exchanged
in the hands of the sea
her ray fell upon the doors which opened
and I walked in the living wood
The leaves turned bronze and the moss to marble

At morning I came back to my cabinet
It was a tree in the daylight
the lizard a scroll of its bark

Green Red Brown and White

Bit an apple on its red
side   Smelled like snow
Between white halves broken open
brown winks slept in sockets of green

Stroked a birch white as a thigh
scar-flecked smooth as the neck
of a horse   On mossy pallets green
the pines dropped down
their perfect carvings brown

Lost in the hairy wood
followed berries red
to the fork   Had to choose
between green and green   High

in a sunwhite dome a brown bird
sneezed   Took the path least likely
and it led me home   For

each path leads both out and in
I come while going   No to and from
There is only here   And here
is as well as there   Wherever
I am led I move within the care
of the season
hidden in the creases of her skirts
of green or brown or beaded red

And when they are white
I am not lost   I am not lost then
only covered for the night

Wingfolk

To be one of the wingfolk our desire:
Waking on certain mornings, before the choir
ceases, and our bones take back their weight,
forsaking our flaxen feathers and our thrones,
we know the meaning of our breath.
As from the becalmed sky our chests are hurled,
our sharp birth re-enacted on this rock,
the dream-harp is broken from memory
and washed aflood . . . But even in heavy daylight,
kite or cloud aloft freshens the dream
that skims us toward our future:
Freedom sleeps like music in our numb limbs.
This ground cannot confine us, while slots of sky,
swan-whiteness and the smile of sleep invite us
where our dense and somber blood shall brighten.
In other air, with night's escape, we nimbly climb
to claim our nakedness away from time,
rehearse our harmonies, prepare the winged act
to make our body's miracle intact.

An Opening

Close to sleep an Opening
    What was wall
    to the light-filled eye
    or panel fingertips could find no groove in
    slides apart
    The Box of Now of Me of only Here unlocks

At once in a landscape limitless and free
    all that my Eye encircles I become
    Trees ponds pastures bullocks grazing there
    silks of my Skin strands of my Hair
    waters of my Body glittering

Then and Forever are my two hands spread
    forgotten by each other
    my Head an orchard where in noons of ebony
    in the white night are mated East and West
    and polar fruits and flowers from the sea
    are harvested together

Now I know I have been Hooded
    On rails my sight has run
    to its Horizon where the future spun
    or tapered to the gray Thread hooked in the past
    And these have dropped away
    like markers lost in corridors of Snow
    I am an eye that without socket looks
    on all sides above below

Where is Wakeness then?
    Rigid these wires and joints and jerky stilts
    when Upright I am stretched in the frame again
    the sky a Lid I cannot pry
    The air a tissue of whispers I cannot tear

When narrowed utterly the final Blind
    box of sleep clapped shut
    unhinged from sight then will I find
    within the pupil of the total deep the Wide
    doorway to fields of Bright
    bristles of the sun to be my hide?

A CAGE OF SPINES
(1958)

I

The form is stone
The dress is rain

Almanac

The hammer struck my nail, instead of nail.
A moon flinched into being. Omen-black,
it began its trail. Risen from horizon
on my thumb (no longer numb and indigo)
it waxed yellow, waned to a sliver that now
sets white, here at the rim I cut tonight.

I make it disappear, but mark its voyage
over my little oval ceiling that again
is cloudless, pink and clear. In the dark
quarter-inch of this moon before it arrived
at my nail's tip, an unmanned airship
dived 200 miles to the hem of space, and
vanished. At the place of Pharaoh Cheops'
tomb (my full moon floating yellow)
a boat for ferrying souls to the sun
was disclosed in a room sealed 5000 years.

Reaching whiteness, this moon-speck waned
while an April rained. Across the street,
a vine crept over brick up 14 feet. And
Einstein (who said there is no hitching
post in the universe) at 77 turned ghost.

The Centaur

The summer that I was ten—
Can it be there was only one
summer that I was ten? It must

have been a long one then—
each day I'd go out to choose
a fresh horse from my stable

which was a willow grove
down by the old canal.
I'd go on my two bare feet.

But when, with my brother's jack-knife,
I had cut me a long limber horse
with a good thick knob for a head,

and peeled him slick and clean
except a few leaves for the tail,
and cinched my brother's belt

around his head for a rein,
I'd straddle and canter him fast
up the grass bank to the path,

trot along in the lovely dust
that talcumed over his hoofs,
hiding my toes, and turning

his feet to swift half-moons.
The willow knob with the strap
jouncing between my thighs

was the pommel and yet the poll
of my nickering pony's head.
My head and my neck were mine,

yet they were shaped like a horse.
My hair flopped to the side
like the mane of a horse in the wind.

My forelock swung in my eyes,
my neck arched and I snorted.
I shied and skittered and reared,

stopped and raised my knees,
pawed at the ground and quivered.
My teeth bared as we wheeled

and swished through the dust again.
I was the horse and the rider,
and the leather I slapped to his rump

spanked my own behind.
Doubled, my two hoofs beat
a gallop along the bank,

the wind twanged in my mane,
my mouth squared to the bit.
And yet I sat on my steed

quiet, negligent riding,
my toes standing the stirrups,
my thighs hugging his ribs.

At a walk we drew up to the porch.
I tethered him to a paling.
Dismounting, I smoothed my skirt

and entered the dusky hall.
My feet on the clean linoleum
left ghostly toes in the hall.

Where have you been? said my mother.
Been riding, I said from the sink,
and filled me a glass of water.

What's that in your pocket? she said.
Just my knife. It weighted my pocket
and stretched my dress awry.

Go tie back your hair, said my mother,
and *Why is your mouth all green?*
*Rob Roy, he pulled some clover
as we crossed the field,* I told her.

The Red Bird Tapestry

Now I put on the thimble of dream
    to stitch among leaves the red node of his body
and fasten here the few beads of his song.

Of the tree a cage of gilded spines
    to palace his scarlet, cathedral his cry,
and a ripple from his beak I sew,
    a banner bearing seven studs,
this scarf to be the morning that received his stain.

I do with thought instead of actuality
    for it has flown.
With glinting thimble I pull back, pull back
    that freak of scarlet to his throne:

To worship him, enchanted cherry to a tree
    that never bore such fruit—
who tore the veil of possibility
    and swung here for a day,
a never-colored bird, a never-music heard,
    who, doubly wanded then, looped away.

To find, in hollow of my throat, his call,
    and try his note on all the flutes of memory,
until that clear jet rinses me
    that was his single play—
for this I wear his daring and his royal eye.

Now perfected, arrested in absence—
    my needle laid by and spread my hand—
his claws on stems of my fingers fastened,
    rooted my feet and green my brow,
I drink from his beak the seven beads dropping:
    I am the cage that flatters him now.

A Lake Scene

So innocent this scene, I feel I see it
   with a deer's eye,
uncovering a first secret from this shore.
   I think of the smoothest thing:
the inside of a young thigh,
   or the line of a torso when, supine,
the pectoral sheathe crosses the armpit
   to the outflung arm;
at the juncture of lake and hills, that zone,
   the lowest hill in weavings
of fainter others overlaid,
   is a pelvis in shadow.

The hazel waves slip toward me,
   the far arcade
honed by the sunset; nothing tears
   the transparent skin that water
and sky and, between them,
   the undulant horizon wears.
No contest here, no roughness,
   no threat,
the wind's lick mild as the lake's,
   the rock I lean on, moss-round
as that silhouette
   in the thwart of the opposite shore;
spruce and fir snug-wool its folds.

My eye goes there, to the source
of a first secret. I would be inheritor
   of the lamb's way and the deer's,
my thrust take from the ground
   I tread or lie on. In thighs of trees,
in recumbent stones, in the loins
   of beasts is found
that line my own nakedness carried.
   Here, in an Eden of the mind,
I would remain among my kind,
   to lake and hill, to tree and beast married.

The Promontory Moment

Think of only now, and how this pencil,
tilted in the sand, might be a mast,
its shadow to an ant marking the sun's place;
little and vast are the same to that big eye
that sees no shadow.

Think how future and past, afloat on an ocean
of breath, linked as one island,
might coexist with the promontory moment
around the sun's disk—for that wide eye
knows no distance or divide.

Over your shoulder in the circular cove, the sea,
woven by swimmers' gaudy heads, pulses an indigo
wing that pales at its frothy edge;
and, far out, sails as slow as clouds
change bodies as they come about.

Look at the standing gull, his pincered beak
yellow as this pencil, a scarlet streak beneath the tip,
the puff of his chest bowl-round and white,
his cuff-button eye of ice and jet
fixed on the slicing waves; shingle-snug, his gray wing
tucked to his side; aloft, that plumpness,
whittled flat, sits like a kite.

Turn to where fishermen rise from a neck
of rock, rooted and still, rods played like spouts
from their hips, until, beneath the chips of waves,
a cheek rips on the barb, a silver soul is flipped
from the sea's cool home into fatal air.

Close your eyes and hear the toss of the waves'
innumerable curls on the brow of the world—
that head is shaggy as Samson's, and three-fourths
furred. And *now* is eternal in beard and tress
piled green, blown white on churned sand,
the brand of the past an ephemeral smutch
of brown seaweed cast back to the sucking surf.

Tomorrow the marge is replaced
by a lace of shells, to be gathered again
by the hairy sea when it swells; here nothing is built
or grown, and nothing destroyed; and the buoyed
mind dares to enmirror itself,
as the prone body, bared to the sun,
is undone of its cares.

The eye, also a sun, wanders,
and all that it sees it owns;
the filled sail, tacking the line between water
and sky, its mast as high as this pencil,
becomes the gull's dropped quill, and the fleece
of the wave, and the sea robin's arc
now stilled on the rock.

Fountain Piece I

A bird
   is perched
      upon a wing

      The wing
    is stone
  The bird
is real

A drapery
   falls about this form
      The form is stone
        The dress is rain

        The pigeon preens his own
      and does not know
    he sits upon a wing
   The angel does not feel
  a relative among her large
 feathers stretch
and take his span

in charge
and leave her there
with her cold
wings that cannot fold
while his fan
in air.

The fountain raining
wets the stone
but does not know it dresses
an angel in its tresses

Her stone cheek smiles
and does not care
that real tears
flow there

The Wave the Flame
the Cloud and the Leopard
Speak to the Mind

Watch and watch and follow me
I am all green mimicry
        In my manyness you see
what engenders my beauty

Dancer red and gold with greed
I am that which does not bleed
    On my rising breath be carried
Twine with me and so be freed

Ride with me and hold my mane
I am chimæra the skein
        of everchange that's lily-lain
above the steady mountain

Go the circle of my cage
I own nothing but my rage
the fixed eye of the savage
This singleness may you assuage

The Engagement

When snow	cross
a wing	to where
is folded	I flow
over everything	in the rainbow
when night	seek me
a net	in the rock
dips us	break
in forget	that lock
when blue	meet me
my eye	in the wheel
leaks into	your thread
a sky	I'll feel
and floss	I'll come
your skin	to where you sink
is what the	in the tiger's
spiders spin	blink
when stone	and catch you
our veins	in the fish
are parted	with my strenuous
chains	wish
when prism	find me
sun	in the flake
bends us	I will
one from one	wake

In the Egyptian Room

Camels, with imperious throats,
prowed on a parchment sea,
that rustling unrolls its dead tide eternally,
have heads like smaller boats
resting on slabs of air;
in hieroglyphic trance the centuries,
cupped in their eyes' soft glance,
might be swept bare with a down-blink
of their lids' coarse shining hair;
their lips, curved too, like keels of ships;
coffin-shaped the sacred jaw,
wrenched open in our fantasy, reveals,
cradled in yellowed ivory, the enwrapt king,
gems and brocade encasing a sack of dust.

Cats the Egyptians made to be their gods,
seated on iron thrones, their chests arched
like keystones of a stygian doorway where,
between their paws as on a grand concourse,
souls passed in absolved of time and lust,
have become but ornaments; the scrollwork
of their claws, the abstruse equation gripped
within their smiles, once graphed the very letters
of the laws on the tablets chipped from ebony;
this the script before man, from beast torn free,
was taught to walk in other bodies,
to be of the temple.

Rubbed out in the murky light of the mind's museum
are the faces of sacred beasts;
the sands and winds of history have smoothed
all but the griffin-look, the pharaohic shoulders;
their mouths smeared closed; yet, the emanation
thrown from their brows like light transposed to force,
projects the everlasting, budgeless and inert,
that dreams the metric of the universe.

The School of Desire

Unloosed, unharnessed, turned back to the wild by love,
the ring you cantered round with forelock curled,
the geometric music of this world
dissolved and, in its place,
alien as snow to tropic tigers, amphitheatric space,
you will know the desert's freedom, wind and sun
rough-currying your mane, the plenitude
of strong caresses on your body nude.

Released to run from me. Then will I stand
alone in the hoof-torn ring,
lax in my hand
as wine leaked out the thin whip of my will,
and gone the lightning-string
between your eye and mine.

Our discipline was mutual and the art
that spun our dual beauty. While you wheeled
in flawless stride apart,
I, in glittering boots to the fulcrum heeled,
need hardly signal: your prideful head
plunged to the goad of love-looks sharper than ice.

I gloated on the palomino of your flanks, the nice
sprightliness of pace,
your posture like Apollo's steed. I stood my place
as in a chariot,
held the thong of studded light, the lariat
that made you halt, or longer leap, or faster.
But you have bridled me, bright master.

On wild, untrampled slopes you will be monarch soon,
and I the mount that carries you to those high
prairies steeped in noon.
In the arena where your passion will be spent
in loops of speed, sky's indigo unbounded
by the trainer's tent,
instead of oboes, thunder's riddle,
rain for the racing fifes, I will be absent.

When orchestras of air shall vault you
to such freedom, joy and power,
I will cut the whip that sent you there, will put
away the broken ring, and shut
the school of my desire.

The Charm Box

As if the knob,
perhaps of porcelain,
of a small calliope
turns around twice:

then a hush,
while the memory
of the dainty fragment
is listened to
by the box itself:

the hermit thrush,
that plain instrument,
not seeming precious,
twice releases
its throb.

This double jewel,
this brief,
lovely jangle
is all there is in it.

One expects the knob
to spin and—in a rush—
a long-looped ornament
of every color to dangle
down the air.

A spoke in there
is not broken.
It's just that stunted
quirk—repeated—

and attention to
the silence in between
that is the amulet
that makes the
charm box work.

The hermit thrush
refuses to be luscious,
to elaborate, to entangle,
to interpret, to defend,
or even to declare a goal.

Only the strict
reiteration of a rarity
from this small calliope,
until it is convinced
its bare beginning
is the end, and the whole.

Waiting for It

My cat jumps to the windowsill
and sits there still as a jug.
He's waiting for me, but I cannot be
coming, for I am in the room.

His snout, a gloomy V of patience,
pokes out into the sun.
The funnels of his ears expect
to be poured full of my footsteps.

It, the electric moment, a sweet
mouse, will appear; at his gray

eye's edge I'll be coming home
if he sits on the window-ledge.

It is here, I say, and call him
to my lap. Not a hair
in the gap of his ear moves.
His clay gaze stays steady.

That solemn snout says: *It*
is what is about to happen, not
what is already here.

The Word "Beautiful"

Long, glossy caterpillar
with softest feet
of audible and inaudible vowels;

dewberry head so black
it's silver;
nippered lip, and fluent rump;

who moves by the T
at his tifted middle,
a little locomotive hump.

His ripple is felt
by the palm ashamed,
and we are loath to name him;

hairs of his back
a halo's paint
we daren't put round objects anymore.

He's tainted,
doomed to sloth, like those
other lunar insects such

as Velvet,
that we must not touch,
or Rose, or Gold.

His Destiny—
a myth or moth—still glows
inside the skull,

although his creep is blue,
the untrusted phosphor
of our sleep.

The Poplar's Shadow

When I was little, when
the poplar was in leaf,
its shadow made a sheaf,
the quill of a great pen
dark upon the lawn
where I used to play.

Grown, and long away
into the city gone,
I see the pigeons print
a loop in air and, all
their wings reversing, fall
with silver undertint
like poplar leaves, their seams
in the wind blown.

Time's other side, shown
as a flipped coin, gleams
on city ground
when I see a pigeon's feather:
little and large together,
the poplar's shadow is found.

Staring at here,
and superposing then,
I wait for when.
What shapes will appear?
Will great birds swing
over me like gongs?
The poplar plume belongs
to what enormous wing?

Cause & Effect

Am I the bullet
or the target,
or the hand
that holds the gun?
Or the whisper
in the brain saying *Aim, Fire?*
Is the bullet innocent though it kill?
Must the target stand unblinking and still?
Can one escape, the other stop, if it will?
Will the trigger-finger obey through force?
If the hand reverse command,
will the pregnant gun abort its course?
The brain,
the brain, surely it can refrain,
unclench the gun, break open
the pod of murder,
let the target rise and run.
But first the whisper must be caught,
before the shot—
the single wasp be burnt out,
before the nest, infested, swarms with
the multiple thought—
each sting the trigger pressed!

The Cloud-Mobile

Above my face is a map.
Continents form and fade.
Blue countries, made
on a white sea, are erased,
and white countries traced
on a blue sea.

It is a map that moves:
faster than real,
but so slow.
Only my watching proves
that island has being,
or that bay.

It is a model of time.
Mountains are wearing away,
coasts cracking,
the ocean spills over,
then new hills
heap into view
with river-cuts of blue
between them.

It is a map of change.
This is the way things are
with a stone or a star.
This is the way things go,
hard or soft,
swift or slow.

Order of Diet

I

Salt of the soil and liquor of the rock
is all the thick land's food and mead.
And jaws of cattle grip up

stuffs of pasture for their bellies' need.
We, at table with our knives,
cut apart and swallow other lives.

2

The stone is milked to feed the tree;
the log is killed when the flame's hungry.
To arise in the other's body?
Flank of the heifer we glut, we spend
to redden our blood. Then do we send
her vague spirit higher? Does the grain
come to better fortune in our brain?

3

Ashes find their way to green;
the worm is raised into the wing;
the sluggish fish to muscle slides;
eventual chemistry will bring
the lightning bug to the shrewd toad's eye.
It is true no thing of earth can die.

4

What then feeds on us? On our blood
and delectable flesh: the flood
of flower to fossil, coal to snow,
genes of glacier and volcano?
And our diamond souls that are bent
upward? To what beast's intent
are we the fodder and nourishment?

Zambesi and Ranee

Because their mothers refused to nurse them, the two female animals in
this compartment were reared together by hand from early infancy...
They are firm friends and strongly resent separation. While Zambesi,
the lion, is inclined to be rough and aggressive, Ranee, the tiger,
easily dominates her.   —From a plaque at the Bronx Zoo

The tiger looks the younger and more male,
her body ribbed with staves as black as Bengal's
    in the next den. Clear green her eyes,
    in the great three-cornered head, set slantwise;
her hips as lean, her back as straight,
she's a velvet table when she walks, and able
    to bound ten feet to the level where her meat
    is flung at feeding time.

The lion, square-bodied, heavy-pelted, less grand,
her maneless, round-eared head held low,
    slouches and rocks in sand-colored nakedness,
    drag-bellied, watchful and slow; her yellow eyes
jealous, something morose in the down-hook
    of her jaw; her tail, balled at the end,
    like a riding crop taps at the bars.

They twine their shared pavilion, each spine
tracing an opposite figure eight. Paired females,
    they avoid each other's touch; but if, passing,
    as much as a whisker of that black-and-orange head
grazes the lion's flank, her topaz eye narrows:
    irascibly she turns with slugger's paw
    to rake the ear of her mate.

Then rampant, they wrestle; rich snarls
in coils pour from their throats and nostrils.
    Like soft boulders the bodies tumble each other down.
    And then, not bothering to rise, they lounge,
entangled chest to chest. Not hate embroils them,
but that neither will be humble to the other;
    nor will the tiger, in earnest, test her quickness
    against the lion's weight.

Few sights can still surprise us in the zoo,
   though this is the place for marvels.
These odd heroines do attract us. Why?
Crouched on sinewy elbows, sphinxes, they project
   vast boredom. Those still heads outstare
   some horizon of catlike time, while we, in vain,
expect a gleam from eye to eye between them,
a posture of affection, or some clue . . .

Bemused at the bars, some watchers smile and read
Zambesi and Ranee upon their card:
   They might ring the bell, introduce themselves
   and be welcome. The life these ladies lead,
upon a stage, repeats itself behind the walls
   of many city streets; silent, or aloud,
   the knowing crowd snickers.

Refused to nurse them, simpering mothers read,
and tighten the hold on Darling's hand: "Look
   at the pussy cats!" they coax, they croon,
   but blushing outrage appals their cheeks—
that this menage calls down no curse,
not only is excused, but celebrated.
   They'd prefer these captives punished, who
   appear to wear the brand some captivated humans do.

The Legend of To Rise

On a certain island
(this was long ago)
among a savage people
when a man died
the others took spears
stones and blazing coals
and punished his body
while gibbering drums
ridiculed his crime

With taunts and curses
 and salivary rage
  they spewed his rigid face
  gouged and flayed
   his bloodless flesh
    burned his hair
     and boiled his eyes
      till the sockets cracked
       When the corpse was chopped
        to chunks and charred
         the ashes and black bones
          were pushed into a hole
           Young boys were made
            to dip their tongues in it
             while the women chanted
              a warning to remember
               the loathsome taste of death
                Anthropologists find
                 that among this people
                  many lived 300 years
                 (some even longer)
                The purest among them
                 a shaman of the tribe
                  who longest had succeeded
                   in avoiding death
                    evolved an Other Body
                     impervious to the weakness
                      that lets a man sink
                       to the lowest crime
                        This wise man taught
                         that the earth is drenched in death
                          the epidemic spreading
                           from a toxin in the stones
                            seething in her belly
                             and that the earth herself
                              a living body once
                               and born without sin
                                has been rotting in her slime
                                 these million years

The shaman it is told
took a small company
of chosen followers
the purest of the tribe
and spent a century
teaching them to Rise
To Rise was a ritual
an exercise
to change their bodies
perfect their control
and make them ready
for the High Journey
to discover a New Earth
innocent of death
And the legend tells
how the shaman rose
but how the others fell
on the High Journey
back to death-ridden earth
and eventually died
There is pictured
in the caves of this people
the shaman in his Other Body
risen to the New Earth
herself an Other Body
with a new Genesis
The New Earth is shown
peopled by the shaman alone
by means of a new genital
fostered within him
through purity and strength

Death, Great Smoothener

Death,
great smoothener,
maker of order,
arrester, unraveler, sifter and changer;
death, great hoarder;

                    student, stranger, drifter, traveler,
             flyer and nester all caught at your border;
                              death,
                         great halter;
                  blackener and frightener,
                     reducer, dissolver,
         seizer and welder of younger with elder,
                     waker with sleeper,
                    death, great keeper
                    of all that must alter;
                              death,
                        great heightener,
                       leaper, evolver,
                     great smoothener,
                      great whitener!

Today in Winter's Town

                                I

Up there we rode
a knife, that slid
through mountains of snow.

It was summer: the snow
was in the sky: great high
solid buttes ahead, piled

on blue—built
of white silence.
But, pierced, were veils:

behind them silver
veils, behind them
denser veils; the gray

layered middle hid
snarled balls of thunder.
The wing we rode on vanished,

the engine's amputated
pupa struggled on—
shuddered up, and out—grew

new blades in the sun,
flash-raced along
a slope of snow again.

2

We passed through mountains
then, our youth swift as
years were insubstantial;

our sharp car lifted
into illusion, or dove
down frighteningly far.

Today in winter's town,
in my motionless chair,
I ride beside a window where

blue motes rush
backwards by me—brick
across the street obliterated

by those thick veils
that glitter as if lightning
stained them still.

Those hills of cloud
are pouring down to earth
in grains that seethe

the air—while, wingless,
I ride the twilight's
center, in my chair.

The Properties

New time is long
Old time short
The old is emptied
And curled up
Now is a full case
The folds expand
Its crowd-shapes
Feel not their end

Used time re-used
Thins and dulls
The strip is thick
If freedom pulls
It from the spool
At first unwinding
Loose and clear
It foresees no rebinding

Future time
As if it stood
In weight its maker
Comes to add
A cube to its structure
Raw and stern
The shadow-fixture
Howls to be born

In motion and feature
And to think
A fresh universe
From the rank
Of old old limit
Is mind's game
And innocent infinity
The same

New time short
Used time is long
Beginning vacant
I end my song
Then what seams
Is only art
Holds wide and narrow
Up and down apart

2

Targets in the brain

At
Breakfast

Not quite
spherical
White
Oddly closed
and without a lid

A smooth miracle
here in my hand
Has it slid
from my sleeve?

The shape
of this box
keels me oval
Heels feel
its bottom
Nape knocks
its top

Seated
like a foetus
I look for
the dream-seam

What's inside?
A sun?
Off with its head
though it hasn't any
or is all head no body
a
One

Neatly
the knife scalps it
I scoop out
the braincap
soft

sweetly shuddering
Mooncream
this could be
Spoon
laps the larger
crescent
loosens a gilded
nucleus
from warm pap
A lyrical food

Opened
a seamless miracle
Ate a sun-germ
Good

Hypnotist

His lair framed beneath the clock
a red-haired beast hypnotic in the room
glazes our eyes draws us close
with delicious snarls and flickers of his claws
We stir our teacups and our wishes feast
on his cruelty

Throw the Christian chairs to him
a wild child in us cries
Or let us be Daniel bared
to that seething maze his mane
Loops of his fur graze the sill
where the clock's face looks scared

Comfort-ensnared and languorous
our unused daring roused resembles him
fettered on the hearth's stage
behind the iron dogs
He's the red locks of the sun
brought home to a cage

Hunched before his flaring shape
we stir our teacups
We wish he would escape
and loosen in ourselves the terrible
But only his reflection pounces
on the parquet and the stair

Was Worm

Was worm
swaddled in white

Now tiny queen
in sequin coat
peacockbright
drinks the wind
and feeds
on sweat of the leaves

Is little chinks
of mosaic floating
or a scatter
of colored beads

Alighting pokes
with her new black wire
the saffron yokes

On silent hinges
openfolds her wings'
applauding hands

Weaned
from coddling white
to lakedeep air
to blue and green

Is queen

An Extremity

Roused from napping in my lap
this nimble animal or five-legged star
parts its limbs sprat-wide
    See where they glide to focus at their base as spokes of a harp
    Blunt and fat the first
sharp-tipped tapping the next
the third authentic and the fourth shy
the least a runt begs pardon for his stature
    Why they're separate beasts I see
and not one beast with legs

    Or a family of dolls
you could dress the tallest as a boy
already his sister wears a silver belt
that's a toy-baby by her curled if you put a bonnet on it
    Here's agile-joint the pointed the smart wife
    Square-head short and papa-perfect
sits apart in dignity a wart at knuckle

    Turned over open inner skin is vellum
    Here's a map
five islands spread from the mainland in the fist
    Seen flat it's a plain
forked rivers thread to the wrist
or call them roads the rosy pattern sprawled in an M
    Forests are stitched with prick-hatched pinetree criss-marks
    Whorled lines are ploughed land
and ending each pentacle beach are U-bands of sea-rippled sand

    Left one looked at
right one writes Star Harp Beast Family of Five
    Map laid live in my lap
    Clapped together the two arrive are stated
the poem made extremities mated

Am I Becoming?

Where I am becoming
  in the square
  am I becoming?
His bristles stroke
  and bristles appear
  to be my brows of umber

His squint tarries
  on the blank square
  then seizing the print
  from the seeing pair
  in the chair
  his wand darts
  to demon blue
Cobalt pupils
  receive their tint

A snitch of white
  of purple a drop
  his soft switch
  leaves nostrils here
I smell what he weaves
  a petal of zinc
  the gloss of jasmine
  and turpentine's ozone
  suggesting the zest
  of a sneeze
With lampblack raw
  as pitch he draws the
  undulation of my jaws

Naples Yellow
  a glistening tail
  muddies itself in ochre
Rough spokes
  he sets in motion
He peers where
  at the side and in the air
  a fugitive light enters
  to spear the iris

Bristles twinkle
  in Chinese White
My double stare suddenly
  sees him!
The square is occupied

Skull feels its roots
Their pull and sprout
  confirm it round
  and able to beckon
From clavicle's ground
  a stem becomes a neck

Alizarin Crimson
  (in Arabic this means
  juice) the lash
  is dipped into its pool
Prickles scour my cheeks
  their small ecstatic slaps
  cool from the peaks
  upon the palette
Now the lips are fed
I taste the smile
  he points with Madder Red

Shade slips with the
  charcoal down my head
Dark Violet and Iron
  oil the eyelid
Opposite in window light
  a spectral chrome
  marks the gnomish snuggle
  of the ear
I hear the scratch
  of that stiff wand
  that dents the pond
  Verd Emeraude
  to match and to begin
  the scarf at my chin

I am becoming
Am I becoming in the square?
I have been transferred
 from my chair

With eyes he made
 I see his wrist

the twist of hair
wade in umber
carried to a corner
to hide his name
and the year's number

Seven Natural Songs

1   Awoke and stretched in all the bodies
    lofted on sinewy air.   Clipped out
    beak-shaped cries and skinned the mist
    from the morning.

2   Stood wooden, wiggled in earth way under.
    A toenail scraped a mammoth's tusk.
    Jounced and jittered all these lippy leaves.

3   Slicked along meddling with rocks.   Tore
    their ears off gradually.   Sparkling made
    them hop and holler down a slate-cold throat.

4   Humped up, sucked in all my thongs
    belly-deep to the roaring core.   Recoiled
    for a big yellow bloom.   Burst and hurled
    wide open pods of light everywhere.

5   Loosened and looled elongate in hammocks
    of blue.   Evasive of shape and the eggshell's
    curve.   Without taint or tint or substance
    dissolved in fleecy sloth.

6   Pricked up out of each pore, urgent, ambitious,
    itching to be even.   Scurried and spread
    so all is kept level.   Forever unfinished
    my mass fernal mystery.   Ants read its roots,
    tell its juices to sand.

7 Once cloud, now all memory my motion.
  Amorphous creeping slow as sleep to a full
  black gulping flood.   The small five-fingered
  blot enlarged beyond identity.   Heavy unslaked,
  still hunting form.   The hiding place,
  the necessary horror.

1 Birds   2 Tree   3 Waterfall   4 Sun
5 Clouds   6 Grass   7 Shadow

To Her Images
(For I. M.)

As if the aimed
            heads of swans
            with reaching necks
            their napes curved
            came to their images
To the glozed
            the sleeping surface
            black-white-beamed
            her hands on sinuous arms
            the wrists reared dipped
Dilations of light ran
            rapid and chill
            from the high splints
            on the panel
Lower the fingers
            spanned plunged like bills
            and slower orbits began
            and opened
A kind of dawn awoke
            clean in the bone
            of the ear
            clear lake-lappings
            against the steady
            breasts of swans

Targets in the brain
            were pierced by rays
            glancing from the poises
            of those scarcely plucking
            beaks on the keys'
            reflected pinions
Then prongs ripped
            a heavy element
            strong muscled like whirlpool
            flinching the heart's drumskin
Whips of light across the eyes
            those swans
            and her body dived
In groans as of great
            stones embracing under water
            she came to her images
Then silence a long
            mirror rose upright

Frontispiece

In this book I see your face and in your face
your eyes holding the world and all else besides
like a cat's pupils rayed and wide
to what is before them and what more alive
ticks in the shadows flickers in the waves

Your hair in a slow stream curves
from your listening brow
to your ear shaped like a sea-thing found
in that water-haunted house where murmurs
your chaste-fierce name   The vow

that corners your mouth
compelled you to that deep between words and acts
where they cross as sand with salt
There spills the layered light
your sockets lips and nostrils drank

before they sank
On stages of the sea the years tall
tableaus build   The lighthouse you commanded
the room the oak and mutable Orlando
reoccur as the sea's pages to land's mind   The wall

the steep and empty slate
your cane indented until you laid it as a mark
above where the tide would darken
in weed and shell is written how you were sane
when walking you wrapped your face

in the green scarf
the gray
and then the black
The waves carve your hearse and tomb
and toll your voyage out again again

R. F. at Bread Loaf
His Hand Against a Tree

His hand on the saw
    ed off should
    er of a tree
Companions he and the cross
    grained bark
    crusted fellow from whose stub
    born t hickness limb
    er switches lean
    and wag young leaves
Lines in that hand
    whorls in that tree re
    cord a brother's chronic
    le the stoic accrual of s
    elfhood from the c ore out
Flat of his palm and flat
    of the cut fork meet fit
    tingly

Lots of trees in the fo
    rest but this one's an O
    a K that's plan
    ted hims elf and nob
    oddy has k nots of that hand
    some polish or the knarl
    edge of ear th or the obs
    tiny ate servation his blueyes
    make or the tr easures his sent
    ient t humb les find
His sig nature's on the he art
    of his time
Snowcrop on rude dy square b
    locked f orehead
    on summer's dreamhead
Snowrims over w him sey t wink
    led blueyes
And veined in autumn g love
    that ax and ax
    iom h ardent hand
Oh may it feel many sp rings
    widening warm hone y ed
    g lad as the c limb of youth

Deciding

Deciding to go on digging doing it
what they said outside wasn't any use
Inside hiding it made it get ambitious
Like a potato in a dark bin
it grew white grabbers for light
out of its navel eyes not priding
itself much just deciding
it wasn't true inside what they said
outside those bumps were

All humped alike dumped inside
slumped in burlap said
roots are no good out of ground

a fruit's crazy to want to be a flower
Besides it's sin changing the given shape
Bursting the old brown skin is suicide
Wishing to taste like a tulip
sip colored light
outside thumps said isn't right

Deciding to keep on striding
from inside bursting the bin-side
poking out wishes for delicious opposites
turning blind eyes to strong fingers
touching meaning more than sight
the navel scars of weaning
used for something finally
Deciding to go on digging doing it

Two-Part Pear Able

I. SOMETHING MISSING

In a country where
every tree is a pear tree
it is a shock to see
one tree
(a pear tree undoubtedly
for its leaves are the leaves
of a pear)
that shows no pears

It is a fairly tall tree
sturdy
capable looking
its limbs strong its leaves glossy
its posture in fact exceptionally
pleasing

but there
among the true pear trees
all of which show pears

the pear tree with no pears
appears (to say the least)
unlikely
and therefore
unlovely

You see
those globes invariably
grow in the trees of that country
There are no other kinds of trees
and pears in the pear trees
are what make them trees
as much
(no even more than)
their leaves
Otherwise they would be named
leaf trees

Pears are what the trees *have*
The leaves are accessory
They are there
to set off the shapes
and colors of the fruits
and shade them
(naturally)
and shelter them
It is as if the trees
were great cool nests for the pears
So that a nest
like the rest (apparently)
but empty
is inconceivable
Like seeing a ghost
or at most a body
without bones

It is a shock
and a pity to see
a pear tree
that can't be
but is

2. SOMETHING ADDED IS WORSE

But in another country
where there
are trees just trees
and no one has ever seen
a fruit tree
of any kind
(much less specifically
a pear tree)
suppose a *pear* tree

(This country must be
entirely imaginary
you say and we agree
The other's unlikely
but could be)

Suppose suddenly
in between leaves
(that are the "fruits" actually)
another sort of a leaf
but differently
shaped and colored
heavier
and depending from a gross
stem were discovered
And then more and more

And finally
it is seen that this tree
is infested with pears
(not yet named of course)
hidden
but obviously
getting bigger
growing there with the leaves

And someone says
How horrible
these leaves are turning into

into *fruits*
(fortuitously
inventing an aggressive
name for it)

There will be
general revulsion won't there?
There will be
demand for expulsion

which could easily
succeed
for the time being

And in that country's
dictionary
it will be
a long while before you see
the word *pear*

Parade of Painters

ASSIGNMENT OF COLORS

Cezanne green
Modigliani orange
Picasso blue
Gauguin brown

Renoir pink
Matisse yellow
Monet violet
Van Gogh red

Manet white
Corot ochre
Millet wheat
Lautrec slate

Vuillard zebra
de la Fresnaye flamingo
Fragonard umber
Poussin taupe

Goya ash
Greco purple
Titian pimento
Hals milk

Rembrandt clove
Velasquez iron
Courbet smoke
Rubens gold

Bonheur poppy
Delacroix iris
Rousseau pepper
Degas clay

Daumier apple
Pissarro marble
Redon maze
Seurat poplar

Derain oak
Dufy azure
Soutine black
Rouault blood

ASSIGNMENT OF TEXTURES

Rouault serge
Soutine plumage
Dufy pearl
Derain froth

Seurat linen
Redon chamois
Pissarro privet
Daumier hair

Degas birch
Rousseau bees
Delacroix viscera
Bonheur snow

Rubens thunder
Courbet onyx
Velasquez gentian
Rembrandt light

Hals pine
Titian leather
Greco quills
Goya coins

Poussin grass
Fragonard wine
de la Fresnaye fleece
Vuillard geranium

Lautrec pears
Millet cobbles
Corot fog
Manet porcelain

Van Gogh talons
Monet moon
Matisse thistles
Renoir moss

Gauguin balsam
Picasso bone
Modigliani ice
Cezanne sea

ASSIGNMENT OF SHAPES

Soutine trumpet
Derain eel
Seurat hourglass

Pissarro dhow
Rousseau corolla
Bonheur conch
Rubens narwhal
Velasquez groin

Titian heron
Goya gnome
Poussin lantern
de la Fresnaye hoof
Millet urn
Monet eye
Van Gogh anvil
Matisse heart

Picasso window
Cezanne javelin
Modigliani mask
Rouault mummy
Gauguin sundial
Dufy glove
Renoir mirage
Redon borzoi

Manet alembic
Daumier pistol

Corot scarab
Degas witchmoth

Lautrec cloak
Delacroix mouth

Vuillard chimera
Courbet acorn

Fragonard whistle

Rembrandt burnoose

Greco knot

Hals caliper

ORDER OF ASSEMBLY

Modigliani mask ice orange
Gauguin sundial balsam brown
Matisse heart thistles yellow

Van Gogh anvil talons red
Corot scarab fog ochre
Lautrec cloak pears slate

de la Fresnaye hoof fleece flamingo
Poussin lantern grass taupe
Greco knot quills purple

Hals caliper pine milk
Velasquez groin gentian iron
Rubens narwhal thunder gold

Delacroix mouth viscera iris
Degas witchmoth birch clay
Pissarro dhow privet marble
Seurat hourglass linen poplar
Dufy glove pearl azure
Rouault mummy serge blood
Cezanne javelin sea green

Picasso window bone blue
Renoir mirage moss pink
Monet eye moon violet
Manet alembic porcelain white
Millet urn cobbles wheat

Vuillard chimera geranium zebra

Fragonard whistle wine umber
Goya gnome coins ash

Titian heron leather pimento

Rembrandt burnoose light clove
Courbet acorn onyx smoke

Bonheur conch snow poppy

Rousseau corolla bees pepper
Daumier pistol hair apple

Redon borzoi chamois maze

Derain eel froth oak
Soutine trumpet plumage black

The Process

Lie down upon your side
 and fold your knees
  Bend your hands at the wrist
   against your chest
    as a cat or dog does in repose

     Close your eyes and feel
      your brow smooth out like a small
       cloth in the wind
        or a brook slipping
         to gentle waterfall

          Now wait for what will happen
           Something will

            Beneath this hill of breathing hair
             a steep mine
              Within this ear
               oracles of echoes seep
                Wide and clear the eyelid's dome
                 a galaxy where suns collide
                  and planets spin and moons begin

Words are birds perceived
in a secret forest
Fed by nerve and vein they hop
from twig to twig and up
an ivory ladder to the top
where it is light and they remain
and are believed

3

A health of yellow

Looking Uptown

All cars run one way: toward the point of the wedge
where the sky is pinched
in the meeting of perpendiculars.
Over mats of shadow, through rents of sun,
the cars run, with a sound of ripping silk
in the gape of the avenue,
to cram where it narrows far uptown.
The metallic back of something scaly
oozes there in its trap.

Here in the foreground: gigantic terraces
of stone to left and right, inlaid with squares
of mirror; and the suede shadows mimic on cement
angular rhomboids, flat parapets,
so that the cars purr over wide checkers.

Along the corridor, the eye, as well, must race,
drawn by a stream of horizontal threads
fastened to that far blue slice.
At every crossing, pairs of hooded lights
decide to let the cars proceed.
But, in the vise, a glinting lizard pack
strangles, drained of speed,
while the free eye dives on, true and straight,
up the open vertical, to swallow space.

Working on Wall Street

What's left of the sunset's watered blood
settles between the slabs of Wall Street.
Winter rubs the sky bruise-blue as flesh.
We head down into the subway, glad
the cars are padded with bodies so we
keep warm. Emptied from tall closets
where we work, on the days' shelves
reached by elevators, the heap of us,
pressed by iron sides, dives forward under
the city—parcels shipped out in a trunk.

The train climbs from its cut to the trestle.
Sunset's gone. Those slabs across the murky
river have shrunk to figurines, reflecting
the blush of neon—a dainty tableau, all
pink, on the dresser-top of Manhattan—
eclipsed as we sink into the tunnel.
The train drops and flattens for the long
bore under Brooklyn.

Night, a hiatus hardly real, tomorrow
this double rut of steel will racket us back
to the city. We, packages in the trade
made day after day, will tumble out of
hatches on the Street, to be met by swags
of wind that scupper off those roofs
(their upper windows blood-filled by the sun).
Delivered into lobbies, clapped into upgoing
cages, sorted to our compartments, we'll be
stamped once more for our wages.

To the Statue

The square-heeled boat sets off for the Statue.
People are stuck up tight as asparagus stalks
inside the red rails (ribbons tying the bunch).

The tips, their rigid head against the fog,
all yearn toward the Statue; dents of waves
all minimize and multiply to where

she, fifteen minutes afar (a cooky-tin-shaped-
mother-doll) stands without a feature
except her little club of flame.

Other boats pass the promenade. It's exciting
to watch the water heave up, clop the pier,
and even off: a large unsteady belly,

oil-scaled, gasping, then breathing normally.
On the curved horizon, faded shapes of ships,
with thready regalia, cobweb a thick sky.

Nearer, a spluttering bubble over the water
(a mosquito's skeletal hindpart, wings detached
and fused to whip on top like a child's whirltoy)

holds two policemen. They're seated in the air,
serge, brass-buttoned paunches behind glass,
serene, on rubber runners, sledding fog.

Coming back, framed by swollen pilings,
the boat is only inches wide, and flat.
Stalk by stalk, they've climbed into her head

(its bronze is green out there, and hugely spiked)
and down her winding spine into their package,
that now bobs forward on the water's mat.

Soon three-dimensional, colored like a drum,
red-staved, flying a dotted flag,
its rusty iron toe divides the harbor;

sparkling shavings curl out from the bow.
Their heads have faces now. They've been to the Statue.
She has no face from here, but just a fist.
(The flame is carved like an asparagus tip.)

Ornamental Sketch with Verbs

Sunset runs in a seam
over the brows of buildings
    dropping west to the river,
turns the street to a gilded stagger,
makes the girl on skates,
    the man with the block of ice,
    the basement landlady calling her cat
    creatures in a dream,

scales with salamander-red
     the window-pitted walls,
hairs the gutters with brindled light,
helmets cars and boys on bikes
and double-dazzles
     the policeman's portly coat,
halos the coal truck where
     nuggets race from a golden sled,

festoons lampposts to fantastic trees,
lacquers sooty roofs and pavements,
floats in every puddle
     pinks of cloud,
flamingos all the pigeons,
grands all dogs to chows,
enchants the ash cans into urns
     and fire-escapes to Orleans balconies.

At East River

| Tugboat: | A large shoe |
| shuffles the floor of water, |
| leaving a bright scrape. |

Floating Gulls: Ballet slippers, dirty-white,
                     walk awkward backward.
                     Bobbing closer: yellow-pointed painted
                     wooden shoes.

The Bay: Flat, shiny, rustling
              like parquet under the bridge's
              balustrade of gray garlands.

On the Bridge: Slow skates of cars (a distant whisper)
                    and the long swishing foot of a train.

A Plane: Turns on its elegant heel:
              a spark, a click
              of steel on blue.

That Steamer: The top of a short boot, red and black,
                  budging deep water wading to the sea.

Brooklyn: A shelf of old shoes,
              needing repair,
              but clean knots of smoke
              are being tied and untied.

Water Picture

In the pond in the park
all things are doubled:
Long buildings hang and
wriggle gently. Chimneys
are bent legs bouncing
on clouds below. A flag
wags like a fishhook
down there in the sky.

The arched stone bridge
is an eye, with underlid
in the water. In its lens
dip crinkled heads with hats
that don't fall off. Dogs go by,
barking on their backs.
A baby, taken to feed the
ducks, dangles upside-down,
a pink balloon for a buoy.

Treetops deploy a haze of
cherry bloom for roots,
where birds coast belly-up
in the glass bowl of a hill;
from its bottom a bunch
of peanut-munching children
is suspended by their
sneakers, waveringly.

A swan, with twin necks
forming the figure 3,
steers between two dimpled
towers doubled. Fondly
hissing, she kisses herself,
and all the scene is troubled:
water-windows splinter,
tree-limbs tangle, the bridge
folds like a fan.

Fountain Piece II

In a circular mirror
of stippled water,
the peculiar color

such waters are—
the shade of shade
or of morbid willow,

the dusk of dusk
or of drowned moss—
a float for lilies,

their white teats
even in sunlight chill,
there stands at center

a double goblet,
a stone cake
or loving cup,

or huge Susan,
twirling, it seems,
with the wind's push

at the crystal ropes
of gauzy water
at the stone rims

of the two bowls;
the lower and larger
being the roof

of a kind of temple
with pleated columns
and miniature arches

she the cake's
intricate pinnacle,
the goblet's frothy

cream of stone,
or the fixture of fortune
on the loving cup;

her wings whipped out
from arrogant shoulders
above the drool

of the blown water
that, bowl to bowl,
lashes the pool

forming a porch
for the jazz of water;
and under the other,

as in a pavilion
of scalloped stone,
still and immune

and heavy waves
clap at her heel;
she the triumph

behind the flicker
of flouncing water,
four grave cherubs

of the twirling Susan,
trailing swags
of clear hysteric water;

holding hands,
press stone buttocks
against stone;

with the sound of harsh
lace being torn,
or shavings of glass,

a tier above them
upon a dais
of saucered stone

wind-shivered and strewn,
that stipples the lower
circle where,

in shifting water,
an angel strides
with full-sprouting wings,

at the foot of the goblet
lilies prick
in the shade of shade,

her determined thighs
shunting the folds
of her robe apart,

in the dusk of dusk,
the color
of drowned moss.

To the Shore

Wheels flee on silky steel. We are seated
in a glass tube that, bullet-headed, cleaves
the scene, tossing a froth of fields and trees
and billowing land alongside.

Paced by idle clouds, we glide on a ruled diameter
of green. Preserved from weather, tidy, on display,
we are chosen fruits in a jar. Too soon, the far
and faded hills become particular in color;
too quickly the sea sparkles between them. The wide,
rough, plough-measured miles are belittled to a park.

In our space-splitting capsule, where the horses
are diesel, time and the sun's heat suddenly seem
indecently excluded, along with natural grime.
Not special plums or pears, wearing blue ribbons
for county fairs, no rare aristocrats of pleasure,
we rompers to a popular shore arrive
only a little chosen above the poor. Below our
shelf of glass, cows brazenly chew, unamazed,
as we pass, and scornfully ogle our wheels,
their boredom real, and reassuring.

Early Morning: Cape Cod

We wake to double blue:
an ocean without sail,
sky without a clue
of white.
Morning is a veil
sewn of only two
threads, one pale,
one bright.

We bathe as if in ink,
but peacock-eyed and clear;
a roof of periwink
goes steep
into a bell of air
vacant to the brink.
Far as we can peer
is deep

royal blue and shy
iris, queen and king
colors of low
and high.
Then dips
a sickle wing,
we hear a hinged cry:
taut as from a sling

downwhips
a taunting gull.
And now across our gaze
a snowy hull
appears;
triangles
along its stays
break out to windpulls.

With creaking shears
the bright
gulls cut the veil
in two,
and many a clue
on scalloped sail
dots with white
our double blue.

The Tide at Long Point

The sea comes up and the sun goes over
    The sea goes out and the sun falls
The stubby shadow of the lighthouse pales
    stretches to a finger and inches east
The wind lifts from off the sea
    and curries and curries the manes of the dunes
The pipers and the terns skate over
    tweaking the air with their talk
In sky clean as a cat-licked dish
    clouds are sandbars bared by ebbing blue

The hourglass is reversed

The sea comes up and the moon peers over
    The sea goes out and the moon swells
The shadow of the lighthouse thick as a boot
    is swiped by a whiskered beam

The wind licks at the jetty stones
    The pipers and terns hunch on the spit
hiding their necks and stilted feet
    The sky has caught a netful of stars
The moon is a dory trolling them in

The hourglass is reversed

The sea comes up and the moon tips under
    The sea goes out and the sun looms
The sun is a schooner making for harbor
    Shallops of cloud are adrift in the west
The wind gallops the waves to a lather
    and lashes the grass that shines on the dunes
The lighthouse looks at its twin in the water
    The pipers and terns preen on its brow

The Even Sea

Meekly the sea
now plods to shore:
white-faced cattle used to their yard,
the waves, with weary knees,
come back from bouldered hills
of high water,

where all the gray, rough day they seethed like bulls,
till the wind laid down its goads
at shift of tide, and sundown
gentled them; with lowered necks
they amble up the beach
as to their stalls.

Sunday in the Country

No wind-wakeness here. A cricket's creed
intoned to the attentive wood all day.
The sun's incessant blessing. Too much gold
weighs on my head where I lay it in light.
Angels climb through my lashes, their wings
so white, every color clings there. Sky,
deep and accusing in its blue, scrapes
my conscience like a nail. I'm glad
for the gray spider who, with torpid
menace, mounts my shoe; for the skittish
fly with his green ass and orange eyes,
who wades in hairs of my arm to tickle
his belly. Long grass, silky as a monk's
beard, the blades all yellow-beamed.
Corporeal self's too shapeful for this manger.
I'm mesmerized by trumpet sun
funneling hallelujah to my veins.

Until, at the tabernacle's back, a blurt
guffaw is heard. An atheistic stranger calls
a shocking word. That wakes the insurrection!
Wind starts in the wood, and strips the pompous
cassocks from the pines. A black and
impudent Voltairean crow has spoiled
the sacrament. And I can rise and go.

Forest

The pines, aggressive as erect tails of cats,
bob their tips when the wind freshens.

An alert breath like purring stirs below,
where I move timid over humps of hair,

crisp, shadow-brindled, heaving as if
exhilarated muscular backs felt

the wisps of my walking. Looking to sky,
glaring then closing between the slow

lashes of boughs, I feel observed:
up high are oblong eyes that know,

as their slits of green light
expand, squeeze shut, expand,

that I stand here. Suddenly I go,
flick-eyed, hurrying over fur

needles that whisper as if they weren't dead.
My neck-hairs rise. The feline forest grins

behind me. Is it about to follow?
Which way out through all these whiskered yawns?

A Haunted House

Evil streams from that corner, beside the bookcase
where the bulging mirror hangs.
When flames rush in the grate
and the paneled room, all tawny, is nude of shadow,
there is a pallor of the air in that corner.

In firelight the wicked eyes of portraits appear
more real than paint; the sallow books
have rubbed cheeks for a hundred years,
yet confess a gold title here and there; the dim carpet
blushes beneath the table and reveals its

threadbare rose. Still, there is a stench of horror
in that corner. Is it evil or awe on a summer day
inhabits the well of the stair, the black jaw
of the chimney empty of fire,
the horsehair sofa, the rug,

the mildewed mahogany walls? Into the dull room
the youthful light from the window,
decantered through leaves, comes queerly.
The convex mirror mimics on its eyeball
a bulging room where everything is small,

and piped with silver as in a mezzotint.
Pinched above the peephole of the window,
the ceiling beams like ribs of a dusty fan
seem to close on the light of the present,
squeezing shut its green, wan frame.

In that thick scope, a glass reversed,
intently aimed upon the past, I can see
my own brown head—remote, wizened as a nut.
Fearfully familiar, it too wears the film of time.
But this is time to come. Wonder,

not horror, should thrum my spine and spike my eye.
There is a haunting here, but not of evil.
It is Time that breathes
in a corner of the future.
Time is the ghost of this house.

News From the Cabin

I

Hairy was here.
He hung on a sumac seed pod.
Part of his double tail hugged the crimson
    scrotum under cockscomb leaves—
    or call it blushing lobster claw, that swatch—
    a toothy match to Hairy's red skullpatch.
Cried *peek!* Beaked it—chiselled the drupe.
His nostril I saw, slit in a slate whistle.
White-black dominoes clicked in his wings.
Bunched beneath the dangle he heckled with holes,
    bellysack soft, eye a brad, a red-flecked
    mallet his ball-peen head, his neck its haft.

2

Scurry was here.
He sat up like a six-inch bear,
    rocked on the porch with me;
    brought his own chair, his chow-haired tail.
Ate a cherry I threw.
Furry paunch, birchbark-snowy, pinecone-brown back,
    a jacket with sleeves to the digits.
Sat put, pert, neat, in his suit and his seat, for a minute,
    a frown between snub ears, bulb-eyed head
    toward me sideways, chewed.
Rocked, squeaked. Stored the stone in his cheek.
Finished, fell to all fours, a little roan couch;
    flurried paws loped him off, prone-bodied,
    tail turned torch, sail, scarf.

3

Then, Slicker was here.
Dipped down, cobalt and turquoise brushes
    fresh as paint. Gripped a pine-tassle,
    folded his flaunts, parted his pointed nib, and scrawled
    jeeah! on the air.
Japanned so smooth, his head-peak and all his shaft:
    harsh taunts from that dovey shape, soft tints—
    nape and chin black-splintered, quilltips white-lashed.
Javelin-bird, he slurred his color,
    left his ink-bold word here; flashed off.
Morning prints his corvine noise elsewhere,
    while that green toss still quivers with his equipoise.

4

And Supple was here.
Lives nearby at the stump.
Trickled out from under, when the sun struck there.
Mud-and-silver-licked, his length—a single spastic muscle—
    slid over stones and twigs to a snuggle of roots, and hid.
I followed that elastic: loose
    unicolored knot, a noose he made as if unconscious.

Until my shadow touched him: half his curd
   shuddered, the rest lay chill.
I stirred: the ribbon raised a loop;
   its end stretched, then cringed like an udder;
   a bifid tongue, his only rapid, whirred
   in the vent; vertical pupils lit his hood.
That part, a groping finger, hinged, stayed upright.
Indicated what? That I stood
   in his light? I left the spot.

The Harp

   Where the trail bends, at morning
   a great harp is strung
   of saplings, and sunlight thrums a chord,
   crystal to jade, a green glissade,
   chrome to lapis lazuli.

   At crescendo of the noon
   a scarlet bird, the strings among,
   dips his passionate sharp wings
   and strokes the furnace-ruddy lyre,
   evoking a daemonic chord,
   the deathless, the death-dealing fire.

   Then, bent by wind, long bows are wrung.
   The clashing leaves
   skirl cymbals with a silver sun.
   Twanging gray in stealthy rain,
   a spent chord shivers and grieves.

   Where the trail to evening bends,
   the moon's back-raveling hand,
   thin its glitter, the spectrum spanned,
   plucks upon a single wire
   a final chord: frail snake-eyes,
   clear burnoose purple and sapphire.

Executions

I walk out on thongs of shadow,
my back to the morning sun,
the pines' dark quivers running up along their bow
of sky: taut blue about to twang
with the anguish of summer, shot.
October's target-mark on every leaf,
on points of dew my shadow rips;
light pierces wings of jays in flight:
they shout my grief.

Ring, locusts: murder is prepared;
shorn fair pine hair litters the ground;
swords already have beheaded mushrooms:
black necks rot in these sunny grottos
that sumac, blood-beaded, drapes.
And ghostly fern here frightens me,
spanned like my light-catching hands,
a design for urns.

By stride escaped to the meadow,
I think that mound, that haul of sun,
a health of yellow, still safe from killer shadow,
but all is beaten flat: torn shucks
in the flogging place, pale corpses
surpliced with light.
Then, hearse-horns of macabre crows sweep over;
gibbet-masks they cut on blue.
I wade in husks, in broken shafts of arrows.

The Day Moon

The day moon, a half ball of snow vaulting
the mountain, was thrown last night by the level east
from a heavy fist.

Its chunk, of metal, passed the pole among the pelting
stars, one curve sliced, the other cupped
in the upright dark, of charcoal. Looped

the parabola of west, lost weight and glamour,
a plaster socket, kneecap-shaped, or as if hammer-
dented. Porous, marrow-old, dawn tossed

it lower. Shrank in the pink net of the sun, a shell
so light no pitch could give it force. Fell
on cold and solid morning, an almost-ball

rolled by a hard hand. Halts
so, until the day aloft the mountain melts,
softens it, bitten wafer, slips it down.

Spring Uncovered

Gone the scab of ice that kept it snug,
the lake is naked.

Skins of cloud on torn blue:
sky is thin.

A cruelty, the ribs of trees
ribboned by sun's organdy.

Forsythia's yellow, delicate rags,
flip in the wind.

Wind buckles the face of the lake;
it flinches under a smack of shot.

Robbed of stoic frost, grass
bleeds from gaffs of the wind.

Rock, ridging the lake,
unchapped of its snowcloth, quakes.

But autumn fruits upon the water,
plumage of plum, and grape, and pumpkin bills:

Two mallards ride, are sunny baskets;
they bear ripe light.

And a grackle, fat as burgundy,
gurgles on a limb.

His bottle-glossy feathers
shrug off the wind.

Her Management

She does not place, relate, or name
the objects of her hall,
nor bother to repair her ceiling,
sweep her floor, or paint a wall
symmetrical with mountains;

cylindrical her tent
is pitched of ocean on one side
and—rakish accident—
forest on the other.
Granular, her rug

of many marbles, or of roots,
or needles, or a bog—
outrageous in its pattern;
the furniture is pine
and oak and birch and beech and elm

the water couch is fine.
Mottled clouds, and lightning rifts,
leaking stars, and whole
gushing moons despoil her roof.
Contemptuous of control,

she lets a furnace burn all day,
she lets the winds be wild.
Broken, rotting, shambled things
lie where they like, are piled
on the same tables with her sweets,

her fruits, and scented stuffs.
Her management is beauty.
Of careless silks and roughs,
rumpled rocks, the straightest rain,
blizzards, roses, crows,

April lambs and graveyards
she *chances* to compose
a rich and sloven manor.
Her prosperous tapestries
are too effusive in design

for our analyses—
we, who through her textures move,
we specks upon her glass,
who try to place, relate and name
all things within her mass.

TO MIX WITH TIME
(1963)

I

· · · then I saw it flow · · ·

The Universe

What
is it about,
the universe,
the universe about us stretching out?
We within our brains
within it
think
we must unspin
the laws that spin it.
We think *why*
because we think
because.
Because we think,
we think
the universe about us.

But does *it* think,
the universe?
Then what about?
About us?
If not,
must there be cause
in the universe?
Must it have laws?
And what
if the universe
is *not* about us?
Then what?
What
is it about?
And what
about *us?*

God

They said there was a	Thing
that could not	Change
They could not	Find
it so they	Named
it	God
They had to	Search
so then it must be	There
It had a	Name
It must exist	Somewhere
The	Name
was	God
the	Thing
that could not	Change
They could not	Find
it What is	Lost
is	God
They had to	Search
for what could not be	Found
What can't be	Found
is	Changeless
It is	God
The	Name
is clue The	Thing
is	Lost
	Somewhere
They	Found
the	Name
The	Name
is	Changeless
	God

Out of My Head

             If I could get
    out   of my
    head   and
    into   the
  world.
             What am I saying?
    Out   of my
    head?
             Isn't my
    head
      in   the
  world?
      In   it I'm
      in   it, a
  round
  place
      in   a bigger
  round
  place
someplace.
             Seems like the
  center.
             Every
    head
      in   there's a
  center,   it
  thinks.
             It
  thinks!
             O.K., let's say I'm
    out   and
      in   the
  round   free
  world:
    Back   there's the tight aluminum sphere
             I jumped
    out   of, slammed the door like an icebox.
             A clean landscape

```
around   me, an inch or two of "snow"—
         rock-dust from those
  peaks
     in   the distance. No colder here,
          even if it is wider. Very few things
around    —just the
peaks.    It'll take weeks to reach them.
          Of course I came here in my
  head.
          I'll be taking it
  back.
          The idea is to make a vehicle
    out   of it.
```


The Wish to Escape into Inner Space

All is too open:
all expands, explodes
and scampers out and speeds apart.
What was a ball, and solid, now balloons,
the outline thin, the core weightless.

What was full, and held to a pole centripetal,
what gathered, while it spun, coherent mass,
seized light, shape, ordered time and motion,
worked upon itself its own proportion:
to be round, smooth in its orbit,
beautifully closed—

spurts loose, erratic, widens,
torn from its core,
feels itself emptied, floats detached . . .
is dragged through galactic vapors:
the cold pain of unwanted growth.

Downward

That there were men.
That we are their ghosts.
That men died long ago.

That there was life.
That ours is merely its shadow.

That we have fallen
from a peak on the high past
and are no longer men.

That this is the reason
for our hopelessness,
the reason our life is crippled.

That we grope
upon the slope of the past
and grasp nothing
but our cravings.

Our forward aims
are but our backward looks.
We can barely remember life
for it belonged to *Them*.

Let Us Prepare

to get beyond the organic
for surely there is something else
to which it is an impediment an opaque pod
What if it is sight that blinds
hearing that deafens
touch that makes us numb?
What if trussed in a jacket of blood
to a rack of bone we smother
in the dungeon of our lungs?
Today we are in our brain

a laboratory
Must we be here
tomorrow?
Are there not
pinnacles
on which to stand
cleanly
without a head?
Between the belly
of the sun and the belly
of the world
must we bounce forever
magnetized generations of the circle?
Let us eat nothing but darkness
refuse our stale orbit
and walk only in sleep
There to descry a crack in the future
and work to widen it
Let us prepare to bare ourselves outside the gibbet-hood
of the world
without excuse of flesh or apology of blood

Landing on the Moon

When in the mask of night there shone that cut,
we were riddled. A probe reached down
and stroked some nerve in us,
as if the glint from a wizard's eye, of silver,
slanted out of the mask of the unknown—
pit of riddles, the scratch-marked sky.

When, albino bowl on cloth of jet,
it spilled its virile rays,
our eyes enlarged, our blood reared with the waves.
We craved its secret, but unreachable
it held away from us, chilly and frail.
Distance kept it magnate. Enigma made it white.

When we learned to read it with our rod,
reflected light revealed
a lead mirror, a bruised shield
seamed with scars and shadow-soiled.
A half-faced sycophant, its glitter borrowed,
rode around our throne.

On the moon there shines earth light
as moonlight shines upon the earth . . .
If on its obsidian we set our weightless foot,
and sniff no wind, and lick no rain
and feel no gauze between us and the Fire,
will we trot its grassless skull, sick for the homelike shade?

Naked to the earth-beam we will be,
who have arrived to map an apparition,
who walk upon the forehead of a myth.
Can flesh rub with symbol? If our ball
be iron, and not light, our earliest wish
eclipses. Dare we land upon a dream?

The Shape of Death

What does love look like? We know
the shape of death. Death is a cloud
immense and awesome. At first a lid
is lifted from the eye of light:
there is a clap of sound, a white blossom

belches from the jaw of fright,
a pillared cloud churns from white to gray
like a monstrous brain that bursts and burns,
then turns sickly black, spilling away,
filling the whole sky with ashes of dread;

thickly it wraps, between the clean sea
and the moon, the earth's green head.

Trapped in its cocoon, its choking breath
we know the shape of death:
Death is a cloud.

What does love look like?
Is it a particle, a star—
invisible entirely, beyond the microscope and Palomar?
A dimension unimagined, past the length of hope?
Is it a climate far and fair that we shall never dare

discover? What is its color, and its alchemy?
Is it a jewel in the earth—can it be dug?
Or dredged from the sea? Can it be bought?
Can it be sown and harvested?
Is it a shy beast to be caught?

Death is a cloud,
immense, a clap of sound.
Love is little and not loud.
It nests within each cell, and it
cannot be split.

It is a ray, a seed, a note, a word,
a secret motion of our air and blood.
It is not alien, it is near—
our very skin—
a sheath to keep us pure of fear.

Each Like a Leaf

Each like a leaf
like a wave
to be replaced
repeated

What do we crave
heated by cerebral
fire?

Transitive as flames
that turn
in a furnace
Or sleet falling
separately settling

to one sheet
Forms faced alike
we dance in some
frame

We are a sea
its waves
cannot name
only be

We are a thick
wood
by its leaves made
not understood

As flames their flight
and snow its white
do not perceive
we weave asleep

a body
and awake unravel
the same veins
we travel

The Primitive

I walk a path that a mountain crosses.
I am walking toward the mountain.
I have been making the path, I suppose.
Its trace is behind me. I see how it goes
ahead of me also. Perhaps I make it with my eyes.

Then have I made the mountain also?
More likely the mountain makes itself,
and lets me walk here. Or it lets the path
come upon it. And whatever may be
on the path may approach . . . Why not?
    Or perhaps, thrown out by the mountain once,
like a stone I fell here. Or I fell
in the path farther back, where it already lay.
And then started on my way,
as now, toward the mountain.
    The thing is, I cannot see over the mountain.
It is there, a gradual great rise of the ground.
As I walk, I am crossing it really, already:
the path is rising ever so gently.
But there is the peak. Do I want to go *over* the mountain?

    I see I have come quite far already.
It is strange to look back . . . as if down a thread
with no knot! Before me the path is almost level,
and narrow. But higher, ahead
on the mountain's wedge, it widens. That is strange.
    What would I prefer, then? To stay here,
midway, facing the mountain? To stop,
and not look up or down? Or to drop
back, downwards? I ask myself such things, *while walking*!
—and smile to myself. *Forward, forward is the only choice.*

    But am I sure of this? What if, for instance,
I do make the path with my eyes?
And since it is on the mountain,
I am making the mountain?
There is no one else on this path, after all.
    All the others—although in some way
it is also theirs—this mountain—
their paths make it a separate mountain.
Yet it is mine, in some same parallel way
as I am all the others. I notice this sometimes.
    They are all around me, beside me, walking.
Or within me, when I remember them.
So that they are myself.

So then I am all alone on this mountain?
It must be that I make it. With my eyes?

   I am walking, and talking to myself as I walk—up—
the mountain. I will come to the summit at last.
There are no separate ways about that . . .
Which ought to be a good thing. Except that,
will I know when I reach the peak?
   Will I see *the other side?* I can't "see"
what it may be like—the other side. Except
as being like *this* side . . . No, no,
that would be too foolish! And then,
there is the omen . . . that I shall go blind.
   It is said that this happens
before reaching the peak, so that no one may know
just when he is crossing the mountain.
Then have my eyes, that made this path, that makes
this mountain, made this fate for themselves?

   Oh, eyes, turn and look at me,
instead of always ahead or behind! No, no, no,
such a thing is insane! Mountain, again
you have thrown me back, and down, like a stone!
You are the One! I am yours.
   There is nothing I can know but you.
And I can never know you. Yet we are each other,
are we not? As a pebble is a fraction of the rock
it came from? I must know you, as I know myself.
Exactly that. *But need you know me?*
   Am I not rolling up to you, mountain, as I walk?
Was I "thrown away" upon your self-forgotten body,
and are you now pulling me into your great head again?
Will you let me, finally, see your other side?
Surely some one may see it, sometime?
   What if I, steadfastly, determine
to reach your peak, *without going blind?*
If you can throw me from yourself,
you can take me as quickly up.
Or I will hurry to climb, faithfully, by myself.

I PROMISE
NEVER
TO TAKE MY EYES
FROM YOUR PEAK.
Mountain, give me a sign!

No . . . I think, rather, that you do not care.
Perhaps it is a small nobility to think this way . . .
Can pebbles expect a summit?
Enough that we have "eyes"—for a time.
Strange enough. *I cannot understand it.*

Night Practice

I
will
remember
with my breath
to make a mountain,
with my sucked-in breath
a valley, with my pushed-out
breath a mountain. I will make
a valley wider than the whisper, I
will make a higher mountain than the cry;
will with my will breathe a mountain, I will
with my will breathe a valley. I will push out
a mountain, suck in a valley, deeper than the shout
YOU MUST DIE, harder, heavier, sharper, a mountain than
the truth YOU MUST DIE. I will remember. My breath will
make a mountain. My will will remember to will. I, suck-
ing, pushing, I will breathe a valley, I will breathe a mountain.

The Surface

First I saw the surface,
then I saw it flow,
then I saw the underneath.

In gradual light below
I saw a kind of room,
the ceiling was a veil,

a shape swam there
slow, opaque and pale.
I saw enter by a shifting corridor

other blunt bodies
that sank toward the floor.
I tried to follow deeper

with my avid eye.
Something changed the focus:
I saw the sky,

a glass between inverted trees.
Then I saw my face.
I looked until a cloud

flowed over that place.
Now I saw the surface
broad to its rim,

here gleaming, there opaque,
far out, flat and dim.
Then I saw it was an Eye:

I saw the Wink that slid
from underneath the rushes
before it closed its lid.

How to Be Old

It is easy to be young. (Everybody is,
at first.) It is not easy
to be old. It takes time.
Youth is given; age is achieved.
One must work a magic to mix with time
in order to become old.

Youth is given. One must put it away
like a doll in a closet,
take it out and play with it only
on holidays. One must have many dresses
and dress the doll impeccably
(but not to show the doll, to keep it hidden).

It is necessary to adore the doll,
to remember it in the dark on the ordinary
days, and every day congratulate
one's aging face in the mirror.

In time one will be very old.
In time, one's life will be accomplished.
And in time, in time, the doll—
like new, though ancient—will be found.

2

· · · touching his toe · · ·

The poems in Part 2, together with *How to Be Old* in Part I, are from a group written in France, Italy and Spain. The author is grateful to the Amy Lowell Travelling Scholarship Fund which enabled them to be made.

Death Invited

Death invited to break his horns
on the spread
cloth. To drop his head
on the dragged flag on the sand.
Death's hoofs slipping
in blood, and a band
of blood down the black side.
Death's tongue, curved in the open mouth
like a gray horn, dripping
blood. And
six colored agonies decking the summit
of his muscled pride.
Death invited to die.

The head
of death, with bewildered raging eye,
flagged down,
dragged down to the red
cloth on the sand.
Death invited to stand,
legs spread,
on the spot of the cape.
To buckle stubborn knees and lie
down in blood on the silken shape.
Beg blindness come to the sun-pierced eye.

The sword, sunk at the top of the shoulder's pride—
its hilt a silver cross—drawn forth now lets
hot radiant blood slide
from bubbling nostrils
through cloth to thirsty ground.

Yearning horns found
fleeing cloth and bloodless pillow,
substance none. Arrogant thighs,
that swiped and turned death by,
now, close as love, above lean lunging,
filling the pain-hot eye.

That stares till it turns to blood.
With the short knife dug
quick!
to the nape.
And the thick
neck drops on the spot of the cape.

Chains are drawn
round the horns, whose points are clean.
Trumpets shout.
New sand is thrown
where death's blood streamed.
Four stout,
jingling horses with gilded hoofs
tug death out.

Life is awarded ears and flowers.
Pelted with hats and shoes, and praise,
glittering life, in tight pink thighs,
swaggers around a rotunda of screams and *Olés*.

Death is dragged from the ring,
a clumsy hide,
a finished thing—
back to his pen.
The gate swings shut.

The gate swings wide.
Here comes trotting, snorting death
let loose again.

Instead of the Camargue

I

We hoped to find wild bulls and flamingos.
There were none there.
At Fos-sur-Mer
the wind whittled the gray sea to shingles

that, slanting, ran the reeds down.
Foils well-tempered,
they flew up again. Wind whimpered
over the fissured ramparts of the town.

We climbed to explore its church.
With the stone head of an elf
for tower, it sat on a stone shelf
high-hinged above the sea. This windy porch

held, as well, an ancient cemetery.
Marble-gabled steep *maisons*,
snug against *toutes les saisons*,
each housed a reliquary.

Tall, windowless sheds of tiny
width, in narrow yards—We wondered, were
the rag-robed bones standing within, for
they could not be lying. Shiny

nickel hearts, wreaths of mineral
flowers, fat sugar-white crosses,
and ceramic brooches bearing verses,
hung behind the ornate fences. No funeral

atmosphere. More like carnival.
For instance, rumps of rosy angels
fringed a tinted image of *Cher Papa*. Spangled
silver lilies blanketed a doll-

faced, smiling child
asleep in an ormolu pavilion; he hugged
a pink lamb that looked like candy. Tugged
by the wind (that failed

to fade or kill them) wax tulips, pansies,
peonies profused out of fix-footed urns.
On gilded grapes and vines
cherubs climbed in delicate frenzies

of carver's art: an arbor
of iron fruit and iron shade
stood over a dead
husband. Widow had built a harbor

durable as could be, for his soul's rest.
A populous white fondant and fuss of graves:
crosses shouldered each other, conclaves
of many identicals of the dying Christ

plastered on the chests
and foreheads of the huts—that stood for
bodies needing no roof and no floor—
a labyrinth, a jagged forest.

And where a flayed, white figurine
twined snakish on an occasional black
cross, or burned black on a gold one, the crack
in conformity frightened; the thin,

writhing form, sweating
in redundant chorused pain
against the dark grain,
was like a voodoo sign. Forgetting

to enter the *église*—outside
a Virgin with downcast eyes and upbent lips
held out the robust Child, her hand beneath His hips—
we wandered the macabre compound where He died

in every yard. And came to a miniature cathedral
with encrusted spires of colored tile,
even a little pointed window, playhouse style,
in the side, leaded and stained—a tetrahedral

tomb caked with carvings. On its gothic portal:
"Ici repose Maman aux bras de Dieu."
A tight embrace, we thought. And were it true,
her head must reach the belfry, she'd displace the altar.

At a neglected gate, two angels, kneeling,
        clapped between broken
wings like violet mussel shells, raised stricken,
        noseless faces to a peeling

        shrine of metal, now corroded,
    roofless. Beneath, a pair of marble beds,
        moss-browned, sunk in weeds,
    could not be read, the inscriptions faded.

        But ovals of porcelain rimmed
            with filigree forget-me-nots
            and painted bleeding hearts,
            their baked designs undimmed,

    depended from the necks of the bitten
            tombstones side by side.
            We leaned to read
        what graceful brush had written:

A Notre Fils   *A Notre Fille*

Il est passé   *Toi qui passa*
Comme un nuage   *Comme un nuage*
Comme un flot   *Emportant au Ciel*
Rapide en son cours   *Notre amour*
Et nos coeurs   *Nos coeurs garderont*
Gardent son image   *Ton image*
Toujours   *Toujours*

    There were many "beds" most
neatly made, side by side and close together,
and unnumbered "houses" that the weather
        would take long to unpost,

        but the cracked stone
covers over these children (who had slept away
    how many hundred birthdays in the clay?)
            would soon be thrown

among the shards and slabs that leaned
in a corner of the wall—
the thick wall around this stone metropole,
that defended and screened

it from the living still at large. We
moved bemused in its gravel alleys, peeping
into curious stalls of the fête the dead were keeping
open above the sea.

Past a mélange of flamboyant and somber things,
butterflies (of pressed paper), hectic flowers,
black-wrapped stars and harps, and wire
hourglasses with wings,

we came to the gate's gap, where the wind squalled
and sun smote the rock stair
going down. In a corner there,
by sharp dark cypress enwalled,

was hidden a tomb square and plain:
A lean and beautiful lion
couched on the lid—rivet-eyed scion
and emblem of France—his mane

a cowl of grim, roughened stone
black from the rains—one paw bent
on the lock of the grave, but negligent,
upturned, the other—as all lions are known

to lie—guardianship
alerting his nostrils, his chest raised.
His cool, secret smile grazed
us, and the ancient patience at his lip.

Chiseled below, on his pedestal:
"Ici Repose Le Gendarme Pierre,
Pecot, Tué Par Un Braconnier,
1752"—within a wreath of laurel.

2

We saw no wild bulls or flamingos that day.
To reach the Camargue, we agreed
we would need
to have gone by another way—

north, then west around the delta of the Rhône.
Descending to the flats, we drove the straight
road between sea and slate
marsh, where rice is grown.

We saw shorebirds wade
near the floating corks
of fishermen's nets. Not Moroccan storks
or Egyptian ibises, as the guidebook had said,

but ordinary checkered sanderlings, and a lone heron.
We turned back through the red hills, *terres rougeâtres*, where,
above the Etang de Berre,
the incessant mistral blows—and came to an environ

of Van Gogh. Great umber faces
headdressed in flames—round
ruffed faces, Indian and profound,
on totem stalks thick as maces—

stared: a company of giant
sunflowers. Like eclipses of the sun,
their plate-heads, almost black, spun
within the yellow aureoles; only the pliant

broad leaves sagged on their spikes in the heat.
East of the divide,
nearing Aix, on the cooler side,
the tranquil valley fell away. Cut wheat

stood in blond hives on the slant
hills. We passed fields of smoky lavender, ditches
full of poppies flaring like lit matches
and young grapevines planted

in ruled brown earth. The road became a funnel: arching
sycamores, their pinto-spotted trunks tan
and gray, with painted white belts, ran
by the car, the low sun torching

through. Beyond the opening of that shade-
striped bower,
Cézanne's mountain, Saint-Victoire,
unfolded its blue knife-blade

on the sky. Against the rind
of evening, its acute shape
blunted, enlarging on the landscape.
We circled fruit and olive orchards, poplar-lined,

and watched how shadows massed
in the concaves of that head,
the impenetrable Pharaoh-face that baffled
all the painters of Provence, until Cézanne in his last

attempt, defined it with simple
brush as tender vapor, a mirage:
"Au lieu de se tasser, immense et sauvage,
elle respire et participe toute bleutée de l'air ample."

3

We never found the blackfaced bulls
and rouge flamingos, except on
postcards . . . We bought one
showing three skulls,

a rosary, and a knapsack
that are among Cézanne's effects
in his studio at Aix,
and twirling the rack

with other tourists on Cours Mirabeau,
also bought views of the exotic Camargue—the small
gray horses in tall
grass, the high-horned, stubborn *taureaux*—

and of gypsies at Fos-sur-Mer.
"La Méditerranée a une couleur comme les maquereaux,"
said the back of a card, quoting Van Gogh,
who used to walk there

"sur la plage déserte." We sat
sipping coffee in the oasis
of Aix, the fountain's breath in our faces,
remembering that

a sign by the cemetery gate had said: "It is forbidden
to photograph the houses of the dead."
We could not buy our lion, spread
dark and lean upon a card. We're glad he's hidden.

Fountains of Aix

Beards of water
some of them have.
Others are blowing whistles of water.
Faces astonished that constant water
jumps from their mouths.
Jaws of lions are snarling water
through green teeth over chins of moss.
Dolphins toss jets of water
from open snouts
to an upper theatre of water.
Children are riding swans and water
coils from the S-shaped necks and spills
in flat foils from pincered bills.
A solemn curly-headed bull
puts out a swollen tongue of water.
Cupids naked are making water
into a font that never is full.
A goddess is driving a chariot through water.
Her reins and whips are tight white water.
Bronze hoofs of horses wrangle with water.
Marble faces half hidden in leaves.

Faces whose hair is leaves and grapes
of stone are peering from living leaves.
Faces with mossy lips unlocked
always uttering water,
water
wearing their features blank
their ears deaf, their eyes mad
or patient or blind or astonished at water
always uttered out of their mouths.

The Alyscamps at Arles

The bodies
that covered the bones
died.
Then the bones
died.
Now the stones
that covered the bones
are dying
in the Alyscamps at Arles.

The lizard darts
between thick lips
of the hollow-bodied
stones.
Under the broken lids
the scorpion lives
transfixed.

A sculptor who forms
by destroying form,
and finds form
beneath,
has peeled the bodies
and found the bones,
has dwindled the bones

till they snapped
in the coffin-beds
of the stones.
Now he crumbles
the heavy limbs
of the stones
that have been dying
for two thousand years
in the Alyscamps at Arles.

Soft bodies
died
soonest.
Flesh
was a colored dew wiped off.
Bones
were chalk to the sculptor,
but he has been rubbing
at these stones
for two thousand years.

See, they have faces
with mouths and sockets!
See, in the shadows
of the poplars
are great square skulls
with noseholes dark,
like caves.
There, where the lizard
spreads his saurean hand.

Moonlight
puts a flesh
around the recumbent ribs
of the stones.
When the passion
of the nightingale begins,
the sculptor
seems to sleep.

Above the Arno

My room in Florence was the color of air.
Blue the stippled wall I woke to,
the tile floor white except where
shadowed by the washstand and my high
bed. Barefoot I'd go to the window to look
at the Arno. I'd open the broad shutters like a book,
and see the same scene. But each day's sky,
or night, dyed it a different light.

The lizard river might be green, or turbid gray,
or yellowish like the stucco palazzi
on the opposite quay.
Boys would be angling with long, lank
poles, sitting on the butts of them, dangling
legs from the paved bank;
they wore handkerchiefs, the corners knotted,
for caps against the strong

sun, and had their dogs along;
the dogs, brown-and-white spotted,
had to lie quiet. But I never saw anything
jerk the lines of the yellow poles.
The boys smoked a lot, and lazed in the sun.
Smaller ones dove and swam in the slow, snaking Arno
right under the sign that read: PERICOLO!
DIVIETO DI BAGNARSI.

Over Ponte Trinità, fiacres would go,
or a donkey-driven cart, among the auto
and popping scooter traffic. Freckled, gray,
blinkered horses trotted the red-and-black
carriages in which the richer tourists rode.
(A donkey looks like a bunny under its load,
with its wigwag ears and sweet expression;
the workman-driver flicks

a string-whip like a gadfly over it.)
I'd hear hoof-clops and heel-clicks
among hustling wheels on the bridge, that curved

like a violin's neck across the Arno.
It had two statues at each end—
white, graceful, a little funny.
One, a woman, had lost her head, but strode
forward holding her basket of fruit just the same.

You could see Giotto's Tower in my "book" and
the gold ball on top of Brunelleschi's Dome
and the clock with one hand
on the campanile of the Palazzo Vecchio,
and a blue slice of the Appenines the color of my room.
One day I slept all afternoon—
it was August and very hot—and didn't wake
until late at night,

or rather, early morning.
My mind was fresh—all was silent.
I crossed the white tiles, barefoot,
and opened the book of the shutters
to faint stars, to a full Arno,
starlight fingering the ripples. Gondola-slim
above the bridge, a new moon held a dim
circle of charcoal between its points.

Bats played in the greenish air,
their wing-joints
soft as moths' against the bone-gray palazzi where
not a window was alight,
the doorways dark as sockets.
Each of the four statues so white
and still,
rose somnambulistic from its hill

of stone, above the dusky slide
of the river. On my side,
a muscular, round-polled
man—naked behind—hugged a drape
against him, looking cold.
His partner, fat,
in short toga and hat
made of fruit, leaned a hand on a Horn

of Plenty. On the opposite bank, in torn
sweeping robes, a Signora
bore sheaves of wheat along her arm.
And, striding beside her with stately charm
in her broken flounces, the Headless One*
offered her wealthy basket, chin
up—though I had to imagine
chin, face, head, headdress, all.

Then a tall
tower began to tell F O U R ,
and another with different timbre spelled it
a minute later. Another mentioned it for the third time
in harsh bronze and slow.
Still another, with delicate chime
countered and cantered it. By now the sky had turned
della Robbia blue, the Arno yellowed silver.

I stood between the covers of my book and heard
a donkey's particular heels,
like syllables of a clear, quick word,
echo over the Arno. Then came the scrape-clink
of milk cans lowered on cobbles. And with the moon still
there, but transparent, the sky began to fill
with downy clouds—pink
as the breasts of Botticelli's Venus—foretinting dawn.

*The head of Primavera was later found in October 1961 by workmen in the
debris of the Arno and restored to the statue.

A Boy Looking at Big David

I'm touching his toe.
I know I'll be brave after this.
His toenail wide as my hand,
I have to stand tall to reach it.

The big loose hand with the rock in it
by his thigh
is high above my head. The vein
from wrist to thumb, a blue strain in the marble.

As if it had natural anatomy all its own
inside it.
Somebody skinned off the top stone,
and there He stands.

I'd like to climb up there on that slippery Hip,
shinny up to the Shoulder
the other side of that thumping Neck,
and lie in the ledge on the collar-bone,

by the sling.
In that cool place
I'd stare-worship that big, full-lipped,
frown-browed, far-eyed, I-dare-you-Face.

I'd like to live on that David for a while,
get to know
how to be immortal like Him.
But I can only reach his Toe—

broad, poking over the edge of the stand.
So cool . . .
Maybe, marble Him,
he likes the warm of my hand?

Notes Made in the Piazza San Marco

The wingéd lion on top of that column
(his paws have been patched, he appears to wear boots)
is bronze but has a white eye—
his tail sails out long . . . Could it help him fly?

On the other column St. Theodore
standing on an alligator,
he and it as white as salt,
wears an iron halo and an iron sword.

San Marco is crusty and curly with many crowns,
or is it a growth of golden thrones?
The five domes
covered, it looks like, with stiff crinkly parachute silk

have gold balls on twigs on turnip-tips,
sharp turrets in between with metal flags that cannot wave.
On all their perches statues gay and grave:
Erect somewhere among the towers a tall-necked woman

wearing an of-course-gold coronet
is helping a beast with baboon's head and lion's body to stand
on hindlegs. She's placing her hand
in his mouth . . . I wonder why.

In recesses of arches half in shade
are robed Venetians made
of red, blue, gold, green mosaics small as caramels,
fishermen encumbered by their robes launching a boat,

their faces all pricked out with those square
skin-colored pores . . .
Above them in a gold sky angels fly standing up.
About to step off the balcony

in the center of the main façade, four
horses exactly as big as horses but consciously more
handsome—gold running in rivulets
from their shoulders to under their bellies, their necks'

curt blade-shaped manes sloping like Roman helmets—
have a pair of heads front
and a pair to the side,
the lips tugged back into wide

loops. The bits are absent.
A pink and white checkered palace relatively plain
with a pleasant loggia half way up
puts a rectangle out to the quay of the Grand Canal:

On one of its corners Adam and Eve look rueful, the Tree
between them—its low branches with leaves attached
happen to cover their genitals. Three
times hugged around the trunk, the serpent laughs.

There's often a rush of pigeons in the Piazza,
a leather scarf swept past your eyes
as if snatched from the ground,
when from the campanile great tongues let loose

and flog you, and flog you with gouts of iron sound.
The air must always burn deep blue here—
a velvet box for all that gold and white.
It turns thin and clear

toward the water. The Canal is a green vase lying down.
Gondolas knock their tethered necks on the quay:
Black, saddled with red, riderless, restless, they
are touching hips and shifting on the single-footing waves.

The Pantheon, Rome

Outside, pacing the sunken ramp around it
are many cats, scrofulous and starving.
The flutings of the columns of the portico
are bitten with age, their bases dark and urinous.
But the circle, the triangle, the square,
a solid geometric with caplike top,
squats here grimly eternal. Sixteen legs,
Corinthian, bear it up under the pronaos,
plain, harmonious. In gouges of the walls,
on accidental pediments of destroyed stone,
the fierce-eyed cats have taken occupation.

On a day of rain I pass into the interior,
through a door of bronze and leather—one slab
of which is agape. Inside is granite dusk
and dungeon cold—the round room no longer lined
with statues, the vault stripped of its gilt tiles.
Yet, there strike upon my chest the radii of grandeur.

The circle is large, the floor an immense coin
of porphyry and pavonazzetto; the dome of lead
is a strong belly; its rows of boxed blind windows
incise the entablature to the open disk at the top—
umbilical and only orifice for light.
That high lidless hole left for the sun to grin through
has not been closed since Agrippa.
Through it, now, rain rushes freely down
on the temple floor, to scour the dull colors
of the pattern that repeats, in giallo antico,
the eternal circle, the just square.

I walk around the tall, splattering column of rain
in the gloom. In a gray niche a dusty Christ
is stretched aloft—feet crossed and twisted,
head shadowed by iron thorns. On a shabby fresco
almost effaced, Mary with a stare of consternation
hears the Angel's smug pronouncement of her state.

Stooping, I discover Raphael's tomb, a bare stone box,
in a recess near the floor. Dust, thick as chalk,
powders the organ pipes, and the crude block
of the altar—installed when the Pantheon
was Christianized by Boniface in 609.
This temple stood before the Popes—
and Jove before Jesus—Minerva before the Virgin.
That empty arched embrasure remembers Bacchus laughing.
The rain that cannot ruin the floor,
the cats with demon eyes that crouch
around these walls, are fitting, are good.

Italian Sampler

Lombardy, Tuscany, Umbria, Calabria.
A spear of leaves. A pear.
A clod-filled pasture dark as a bear.
Yellow blazes around a crown.

Lombardy, Tuscany, Umbria, Calabria.
Somber oxen. September flares.
Wind and silk, parchment and candles.
Slumberous, plushy, ponderous, elaborate.

A tree, a fruit, a pigment, an ornament.
Plumes, juices, bristles, crystals.
A mast. A horn. A bramble. A bride.
Lombardy, Tuscany, Umbria, Calabria.

While Sitting in the Tuileries and Facing the Slanting Sun

There is the	Line
There is the	Circle
the bending	Line
the expanding	Circle
There is the moving	Line
but the still	Circle
but the enlarging	Circle
the lengthening	Line

The	Crack
and the	Particle
the deepening	Crack
the doubling redoubling	Particle
the	Splitting
and	Resplitting

then the	Multiple
the opening	Closing
then the closure	Opening

There is a	Swaddled Thing
There is a	*Swaddled Thing*
There is a	Rocking Box
There is a	*Covered Box*

The	Unwrapping
the	Ripening
Then the	Loosening
the	Spoiling
The	Stiffening
then the	Wrapping
The	Softening
but the long long	Drying

The	Wrapping
the	Wrapping
the	Straightening
and	Wrapping
The rigid	Rolling
the gilded	Scrolling
The	Wrapping
and	Wrapping
and careful	Rewrapping
The	Thinning
and	Drying
but the	Wrapping
and	Fattening

There is the worm	Coiled
and the straw	Straightened
There is the	Plank
and the glaucous	Bundle
the paper	Skull
and the charred	Hair
the linen	Lip
and the leather	Eyelid

There is a	Person
of flesh that is *a rocking*	*Box*
There is a	Box
of wood that is a *painted*	*Person*

NOTE FROM A DIARY: I sat an hour on a bench in the Tuileries by a frozen flower bed. The sunrays striking between my lashes made gilt slits, black dots. I felt rolled up in a spool of light—face warm, feet numb—a kind of mesmerization . . . And remembered Giotto's fresco *Birth of the Virgin* in a cloister in Florence: the "Mother of God" was a swaddled infant held upright, like a board or plaque, by her nurse—the halo a gilt bonnet around the tiny head with its fugitive eyes . . . And I remembered a mummy in the Vatican Museum in Rome: in her sarcophagus shaped and painted like herself, an Egyptian girl 2000 years old lay unwrapped to the waist, and with hands and feet bare—her nails, hair, lips and eyelids frangible as tobacco leaf, but intact. Still exquisite, merely dried and darkened, was her youth.

A Hurricane at Sea

Slowly a floor rises, almost becomes a wall.
Gently a ceiling slips down, nearly becomes a floor.
A floor with spots that stretch, as on a breathing
animal's hide. It rises again with a soft lurch.

The floor tilts, is curved, appears to be racing north
with a pattern of dents and dips
over slashes of dark. Now there are white lips,
widening on the wall

that stands up suddenly. The ceiling is all
rumpled, snarled, like a wet animal's fur.
The floor hardens, humps up like rock,
the side of a hill too slant to walk.

White teeth are bared where lazy lips swam.
The ceiling is the lid of a box about to slam.
Is this a real floor I walk? It's an angry spine
that shoots up over a chasm of seething

milk—cold, churned, shoving the stern around.
There's the groaning sound
of a cauldron about to buckle, maybe break.
A blizzard of glass and lace

shivers over this dodging box.
It glides up the next high hissing alp—halts
on top. But the top turns hollow while the hollow spins.
I run down a slope and feel like twins,

one leg northeast, one west.
The planks pitch leeward, level an instant, then
rear back to a flat, stunned rest.
It's frightening, that vacant moment. I feel

the Floor beneath the floor reel,
while a thickening wilderness is shunted aft, under.
I'm in a bottle becalmed, but a mountain bloats
ahead, ready to thunder

on it. The floor is rushed into the pit.
Maybe there's no bottom to it.
I'm buried in a quarry, locked in a bucking
room—or bottle, or box—near cracking,

that's knocked about in a black,
enormous, heavy, quaking Room.
Is there a bottom to it? I'm glad not to have to know.
Boulders, canyon-high, smash down on the prow,

are shattered to snow, and shouldered off somehow.
Tossed out again on top. Topside bounced
like a top, to scoot the bumpy floor . . .
Out there, it's slicked to a plane almost, already,

though chopped with white to the far baseboard.
The ceiling is placing
itself right, getting steadier,
licking itself smooth. The keel

takes the next swollen hills along their backs—
like a little dog gripped
to a galloping horse—slipping
once in a while, but staying on.

3

· · · cubes and cones · · ·

Snow in New York

It snowed in New York. I walked on Fifth
Avenue and saw the orange snowplow cut the drifts
with rotary sickles, suck up celestial clods into its turning
    neck,
a big flue that spewed them into a garbage truck.
This gift from the alps was good for nothing, though scarcely
    gray.
The bright apparatus, with hungry noise,
crumbled and mauled the new hills. Convoys
of dump-cars hauled them away.

I went to Riker's to blow my nose
in a napkin and drink coffee for its steam. Two rows
of belts came and went from the kitchen, modeling scrambled
eggs, corn muffins, bleeding triangles of pie.
Tubs of dirty dishes slid by.
Outside the fogged window black bulking people stumbled
cursing the good-for-nothing whiteness. I thought
of Rilke, having read how he wrote

to Princess Marie von Thurn und Taxis, saying: "The idea
    haunts me—
it keeps on calling—I must make a poem for Nijinski
that could be, so to say, swallowed and then danced." Printed
as on the page, in its
remembered place in the paragraph, that odd name with
    three dots
over the *iji*, appeared—as I squinted
through the moist window past the traveling
dishes—against the snow. There unraveled

from a file in my mind a magic notion
I, too, used to play with: from chosen words a potion
could be wrung; pickings of them, eaten, could make you fly,
    walk
on water, be somebody else, do or undo anything, go back
or forward on belts of time. But then I thought:
Snow in New York is like poetry, or clothes made of roses.

Who needs it, what can you build with snow, who can you feed?
Hoses
were coming to whip back to water, wash to the sewers the
    nuisance-freight.

From the Office Window

My attention the frame for
a complication of city roofs:
Various levels, shapes,
perspectives, angles. Puffs

from chimneys, ruffled flags
on a school tower. Ectomorphic
shadows, flats of late light.
Distant pigeons diving, cloud surf

slow-unrolling. A red
construction crane north-leaning,
then south. Scrawl of a jet
half-circling, caning

the sky. A monster of many surfaces
rises to the split-second net
of my eye. How to beach it?
Strokes of a pen, fleet

washes of a brush would
fetch it eventually almost exact.
The process would be tedious,
the body stiff, unlit

at capture. A camera might
harpoon, arrest
the big thing whole—but gray
and small. A cinema projector

would gulp and then expel
it life-sized, intact in all

details, the entire whale
still swimming. But the soul

would be hooked, and have to repeat
itself just like that:
Chimneys never
ceasing their white

evacuations. Shadows
never slipping.
Flicking flags
forever flicking.

Pigeons always slanting
at that distance. The brick whale
never darkening. *Its many scales
are already lamplit,*

the spouts and towers dark.
Words? Let their
mutations work
toward the escape

of objects into the nearest next
shape, motion, assembly,
temporal context;
let the progeny of interlapping

shadows multiply . . .
*Façades of light!
Another cumbrous monster
has risen to my eye.*

At the Museum of Modern Art

At the Museum of Modern Art you can sit in the lobby
on the foam-rubber couch; you can rest and smoke,
and view whatever the revolving doors express.
You don't have to go into the galleries at all.

In this arena the exhibits are free and have all
the surprises of art—besides something extra:
sensory restlessness, the play of alternation,
expectation in an incessant spray

thrown from heads, hands, the tendons of ankles.
The shifts and strollings of feet
engender compositions on the shining tiles,
and glide together and pose gambits,

gestures of design, that scatter, rearrange,
trickle into lines, and turn clicking through a wicket
into rooms where caged colors blotch the walls.
You don't have to go to the movie downstairs

to sit on red plush in the snow and fog
of old-fashioned silence. You can see contemporary
Garbos and Chaplins go by right here.
And there's a mesmeric experimental film

constantly reflected on the flat side of the wide
steel-plate pillar opposite the crenellated window.
Non-objective taxis surging west, on Fifty-third,
liquefy in slippery yellows, dusky crimsons,

pearly mauves—an accelerated sunset, a roiled
surf, or cloud-curls undulating—their tubular ribbons
elongations of the coils of light itself
(engine of color) and motion (motor of form).

A Fixture

Women women women women
in a department store
with hats on (hats in *it*)
and shoes on (shoes in *it*)
dresses coats gloves on (and *in*
all the departments)

In the lobby (in a niche)
between two glass revolving doors
sluff sluff sluff sluff
(rubber bottoms of whirling doors)
flick flick click click
(women in women out) sits a nun

In the mid-whirl (a station)
white black wooden (a fixture)
holding a wooden cup she sits
between the glitter of double doors
hexagonal glasses glittering
over glassy fixed eyes

A garter snake of black
beads (wooden?) catching light
crawling (clicking) crawling
(clicking) up her draped
fixed short carved
black knees (thighs)

Her white hat (hood) a head cover
her shoes short black
flat (foot covers)
her dress a black curtain (cape)
over a longer curtain shape
she is the best dressed

Riding the "A"

I ride
the "A" train
and feel
like a ball-
bearing in a roller skate.
I have on a gray
rain-
coat. The hollow
of the car
is gray.

My face
a negative in the slate
window,
I sit
in a lit
corridor that races
through a dark
one. Strok-
ing steel,
what a smooth rasp—it feels
like the newest of knives
slicing
along
a long
black crusty loaf
from West 4th to 168th.
Wheels
and rails
in their prime
collide,
make love in a glide
of slickness
and friction.
It is an elation
I wish to pro-
long.
The station
is reached
too soon.

Pigeon Woman

Slate, or dirty-marble-colored,
or rusty-iron-colored, the pigeons
on the flagstones in front of the
Public Library make a sharp lake

into which the pigeon woman wades
at exactly 1:30. She wears a
plastic pink raincoat with a round
collar (looking like a little

girl) and flat gym shoes,
her hair square-cut, orange.
Wide-apart feet carefully enter
the spinning, crooning waves

(as if she'd just learned how
to walk, each step conscious,
an accomplishment); blue knots in the
calves of her bare legs (uglied marble),

age in angled cords of jaw
and neck, her pimento-colored hair,
hanging in thin tassels, is gray
around a balding crown.

The day-old bread drops down
from her veined hand dipping out
of a paper sack. Choppy, shadowy ripples,
the pigeons strike around her legs.

Sack empty, she squats and seems to rinse
her hands in them—the rainy greens and
oily purples of their necks. Almost
they let her wet her thirsty fingertips—

but drain away in an untouchable tide.
A make-believe trade
she has come to, in her lostness
or illness or age—to treat the motley

city pigeons at 1:30 every day, in all
weathers. It is for them she colors
her own feathers. Ruddy-footed
on the lime-stained paving,

purling to meet her when she comes,
they are a lake of love. Retreating
from her hands as soon as empty,
they are the flints of love.

Cat & the Weather

Cat takes a look at the weather:
snow;
puts a paw on the sill;
his perch is piled, is a pillow.

Shape of his pad appears:
will it dig? No,
not like sand,
like his fur almost.

But licked, not liked:
too cold.
Insects are flying, fainting down.
He'll try

to bat one against the pane.
They have no body and no buzz,
and now his feet are wet;
it's a puzzle.

Shakes each leg,
then shakes his skin
to get the white flies off;
looks for his tail,

tells it to come on in
by the radiator.
World's turned queer
somehow: all white,

no smell. Well, here
inside it's still familiar.
He'll go to sleep until
it puts itself right.

De Chirico: Superimposed Interiors

1

A cannon's mouth. A
clock. The heads of
two gargoyles on a
butcher's block. No blood,
however. Blue and green
opaque panels pretend to
be   air.

2

If a window were there,
we'd breathe pebbles.
The night tastes burrs
in the full moon's hair.

3

A
queen
 has
 just
  passed
  by
 for
 the
 spore
of
 her
  train
  is
   seen
    on
  the
  floor.

4

This
yellow
rectangle
might be light
except it's thick;
you could stir
it with a
stick
had
you
come
sooner.

5

Sir: High up on a trestle created by your eyelashes
when you blink, a very tiny train, the kind that
chugs,
and a
white
scald
above
its
bald
head,
is moving, making you think several black bugs   bump
softly.

6

Several black bugs bump softly.
Several
black
bugs
bump
softly.

7

Yes, elephant
gray   is
d o m i n a n t .

8

Although these arches d w i n d l e
alarmingly, there's no harm. Try the
doorknobs; the sea won't leak through.

9

The foreground's reassuring—
it slants backward.
That
shadow
is
a
hill
of flowing sand.

Slick in places.
Take my hand.   Ah, here's the
escalator
                leading
                        down
                            to
                              sleep.

10

Kick
Kick
Kick
Kick
Kick
Kick
Kick
Kick
Kick
these
eggs
out
of
the
way
without breaking any.
Not difficult—they're
flat—only pasted on;
they can't roll, for
the tiles are rose.
But the toes of our
boots must be reno-
vated accordingly.

11

One more trapezoid left to be
crossed—the sole piece of
furniture on the lower
level. A stern jerk at
the bit will do it . . .
There might be a
rubber   mitten
nailed   beside
the brow of a
Greek   in
plaster,
b u t
don't
stop
for
that
now.

12

                    doll.
                of ª With stitches
        body   prominent
    the kid   from
around   crotch
Gallop   to navel.

The double gleam of needles lifts
the horizon
to stilts.

13

Then the

Stop! Notice
that the
ground is
S   K   Y
s o l i d i f i e d .

path, or
slab, or
wall wilts. We^{flounder}in^{melted}cheese or
candle-droppings.

14

Let us recall that the infinite number
resembles the Figure 6, reflected in
any smooth convex surface well-buffed.
The frame is only lumber. Let us e-
merge. E-merge on the threshold of
the unexpected, where all rays, all
rays, all rays employed here, converge.

Southbound on the Freeway

A tourist came in from Orbitville,
parked in the air, and said:

The creatures of this star
are made of metal and glass.

Through the transparent parts
you can see their guts.

Their feet are round and roll
on diagrams—or long

measuring tapes—dark
with white lines.

They have four eyes.
The two in the back are red.

Sometimes you can see a 5-eyed
one, with a red eye turning

on the top of his head.
He must be special—

the others respect him,
and go slow,

when he passes, winding
among them from behind.

They all hiss as they glide,
like inches, down the marked

tapes. Those soft shapes,
shadowy inside

the hard bodies—are they
their guts or their brains?

When You Lie Down, the Sea Stands Up

Thick twisted cables
                    of bottle glass at the base,
gunbarrel-blue higher up,
  are quickly being braided and stretched,
their condition molten,
                            their surface cold.
Or they are the long smooth logs of a pile
            being built from the top down.
The trunks of greatest girth
                            arrive at the bottom
with silver rips and ridges in their bark.
                    There is a wall in motion
like a lathe of light
                        and dark galvanic blue
layers which are twirling,

extending beyond your eye-points.
You cannot see their ends.
    Watch the topmost thinnest strand,
too taut to quiver:
        Above is a calcimined ceiling,
heliotrope . . . steady . . .
            delicate as for a bedroom.

The Contraption

Going up is pleasant. It tips your chin,
    and you feel tall and free
as if in control of, and standing in
a chariot, hands feeling the frisky

reins. But, doubled in your seat,
knuckled to the fun-car's handrails,
you mount baby-buggied, cleat by cleat,
to that humped apogee your entrails

aren't ready for. Wind in your
ears, clouds in your eyes, it's easy
to define the prophetic jelly at your core
as joy. The landscape of amusement goes queasy

only when the gilded buckboard juts straight out
over undippered air. A jaw of horror will spill
        you? Not yet. The route
becomes a roaring trough for the next hill

hairpinning higher. You wish you had
the chance to count how many ups,
downs and switchbacks the mad
rattler, rearing its steel hoops, has. The divan hiccups

over a straightaway now, at mild speed.
Then you look: Jolly carousel and ferris wheel, far
years beneath, are cruel gears you can be emptied
into over the side of the hellish sled. Star-

beaded sky! (It feels better to look higher.) How
did the morning, the whole blue-and-white day
    go by in what seems one swoop? You vow
to examine the contraption and its fairway,

    measure the system of gruesome twists,
the queer dimensions, if ever you get down. Going
        down is a dull road. Your fists
    loosen, pretend no longer, knowing

they grip no stick of purpose. The final chutes are
    unspectacular, slower repetitious of past
        excitements. A used and vulgar car
shovels you home in a puzzling gloom. The vast

    agitation faded in your bowels, you think
    that from the ground you'll trace the rim
        your coaster sped and crawled, the sink
    and rise, the reason for its shape. Grim

        darkness now. The ride
is complete. You are positioned for discovery, but,
your senses gone, you can't see the upper arching works.
                Wide
    silence. Midnight. The carnival is shut.

Trinity Churchyard, Spring

Thin shoulders of the old stones,
rude weathered signals of the dead,
armless and as if wearing square
robes, some with an outcrop rounded

as the head once was. Some dark
and marred as charcoal, slices broken,
are torsos rugged earth holds steady here,
perpetual in rain and wind and under

the shrill file of the years.
Some that were white have yellowed
in the sun, bent back in a stasis,
tipped by time, as candles lopped

or shortened with their use. The names
have run awry as melted wax.
Their burning has been opposite to green
and flame-shaped buds exploding now.

Gaunt remnants of one great skeleton
awaiting assembly by the church's side,
(she herself a saintly corpse
hidden in a corner of the town,

a soot-cowled ornament among the tall,
smooth-sided tombs of glass
whose ostentatious signals on the sky
heedless ask their own erasure)

their shadows grow and, longer than themselves,
repeat them on their owned and ancient grass.
Among the dead-to-be, that multiply,
huddle the frail dead undestroyed.

The Totem

We live in the
radius of this
tower. Cocked
at heaven, its
pike is visible
from every quarter.
At night, sabers of
light from its tip
encompass two rivers.
Every forty seconds
the wide shears separate;
raised arms in bishop's
robes impose a mechanical

blessing on all roofs.
By day, the arrogant flint-gray
stock—square, printed with
windows—takes aim at the sun.
Or else, ethereal, decapitated by
fog, it sits, a pale alp
on false distance. From high in
the sides of lesser towers, its
naked neck and shoulders of an obese
bottle occupies the frame of every
window. On any corner—north, south,
east, west—a lift of the head finds
the totem-shape, the boss-god's profile
regnant, its four faces caressed by cloud,
granite, ever the same.
From the apex of
this tower, on a parapet, our bodies boxed by
the wind, we feel the tremor of the heavy stake
screwed into the engine of the city. It quivers
as if transmitting the rub of our planet's axial
twist. Here we scan our compact kingdom: a geometrized
platform, one wedge in the sea, loaded with cubes
and cones, a chaos of knives flashing upright to the
south. In the north, straight-edged blocks and rulers,
within which, quaintly, a yard—a quadrangle of actual
earth—retains the nap of trees and grass. To east and
west, curving skeins of rails and highways, bridges webbing
the rivers; serene, arrowed with craft, they hug our island's
sides. Straight down a hundred floors, in fissures and
crossing furrows, diagonals of shadow and dusty light,
vehicles stitch the redundant maze. A human rug moves,
mottling the pavements. Foreshortened, we pour around our
totem's pedestal, and we pour in and out of its broad, hollow core.

We live in the radius of this tower. It is the hub of our
flat wheel of days. The semaphore at the ends of all our
avenues. Its head a vector, the terminal of our groundling
sight. Landmark and seamark. Sky-peg in the pilot's eye
as he glides down tilting floors of air. Moon and sun are midgeted
by its radiant, constant shaft. Its real sides we lean against—
neighbor and titan—stone, obedient glass and concrete
that is our home. Secure in the shadow—dense, pyramidal
dipped over the city that dyes us—we are content to be tiny—
proud in the beacons that bless us with a god's bayonet gaze.

Distance and a Certain Light

Distance
and a certain light
makes anything artistic—
it doesn't matter what.

From an airplane, all
that rigid splatter of the Bronx
becomes organic, logical
as web or beehive. Chunks

of decayed cars in junkyards,
garbage scows (nimble roaches
on the Harlem), herds of stalled
manure-yellow boxes on twisting reaches

of rails, are punched clean and sharp
as ingots in the ignition of the sun.
Rubbish becomes engaging shape—
you only have to get a bead on it,

the right light filling the corridor
of your view—a gob of spit
under a microscope, fastidious
in structure as a crystal. No contortion

without intention, and nothing ugly.
In any random, sprawling, decomposing thing
is the charming string
of its history—and what it will be next.

4

· · · colors take bodies · · ·

The Snow Geese at Jamaica Bay

A great wedge of snow geese wafted over,
their wings whiter than the white air,
thinned to a long line at one hypotenuse,
as the caravan turned, and pointed north,

a needle their leader, trailing two wavering
threads. Each pair of wings powerful and large,
but in the air, high, weightless as fleece
or petals blown, to lift within the pattern.

Arrowed, yet curved, their course unveering,
varying but carried forward in a ventral glide,
all the star-sharp forms taking their own tilt,
undulant crests on a proud swell, heaving,

hoisting its feather-body toward a divined coast.
And a blue goose flew with them in the dwindling
end of their line. Cooler his color
than the buttermilk breasts of the others,

his dark feet stretched out, his wings
of evening snow. A strange and related other,
denser chip let go, to weight a pure design,
in the wild wedge melted last into the sky.

Living Tenderly

My body a rounded stone
with a pattern of smooth seams.
My head a short snake,
retractive, projective.
My legs come out of their sleeves
or shrink within,
and so does my chin.
My eyelids are quick clamps.

My back is my roof.
I am always at home.
I travel where my house walks.
It is a smooth stone.
It floats within the lake,
or rests in the dust.
My flesh lives tenderly
inside its bone.

The Woods at Night

The binocular owl,
fastened to a limb
like a lantern
all night long,

sees where all
the other birds sleep:
towhee under leaves,
titmouse deep

in a twighouse,
sapsucker gripped
to a knothole lip,
redwing in the reeds,

swallow in the willow,
flicker in the oak—
but cannot see poor
whippoorwill

under the hill
in deadbrush nest,
who's awake, too—
with stricken eye

flayed by the moon
her brindled breast
repeats, repeats, repeats its plea
for cruelty.

Another Spring Uncovered

Colors take bodies,
become many birds.
Odors are born
as earliest buds.
Sounds are streams,
the pebbles bells.
Embraces are
the winds and woods.

Hills of lambskin
stroke our feet.
We move in an amnion
of light,
fondle moss
and put our cheeks
to birches
and warm slate

sides of rocks.
Cardinal on a limb
gripped: if we
could take him
into our hand,
the whistling red
feather-pulse,
the velvet plum—

and seize those other
hues, hot, cool:
indigo bunting sky-piece,
olive thrush
in brown shadow,

oriole apricot-breasted,
hush-wing harlequin
towhee—alive!

If we could eat snowdrops,
sip hyacinths,
make butterflies
be bows in our hair,
wade the tinkling streams
of innocence,
wear lambskin grass,
and suck but milk of air!

One Morning in New Hampshire

We go to gather berries of rain
(sharp to the eye as ripe to the tongue)
that cluster the woods and, low down
between rough-furrowed pine
trunks, melons of sunlight. Morning, young,
carries a harvest in its horn:
colors, shapes, odors, tones
(various as senses are keen).
High in a grape-transparent fan
of boughs are cones
of crystal that were wooden brown.

Two by two, into our ears
are fed sweet pips from a phoebe's throat,
and buzzy notes from a warbler pair,
nuts chuckled from the score
of the thrasher. Gauzing afloat,
a giant moth comes to the choir,
and hums while he sips
from spangles of fern. Insects whir
like wheat in a circular
bin of light; we hear skip
the husking chipmunks in their lair.

Goblin pears, or apples, or quaint
eggs, the mushrooms
litter the forest loft
on pungent mats, in shade still wet,
the gray of gunny in the gloom—
in sun, bright sawdust.
Here's a crop for the nose:
(relish to sight as motley to scent):
fume of cobwebbed stumps, musky roots,
resin-tincture, bark-balm, dayspring moss
in stars new-pricked (vivid as soft).

Day heats and mellows. Those winking seeds—
or berries—spill from their pods; the path's dry
from noon wood to meadow. A speckled
butterfly on top of a weed is a red
and yellow bloom: if that two-ply
petal could be touched,
or the violet wing of the mountain!
Both out of reach—too wary,
or too far to stroke, unless with the eye.
But in green silk of the rye
grain our whole bodies are cuddled.

In the sun's heart we are ripe
as fruits ourselves, enjoyed
by lips of wind our burnished slopes.
All round us dark, rapt
bumble-eyes of susans are deployed
as if to suck our honey-hides. Ants nip,
tasting us all over
with tickling pincers. We are a landscape
to daddy-long-legs, whose ovoid
hub on stilts climbs us like a lover,
trying our dazzle, our warm sap.

A Couple

A bee
rolls
in the yellow
rose.
Does she
invite his hairy
rub?
He scrubs
himself
in her creamy
folds.
A bullet soft imposes
her spiral and, spinning, burrows
to her dewy
shadows.
The gold
grooves almost
match
the yellow
bowl.
Does his touch
please
or scratch?
When he's
done
his honey-
thieving
at her matrix,
whirs free
leaving,
she
closes,
still
tall, chill,
unrumpled on her stem.

Japanese Breakfast

The table of the pool is set.
Each cup quivers by a plate.

Some are filled with tea of sun,
some have pinks of liquor in;

some, thick and white, look upside down
as if put out to dry,

or not to use till morning
pours a thinner cream.

Lying out lopsided,
all the plates are green.

Immaculate as in Japan
the food is only dew,

but fountain-flounce, the table cloth,
shows a rainbow stain.

Some black-nosed goldfish passing through
on their way to shade

nudge the rocking saucers.
A wet ceramic toad,

descending stairs of moss
to breakfast on an insect,

upsets the level table top
but leaves the cups intact.

Seeing the Frog

Seeing the frog
and on its back
embroidery like eyes,
I felt it "see" me
also as shadow
in disguise.

Lengthening
without motion
carefully my hand
lowered a socket—
and unclosed a pond.

Memory handed me
a frog,
pulse under thumb:
how to hold
a loose thing tight,
yet not lame.

The jerk, the
narrow hips' escape
happened again.
I felt the chill
embossment and
the ticking chin.

Before the splash
a hand spread
in whole design,
tan and shadow-
patched, the warts
of water mine!

Fireflies

Fireflies throw
love winks
to their kind
on the dark, glow
without heat,
their day bodies
common beetles.
In a planetarium
of the mind
sparks lit
when logic has gone
down
faint in the dawn
of intellect.
Instinct
makes luminous
the insect.
Idea's anonymous
ordinary mark,
that cryptic
in daylight crept,
can rise an asterisk
astonishing others out.
If the secret
of the dark
be kept,
an eagerness
in smallest, fiercest
hints
can scintillate.

The Crossing

With stealthy wing
the hawk crossed over
the air I breathed
and sank in some cover.

Through water I drank
the deer stepped slow
without chinking a stone
and slid into shadow.

The mountain's body ahead.
the same ground
I walked, hurried up
and out, away, and around

to where the distance stood.
It could not flee or hide.
I filled it. It filled me
and was satisfied.

The Exchange

Now my body flat,
the ground breathes,
I'll be the grass.

Populous and mixed is mind.
Earth take thought,
my mouth be moss.

Field go walking,
I a disk
will look down with seeming eye,

I will be time
and study to be evening.
You world, be clock.

I will stand,
a tree here,
never to know another spot.

Wind be motion,
birds be passion,
water invite me to your bed.

HALF SUN HALF SLEEP
(1967)

For J., the first to read this book.

After the Dentist

My left upper
lip and half

my nose is gone.
I drink my coffee

on the right from
a warped cup

whose left lip dips.
My cigarette's

thick as a finger.
Somebody else's.

I put lip-
stick on a cloth-

stuffed doll's
face that's

surprised when one
side smiles.

After the Flight of Ranger VII

Moon
old fossil
to be scrubbed
and studied
like a turtle's stomach

prodded over on your back
Invulnerable hump
that stumped us

pincers prepare to
pick your secrets
bludgeons of light
to force your seams

Old fossil
glistening
in the continuous rain
of meteorites
blown to you from
between the stars
Stilt feet
mobilize to alight upon you
Ticking feelers
determine your fissures

to impact a pest
of electric eggs in the
cracks of your cold
volcanoes
Tycho Copernicus Kepler
look for geysers

strange abrasions
zodiacal wounds

All That Time

I saw two trees embracing.
One leaned on the other
as if to throw her down.
But she was the upright one.
Since their twin youth, maybe she
had been pulling him toward her
all that time,

and finally almost uprooted him.
He was the thin, dry, insecure one,

the most wind-warped, you could see.
And where their tops tangled
it looked like he was crying
on her shoulder.
On the other hand, maybe he

had been trying to weaken her,
break her, or at least
make her bend
over backwards for him
just a little bit.
And all that time
she was standing up to him

the best she could.
She was the most stubborn,
the straightest one, that's a fact.
But he had been willing
to change himself—
even if it was for the worse—
all that time.

At the top they looked like one
tree, where they were embracing.
It was plain they'd be
always together.
Too late now to part.
When the wind blew, you could hear
them rubbing on each other.

April Light

Lined with light
the twigs are stubby arrows.
A gilded trunk writhes
upward from the roots,
from the pit of the black tentacles.

In the book of spring
a bare-limbed torso
is the first illustration.

Light teaches the tree
to beget leaves,
to embroider itself all over
with green reality,
until summer becomes
its steady portrait,
and birds bring their lifetime
to the boughs.

Then even the corpse
light copies from below
may shimmer, dreaming it feels
the cheeks of blossom.

At First, At Last

At first the dips are shallow,
the peaks ever higher.
Until at last the peaks

are lower.
The valleys deepen.
It is a wave

that mounts and recoils.
Coming then to shadows
on the slopes,

rifts in the concaves,
what is there to do
but lie open-eyed and love

the wave? The wave that gave us
high joys
never again to be matched,

and shall give us,
till it breaks,
oh what

surprises, releases, abysses?
To feel, to feel,
To be the implement

and the wound of feeling.
To lie open to feeling
on the exploding breast, the wave.

At Truro

The sea is unfolding scrolls
and rolling them up again.
It is an ancient diary

the waves are murmuring.
The words are white curls,
great capitals are seen

on the wrinkled swells.
Repeated rhythmically
it seems to me I read

my own biography.
Once I was a sea bird.
With beak a sharp pen,

I drew my signature on air.
There is a chapter when,
a crab, I slowly scratched

my name on a sandy page,
and once, a coral, wrote
a record of my age

on the wall of a water-grotto.
When I was a sea worm
I never saw the sun,

but flowed, a salty germ,
in the bloodstream of the sea.
There I left an alphabet

but it grew dim to me.
Something caught me in its net,
took me from the deep

book of the ocean, weaned me,
put fin and wing to sleep,
made me stand and made me

face the sun's dry eye.
On the shore of intellect
I forgot how to fly

above the wave, below it.
When my foot
touched land's thick back

it stuck like stem or root.
In brightness I lost track
of my underworld

and put night away.
The sea is unfolding scrolls,
and rolling them up.

of ultraviolet wisdom.
My fiery head furled
up its cool kingdom

As if the sun were blind
again I feel the suck
of the sea's dark mind.

August 19, Pad 19

. . . . 8 days without weighing anything.
Not knowing up from down.
Positioned for either breech birth
or urn burial. My mission the practice
of catching up by slowing down,
I am the culmination of a 10-storey bottle,
in 3 disconnectable parts,
being fueled with seething vapor
becoming water becoming fire.
I am the throbbing cork about to pop.

. . . . About to be dragged backward
through 121 sunsets,
not to bathe or drink bare light raw air.
My $75 pencil in my grotesque hand
prepares to float above the clipboard
strapped to my right knee.

. . . . T minus 10 and counting.
Over my obsolete epiderm redundant with
hairs and pits of moisture
I wear my new, rich, inflatable skin,
the bicep patch a proud tattoo,
a galaxy of 50 States,
my telemetric skull, a glossy cupola
resembling the glans of an Aztec god.
My sliding jaw, my safe transparent face
closes. Lungs, you will learn
to breathe hydrogen.

. . . . T minus 10 and counting.
Belted and bolted in, the capsule plugged,
when my 2 umbilical hoses tear free,
I shall increase to the bulk of 7 men,
be halfway to Africa in 12 minutes,
40 seconds. A bead beyond the bulge of earth,
extruded, banished. Till hooked to
the swivel of my ellipse,
I'm played through day and night and east
and west, reeled between apogee and perigee.

. . . . The erector stiffly swoons to its
concrete grave.

. . . . T minus 10 and holding.
Below in the blockhouse, pressed to the
neck of flame, a thumb on the piston
pulses LIFT OFF or ABORT.
My teleological aim the ovary moon,
will I ignite, jump, inject into the sky today
my sparkle of steel sperm?

. . . . Never so helpless, so choked with power.
Never so impotent, so important.
So naked, wrapped, equipped, and immobile,
cared for by 5000 nurses.
Let them siphon my urine to the nearest star.
Let it flare and spin like a Catherine.

. . . . T minus 10 . . . . The click of countdown stops.
My pram and mummycase, this trap's
tumescent tube's still locked to wet,
magnetic, unpredictable earth.
All my systems go, but oh,
an anger of the air won't let me go.
On the screen the blip is MISSION SCRUBBED.

. . . . Be dry my eye for nothing must leak
in here. If a tear forms, instruct the duct
to suck it back. Float, tadpole heart,
behind your slats of bone.

Keep your vibration steady, my switch of blood.
Eyeball in your nook of crepe
behind the ice shield of my window-face,
and ear within your muff of radio,
count taps against the hatch's darkening pane.
Out on the dome some innocent drops of rain.
A puny jolt of thunder. Lightning's golden sneer.

Note: On August 19, 1965, the launch of Gemini 5 from Pad 19 at Cape
Canaveral was "scrubbed" because of weather.

A Basin of Eggs

Their cheeks touching,
their cheeks being
their bellies, their
bellies being undimpled,
dimples of dark being
blue chinks between
their touchings—
eggs in a basin in
a butcher's window

in strong sunlight
being elliptical
loops of primary whiteness.
In a pan their nudity
painful! Potential pain
of their being
damaged deranged de-arranged
against each other's
cheeks-and-bellies

or sides of the pan.
My like-curved eyeballs'
nooses chase their
smoothnesses
in the lattice-pattern's
blond and round design,

hunting clarities of being
yawed and yawned beyond
such birth-loops,

hinting at girths unpinched
by bruises of eclipse.
Sliced by blind rifts
between, my eyeballs
hurt from long looking
at the bone-looking
skin-thin bins
as yet uncracked,
and from yearning to exact

the fact of being
from white-bellied berries'
oblongs of light.
I feel how their cheeks
might grate like
bearings but for
buffers of my seeing
pads of shadow's bruise-
blue chinks between!

A Bird's Life

Is every day a separate life to a bird?
Else why,
as dawn finds the slit lid of starling- or sparrow-eye,
spurts that mad bouquet from agape bills?
Streamered, corkscrew, soprano tendrils
riot in the garden—
incredulous ejaculations at the first pinches
of birth—tiny winches
are tightened, then hysterically jerked loose.
There is produced
a bright geyser of metal-petaled sound
that, shredding, rubs its filings into my sleep.

As the sun, Herself, bulges from a crack in the cloud-shell,
a clamp is applied to every peep—
a paralysis of awe, at the ovening
under feathers of Mother Light—
a stun
of silence—then the reversion
to usual.

When the sun
is higher, only a blurt
of chitters, here and there,
from the sparrows—
sassy whistles, sarcastic barks from the starlings.
By noon they're into middle age
and the stodgy business of generation.

Evening, though, leaks
elegy from a few pathetic beaks.
Chirks of single-syllable despair
that the sky is empty and their
flit-lives almost done.
Their death is the death of light.
Do they lack memory, and so
not know
that The Hen
of the sun
will hatch them again
next morning?

The Blindman

The blindman placed
a tulip on his tongue for purple's taste.
Cheek to grass, his green

was rough excitement's sheen
of little whips.
In water to his lips

he named the sea blue and white,
the basin of his tears and fallen beads of sight.
He said: This scarf is red;

I feel the vectors to its thread
that dance down from the sun. I know
the seven fragrances of the rainbow.

I have caressed
the orange hair of flames. Pressed
to my ear,

a pomegranate lets me hear
crimson's flute.
Trumpets tell me yellow. Only ebony is mute.

Cardinal Ideograms

o   A mouth.   Can blow or breathe,
be funnel, or Hello.

1   A grass blade or a cut.

2   A question seated.   And a proud
bird's neck.

3   Shallow mitten for two-fingered hand.

4   Three-cornered hut
on one stilt.   Sometimes built
so the roof gapes.

5   A policeman.   Polite.
Wearing visored cap.

6   O unrolling,
tape of ambiguous length
on which is written the mystery
of everything curly.

7   A step,
      detached from its stair.

8   The universe in diagram:
      A cosmic hourglass.
      (Note enigmatic shape,
      absence of any valve of origin,
      how end overlaps beginning.)
      Unknotted like a shoelace
      and whipped back and forth,
      can serve as a model of time.

9   Lorgnette for the right eye.
      In England or if you are Alice
      the stem is on the left.

10   A grass blade or a cut
      companioned by a mouth.
      Open? Open. Shut? Shut.

A City Garden in April

THE MAGNOLIA
In the shade
each tight cone

untwists to a goblet.
Under light

the rim widens,
splits like silk.
Seven spatulate

white flakes
float open, purple
dregs at the nape.

THE OLD AILANTHUS
Impossible to count
your fingers,

and all of them crooked.
How many tips

intending further tender
tips, in rigid grapple-

clusters weave with the
wind, with the shift

of the puffy rain cloud?
With the first big

honey-heat of the sun
you'll unloose

your secret explosion.
Then impossible to
count

all the lubricious torches
in your labyrinth of arms.

DAFFODILS
Yellow telephones
in a row in the garden
are ringing,
shrill with light.

Old-fashioned spring
brings earliest models out
each April the same,
naïve and classical.

Look into the yolk-
colored mouthpieces
alert with echoes.
Say hello to time.

THE LITTLE FOUNTAIN
The sun's force
and the fountain's

cool hypnosis—
opposed purities

begin their marathon.
Colorless and motionful

the bowl feels twirl
a liquid hub,

the soft, incessant wheel
slurs over marble

until the dilation frays,
dribbling crystal strings.

The circle encircled,
the reborn circle

synchronized,
repeats the friction,

plash and whisper,
as of feathers rubbed

together or glossy hair.
Bounced from the sun's

breastplate, fierce colors
of flowers, fat leaves,

flinching birds—
while the gray dial

of water keeps all day
its constancy and flicker.

THE VINE
You've put out
new nooses since
yesterday.

With a hook and
a hook and a hook
you took territory

over brick,
seized that side
and knitted

outward to snare
the air with knots
and nipples of leaves.

Your old rope-root,
gray and dried,
made us think you'd

died self-strangled.
One day you inflated
a green parachute,

then breezily invented
a tent, and in five
you've proliferated

a whole plumed pavilion.
Not only alive
but splurging

up and out like a geyser.
Old Faithful,
it's worth a winter

hung up stiff
in sullen petrifaction
for such excess.

Colors Without Objects

Colors without objects—colors alone—
wriggle in the tray of my eye,

incubated under the great flat lamp
of the sun:

bodiless blue, little razor-streak,
yellow melting like a firework petal,

double purple yo-yo
in a broth of murky gold.

Sharp green squints I have never seen
minnow-dive the instant they're alive;

bulb-reds with flickering cilia
dilate, but then implode

to discs of impish scotomata
that flee into the void;

weird orange slats of hot thought
about to make a basket—but

there is no material here—they slim
to a snow of needles, are erased.

Now a mottling takes place.
All colors fix chromosomic links

that dexterously mix,
flip, exchange their aerial ladders.

Such stunts of speed and metamorphosis
breed impermanent, objectless acts,

a thick, a brilliant bacteria—
but most do not survive.

I wait for a few iridium specks of idea
to thrive in the culture of my eye.

*Dear Elizabeth**

Yes, I'd like a pair of *Bicos de Lacre*—
meaning beaks of "lacquer" or "sealing wax"?
(the words are the same in Portuguese)
". . . about 3 inches long including the tail,
red bills and narrow bright red masks . . ."
You say the male has a sort of "drooping
mandarin-mustache—one black stripe"—

otherwise the sexes are alike. "Tiny but
plump, shading from brown and gray on top
to pale beige, white, and a rose red spot
on the belly"—their feathers, you tell
me, incredibly beautiful "alternating
lights and darks like nearly invisible
wave-marks on a sandflat at low tide,

*A reply to Elizabeth Bishop in Brazil.

and with a pattern so fine one must put on
reading glasses to appreciate it properly."
Well, do they sing? If so, I expect their
note is extreme. Not something one hears,
but must watch the cat's ears to detect.
And their nest, that's "smaller than a fist,
with a doorway in the side just wide enough

for each to get into to sleep." They must
be very delicate, not easy to keep. Still,
on the back porch on Perry St., here, I'd
build them a little Brazil. I'd save every
shred and splinter of New York sunshine
and work through the winter to weave them
a bed. A double, exactly their size,

with a roof like the Ark. I'd make sure to
leave an entrance in the side. I'd set it
in among the morning-glories where the
gold-headed flies, small as needles' eyes,
are plentiful. Although "their egg is apt
to be barely as big as a baked bean . . ."
It rarely hatches in captivity, you mean—

but we could hope! In today's letter you
write, "The *Bicos de Lacre* are adorable as
ever—so tiny, neat, and taking baths
constantly in this heat, in about ¼ inch
of water—then returning to their *filthy*
little nest to lay another egg—which
never hatches." But here it might! And it

doesn't matter that "their voice is weak,
they have no song." I can see them as I
write—on their perch on my porch. "From
the front they look like a pair of half-
ripe strawberries"—except for that stripe.
"At night the cage looks empty" just as
you say. I have "a moment's fright"—

then see the straw nest moving softly.
Yes, dear Elizabeth, if you would be so
kind, I'd like a pair of *Bicos de Lacre*—
especially as in your P.S. you confess,
"I already have two unwed female wild
canaries, for which I must find husbands
in order to have a little song around here."

Drawing the Cat

Makes a platform for himself:
forepaws bent under his chest,
slot-eyes shut in a corniced head,
haunches high like a wing chair,
hindlegs parallel, a sled.

As if on water, low afloat
like a wooden duck: a bundle not
apt to be tipped, so symmetrized
on hidden keel of tail he rides
squat, arrested, glazed.

Lying flat, a violin:
hips are splayed, head and chin
sunk on paws, stem straight out
from the arched root
at the clef-curve of the thighs.

Wakes: the head ball rises.
Claws sprawl. Wires
go taut, make a wicket of his spine.
He humps erect, with scimitar yawn
of hooks and needles porcupine.

Sits, solid as a doorstop,
tail-encircled, tip laid on his toes,
ear-tabs stiff, gooseberry eyes
full, unblinking, sourly wise.
In outline: a demijohn with a pewter look.

Swivels, bends a muscled neck:
petal-of-tulip-tongue slicks
the brushpoint of his tail to black,
then smooths each glossy epaulette
with assiduous sponge.

Whistle him into a canter
into the kitchen: tail hooked aside,
ears at the ready. Elegant copy
of carrousel pony—
eyes bright as money.

11th Floor, West 4th Street

From a little window high in a shaft
I look at many-windowed giant crates,
lit factories jumbled in the loft
of beginning night. Sluggish coils of
sundown low on the wall of sky
behind the river—its glimmer moves,
a stamp-sized square of prickled waves
between tall rulers of the western street.
Blue-white light in the shells of the
crates that bulk their corners on the valley
of beginning night; light-riddled the trough
of the southern street where trinket-vehicles
double-trickle to the anvil-end of Manhattan,

toward the squat trunks of towers;
their jutting tops curved or coned,
crossed with wires of windowed light,
lift stiff and slender into the high apse
of night. In space, at level of my eye,
the early dark is clean of objects,
except three: the new emphatic moon
a comma of light, and two flies of light
that wigwag red and green, crawling a pane
of slate into the east.

                              The ruddy smudge
has darkened on the wall now, low by the river.
Copper-green, the drape of maturing night
rides down in loops of shadow to the street.
I see along its edges slow dolls,
dressed in thickening cloth of dark,
pushing their shades like barrows as they walk
beneath the trinket-lamps. And all the upright
radiant walls, the jagged lighted gorge
of the southern street, is theirs—
their scene, their stage, their making—
soft innocuous puppets there below
wobbling on the sidewalks of their show.

Fable for When There's No Way Out

Grown too big for his skin,
and it grown hard,

without a sea and atmosphere—
he's drunk it all up—

his strength's inside him now,
but there's no room to stretch.

He pecks at the top
but his beak's too soft;

though instinct and ambition shoves,
he can't get through.

Barely old enough to bleed
and already bruised!

In a case this tough
what's the use

if you break your head
instead of the lid?

Despair tempts him
to just go limp:

Maybe the cell's
already a tomb,

and beginning end
in this round room.

Still, stupidly he pecks
and pecks, as if from under

his own skull—
yet makes no crack . . .

No crack until
he finally cracks,

and kicks and stomps.
What a thrill

and shock to feel
his little gaff poke

through the floor!
A way he hadn't known or meant.

Rage works if reason won't.
When locked up, bear down.

Flag of Summer

Sky and sea and sand,
fabric of the day.
The eye compares each band.

Parallels of color on bare
canvas of time-by-the-sea.
Linen-clean the air.

Tan of the burlap
beach scuffed with prints
of bathers. Green and dapple,

the serpentine swipe
of the sea unraveling
a ragged crepe

on the shore. Heavy satin
far out, the coil,
darkening, flattens

to the sky's rim.
There a gauze screen,
saturate-blue, shimmers.

Blue and green and tan,
the fabric changes hues
by brush of light or rain:

sky's violet bar
leans over flinty waves
opaque as the shore's

opaline grains; sea silvers,
clouds fade to platinum,
the sand-mat ripples

with greenish tints
of snakeskin, or drying,
whitens to tent-cloth

spread in the sun. These bands,
primary in their dimensions,
elements, textures, strands:

the flag of summer,
emblem of ease, triple-striped,
each day salutes the swimmer.

Flying Home from Utah

Forests are branches of a tree lying down,
its blurred trunk in the north.
Farms are fitted pieces of a floor,

tan and green tiles that get smoother,
smaller, the higher we fly.
Heel-shaped dents of water I know are deep

from here appear opaque, of bluish glass.
Curl after curl, rivers are coarse locks
unraveling southward over the land;

hills, rubbed felt, crumpled bumps
of antlers pricking from young bucks' heads.
Now towns are scratches here and there

on a wide, brown-bristled hide.
Long roads rayed out from the sores of cities
begin to fester and crawl with light—

above them the plane is a passing insect
that eyes down there remark, forget
in the moment it specks the overcast.

It climbs higher. Clouds become ground.
Pillows of snow meet, weld into ice.
Alone on a moonlit stainless rink

glides the ghost of a larva, the shadow
of our plane. Lights go on
in the worm-belly where we sit;

it becomes the world, and seems to cease
to travel—only vibrates, stretched out tense
in the tank of night.

The room of my mind replaces the long, lit room.
I dream I point my eye over a leaf
and fascinate my gaze upon its veins:

A sprawled leaf, many-fingered, its radial
ridges limber, green—but curled,
tattered, pocked, the brown palm

nibbled by insects, nestled in by worms:
One leaf of a tree that's one tree of a forest,
that's the branch of the vein of a leaf

of a tree. Perpetual worlds
within, upon, above the world, the world
a leaf within a wilderness of worlds.

Four-Word Lines

Your eyes are just
like bees, and I
feel like a flower.
Their brown power makes
a breeze go over
my skin. When your
lashes ride down and
rise like brown bees'
legs, your pronged gaze
makes my eyes gauze.
I wish we were
in some shade and
no swarm of other
eyes to know that
I'm a flower breathing
bare, laid open to
your bees' warm stare.
I'd let you wade
in me and seize
with your eager brown
bees' power a sweet
glistening at my core.

Gods | Children

They are born naked,
and without tails.
They cannot fly.
Their blood is red.
They are children until they die,
and then "are God's children."
Are gods . . . children . . .
Are *gods children?*

Worlds are their heads,
oceans infants' serene eyes.
Blue and green they invented.
Leaves did not grow
or the wind blow
until their spine
lifted like a tendril.
Their tongue curled.
Their hand made a sign.

They are not like fruit
though their skin is sweet.
Though they rot they have wrought
the numbers one to ten.
They founded the sun.
When the sun found them
it undertook its path and aim.
The moon, also,
when it received its name.
The air first heard itself called glory
in their lungs.

Beasts they placed in the sky
and in their caves
and on their platforms,
for they remembered their cradles,
their blood in flow
told them their beginnings.
The beloved hoofs,
massy necks,

rich nostrils,
sex, a red coal in the groin,
they worshipped.
Also their helical rod
called evil and sapience.

They ensorcelled angels,
dreamed queerer forms,
on the brain's map fixed a junction, "Infinity,"
in the entrail's maze, "Prophecy,"
and made "Measure"
and the dance of "The Particles,"
with a switch the system, "Time," turned on,
a braided chain,
torque for the whole of space
their game.

They play,
are flexible jugglers and jongleurs,
fashioners of masks;
are mirror-makers
and so dupe themselves,
dress themselves,
are terrified at flesh,
think each other phantoms,
idols, demons, toys;
make of each other handles, ladders, quicksands;
are to each other houses of safety,
hammocks of delight.

They cannot fly,
but nest themselves in bullets
and, dressed as embryos,
shoot out to a circle beyond their ball.
And can breathe with such a placenta,
their foot floating
far separate from its ground.

Before, in iron capsules
lived under the sea,

in baskets inflated rode the air.
Many other marvels built besides.
Are mysterious charts
beneath their skulls' membranes.
And have invented madness.

Under their bodies' casings
in intricate factories
work their strong, soft engines.
Their blood is red.
Color and name they invented,
and so created it.
And have named themselves.

And it is even so
that they operate upon one another,
and increase,
and make replicas,
and replace one another,
new for old,
and tick to death
like moments.

When they are dead,
they are made naked,
are washed and dressed.
They do this for each other
like children.
And are fixed into fine boxes
like children fix their dolls.

And then?
"Are God's children."
Are gods . . . children . . .
Then are gods children?

Hearing the Wind at Night

I heard the wind coming,
transferred from tree to tree.
I heard the leaves
swish, wishing to be free

to come with the wind, yet wanting to stay
with the boughs like sleeves.
The wind was a green ghost.
Possessed of tearing breath

the body of each tree
whined, a whipping post,
then straightened and resumed
its vegetable oath.

I heard the wind going,
and it went wild.
Somewhere the forest threw itself
into tantrum like a child.

I heard the trees tossing
in punishment or grief,
then sighing, and soughing,
soothing themselves to sleep.

His Suicide

He looked down at his withering body and saw a hair
near his navel, swaying.

And now he saw his other hairs rise up.

He felt a hectic current in his veins.
Looking within, he saw the bubbling of his blood.

He cursed his fever, saying:
"It is the chemistry of prayer.

It increases in frequency,
seeding panic to all my being.
My cells swell with the liquid of guilt they fabricate,
juices of hatred eat my belly
my corpuscles make war in me as they devour each other.
My head heats in the combustion of anxiety,
I am polluted by the secretions of my soul's decay,
while my brain wears away
with the scratching night and day
on the encephalograph of prayer.
I grow monstrous with the leukemia of the world."

And he heard the hair say: "Hear me."
And he saw it grow gray as it waved.
All his hairs he saw whiten,
and, numberless, wilt from their erect electric listening.
He saw them topple from their roots.
"How dare you!" he cursed them.
There surged a brief resuscitation to his body.
His heart took heart and pounded twice
with the health of fear.
But then the plague of prayer redoubled and overwhelmed
    him.

In his feebleness he raged, and said:
"I will tear out this evil and free it."
With his withered hands he tore the remaining hairs
from his body and head.
With his nails he opened his breast,
and with his fist he exploded his heart,
which erupted, a black and red volcano.

As his brain tasted, for the first time,
the birth of his doom,
he became a rolling tide, a floating mountain of ecstasy.
"I see you! I love you!" his eyes cried,
overflowing with his bright blood.
"You were the light of the world
that are now my gushing tears—
the kind and fiery tears of chaos, that wash my eyes
with the cure of oblivion."

"He hears us!" cried his sick blood
pouring from his ears.
"Even as of old he heard our hair before it perished."

With his last strength, the chemistry of prayer,
a few drops of his blood coagulated.
That clot whirled out, free, in the vortex of the universe.

In a Museum Cabinet

Like some kind of ruin, but domed
like an igloo . . . Midway in the mound
are two deep punctures of darkness
more square than round—thick-walled
"casements," those transparencies

that filtered light lost long ago.
Where the nose was, a rough diamond-shape
positioned on the sill of the lip-ridge,
I can see, as through a "front door"
agape, thin steps of debris within.

Heavy, squat, like a blockhouse,
but bombed out . . . This makes it look frail.
The card says: *Unearthed in London.*
Roman. 100 A.D. It could also be
some wild den, scoured by a hurricane,

its stones so stubborn they settled
into fissures where the cheekbones hinge,
did not quite crumble. Or, again,
it could be the beast of that den
petrified to rock. It crouches

on side-teeth still strong. The wide
underjaw is gone. The forehead
is whole, smooth, and round. But an old
fracture slants from the left socket
to a tooth-root, like a trench for tears.

It crouches, gripping the glass ground
with teeth and the blunt points of the
neck-pocket. Looking at it, I hear
an eerie wind whirl in and out,
as through gray caves, of coral, by the sea.

In the Hair of the Night

The hound's eye of the sun
and the cat's eye of the moon
watch the earth's eye
the iris of a mouse
in the cloudy hair of the night

The sun's eye sees
In the hair of the night
the cloudy head of a sphinx
whose face is a herd of eyes
in the monstrous hair of the night

The moon's eye sees a snake
in the cloudy mouth of the night
that uncoils, uncovers the nine
diamonds of its eyes
in the monstrous face of a sphinx

The earth's eye is the iris of a mouse
in the cloudy mouth of a snake
in the face of a sphinx
whose head is a herd of monstrous eyes
in the hair of the night

The Kite

Triangular face, or mask,
dangling a spinal cord,

or like the diagram of a spirochete,
the tail wiggling.

Desperate paper pollywog, aloft,
pushing upstream,

alive because wind pours over, under
it, like water.

The sky with invisible wind,
the frame of Being around a face;

behind the unprobed surface
the mirror's space.

"Perhaps all things are inanimate
and it is the void that lives,"

I think, until I remember
that a string,

not seen in the white air,
is tied to a finger below.

The paper face is fixed
in a magnetic flow

on which it depends,
by which it is repelled.

The tug of the void,
the will of the world

together declare
placement for the shivering mask.

The Lightning

The lightning waked me. It slid unde r
my eyelid. A black book flipped ope n
to an illuminated page. Then insta   ntly
shut. Words of destiny were being ut-
tered in the distance. If only I   could
make them out! . . . Next day, as I   lay
in the sun, a symbol for concei   ving the
universe was scratched on my e   yeball.
But quickly its point eclipse   d, and
softened, in the scabbard of   my brain.

My cat speaks one word: Fo   ur vowels
and a consonant. He rece   ives with the
hairs of his body the wh   ispers of the
stars. The kinglet spe   aks by flashing
into view a ruby feath   er on his head.
He is held by a threa   d to the eye of
the sun and cannot   fall into error.
Any flower is a per   fect ear, or else it
is a thousand lips   . . . When will I grope
clear of the entr   ails of intellect?

The Little Rapids

Over its cliff
splashes the
little rapids,
a braid of glossy
motion in perpetual
flow and toss,
its current rayed
flashing down
crayon veins.

Life-node of my
precipice of bone,
a snake-mouth muscle

spills urgent venom
to soft hills,
to flesh-warm stone.

A replica of all
power's crotched
here in the ribs,
knot and nubbin
of the jutting flood.
Leaps and drops
are instants in
the swirling hour
reiterated from
this hub:

Grief-gusher,
freshet of desire,
snug nest of joy
and fear,
its zest constant
even in sleep,
its padded roar
bounding in the
grotto of the breast.

Hinge of hate and
love, steep springhead,
riddle of my blood,
primal pool of
cruelty, and all
queer sweet thrills . . .
Ravine of my body,
red, incredulous
with autumn,
from here curt death
will hurl me delirious
into the gorge.

More Rich

When I go blind I shall see
my dreams

that round the edges of my mind
flash sometimes

then sink in the inverted sea.
Each thing the sun

makes hard and my hand takes
shall dissolve

a pure void underhemisphere
reveal its pole

When tensions of the light
relax there'll be

a waveless plunge. I'll cast
my shape

and weight and have no hinge
and have no

mental hook. Blind I'll dive
and read

the colored flood.
A world

more rich than blood shall be
my book.

Motherhood

She sat on a shelf,
her breasts two bellies
on her poked-out belly,
on which the navel looked
like a sucked-in mouth—
her knees bent and apart,
her long left arm raised,
with the large hand knuckled
to a bar in the ceiling—
her right hand clamping
the skinny infant to her chest—
its round, pale, new,
soft muzzle hunting
in the brown hair for a nipple,
its splayed, tiny hand picking
at her naked, dirty ear.
Twisting its little neck,
with tortured, ecstatic eyes
the size of lentils, it looked
into her severe, close-set,
solemn eyes, that beneath bald
eyelids glared—dull lights
in sockets of leather.

She twitched some chin-hairs,
with pain or pleasure,
as the baby-mouth found and
yanked at her nipple;
its pink-nailed, jointless
fingers, wandering her face,
tangled in the tufts
of her cliffy brows.
She brought her big
hand down from the bar—
with pretended exasperation
unfastened the little hand,
and locked it within her palm—
while her right hand,
with snag-nailed forefinger

and short, sharp thumb, raked
the new orange hair
of the infant's skinny flank—
and found a louse,
which she lipped, and
thoughtfully crisped
between broad teeth.
She wrinkled appreciative
nostrils which, without a nose,
stood open—damp holes
above the poke of her mouth.

She licked her lips, flicked
her leather eyelids—
then, suddenly flung
up both arms and grabbed
the bars overhead.
The baby's scrabbly fingers
instantly caught the hair—
as if there were metal rings there—
in her long, stretched armpits.
And, as she stately swung,
and then proudly, more swiftly
slung herself from corner
to corner of her cell—
arms longer than her round
body, short knees bent—
her little wild-haired,
poke-mouthed infant hung,
like some sort of trophy,
or decoration, or shaggy medal—
shaped like herself—but new,
clean, soft and shining
on her chest.

Naked in Borneo
(From a painting by Tobias)

They wear air
or water like a skin,
their skin the smoothest suit.
Are tight and loose
as the leopard, or sudden
and still as the moccasin.
Their blouse is black

shadows of fronds
on a copper vest of sun.
Glossy rapids are
their teeth and eyes
beneath straight harsh blonds
of rained-on grain that thatch
their round head-huts.

Long thongs their bodies, bows
or canoes. Both tense and lax
their bodies, spears
they tool, caress, hoard, decorate
with cuts. Their fears
are their weapons. Coiled or
straight they run up trees

and on jungle thorns; their feet
are their shoes, fierce hair
their hats that hold off sun's hate.
They glide, muscles of water
through water, dark oil-beads
pave their lashing
torsos. Are bare in air,

are wind-combed, armpit and groin;
are taut arrows turned sinuous reeds
for dancing on drumskin ground.
Rasped by the sun's tongue, then moon-licked

all their slick
moist feathered shafts
in the hammocks of tangled thighs

the silks of night plash among.
Their joys, their toys are their children
who like kittens ride
their mother's neck, or wrestle
with the twins of her breasts
where she squats by the meal pot.
At hunter's naked side

little hunter stalks fix-eyed,
miniature poison-dart
lifted, learning the game:
young pointer in the bush,
fish-diver in the river,
grave apprentice in the art
of magic pain

when the blood pines
to be let a little,
to sharpen the friction of Alive,
in the feckless skin
leave some slits and signs
that old spirit leaked out,
new spirit sneaked in.

Ocean, Whale-Shaped

Ocean, whale-shaped, rocking between the dunes,
in the gateway of their great naked knees,
horizon chafing a tame sky,

your vast back purple, your shoreward side
wallowing blue, fretted with racing foam,
green, then diamond your fin flashes on sand.

Glazed monuments of the wind, the dunes,
their sprawling limbs Olympian lift and fall
to slopes and platforms seeming hard as bone,

but footsteps scar their flanks like snow;
their white bodies shift,
are shunted by you, blue-black, boisterous whale—

and whittled, are rewhittled by the wind
unsatisfied with any shape or perpetuity.
The land, the sand we tread is not the steady

element our feet believe.
Indelible ocean, humped beside the sky,
you unsubstantial we can't grasp or walk on,

you pry at these gates and break them when you will—
overwhelming whale of water, mover and shaper,
over and over carving your cradle here.

October Textures

The brushy and hairy,
tassely and slippery

willow, phragmite,
cattail, goldenrod.

The fluttery, whistley
water-dimpling divers,

waders, shovelers,
coots and rocking scaup.

Big blue, little green,
horned grebe, godwit,

bufflehead, ruddy,
marsh hawk, clapper rail.

Striated water
and striated feather.

The breast of the sunset.
The phalarope's breast.

Of Rounds

MOON
        round
            goes around while going around a
                                    round
                                    EARTH
EARTH
        round
            with MOON
                    round
                        going around while going around
        goes around while going around a
                        round
                        SUN
SUN
        round
            with EARTH
                        round
                            with MOON
                                    round
                                        going around while going
around, and MERCURY
                    round
                        and VENUS
                                round
                                    going around while
going around, and MARS
                    round
                        with two MOONS
                                    round
                                    round
                                        going around
while going around, and JUPITER
                        round

with thirteen MOONS

round
round
round
round
round
round
round
round
round
round
round
round
round

going around while going around, and SATURN

round

with nine

MOONS

round
round
round
round
round
round
round
round
round

going around while going around, and URANUS

round

with five MOONS

round
round
round
round
round

going around while going around, and NEPTUNE

round

with two MOONS

round
round

going around while going around, and

PLUTO

round

going around while going around, goes around while

going around

A   OF ROUNDS

Round

On Handling Some Small Shells
from the Windward Islands*

Their scrape and clink
together of musical coin.

Than the tinkling of crickets
more eerie, more thin.

Their click, as of crystal,
wood, carapace and bone.

A tintinabular fusion.
Their friction spinal and chill

as of ivory embryo
fragments of horn

honed to whistles and flutes.
Windy Eustachian coils

cold as the sea till held,
then warm as the palm,

and snuggled naturally there
smoother than skin.

The curve and continuous
spiral intrinsic, their

role eternal inversion,
the closed, undulant scroll.

Even when corrugate,
sharpness rubbed from

their forms, licked by
the mouth of the sea

*A gift from N.B. and D.E.

to tactile charms.
Some blanched by the eye

         of the sun, a pumice shine
         buffing their calcareous

nakedness clean as a tooth.
Some colored like flesh,

         but more subtle than
         corpuscle dyes. Some

sunsets, some buttermilk
skies, or penumbras

         of moons in eclipse.
         Malachite greens, fish-eyed

icy blues, pigeon-foot pinks,
brindled fulvous browns,

         but most white like tektites.
         Gathered here in a bowl,

their ineradicable inks
vivid, declarative

         under water. Peculiar fossil-
         fruits that suck through ribbed

lips and gaping sutures
into secret clefts

         the sweet wet with a tame taste.
         Vulviform creatures, or

rather, their rocklike
backs with labial bellies.

Some earhole shaped, or
funnels with an overlap,

some stony worms curled up
and glazed, the egress

like a trumpet. Some cones
with tight twisted sphincters

rugos and spiculate,
cactus-humped or warted,

others slick and simple
pods where tender jellies hid.

The frigid souls, the
amorphous ones, emptied

from out their skeletons
that were their furled caves.

Each an eccentric
mummy-case, one facet mute

and ultimate, one baffling
in its ruffles as a rose.

The largest, a valve of
bone streaked like a cloud,

its shadowy crease a pinched
ambiguous vestibule, a puckered

trap ajar: the sly inviting
smile into the labyrinth.

On Seeing Rocks Cropping Out
of a Hill in Central Park

Boisterous water arrested, these rocks
are water's body in death. Transparent

water falling without stop makes a wall,
the frenzied soul of rock its white breath.

Dark water's inflated wave, harsh spray
is ghost of a boulder and cave's

marble, agitated drapery. Stillness
water screams for, flying forth,

the body of death. Rock dreams
soul's motion, its hard birth.

Out of the Sea, Early

A bloody
egg yolk. A burnt hole
spreading in a sheet. An en-
raged rose threatening to bloom.
A furnace hatchway opening, roaring.
A globular bladder filling with immense
juice. I start to scream. A red hydrocepha-
lic head is born, teetering on the stump of
its neck. When it separates, it leaks rasp-
berry from the horizon down the wide esca-
lator. The cold blue boiling waves cannot
scour out that band, that broadens, slid-
ing toward me up the wet sand slope. The
fox-hair grows, grows thicker on the
upfloating head. By six o'clock,
diffused to ordinary gold,
it exposes each silk thread and rumple in the carpet.

The People Wall*

Prodded by the smiles of handsome clerks,
they file into the narrow slits, and are filed,
500 every 20 minutes on 12 varicolored shelves.
All are carefully counted; all but their names are known.

It's been shown that 50 hips from the Midwest,
mainly female, with a random sprinkling of male and
juvenile, can fit into any given row, elbow to elbow
along the rail, heels hooked under the padded

8-inch-wide seat bar. Now the steep drawer
is filled, all the heads are filed, the racks closed
by the clerks at the ends of each aisle.
"Hello there!" calls the sartorially perfect head

clerk, let down on a circular podium to stand as if
in the air. He's propped like a stopped pendulum
in front of the wall of people all filed and smiling.
It's a colorful assortment of United States faces, good-

looking for the most part, fun-ready, circus-
expectant, and bright as a box of glazed marzipan.
"Hello there, all you people!" Twirling his
microphone cable like a lariat: "Do you know

where you're going on this Fair day? You're
going to be lifted . . . by mighty hydraulic arms . . .
straight up . . . 90 feet . . . up into The Egg!
In there you're going to learn how your mind works . . .

in color . . . on 15 separate screens . . . a show
that will show you how you all think! What do you think
of that? Now, just relax. Lean back. And no
smoking, please. Everybody comfortable? No need

to hold on to anything. Don't hold on to your hats,
or even your heads. Just lean back and get ready

*At the IBM pavilion, New York World's Fair, 1965.

for a pleasant ride backwards . . . There you go!
Up . . . up . . . up into the World of the Computers!"

Down on the ground, thousands of identical plastic
balls cascade through the maze of the Probability
Machine, repeatedly testing the Theory of the
Frequency of Errors. Clicking musically, they choose

their individual ways down, bouncing once before they
settle into the common heap. Each ball might
land in any one of 21 chutes, yet each chute fills
to about the same height each time the balls descend.

The magic curve completes itself. All balls
have fallen, and form a more or less symmetrical
black hill. A cheerful bell trills. The People Wall
rises. All heads, filed and smiling, are fed into The Egg.

The Pregnant Dream

I had a	dream in which I had a dream,
and in my	dream I told you, "Listen, I will tell you my dream." And I began to tell you. And
you told me, "I haven't time to	listen while you tell your dream."
Then in my	dream I dreamed I began to forget my dream.
And I	forgot my dream.
And I began to tell you,	"Listen, I have forgot my dream."
And now I tell you:	"Listen while I tell you my dream, a dream
in which I	dreamed I forgot my

dream,"
and I begin to tell you: "In my   dream you told me, 'I haven't time to
                                          listen.'"

And you tell me: "You   dreamed I wouldn't
                               listen to a
                               dream that you
                               forgot?
I haven't time to   listen to
                           forgotten
                           dreams."

"But I haven't   forgot I
                        dreamed," I tell you,
"a   dream in which I told you,
            'Listen, I have
            forgot,' and you told me, 'I haven't time.'"
"I haven't time," you tell me.

And now I begin to   forget that I
                            forgot what I began to tell you in my
                            dream.
And I tell you,   "Listen,
                         listen, I begin to
                         forget."

Rain at Wildwood

The rain fell like grass growing
upside down in the dark,
at first thin shoots,
short, crisp, far apart,

but, roots in the clouds,
a thick mat grew
quick, loquacious, lachrymose blades
blunt on the tent top.

The grass beneath ticked,
trickled, tickled like rain
all night, inchwormed
under our ears,

its flat liquid tips slipping
east with the slope.
Various tin plates
and cups and a bucket filled

up outside,
played, plinked, plicked,
plopped till guttural.
The raccoon's prowl was almost

silent in the trash,
soggy everything but eggshells.
No owl called.
Waking at first light

the birds were blurred,
notes and dyes of jay and towhee
guaranteed to bleed.
And no bluing in the sky.

In the inverted V
of the tent flaps
muddy sheets of morning
slumped among the trunks,

but the pin oaks' viridian
dripping raggedy leaves
on the wood's floor released
tangy dews and ozones.

The Secret in the Cat

I took my cat apart
to see what made him purr.
Like an electric clock
or like the snore

of a warming kettle,
something fizzed and sizzled in him.
Was he a soft car,
the engine bubbling sound?

Was there a wire beneath his fur,
or humming throttle?
I undid his throat.
Within was no stir.

I opened up his chest
as though it were a door:
no whisk or rattle there.
I lifted off his skull:

no hiss or murmur.
I halved his little belly
but found no gear,
no cause for static.

So I replaced his lid,
laced his little gut.
His heart into his vest I slid
and buttoned up his throat.

His tail rose to a rod
and beckoned to the air.
Some voltage made him vibrate
warmer than before.

Whiskers and a tail:
perhaps they caught
some radar code
emitted as a pip, a dot-and-dash

of woolen sound.
My cat a kind of tuning fork?—
amplifier?—telegraph?—
doing secret signal work?

His eyes elliptic tubes:
there's a message in his stare.
I stroke him
but cannot find the dial.

Sightseeing in Provincetown

If your elbow were	an eagle's head
and your loins	the mouth of a cat
its tongue	many ripped tongues of flame

and if your ribs were the membranous wings of a dragon
and if one leg were of black leather
the bloody claw of a chicken grafted to the knee

and if your buttocks were the cheeks of a laughing insane face
the lips clasping a trumpet
from which wasps were flying the wasps' eyes clearly seen

glossy with mad hilarity and if although you were male
your left breast were a large pale polyp
with numerous nipples and the other breast a dog's head

its jaws straining to swallow a severed thigh
and if from your slick head that of a rhinoceros
with inrolled eyes there curved instead of a snout

a snake with a fishhook through its neck
and if rags of flame flew from your navel
it being the unhinged door of a furnace

and if looking down
you saw a cat's mouth between your legs
giving birth to the dripping lower half

of a face whose skin peeled back hung from the earlobes
with raw lips stretched in a sonorous scream
and if in the gullet's vortex there bobbed

a tiny figure scalded red a Janus-faced child
both girl and boy impaled through one armpit
by a tooth then you'd be elected

Chief Lucifer   of S. H. Masters' Hell
the colors like flesh   like silk like fruit
under an exceptionally clear patina   smooth as petunia

"The Last Judgment"   (Austria c. 1480)
gilt-framed   on a plum-velvet-covered wall
in Provincetown   1965

Sleeping Overnight on the Shore

Earth turns
          one cheek to the sun
while the other tips
          its crags and dimples into shadow.
We say sun comes up,
          goes down,
but it is our planet's incline
          on its shy invisible neck.
The smooth skin of the sea,
          the bearded buttes of the land
blush orange,
          we say it is day.
Then earth in its turning
          slips half of itself away
from the ever burning.
          Night's frown
smirches earth's face,
          by those hours marked older.
It is dark, we say.
          But night is a fiction
hollowed at the back of our ball,
          when from its obverse side
a cone of self-thrown shade
          evades the shining,
and black and gray
          the cinema of dreams streams through
our sandgrain skulls
          lit by our moon's outlining.

Intermittent moon
        that we say climbs
or sets, circles only.
        Earth flicks it past its shoulder.
It tugs at the teats of the sea.
        And sky
is neither high
        nor is earth low.
There is no dark
        but distance
between stars.
        No dawn,
for it is always day
        on Gas Mountain, on the sun—
and horizon's edge
        the frame of our eye.

Cool sand on which we lie
        and watch the gray waves
clasp, unclasp
        a restless froth of light,
silver saliva of the sucking moon—
        whose sun is earth
who's moon to the sun—
        To think this shore,
each lit grain plain
        in the foot-shaped concaves
heeled with shadow,
        is pock or pocket
on an aging pin
        that juggler sun once threw,
made twirl among
        those other blazing objects out
around its crown.
        And from that single toss
the Nine still tumble—
        swung in a carousel of staring light,
where each rides ringleted
        by its pebble-moons—

white lumps of light
        that are never to alight,
for there is no down.

Spectrum Analysis

When I say
     I
     I swim
in a yellow
     room.
When I think
     my mind
     my mind
pulls to me a
     sun
that magnetizes to itself a
     million
     million
butterflies dandelions and
coins eggyolks strands
of ambergris the eyes
of cats and owls and
beakers ampouls beads
of topaz and of honey and of
     urine.

Have I arrived from
     left or
     right to hover here
in the clear permission of my
     temperature? Is my
     flow a fading
     up or
     down—my glow
     going? Or is my flush
     rushing to a rose of ripe
     explosion?

Outside the wall
    I call
    east the scene is
    green
    I name
    naming *my*
    name. And
    west beyond this
  room looms brazen in heathaze
of imagination an
    orange doom
if my destiny's so spelled.

Saying
    I feel
    I feel
    I flicker out toward cooler
    cells through
    green down
    blue to darkening
    indigo wells—
if these are
    downhills and not
    upslants I'm engulfed
in the throat of a vast
    petunia unknown
    to bone or
    moon.

In that atmosphere immeasurably rare—
and is it
    high or
    deep?—
have I already been iced an
    ultraviolet inkling
in my narrowest
    sleep?
    Unless the pass is
    counterwise and
    I whirl—not

    grassward but
    brassward
rammed with the rusty
        dust through spirals of
        radiation
crammed flaked corroded dispersed
        particulated
to electron
        pits my
        I dissected
        naked
frayed to anonymous
        its—reversed and
        tossed out
        lost—so
        around in the
        boundless loosed.

Yet while
        I say
        I
        I swim
defined in a
        yellow
        room. Though
        I know not what
        point *my*
        point
        points to
        it is a
        point intent upon
        itself and in
        its speed so steady bent
        it seems entirely still.
        Pointing
        its
        it to
        itself
        it's spent
upon its journey
the jagged jig around the centrifuge.

Until
       I say
       I
       will
       will
       I be distilled in the
       red
       room there next
       door within the
       core of an
       orbital rose that
       decaying to
       its bud will freeze to
       its seed?
       Yes
       I say
       yes and consent to
       less and
       less.

       Unless
the race is to unfurling where
       lips within
       lips proliferate
their lace outleaping all edges
to compel gigantic
       bloom. Then
       blood again? *My*
       blood beneath my skin?

When I taste
       I
       I taste something akin
to suprafruit or neutronic
       flower
a solar heart engorged with light's rich
       juice
       infrared.

Still Turning

Under a round roof the flying
horses, held by their heels to the disk of the
floor, move to spurts from a pillar of
    music, cranked from the past like grainy

    honey. Their ears are wood, their nostrils
painted red, their marble eyes
startled, distended with effort, their
    jaws carved grimaces of

    speed. Round and round go the flying
horses, backs arched in utmost
leaps, necks uptossed or stretched
    out, manes tangled by a wooden

    wind. As if lungs of wood inside their
chests pumped, their muscles
heave, and bunch beneath the colored
    traces. Round and round go the flying

    horses. Forked in the saddles are thrilled
children, with polished cheeks and fixed
eyes, who reach out in a stretch of
    ambition, leaning out from the turning

    pillar. They lean out to snatch the
rings, that are all of wood. But there's one of
brass. All feel lucky as, pass after
    pass, they stay fixed to the flying

    horses. The horses' reins and stirrups are
leather. Holes in the rumps spout actual
hair, that hangs to the heels that are held to the
    floor that wobbles around to the reedy

    tune. Their tails sweep out on a little
wind, that stirs the grass around the
disk, where the children sit and feel they
    fly, because real wind flies through their

hair. There is one motion and it is
round. There is one music, and its
sound issues from the fulcrum that
    repeats the grainy tune, forever

    wound in the flutings of wooden
ears. There is one luck (but it is
rare) that, if you catch, will grant
    release from the circle of the flying

    horses. But round and round on the fixed
horses, fashioned to look as if running
races, the children ride as if made of
    wood, till wrinkles carve their smiling

    faces, till blindness marbles all their
eyes. Round and round to the sagging
music, the children, all bewitched by their
    greeds, reach out to gather the wooden

    rings. And each ring makes a finger
stiff, as oil from the fulcrum blackens the
grass. Round and round go the flying
    hearses, carved and colored to look like steeds.

Swimmers

Tossed
by the muscular sea,
we are lost,
and glad to be lost
in troughs of rough

love. A bath in
laughter, our dive
into foam,
our upslide and float
on the surf of desire.

But sucked to the root
of the water-mountain—
immense—
about to tip upon us
the terror of total

delight—
we are towed,
helpless in its
swell, by hooks
of our hair;

then dangled, let go,
made to race—
as the wrestling chest
of the sea, itself
tangled, tumbles

in its own embrace.
Our limbs like eels
are water-boned,
our faces lost
to difference and

contour, as the lapping
crests.
They cease
their charge,
 and rock us

in repeating hammocks
of the releasing
tide—
until supine we glide,
on cool green

smiles
of an exhaling
gladiator,
to the shore
of sleep.

The Tall Figures of Giacometti

We move by means of our mud bumps.
We bubble as do the dead but more slowly.

The products of excruciating purges
we are squeezed out thin hard and dry.

If we exude a stench it is petrified sainthood.
Our feet are large crude fused together

solid like anvils. Ugly as truth is ugly
we are meant to stand upright a long time

and shudder without motion
under the scintillating pins of light

that dart between our bodies
of pimpled mud and your eyes.

Things in Common

We have a good relationship, the elevator boy and I.
I can always be cheerful with him.
We make jokes. We both belong to the TGIF Club.
No matter how artificial and stiff I've had to be in the office,
seems like I can be natural with *him*.
We have basic things in common—
the weather, baseball, hangovers,
the superiority of Friday over Monday.

It's true I make it a point to be pleasant to him. Why?
Honest, it's because I really like him.
Individually, I mean.
There's something about him—relaxed and balanced
like a dancer or a cat—
as if he knows who he is and where he's at.
At least he knows how to act like that.
Wish I could say the same for myself.

I like his looks, his manner, his red shirt,
the smooth panther shape to his head and neck.
I like it that he knows I don't mean to flirt—
even though I really like him.
I feel he knows I know the score.
It's all in the gleam of his eyes,
the white of his teeth, when he slides back the door
and says, "TGIF, Ma'am, have a nice weekend."

He's strong muscled, good looking—could be 35—
though with his cap off he's 50, I suppose.
So am I. Hope he thinks I look younger too.
I want him to like it that my eyes are blue—
I want him to really like me.
We look straight at each other when we say goodnight.
Is he thinking it's only an accident I'm white?
"TGIF," we say. "Have a nice weekend."

That's the way it's been so far.
We have a good relationship, just the two of us
and the little stool on which he never sits, in the car.

Fridays I work late. I'm the last one down.
Been, let's see, 11 years now . . .
These days I hug the newspaper to me so the headlines won't
    show.
Why he never has a paper I don't know.
Probably not supposed to read in the elevator.

Lately I've asked myself why don't I say:
"What do you think of the mess down South, Willie?
Or for that matter, right here in D.C.?"
Wish I dared ask him. Or that he'd find a way to put it to me.
I'd like to say bluntly, "Willie, will there be war?"
Neither of us has been able to say it so far.
Will I dare, someday? I doubt it . . . Not *me*, to *him*. . . .
"Thank God It's Friday," we say. "Have a nice weekend."

Models of the Universe

1

At moment X
the universe began.
It began at point X.
Since then,
through the Hole in a Nozzle,
stars have spewed. An
inexhaustible gush
populates the void forever.

2

The universe was there
before time ran.
A grain
slipped in the glass:
the past began.
The Container
of the Stars expands;
the sand
of matter multiplies forever.

3

From zero radius
to a certain span,
the universe, a Large Lung
specked with stars,
inhales time
until, turgid, it can
hold no more,
and collapses. Then
space breathes, and inhales again,
and breathes again: Forever.

To Make a Play

To make a play
is to make people,
to make people do
what you say;

to make real people
do and say
what you make;
to make people make

what you say real;
to make real
people make up
and do what you

make up. What you
make makes people
come and see
what people do

and say, and then
go away and do
what they see—
and see what

they do. Real
people do and say,
and you see and
make up people;

people come to see
what you do.
They see what *they*
do, and they

may go away undone.
You can make
people, or you
can unmake. You

can do or you
can undo. People
you make up make up
and make people;

people come to
see—to see
themselves real,
and they go away

and do what you
say—as if they
were made up,
and wore makeup.

To make a play
is to make
people; to make
people make

themselves; to
make people
make themselves
new. So real.

The Truth

A thick serpent
    doubled up with and tangled upon itself.
        So twisted, reiterated a heap,
    the length and girth and weight appear impossible
to assess.

Speculations about shape amount to a counting
of the coils.

    But crawling out or crawling in?

    The head is buried
        in the muddy middle there.
            If that darkest lump *is* a head.
                The tail or tails potential everywhere,
                    cuddled into the interstices.

                    Part of the difficulty
                        is the dim light furnished for this
                        exhibit—
                        part the heavy glass interposed,
                        misted with humidities and
                        exhalations.
                    All the offal of the opulent awful
                    occupant on *its* side,
                our own smears on ours.

            But in the rivet of our stare and vigil
                rare satisfaction.
            That it exists,
        apparently captured,
        apparently alive.
    Though disinclined to display
any kind of dramatic movement today.

Could we stay till feeding time, indeed there'd be a show.
But no, that's only every thousand years.

   A wonder in itself,
      and titillation to our fears.

           Reluctant mobility,
             blunt ambiguity,
              indeterminate extent,
               obscure function,
              undefinable source!

            Rigid, yet oozing contradictory power,
          the undemonstrative monster roils
          our custard-slithery guts.

           Sluggish gigantic whip we curse and worship.
           Great gray boredom!
           When will it lift, strike,
             straighten into motion?

Untitled

I will be earth you be the flower

You have found my root you are the rain

I will be boat and you the rower

You rock you toss me you are the sea

How be steady earth that's now a flood

The root's the oar's afloat where's blown our bud

We will be desert pure salt the seed

Burn radiant sex born scorpion need

Waking from a Nap on the Beach

Sounds like big
rashers of bacon frying.
I look up from where I'm lying
expecting to see stripes

red and white. My eyes drop shut,
stunned by the sun.
Now the foam is flame, the long
troughs charcoal, but

still it chuckles and sizzles, it
burns and burns, it never gets done.
The sea is that
fat.

The Watch

When I
took my
watch to the watchfixer I
felt privileged but also pained to watch the operation. He
had long fingernails and a voluntary squint. He
fixed a magnifying cup over his
squint eye. He
undressed my
watch. I
watched him
split her
into three layers and lay her
middle (a quivering viscera) in a circle on a little plinth. He
shoved shirtsleeves up, and leaned like an ogre over my
naked watch, and with critical pincers poked and stirred. He
lifted out little private things with a magnet too tiny for me
to watch, almost. "Watch out!" I
almost said. His
eye watched, enlarged, the secrets of my
watch, and I

watched anxiously. Because what if he
touched her
ticker too rough, and she
gave up the ghost out of pure fright? Or put her
things back backwards so she'd
run backwards after this? Or he
might lose a minuscule part, connected to her
exquisite heart, and mix her
up, instead of fix her.
And all the time,
all the time
pieces on the walls, on the shelves told the time,
told the time
in swishes and ticks,
swishes and ticks,
and seemed to be gloating as they watched and told. I
felt faint, I
was about to lose my
breath (my
ticker going lickety-split) when watchfixer clipped her
three slices together with a gleam and two flicks of his
tools like chopsticks. He
spat out his
eye, and lifted her
high, gave her
a twist, set her
hands right, and laid her
little face, quite as usual, in its place on my
wrist.

The Wave and the Dune

The wave-shaped dune is still.
Its curve does not break,
though it looks as if it will,

like the head of the dune-
shaped wave advancing,
its ridge strewn

with white shards flaking.
A sand-faced image of the wave
is always in the making.

Opposite the sea's rough glass
cove, the sand's smooth-whittled cave,
under the brow of grass,

is sunny and still. Rushing
to place its replica
on the shore, the sea is pushing

sketches of itself
incessantly into the foreground.
All the models smash upon the shelf,

but, grain by grain, the creeping sand
reërects their profiles
and makes them stand.

Seated in a Plane

On a kicked-up floor of cloud
a couch of cloud, deformed and fluffy;
far out, more celestial furniture—fat chairs

slowly puffing forth their airy stuffing.
On dream-feet I walked into that large
parlor on cool pearl—but found it far

between the restless resting places.
Pinnacles, detaching, floating from their bases,
swelled to turbulent beds and tables,

ebbed to ebullient chairs,
then footstools that, degraded,
flowed with the floor before I could get there.

One must be a cloud to occupy a house of cloud.
I twirled in my dream, and was deformed,
and reformed, making many faces,

refusing the fixture of a solid soul.
So came to a couch I could believe,
although it altered

its facile carvings, at each heave
became another throne.
Neither dissolved nor solid, I was settled

and unsettled in my placeless chair.
A voluntary mobile, manybodied, I traded
shape for the versatility of air.

A Yellow Circle

A green
string
is fastened
to the earth,
at its apex
a yellow
circle
of silky
superimposed
spokes.
The sun
is its mother.

Later,
the string
is taller.
The circle
is white—
an aureole
of evanescent

hairs
the wind
makes breathe.

Later still,
it is altered;
the green
string
is thicker,
the white
circle
bald
on one side.
It is a half
circle
the wind lifts away.

ICONOGRAPHS
(1970)

ICONOGRAPHS

SECTION ONE

Bleeding

Stop bleeding   said the knife.
I would if I   could said the cut.
Stop bleeding   you make me messy with this blood.
I'm sorry   said the cut.
Stop or   I will sink in farther said the knife.
Don't   said the cut.
The   knife did not say it couldn't help it but
it   sank in farther.
If   only you didn't bleed said the knife I wouldn't
have   to do this.
I know   said the cut I bleed too easily I hate
that I   can't help it I wish I were a knife like
you and   didn't have to bleed.
Well   meanwhile stop bleeding will you said the knife.
Yes you   are a mess and sinking in deeper said the cut I
will have   to stop.
Have you   stopped by now said the knife.
I've almost   stopped I think.
Why must you   bleed in the first place said the knife.
For the same   reason maybe that you must do what you
must do said   the cut.
I can't stand   bleeding said the knife and sank in farther.
I hate it too said   the cut I know it isn't you it's
me you're lucky to be   a knife you ought to be glad about that.
Too many cuts around   said the knife they're
messy I don't know how   they stand themselves.
They don't said the cut.
You're bleeding again.
No I've stopped said the cut   see you are coming out now the
blood is drying it will rub   off you'll be shiny again and clean.
If only cuts wouldn't bleed   so much said the knife coming
out a little.
But then knives might become   dull said the cut.
Aren't you still bleeding a   little said the knife.
I hope not said the cut.
I feel you are just a little.
Maybe just a little but I can   stop now.
I feel a little wetness still   said the knife sinking in a
little but then coming out a   little.
Just a little maybe just enough   said the cut.
That's enough now stop now do   you   feel better now said the knife.
I feel I have to bleed to   feel I   think said the cut.
I don't I don't have to   feel said   the knife drying now
becoming shiny.

Women

Women   Or they
   should be   should be
      pedestals   little horses
         moving   those wooden
           pedestals   sweet
            moving   oldfashioned
          to the   painted
           motions   rocking
           of men   horses

       the gladdest things in the toyroom

        The   feelingly
       pegs   and then
      of their   unfeelingly
     ears   To be
    so familiar   joyfully
   and dear   ridden
  to the trusting   rockingly
fists   ridden until
To be chafed   the restored

egos dismount and the legs stride away

   Immobile   willing
    sweetlipped   to be set
     sturdy   into motion
      and smiling   Women
       women   should be
        should always   pedestals
        be waiting   to men

Things I Can Do in My Situation

1. I can shift my weight,
 eventually turn myself
  over.

   2. I can stretch
   my foot, touch
    the one
     next to
      me
     (he
     is
    something
   like a rock—)
   and attach myself
  to him.

  3. I can investigate the edges
 of my outer body, exude some moisture,
and make the gesture of climbing out upon
myself.

 4. Or, I can suck myself in tighter here, ignore
the exposure to the light, relax in this position,
uncomfortable as it is, and wait.

The first is what I ought to do. That's why
 it occurred to me first. But this is the hardest. I have
  to thrust and turn, get my inner weight into motion,
   swivel around inside here, and reach outside—although
    I'm attached to myself inside,
     at the deepest pinched point.
     I have literally to turn my inside out—
      which is against my nature—
       and then *heave* at the critical moment,
        just before disequilibrium.
        . . . Risk of tumbling back and rolling . . .
        downhill somewhere . . . of suffering
         trauma, and of getting lost . . .

   While I have been making these
   notes, the tide has been coming
  in, silently, reaching around
 and over the rocks.
  How could this
   happen so
    quickly

                and
              secretly?
            When I began
            these notes—it
          seems only a moment ago—
        lazy waves had barely begun
      to touch the farthest rocks.
        "Our rock"—on which
          we were born, I
            suppose—on
              which we
                have today
                            somehow been turned
                            upside down, our
                            tendernesses
                              exposed to
                                light—
                                  is
                                already
                              being wetted
                            on all sides,
                          is shrinking in
                        top-room, and will
                      be entirely covered,
                    will vanish under water.

              We are not prepared for this new
              situation. I don't know about the
              others, but I do not remember ever
              being *covered* by the tide!
            The little liquid I have in here of my
          own—can tide-water be anything like it?
        In any case, it is all beyond my control.
      What's worse, *I* am beyond my control. We
    are stuck to this rock, which is stuck in
  the sand, I suppose, and the swell of the
tide is going to obliterate it.

    Now that it is too late, and there is nothing
      I can do to restore my former situation, I am free
        to withdraw my attention to myself
          and to stop taking notice of what will happen.
            Which has always been my natural state anyway . . .

        As I again
      take note, my
    situation is much
  as it used to be. The

rock is dry, is warm. I
am comfortable. Light strikes
the surface of the water far out.
I never used to notice that. I did
notice the warmth, against my foot—
supposed it came out of the rock. Light
comes from *heat*, which comes from above!
I have a good foothold. There is plenty
to eat. My lips have only to open
and something to eat squeezes its way
between them . . .

What happens happens again. And again.
My companions are not the same *ones.*
Maybe this rock is not the same *one.*
But that is irrelevant . . .
The tide comes in and goes out.
Alternately wet and dry, wet and dry.
A shock now and then. And afterward
a trauma-nodule adds itself to the
others on my back.
I
have
not changed
in character,
only size, I think
with this accrual . . .

I seldom worry, or wish,
anymore. I no longer
even congratulate
myself on my
graduation
to near-
perfect
sluggishness.
What continues to upheave
and recede cannot help itself
probably, anymore than I can.
When it learns this, perhaps it will
stop. When all expectation stops, perhaps
then there will be a change. A real overturn!

I may be very large and heavy then, inside and outside. For instance,
as large as this rock. Or larger. And it a nodule on my back?
Suppose then I were to shift my weight?
But I must forget that this occurred to me . . .
I must stop these notes . . .

It will be easy to shift, only if the memory of the
　possibility is dead . . .
　　In order for it to happen, in fact, the
　　possibility must never have existed.

　　　　I will suck myself in,
　　　forget that I am
　　　　growing . . .
　　　　　the ludicrous
　　　　　　evidence
　　　　　　　　that . . .
　　　　　　　　. . . that
　　　　　　　space is
　　　　　　curved,
　　　　　the universe a
　　　　　snail.

Over the Field

They have
a certain
beauty, those
wheeled
fish, when over the field, steel fins stiff
out from
their sides,
they grope,

and then
through cloud
slice
silver snouts,
and climb,
trailing glamorous veils like slime.

Their long abdomens cannot curve, but
　arrogant cut
　blue, power
　enflaming

their gills.
They claim
that sea where no fish swam until they flew
    to minnow it
    with their
    metal.

The inflexible bellies carry, like roe,
    Jonahs
    sitting
    row on row.
    I sit by the
    fin, in

one of those whale-big, wheeled fish, while
    several silver
    minnows line
    up, rolling
    the runway way
    below.

Earth Will Not Let Go

Earth will not let go our foot
except in her sea cup she lets us float.

Thistle seed, first parachute,
and dragonfly, the glider, use wind for skate.
So does flying squirrel, and helicopter
hummingbird, and winged lizard.

But wind is earth's streamered wake where she whirls,
where pterodactyl in leather suit,
and soaring albatross, white yacht, proved
not grace nor corpulence to extremes brought
breaks the sac earth wraps her creatures in, marsupial.

"Only mammal capable of true flight, the bat,"
equipped with sensory parts (modern instrument craft)
swoops blind of blue, unconscious, a closet his orbit,
or a cave; construes by echo, which is radio.
For Icarus is not yet.

The Wright Aeroplane of 1903 was nothing but a big
box kite "in which the pilot lay prone, head forward,
his left hand operating the lever, his hips
in a saddle. Shifting the hips sideways pulled wires
by which the wing tips were warped and the rudder
turned . . . a double action from one movement
controlling balance and direction."

Blue pilot cap cocked like kingfisher's beak,
and heavy round-toed shoes, how droll, he wore.
Belly-down, on the floor of the long, frail, open box,
he steered with his hips' wiggle. Not merely
the magic carpet, but the whole room he took with him,
trusting loops and fickle twists of air.

Lindbergh sat in a wicker chair
in the Cabin of the Spirit, and solo-crossed
the Atlantic in 1927. ". . . Impossible to photograph
the cabin in one view, the actual distance
from back of the seat to face of instrument board
being only thirty-two inches . . . His feet rested
on the rudder control pedals under the instrument
panel. To see ahead, he either used the periscope or
steered to one side while looking out the window."

Enclosed in a sort of kayak, in wicker to save
weight, the single wing his roof, head bonneted and
goggled, like a plucky scaup with swiveled neck
he swam on swells of ocean wind.

Not unencumbered ever, or by muscle and buoyancy
alone, may we climb loose out of earth's rings,
her atmospheres, ionospheres, pastures to our lungs.

Rejecting wings, props, wheels for landing, all bird
and insect things, John Glenn, snug in the tip
of a cartridge, was discharged in 1962; like a spore
within its pod, was launched by blowgun of pure
energy. His lungfood he took with him. His suit
and embryonic sac, the capsule hugged him uterus-tight.

So, tumbling backwards by propulsion, he tore
the planet's web to the edge. But a last elastic
caught him, kept him to its circle. Implosion,
inbuilt, homeward sucked him back, to splashdown
in her sea cup, that salty womb that spewed
the stillborn moon.

To that rock Apollo astronauts would reach,
they must take the earthpouch simulated. And it
may not breach. For earth will not let go our foot,
though headfirst to be born in angel space we make wings,
jets, rockets, orbit tables, spider landing legs.

The DNA Molecule

The DNA Molecule is The Nude Descending a Staircase,
a circular one. See the undersurfaces of the spiral
treads and the space in between. She is descending
and, at the same time, ascending, and she moves
around herself. For she is the staircase, "a proto-
plasmic framework that twists and turns." She is a
double helix, mounting and dismounting around the
swivel of her imaginary spine.

The Nude named DNA can be constructed as a model with
matches and a ribbon of tape. Be sure to use only
four colors on two white strands of twistable tape.
"Only matches of complementary colors may be placed
opposite each other. The pairs are to be Red and Green,
and Yellow and Blue." Make your model as high as the
Empire State Building, and you have an acceptable

replica of The Nude. But (and this is harder) you
must make her move in a continuous coil, an alpha helix,
a double spiral downward and upward at once, and you
must make her increase while, at the same time, occupy-
ing the same field. She must be made to maintain
"a basic topography," changing, yet remaining stable,
if she is to perform her function, which is to produce
and reproduce the microsphere.

Such a sphere is invisible to, but omnipresent in, the
naked eye of The Nude. It contains a "central region
and an outer membrane," making it both able to divide
and to make exact copies of itself without limit.
The Nude "has the capacity for replication and trans-
cription" of all genesis. She ingests and regurgitates
the genetic material, it being the material of her own
cell-self. From single she becomes double, and from
double single. As a woman ingests the demon sperm and,
with the same membrane, regurgitates the mitotic double
of herself upon the slide of time, so The DNA Molecule
produces, with a little pop, at the waistline of its
viscous drop, a new microsphere the same size as herself,
which proceeds singly to grow in order to divide and
double itself. So, from single to double and double to
single, and mounting while descending, she expands
while contracts, she proliferates while disappearing,
at both of her ends.

Remember that Red can only be opposite Green, and Blue
opposite Yellow. Remember that the complementary pairs
of matches must differ slightly in length, "for nature's
pairs can be made only with units whose structures
permit an interplay of forces between the partners."

I fixed a Blue match opposite a Red match of the same
length, pointed away from the center on the double strand
of tape. I saw laid a number of eggs on eggs on the
sticky side of a twig. I saw a worm with many feet
grow out of an egg. The worm climbed the twig, a single
helix, and gobbled the magnified edge of a leaf in quick

enormous bites. It then secreted out of itself a gray
floss with which it wrapped itself, tail first, and
so on, until it had completely muffled and encased
itself, head too, as in a mummy sack.

I saw plushy, iridescent wings push moistly out of the
pouch. At first glued together, they began to part.
On each wing I saw a large blue eye, open forever
in the expression of resurrection. The new Nude
released the flanges of her wings, stretching herself
to touch at all points the outermost rim of the
noösphere. I saw that, for her body, from which the
wings expanded, she had retained the worm.

I Look at My Hand

I look at my hand and see
it is also his and hers;
the pads of the fingers his,

the wrists and knuckles hers.
In the mirror my pugnacious eye
and ear of an elf, his;

my tamer mouth and slant
cheekbones hers.
His impulses my senses swarm,
her hesitations they gather.
Father and Mother
who dropped me,

an acorn in the wood,
repository of your shapes
and inner streams and circles,

you who lengthen toward heaven,
forgive me
that I do not throw

the replacing green
trunk when you are ash,

When you are ash, no
features shall there be,
tangled of you,
interlacing hands and faces

through me
who hide, still hard,
far down under your shades—

and break my root, and prune my buds,
that what can make no replica
may spring from me.

I'll Be

Young,
I was   too   young
to see and think and say: "I   am   young
I am   too   young."

Old,
I   am   too   young
to see and think,   and say: "I   am   old,
I   was   young.
I   am   too   old."

Older,
I'll   be   too   old
to see,   and think,   and say: "I   was   too   young,
too   old."

Older,
I'll   be   too   old
to . . .   I'll   be   dead,
too.   Be   dead
to . . .   Dead
I'll   be!   Dead,
I'll   be.

The Mobile in Back of the Smithsonian

glanced at is not realized
to be in motion.

Rotates so slowly silently twists
gradually mutates.

A steel ribbon an altering bow
on a pin on a tall triangle its black pediment.

Passing toward it around it antstreaming under it
on into the doorways or away they do

not notice
except as obstruction

perhaps decoration
what

is dismissed with
a shift to the

next objective
next object.

Or if they fasten
upon it their glances

take off.
their eyes inattentive

flick too quick to find it
moves.

Nor stop in the strolling cloud
of mind to claim how it

moves.
How slow how secret as time.

Never to follow its transforms to
count its changes

eyeflow with its outlines eyesit central
in its inspaces anticipate the uncurling

jointures of a figure forever unstable.
Never to know.

The bridge of Discover they do not lift an eye
to and climb

but crawl eyes across other eyes crawling where
others cross.

Automatic feet follow feet follow
groupmobile sightstoppered see-ers

steered streaming to the Labels
directed to collected at the Plaques the

information Frames the strips of Print
eyelevel.

Not to the object but to the explanation of
the object.

Not to the mirror declaring the corridor of
the pupil plunging straight horizontal a

drawbridge into the palace of the mind
where at the point of a triangle Universe

unloops entwines unknots involutes
coexistent beginsgrowsdiesendsbegins.

But to the title on the bottom frame
of the mirror the signature in the

righthand corner to the type on the strip
under glass beside the thing on the wall.

To the bronze lettering on the base of the pediment.
At which they have to stoop.

A double deviational Möbius band of steel
persuasively merges emerges expands in an

undefined sequence of changes.
An elegance unnoticed by no seam

deciding beginning
by no limit denoting end

or whether or if or where
is completion or source

for its permutations.
What without label

rears invisible
without sound below

the speed of sight
covertly turns.

Nor does the man at the
lobby desk know if you

ask him Who made it.
Too slowly for my eye

at first to see that it
moves

when I move
my pencil to diagram

its alterations it
moves

too fast to track
them all to trace

them a sidewinder
eluding all my

eye'shand's computations.
Now some of them notice

me motionless looking
up at unnoticeable motion.

They stop and look
at me.

And then at what I look
at but then at me.

And then at each other looking
at me.

And then at each other walking on walk on
look back at me.

NOTE: The Mobile is by Jose de Rivera, mounted outside the new wing of the Smithsonian Institute in Washington, D.C.

Welcome Aboard the Turbojet Electra

Why do they say 31,000 feet? Why
not yards or miles? Why four
cigarettes and no match? Fly
Winston and see the world—red, white,
filtered, slick in cellophane. We goose
our yellow corntips into the pink
leftover straw(sic)berry mousse
sequined with ash. Coffee comes
in a plasti-cup and sunlight
drills the rivets on the jet-
stream stack just inches beyond
the window and our nose, yet
the inner pane is cool, a breeze—
is it from outer space?—
pleasantly swizzles our face.

Is that St. Louis and the Gateway
to the West? Strident aluminum
hairpin the light tweaks down there.
No, no hairpins anymore. No
bobby pins. No
bobs. What do they call them, those
wire sausage things that build high hair?
Now sun is staining a cleft in cloud
like dogpiss on snow.

What do we do, our coffee's cold, it's
  bumpy over Texas? Stewardess
    wipes an old man's front, he spilled
      his tray. We sneak to set
        ours on the floor. The nose
          lifts, bucks, beginning banking,
            wing slips down. A shoe
              ahead gets soaked under the seat,
                the foot pretending sleep pretends
                  no notice. Maybe that's the U.
                    of Texas Tower, its stone prick due
                      visible in five minutes, which
                        would mean this mother'll be on time.
                          Around which how many people was it died?
                            Hope when the pilot circles
                              Austin we're on the right side.

The James Bond Movie

The popcorn is greasy, and I forgot to bring a Kleenex.
A pill that's a bomb inside the stomach of a man inside

The Embassy blows up. Eructations of flame, luxurious
cauliflowers giganticize into motion. The entire 29-ft.

screen is orange, is crackling flesh and brick bursting,
blackening, smithereened. I unwrap a Dentyne and, while

jouncing my teeth in rubber tongue-smarting clove, try
with the 2-inch-wide paper to blot butter off my fingers.

A bubble-bath, room-sized, in which 14 girls, delectable
and sexless, twist-topped Creamy Freezes (their blond,

red, brown, pinkish, lavender, or silver wiglets all
screwed that high, and varnished), scrub-tickle a lone

male, whose chest has just the right amount and distribu-
tion of curly hair. He's nervously pretending to defend

his modesty. His crotch, below the waterline, is also
below the frame—but unsubmerged all 28 slick foamy boobs.

Their makeup fails to let the girls look naked. Caterpil-
lar lashes, black and thick, lush lips glossed pink like

the gum I pop and chew, contact lenses on the eyes that are
mostly blue, they're nose-perfect replicas of each other.

I've got most of the grease off and onto this little square
of paper. I'm folding it now, making creases with my nails.

It Rains

It rains
       Write a rain poem
It stops
       Write a stop poem
  Shit
       Write a shit   poem
I love you
       Write a love poem
  Die
       Write a dead poem
Fight
       Write a fight poem
Hate
       Write a hate poem
Write
       Write a write poem
Wait
       Make a wait poem
Sleep
       Sleep a   poem
  Wake   a   poem

Feel Me

"Feel me to do right," our father said on his deathbed.
We did not quite know—in fact, not at all—what he meant.
His last whisper was spent as through a slot in a wall.
He left us a key, but how did it fit? "Feel me
to do right." Did it mean that, though he died, he would be felt
through some aperture, or by some unseen instrument
our dad just then had come to know? So, to do right always,
we need but feel his spirit? Or was it merely his apology
for dying? "Feel that I do right in not trying,
as you insist, to stay on your side. There is the wide
gateway and the splendid tower, and you implore me
to wait here, with the worms!"

Had he defined his terms, and could we discriminate
among his motives, we might have found out how to "do right"
before *we* died—supposing he felt he suddenly knew
what dying was. "You do wrong because you do not feel
as I do now," was maybe the sense. "Feel me, and emulate
my state, for I am becoming less dense—I am feeling right
for the first time." And then the vessel burst,
and we were kneeling around an emptiness.

We cannot feel our father now. His power courses through us,
yes, but *he*—the chest and cheek, the foot and palm,
the mouth of oracle—is calm. And we still seek
his meaning. "Feel me," he said, and emphasized that word.
Should we have heard it as a plea for a caress—
a constant caress, since flesh to flesh was all that we
could do right if we would bless him?
The dying must feel the pressure of that question—
lying flat, turning cold from brow to heel—the hot
cowards there above protesting their love, and saying,
"What can we do? Are you all right?" While the wall opens
and the blue night pours through. "What can we do?
We want to do what's right."

"Lie down with me, and hold me, tight. Touch me. Be
with me. Feel with me. *Feel* me to do right."

The Fingers

"If it moves you, move." The fingers
on the upturned bell-shaped glass, three strangers

to each other, waited. In an oval on the table
the alphabet, strung on squares from the Scrabble,

waited for the spirit to choose. Two signs,
like small grave-slabs, of paper with blue lines,

fixed YES and NO at the orbit's ends.
The fingers felt like fools together. The hands

separately trembled. Anticipation's cold
tickled the elbows. Willing to be fooled

wanting a happening, a three-part ghost
gathered itself under the glass from the moist

swirls of the fingertips. "Is anybody there?"
Alert for intentions, three pairs

of eyes, meeting above the lot
in the lamplight, declared no plot.

"Is anybody there? Let us know."
The giggling glass slid around to NO.

"Nobody there? But you're speaking.
Tell us if any of us here is faking.

"Spell out the name—but first, answer if YES."
"G"—the ghost walked out its word—"U E S S."

Unlikely a king finger rode the joking throne.
Not acquainted till tonight, each felt pawn

to the others. But some compound sprite wanted
to rule, without detection from its "bodies," and hinted

at cheating as a distraction.
Would it produce some sort of resurrection?

"Let's ask it a personal question. What is a ghost
made of? What element is there most

like it? Tell us now, so we can understand."
The fingers throbbed as brothers on one hand,

that swept the glass out: It touched "B"
then stammered "L" and "O"—"O" again, then "D."

Moved? We were so moved, we grew
hysterical. A poltergeist must have hopped aboard, too.

Jumping, the glass moved round to spell JUMPS, JUMPS—until
it fell. BLOOD JUMPS is what the fingers had to tell.

Electronic Sound

A pebble swells to a boulder at low speed
                    At 7½ ips a hiss is a hurricane.
                                The basin drain
is Charybdis sucking
                        a clipper down, the ship
                                a paperclip
whirling. Or gargle, brush your teeth, HEAR
                    a winded horse's esophagus lurch
                            on playback at ¹⁵⁄₁₆. Perch
a quarter on edge on a plate, spin:
                a locomotive's wheel is wrenched loose,
            wobbles down the line to slam the caboose,
keeps on snicking over the ties
                        till it teeters on the embankment,
                            bowls down a cement
ramp, meanders onto the turnpike
                            and into a junkhole
                    of scrapped cars. Ceasing to roll,
it shimmies, falters . . .
                        sudden inertia causes
                            pause.
Then a round of echoes
                    descending, a minor yammer
as when a triangle's nicked by the slimmest hammer.

The Grain of Our Eye
(A Scientific Abstract)

Anti-matter it is called.
Awkwardness in naming the
    nonthing unnoticeably not
    occurring anywhere.
Mistaken to assume it (the
non-it) an unoccupant of
    nospace, a simple non-x-
    istent. No, it's (non-it's
not yes) the very grain
of our eye. As hair-crack
    in microscope adds x-tra
    leg to fly, proliferating
nonlegs in all inconsequent
offspring. Or subtracting
    an ex and so re-non-producing
    onspring. No is On by
mirror-proof, and Yes is
almost Eyes. A ton (or not
    notice) of anti-matter weighs
    (some ways, the sum's) the
same as empty sack of non-
feathers, and is the size
    of Between, which varies by
    a pivot (as on schoolboy's
compass) x-cept that this
tool's aim's to make ends
    meet meticulously in-x-act.
    What's its (non-its or nits)
anti-shape? Well, turn in
itside out and cross out
    out. Now print if you can't
    a non-positive pro-negative
of the after-image (or pre-
if-you-fer) of O in the
    word *word*, when warped by
    a million or so small but
unappreciable elisions,

collisions, incisions and
   noninverted visions between
   (*between* being the wee-in
intwixt the hole problem)
o and the nonidentical
   rag content of unavoidably
   aging pages in that thick
folio entitled to no title
unless Void. We learn not
   how, but how Not, since
   one is almost own, knot
two. (That's nearer out.)
To avoid a void, forget
   get, take care to be care-
   less. Lesscare takes
development, requires a
dark room in the nonbrain
   that's tense, prehensile,
   unintentionally indented
with dense pre-eidetic non-
ideas. Taodal blindness
   by its elf won't do.

Science and Religion—A Merger

When Galileo Galilei first turned a telescope on the heavens,
                          Was St. Peter buried on Vatican hill,
400 years ago, his revelations were astounding. Jupiter,
                    the site of the great Roman Catholic basilica
he found, has its own miniature system of planets,
                 that bears his name? Last week Pope Paul. . . .
or moons. He saw the mountains of the moon,
           gave his support to that theory, announcing that bones
spots on the sun and the crescent shape of Venus.
                  discovered in 1953 under the basilica
He found that the Milky Way Galaxy
            had been identified to his satisfaction as those of
of which we are a part is actually formed from billions of
        the saint. For Christians. . . . it is not an idle question. . .

distant, dim stars. Since then, telescopes have gradually increased

                        The claims. . . . rest on two arguments

in size and quality, culminating in 1948

                        concerning Peter: First, that the statement

in completion of the great reflector on Mount Palomar

                        of Jesus quoted by Matthew: "Thou art Peter, and

in California. This instrument, with a parabolic mirror

                        upon this rock I shall build my church"

200 inches in diameter, has been to modern astronomy what

                        is literally true. . . and second, that the apostle

Galileo's instrument was to science in the 17th Century.

                        Peter was bishop of Rome, and thus the first

It has carried man's ken toward the outer fringes

                        in an unending series of Roman bishops—or—popes,

of the universe and it has enlarged his knowledge of the galaxies.

                        who embody the full authority to guide

It first identified the strange quasars that seem to be the

                        the Christian Church. In 1939, the

most distant observable objects and the light-collecting power of

                        Vatican excavations beneath the main altar of St. Peter's

its huge mirror has brought into view peculiar stars,

                        began to uncover a series of tombs, which

that, while not very distant, are too dim to be observed with

                        was held to include the tomb of Peter. But

other instruments. . . . While others are being built, none comes close to

                        the first announcement

the 200-inch Hale Telescope—with one exception. That is

                        came only in 1949, when Pope Pius XII stated that

the 236-inch reflector being built by the Soviet Union near Zelenchuk

                        an urn containing the remains of the apostle

in the Caucasus. . . . Apparently the Russians hope to dazzle the world

                        had been uncovered. . . . Later, however, the bones

as they did with their Sputnik in 1957, by a surprise announcement after

                        in the urn were shown to be those of a woman.

their first look into realms previously beyond reach. . . .

                        During the 1950's, Professor Margherita Guarducci,

While the Russians, with their new instrument, will be able to see things

                        a Vatican expert on inscriptions, argued that

no one else can, their field of view will be limited by

                        writings on walls beneath the altar pointed to

their geography. . . . Because almost all of the world's great observatories

                        a particular niche as the resting place

are north of the Equator, the southern part of the sky

                        of Peter's remains. Earlier a team of Vatican archeologists

is by far the least explored. The center

        had reported secretly to the Pope that the niche,

of the Milky Way Galaxy lies there

        and a box in it, were empty. But Professor Guarducci—

plus the two nearest baby-galaxies (the Clouds

        persisted, reporting that Monsignor Kaas, then secretary

of Magellan). . . . One of the dreams of American astronomers

        and administrator for the Fabric of St. Peter's, told her

is the placing of a large telescope

        that he and two workmen had removed some bones

into orbit above the earth's atmosphere.

        from the niche without the knowledge of Vatican

This has become possible with the giant Saturn

        archeologists. It was these bones that Pope Paul

rockets designed to send men to

        last week identified as those of St. Peter.

the moon. Our present view of

        European archeologists familiar with the

the heavens can be likened to that of a lobster beneath the

        Vatican diggings remain privately skeptical but publicly

murky waters of Long Island Sound.

        silent. . . . Further investigations will likely be

A telescope above the ocean of air would open

        colored by the Pope's decision to commit some of

new realms of knowledge concerning our

        his prestige to a circumstantial argument the

nearest neighbors in space, as well as

        bones in question are indeed Peter's. The Vatican

the nature of the universe as a whole.

        has got itself into a position where its case can't be

However, as with other grandiose science projects, the problem is

        proved 'scientifically,' an American archeologist. . .

cost. . . . American action may be delayed until

        said last week. He said, "We'll probably never know

the Russians have done it first.

        whose bones they are."

Note: The text is taken verbatim (except for deletions where indicated) and interwoven from two columns by Walter Sullivan and John Leo, respectively, in the *New York Times* of Sunday, June 30, 1968, p. 10-E.

The
Power
House

Close to my
place is the
power house.
I knew there
wouldn't be
anybody in it.
It's beauti-
ful. Like a
church. It
works all by
itself. And
with almost no
sound. All glass.
And a tall square
tower on it.
Colored lights
shine from within.
They color the
glass. Pink. Pale
green. Not stained.
Not that kind. And
not fragile. Just
light. Light weight.
  A red rod erect
  from the tower
blinking on top red. Behind it gray wings of motion. A fan
of light opening and folding somewhere in the west of town.
Periodic as a metronome.
The crickets were talking electricity. A white Spitz barked
at me though my sneakers made no noise. I walked up the
slight slope—it's wide—to the power house. Went past
the doorway. Big as a barn door squared. Big horse I thought.
I saw through the doorway gray metal coils. All the clean
machinery and engines. I don't know what to call it all. I
don't know the names.
  Painted pretty colors slick and clean. I knew there
wouldn't be anybody there. Nobody needs to work there
I thought. And walked past that door farther on.
  White lights icy and clean. Not blazing. Cool.
Gossamer. The pink and green like-sherbet-colors bathing the gray machines.
Came to a place where vapor cooled my skin. A breeze made by waterspray
up high. And there was white steam unfurling
  evaporating against the dark.

Down lower a red transparent ball on a pedestal. Incandescent. Big. A
balloon mystery. Inside through another doorway I saw a hook painted
yellow. Huge and high enough to lift a freight car.

    I stood looking in—my shadow so long and black
from the streaming lights.
        And I was wrong. Somebody moved in the powerhouse.
        Came from between the coils and giant tubes.
        Down off the balcony on the steel stairway smooth
        and slow. Like floating. Like not having to
        look or think. I thought he'd be a Negro but he
        wasn't. He didn't see me. Didn't need to see
        anything. He had a red face and a blue uniform.

Orbiter 5 Shows
How Earth Looks from the Moon

There's a woman in the earth, sitting on
her heels. You see her from the back, in three-
quarter profile. She has a flowing pigtail. She's
holding something
in her right hand—some holy jug. Her left arm is thinner,
in a gesture like a dancer. She's the Indian Ocean. Asia is
light swirling up out of her vessel. Her pigtail points to Europe
and her dancer's arm is the Suez Canal. She is a woman
in a square kimono,
bare feet tucked beneath the tip of Africa. Her tail of long hair is
the Arabian Peninsula.   A woman in the earth.

               A man in the moon.

Note: The first telephoto of the whole earth, taken from above the moon by
Lunar Orbiter 5, was printed in the *New York Times*, August 14, 1967. Poem
title is the headline over the photo.

BLACKTUESDAYBLACKTUESDAYBLACKTUESDAYBLACKTUESDAYBLACKTUESDAYBLACKTUESDAYBLACKTUESDAY

Blesséd is the man of color
for his blood is rich with
the nuclear sap of the sun.
Blesséd is his spirit which
a savage history has
refined to intercept
whitest lightnings of
vision. Blesséd the neck
of the black man made
muscular by the weight of
the yoke made proud
bursting the lynch rope.
Blesséd his body meek on
the slave block thunderous
on the porch of revolt.
Blesséd his head hewn with
animal beauty for he has
grappled as the lion bled
as the lamb and extracted
the excellence of each for
his character. Blesséd the
black and the white of his
eye.

For Martin Luther King
April 4, 1968

The Lowering*

The flag is folded
lengthwise, and lengthwise again,
folding toward the open edge,
so that the union of stars on the blue
field remains outward in full view;
a triangular folding is then begun
at the striped end,
by bringing the corner of the folded edge
to the open edge;
the outer point, turned inward along the open edge,
forms the next triangular fold:
the folding continued so, until the end is reached,
the final corner tucked between
the folds of the blue union,
the form of the folded flag is found to resemble that
of a 3-cornered pouch, or thick cocked hat.

Take this flag, John Glenn, instead of a friend;
instead of a brother, Edward Kennedy, take this flag;
instead of a father, Joe Kennedy, take this flag;
this flag instead of a husband, Ethel Kennedy, take this flag;
this 9-times-folded red-white-striped, star-spotted-blue flag,
tucked and pocketed neatly,
Nation, instead of a leader, take this folded flag.
Robert Kennedy, coffin without coverlet,
beside this hole in the grass,
beside your brother, John Kennedy,
in the grass,
take, instead of a country,
this folded flag;
Robert Kennedy, take this
hole in the grass.

*Arlington Cemetery
June 8, 1968

An Old Field Jacket

At the Army Surplus Store I bought an old field jacket,
  because of the snapdown pockets and the attached hood
    rolled up and zippered inside the collar. Good
      for fishing, camping, wet days on the beach.
        Wrinkled, buckled, faded to swamp-mud-green,
          the harsh cloth's wonderfully softened, sateened
            by wear and machine cleaning.

        Sticky resinous marks still on it, above the breast
          pockets and on the arms, are where ID patches, chevrons,
        and whatnot, were ripped off. A blue-white phosphorescent strip
      sewn down the back, when it walks in the dark, still glows.

    Has it single-filed on sinister muck and brush patrols,
      hunched in hot foxholes? Has the hood
        under a hard hat heard mortar rain?
          For all I know, it used to smell of cold
            gun grease, cartridge powder, maybe blood. Smears of paint,
              or something, are on it, and other not quite washed out stains.

        It's loose on me, practical, a good
          wind-breaker, and not too long.
        Came cheap, and will last forever, the cloth's that strong.
      But the best is those four big pockets
    to keep cigarettes and matches dry
  in, carry car keys, flashlight, a fishknife, sinkers and bait—
a bird book, even—anything I want.

  Don't know why it fits my shoulders. Must have shrunk
    getting processed, disinfected, drycleaned for
      the Army Surplus Store. Wonder who wore
        it, and what for? A label by the hang-up loop in the lining says:
          Cotton OG 107 Mil-J-4883C US Army—and then *September 1962*.

      Don't know how near it came to a shooting war—
        and wearing it, I hope, is the closest I'll ever get—
      women not being drafted yet.
    (But if we start using their garb, is that what we're asking for?)

  Standing up out of a tent into the rain
    this summer, Montauk or Maine—
      taking a lungful of dark before light,
        tying the drawstring on the hood,
          out in the open, feeling equipped, protected good,
            I might say:
              Let's start the dirty day
                early. Let's imagine military dawn.

Spring *by Robert Lowell*
(Photograph by Trudi Fuller)

. . . only an ear is in the spring.

Sunlight in Central Park it could
be:yond his shoulders the bench back
a field for play: that's over
exposed as video: fuzzy. Or is it Boston
Common: maybe May be:hind him?
Well: well light's be:hind him. Gray
shades his face: is it a tree
trunk's toppled roots' dark riot he sees
casts shadow on him: be:fore him? Only

an ear and flesh of part
of a neck in sunlight: some
of the right side of his shirt. A wish
bone drawing pinches brows:
parenthe-seizes lips: the eyes
dim be:cause of shadow: not him:
fright light white tight
pellets in pupils: absent in photo

flash his gaze that must be:spectacled.
Be:fore head shows a setting
sun reflected: light's spot on wavelet
thought not sinking yet. A warm
ear's drinking infant
light. Be:side him's morning in the spring
Park: a hot beam rubbing the right
side of his dark coat: baring
as if a gray breast there.

Notice
(On reading Paul Goodman's poem in The New York Review, *9/14/67)*

Now we are talking
straight out to each other,
and for all to hear.
The common stream of our heads (our heart)
till now compartmented
perhaps begins to combine. Maybe to flow
unsurreptitiously together,
unembarrassed to know
we are one body (human)
helplessness and potency
the same circulation systeming
our veins. Paul Goodman
(well known, whom I don't know, and know
so well) breathing and thinking with you
in the same current (electric placenta
we all feed into, drink out of,
charger of every brain,
all blood) just now right here, I read
(with all the others who read)
your poem-prayer
on the death of your son,
so soon on reading
of his death, in the news. Then falling
(with him, with you, with all
the others who fall) a constant
mystery, the mountain down,
again I notice: Since mind first noticed
death, we fall. And how all
feel it (and conceal it)
the same tick-away, our massive
common heart in labor day after day.
Daring from now, perhaps,
to let go,
(the pretence of separate cells,
privacies, prides, singularities) let flow
away, like you, Goodman, we
(who are you, as you are us) may
(in the crack of recognition hurtling) publish
a piece of that heart.

MAsterMANANiMAl

ANiMAte MANANiMAl MAttress of Nerves
MANipulAtor Motor ANd Motive MAker
MAMMAliAN MAtrix MAt of rivers red
MortAl MANic Morsel Mover shAker

MAteriAl-MAster MAsticAtor oxygeN-eAter
MouNtAiN-MouNter MApper peNetrAtor
iN MoNster MetAl MANtle of the Air
MAssive wAter-surgeoN prestidigitAtor

MAchiNist MAsoN MesoN-Mixer MArble-heAver
coiNer cArver cities-idols-AtoMs-sMAsher
electric lever Metric AlcheMist
MeNtAl AMAzer igNorANt iNcubAtor

cANNibAl AutoMANANiMAl cAllous cAlculAtor
Milky MAgNetic MAN iNNoceNt iNNovAtor
MAlleAble MAMMAl MercuriAl ANd MAteriAl
MAsterANiMAl ANd ANiMA etheriAl

M=52
A=73
N=40

theBEAM

How things really are we would like to know.
Does
       T i m e
               flow, is it elastic, or is it
atomized in instants hammered around the
     clock's face? And
                  S p a c e ,
                        is it
what we find around us in our place, or
"a symbol, suitably haunted, of the

    M i n d ?"

The
Mind?
A beam
fitfully focused, then dragged on. So
all material in its ken is lit,
consistent, tranquil as far as
that visitation lasts. When it is
withdrawn, when all we think and
know "goes out" where does it go? Into
a blind sink? No. It must find and drag
into its circle new material for its
being. Moving by
M i n d ' s
light,
which is slow,
M i n d
must move and warm
the groove, spot particles for another
seeing.

Redundant Journey

I'll rest here in the bend of my tail
said the python having traveled
his own length
beginning with his squared snout
laid beside his neck
O where does the neck
end and the chest begin
O where does the stomach
end and the loins begin
O where are the arms and legs
Now I'll travel between myself
said the python lifting his snout
and his blue eyes saw lead-gray
frames like windows on his hide
the glisten of himself the chill

pattern on each side
of himself and as his head slept
 between the middles of himself
        the end of his outer self still crept
        The python reared his neck and yawned
    his tongue was twins his mucous membrane
                purple pink hibiscus sticky
        He came to a cul de sac in the lane
                of the center of his length
            his low snout
         trapped between twin windowed
      creeping hills of himself
      and no way out
         I'll travel upon myself said the python
         lifting his chin to a hill
                of his inner length and while
           his neck crossed one half of his
             stomach his chest crossed his
             loins   while   his   tail   lay   still
                   But then he thought
                I feel uncomfortable in
             this upright knot
          and he lowered his chin
       from the shelf of himself
       and tucked his snout in
           How get away from myself said
             the python beside himself
                    traveling his own side
         How recognize myself as just myself
         instead of a labyrinth I must travel
                   over and over stupefied
                His snout came to the end
       of himself again to the final leaden bend
          of himself
      Said the python to his tail
    Let's both rest till all
       the double windowed middle maze
       of ourself
         gets through crawling

SECTION TWO

IONOGRAPHS

Unconscious
came a beauty to my
wrist
and stopped my pencil,
merged its shadow profile with
my hand's ghost
on the page:
Red Spotted Purple or else Mourning
Cloak,
paired thin-as-paper wings, near black,
were edged on the seam side poppy orange,
as were its spots.

CAME A BEAUTY

I sat arrested, for its soot-haired
body's worm
shone in the sun.
It bent its tongue long as
a leg
black on my skin
and clung without my
feeling,
while its tomb-stained
duplicate parts of
a window opened.
And then I
moved.

Catbird in Redbud

Catbird in the redbud this morning.
No cat could
mimic that rackety cadenza he's making.
And it's not red,
the trapeze he's swaying on.
After last night's freeze, redbud's violet-pink,
twinkled on by the sun.
That bird's red, though, under the tail he wags,
up sharply, like a wren.
The uncut lawn hides blue violets
with star-gold eyes on the longest stems I've ever seen.
Going to empty the garbage, I simply have to pick some,
reaching to the root of green,
getting my fist dewy,
happening to tear up a dandelion, too.

Lilac, hazy blue-violet, nods buds over the alley fence,
and, like a horse with a yen
for something fresh for breakfast,
I put my nose into a fragrant pompom,
bite off some,
and chew.

Geometrid

Writhes, rides down
on his own spit,
lets breeze twist

him so he chins,
humps, reels up it,
munching back

the vomit string.
Some drools
round his neck.

Arched into a staple
now, high on green
oak leaf he punctures

for food, what
was the point
of his act? Not

to spangle the air,
or show me his trick.
Breeze broke

his suck,
so he spit
a fraction of self's

length forth, bled
colorless from within,
to catch a balance,

glide to a knot
made with his own mouth.
Ruminant

while climbing, got
back better than bitten
leaf. Breeze

that threw
him snagged him
to a new.

Rough Triplets

MY FACE THE NIGHT

My eyes seeing nothing
but night in my head
sent two tears south

toward inlets of my mouth.
North in the height
there swam forth two stars

as if from far pupils,
My tongue licked up two
salt drops of light.

ADMIRE

Amphibian bird and mammal cannot shine
by own light as can some uglies
of the undersoil and brine: Chill

toadstool clam and worm. But one bug
of fire's wink and sprinkle's printed
higher on the chart of night. Why?

Mammals think that cannot shine. Admire
the airy faery firefly. Know
one grub aglow a blink above the mire.

WHAT'S SECRET

Always the belly lighter than the back.
What grows in the shade pales,
what's secret keeps tender.

Inversion saves the silk of innocence.
Fierce melanosis of the adult coat
from whips of sun. The overt coarsens,

stripes and grins with color.
Exposure, experience thicken half the beast
who, shy as snow, stays naked underneath.

ROSIGNOLE TO THE CRITIC

Cats have only
their lives to save, while we
our souls (this means our

egos) must keep unslain. Power,
soul's blood, let from some slit
(a stab unnoticed until infected, it

made by the claw of Sneak,
the Cat) may leak
long poison, become a pustulate of self-hate,

paralyze the wings
and lock the little jaw
of Rosignole that sings.

Window in the Tail

Nap of cloud	ked and puff-
as thick	ed and white
as stuff-	as kid-
ing tight	shear-
pack-	ed bel-
ed for	ly ruff
a mat-	
tress tick-	is the floor
ing pick-	and is the ceil-
anin-	ing o'er
ny kin-	which we're

keel-   euverable
ed and sail-   by am-
ing on flat   ple ram-
pin-   ps that
ion not   bevel
of feather   up or slide
but   out wide
slat-   and glide
ted alum-   our car-
in-   riage level
um
or other   Over
                                       fur
met-   of cloud
al man-   we travel

Nap of cloud, as thick as stuffing
tight packed for a mattress ticking,

pickaninny kinked and puffed
and white as kid-sheared belly ruff,

is the floor and is the ceiling
over which we're keeled and sailing,

on flat pinion—not of feather—
but slatted aluminum or other

metal maneuverable
by ample ramps that bevel

up, or slide out wide
and glide

our carriage level.
Over fur of cloud we travel.

On Park Avenue at 52nd Street

Spirits	Each	They
are	strains	lurch
dancing	to	laughter
here—	be	and
are	whitest,	hiss
forced	most	wind
to	festive,	white
dance.	effervescent,	as
They	tossing	the
are	sparks	north.
forced	and	Their
up	gouts,	force
out	white	is
of	"works	perpetual
brass	of	mirth,
rectums.	fire."	pressed
Pressed	Throwing	out
from	up	of
rigid	their	brass
slits,	heads,	rectums.
they	they	They
shoot	catch	juggle
tall,	their	the
out	heads	globulous
of	on	white
the	shoulders	expectorations,
floor	they	the
of	form	flakes
their	over	of
dark	and	their
basin.	over.	heads.

"Merry Christmas. You're on the Right."

I'm looking at those two raffish child-angels
by Raphael, a section of his sky this corner
transaction cropped for close-up on a picture card.

Sunwarmed, well-fleshed, naked except for wings,
(the plum-red bows unpleating from their shoulder-blades,
so short they couldn't hold a robin up, are pure

convention), they rest their elbows on a beam
that looks like wood, not light—some plank in middle
heaven they've seized for perch, or, breaking surface,
    reached arms up over, like a raft or rafter. There
    they dawdle, hips immersed, unseen from behind,
    kissed, blown on, spanked by waves that could be either

    wind or water. The object they contemplate in the high
    foreground they're free to imagine, since it's out
    of view: a new assumption, ritualistic but not serene,
that will not set, nor need it tarnish noticeably.
(I'll paint it so, as were those two angels in impudent
postures long ago.) Beatitudinally turned aloft,

the eyes, of the one with ruffed hair, chin in hand,
look devil-wise. Innocence on the round brow
and quirky mouth of the other's a mask, no doubt,
    for cupid acts practiced toward the dart board's center,
    simultaneous with the stare of adoration. The canvas
    being infinite, how relatively small or large is this

    detail? Dimensions are, in fact, neglected on the card,
    the frame that snares and magnifies encounter into
    permanence. From in front, two plump, spunky angels
seem intent (while carefully not looking at each other)
on adoring whatever I choose to place up there,
their propinquity accidental. Well, angels need no

conscience. The mysterious rail (the color of altar cloth
I suddenly realize) is charged. Between elbow and naked
elbow's a light-gap, electric white. And, in the gray-blue
    robelike flowing of cloud inflations far out, a green
    brush-streak seems to brighten—a freezing omen. Have
    the angels just heard thunder? Or are they about to hear?

A Trellis for R.

B
L
U
E but you are R
       o
       s
       e too
and buttermilk but with blood
dots showing through.
A little salty your white

nape boy-wide. Glinting hairs shoot
back of your ears' R
          o
          s
          e that
tongue likes to feel
the maze of slip into
the funnel tell a thunder whisper to.
When I kiss

your eyes' straight lashes
down crisp go like doll's
blond straws. Glazed
iris R
    o
    s
    e
    s your lids unclose
to B
    l
    u
    e ringed targets their dark
sheen spokes almost green. I sink in
B
l
u
e black R
       o
       s
       e heart holes until
you blink.

Pink lips the serrate
folds taste smooth
and R
    o
    s
    e
    h
    i
    p round the center
bud I suck. I milknip

your two B
       l
       u
       e skeined blown R
             o
             s
             e
beauties too to sniff their
berries' blood up stiff pink tips.
You're white

in patches only mostly R
                o
                s
                e
buck skin and salty
speckled like a sky. I
love your spots your white neck R
                     o
                     s
                     e
your hair's wild straw splash
silk spools for your ears.
But where white spouts out spills

on your brow to clear
eyepools wheel shafts of light
R
o
s
e you are B
       l
       u
       e.

Wednesday at the Waldorf

Two white whales have been installed at
the Waldorf. They are tumbling slowly
above the tables, butting the chandeliers,
submerging, and taking soft bites
out of the red-vested waiters in the
Peacock Room. They are poking *fleur-de-lys*
tails into the long pockets on the
waiters' thighs. They are stealing
breakfast strawberries from two eccentric
guests—one, skunk-cabbage green with
dark peepers—the other, wild rose and
milkweed, barelegged, in Lafayette loafers.
When the two guests enter the elevator,
the whales ascend, bouncing, through all
the ceilings, to the sixth floor. They
get between the sheets. There they turn
candy-pink, with sky-colored eyes, and
silver bubbles start to rise from velvet
navels on the tops of their heads.
Later, a pale blue VW, running on poetry,
weaves down Park Avenue, past yellow
sprouts of forsythia, which, due to dog-do
and dew, are doing nicely. The two
white whales have the blue car in tow
on a swaying chain of bubbles. They are
rising toward the heliport on the Pan Am
roof. There they go, dirigible and slow,
hide-swiping each other, lily tails flipping,
their square velvet snouts stitched with
snug smiles. It is April. "There's
a kind of hush all over the world."

In the Yard

Dogwood's s n o w. Its ground's air.
R e d h e a d e d ' s   riddling the phone pole.

Fat-tailed she-dog grinning's
t h r a s h e r - r e d.

It's the oriole there by the feeder
c h e d d a r   under b l a c k bold head.

Neighbor doing yardwork's getting r e d.
Lifts tiles to a barrow.

L.I.R.R.'s four cars rollskate by
w h i t e   potato blooms farside the field.

That square's our bedroom window.
You're not there. You're away

looking for nails or such
to put up a mirror frame the Adam

and Eve bright hair held back by a
r o b i n ' s - e g g - b l u e   band.

Or you're at the body shop about
the broken bumper.

C a b b a g e   b u t t e r f l y ' s   found
h o n e y he thinks on r i n g

g l i n t s on my hand. I wait
for the r i n g n e c k who

noseblows twice parades his mate. She's g r a y.
Until comes the B l u e Bug crunching driveway.

You're back barefoot brought some fruit.
Split me a n a p p l e. We'll get r e d

w h i t e halves each our
juice on the Indian spread.

Year of the Double Spring

Passing a lank boy, bangs to the eyebrows,
licking a Snow Flake cone, and cones on the tulip tree
    up stiff, honeysuckle tubelets weighting a vine,
and passing *Irene Gay—Realtor, The Black Whale, Rexall,*
    and others—(Irene, don't sue me, it's just your sign
I need in the scene)—
    remembering lilac a month back, a different faded shade,
buying a paper with the tide table instead of the twister
    forecast on page three,
then walking home from the village, beneath the viaduct,
    I find Midwest echoes answering echoes
that another, yet the same train, waked here out East.
    I'm thinking of how I leaned on you, you leaning
in the stone underpass striped with shadows of tracks
    and ties, and I said, "Give me a kiss, A.D.,
even if you are tranquilized," and I'm thinking
    of the Day of the Kingfisher, the Indigo Day of the Bunting,
of the Catfish Night I locked the keys in the car
    and you tried to jimmy in, but couldn't, with a clothes hanger.
The night of the juke at Al's—*When Something's Wrong*
    With My Baby—you pretended to flake out on the bench,
and I poured icy Scotch into the thimble of your belly,
    lifting the T-shirt. Another night you threw up
in a Negro's shoe. It's Accabonac now instead of
    Tippecanoe. I'm remembering how we used to drive
to *The Custard* "to check out the teenage boxes."
    I liked the ones around the Hondas, who
from a surly distance, from under the hair in their eyes,
    cruised the girls in flowered shorts.

One day back there, licking cones, we looked in
    on a lioness lying with her turd behind the gritty window
of a little zoo. I liked it there. I'd like it
    anywhere with you.
Here are the gorgeous pheasants, no hogs, blond horses,
    and Alec Guinness seen at *The Maidstone* Memorial Eve—
and also better dumps. You scavenged my plywood desk top,
    a narrow paint-flecked old door, and the broad white
wicker I'm sitting in now.
    While you're at the dump hunting for more—
maybe a double spring good as that single you climbed to
    last night (and last year)—I sit in front of a house,
remembering a house back there, thinking of a house—
    where? when?—by spring next year?
I notice the immature oak leaves, vivid as redbud almost,
    and shaped like the spoor of the weasel we saw
once by the Wabash.
    Instead of "to the *Readmore*" riffling *Playboy*, I found
you yesterday in that Newtown Lane newspaper store
    I don't yet know the name of. Stay with me, A.D.,
don't blow. Scout out that bed. Go find tennis
    instead of squash mates, surfboarders, volleyball
boys to play with. I know you will, before long—
    maybe among the lifeguards—big, cool-coned,
straight-hipped, stander-on-one-finger, strong.

Five Horses

Midday, midsummer, the field is watercolor green.
  In the center, slats of an open paddock frame.
   A rusty bathtub for water trough in foreground shade.
    Five horses—two brown, two pinto, one a buckskin—wade

       the wide green. They are made short by the stature
        of the grass—hoofs and half their muzzles unseen.
       They keep the composition balanced by their ease
      and placement. On a rectangle of sun, the two brown
     backs, like polished tables, solid, reddish rove.

          The black-on-whites, turned hinders to the wood,
           necks down, feel a slow breeze drag the scarves
            of their manes aslant. One's whole head is a dark hood
             through which the ears, unpainted, point. The other's a mare
              with astonishing blue eyes, and all blond, except for a pale

        tan patch over the stifle and loin. The buckskin, youngest,
         crops in shade alone, tail thrown over tawny rump
        in a constant feathery rotor against flies.
       They move and munch so gradually, the scene
      seems not to change: clean colors outlined on mat-green,

             under a horizontal wash of steady blue
              that ink-sharp darker swallows, distant, dip into.
               That pasture was the end of one of our walks.
                We brought carrots that we broke and passed
                 on the flats of our hands, to the lips of Buck and Blue,

        to Spook, Brown I and Brown II, who nipped and jostled
         each other over the gate to get them.
        They'd wait while we stroked their forelocks and smooth jaws.
       I could look into the square pupils of the palfrey, Blue,
      her underlip and nostrils, like a rabbit's, pink.

             Pied spots, as on a cheetah, showed faint under the hair
              of Buck, your horse: you liked him best.
               Close up, we rubbed the ragged streaks and stars on their
                foreheads and chests, slapped their muscular necks,
                 while they nudged us, snuffling our pockets for more.

        Now we've gone past summer and the green field, but I could draw
         their profiles, so distinguished the five faces stay in view,
        leaning over the gate boards toward our coming,
       waiting for carrots, staring, yearning in a row.

How Everything Happens
(Based on a study of the Wave)

                                                happen.
                                          to
                                        up
                                  stacking
                              is
                        something
When nothing is happening

When it happens
                  something
                        pulls
                              back
                                  not
                                      to
                                        happen.

When   has happened.
      pulling back   stacking up
                    happens

          has happened   stacks up.
When it   something   nothing
                          pulls back while

Then nothing is happening.

                                    happens.
                                and
                        forward
                    pushes
                up
          stacks
      something
Then

A Pair

A he
and she,
prowed upstream,
soot-brown
necks,
bills the green
of spring
asparagus,

heads
proud figure-
heads for the boat-
bodies, smooth
hulls on feathered   the two,
water,   browed with light,
steer ashore,
rise; four
web-
paddles pigeon-
toe it
to the reeds;

he
walks first,
proud, prowed
as when light-
browed, swimming,
he leads.

Camoufleur

Walked in the swamp   His cheek vermilion
A dazzling prince
Neck-band white   Cape he trailed
Metallic mottled
Over rain-rotted leaves   Wet mud reflected
Waded olive water
His opulent gear   Pillars of the reeds
Parted the strawgold
Brilliance   Made him disappear

Beginning to Squall

A Buoy like a man in a red sou'wester
is uP to the toP of its Boots in the water
 leaning to warn a Blue Boat

    that, BoBBing and shrugging, is nodding "No,"
    till a strong wave comes and it shivers "Yes."
        The white and the green Boats are quiBBling, too.
          What is it they don't want to do?

The Bay goes on Bouncing anchor floats,
their colors tennis and tangerine.
Two ruffled gulls laughing are laughing gulls,
 a finial Pair on the gray Pilings.

    Now the Boats are Buttoning slickers on
      which resemBle little tents.
        The Buoy is jumPing uP and down
          showing a Black Belt stenciled "1."

A yellow Boat's last to lower sail
to wraP like a Bandage around the Boom.
 Blades are sharPening in the water
    that Brightens while the sky goes duller.

A Subject of the Waves

Today, while a steamshovel rooted in the cove,
leveling a parking lot for the new nightclub,
and a plane drilled between clean clouds in the October sky,
and the flags on the yachts tied in the basin flipped in the wind,
I watched my footsteps mark the sand by the tideline.
Some hollow horseshoe crab shells scuttled there,
given motion by the waves. I threw a plank back to the waves
that they'd thrown up, a sun-dried, sea-swollen stave
from a broken dinghy, one end square, one pointed, painted
  green.

Watching it float, my attention snagged and could not get off
the hook of its experience. I had launched a subject
of the waves I could not leave until completed.

Easily it skipped, putting out, prow-end topping every smack
and swell. It kept its surface dry, and looked to float
beyond the jetty head, and so be loose,
exchange the stasis of the beach
for unconceived fluidities and agitations.
It set sail by the luck of its construction.
Lighter than the forceful waves, it surmounted their shove.
Heavier, steadier than the hollows they scooped behind them,
it used their crested threats for coasting free.
Unsplashed by even a drop of spray, it was casual master
of the inconsistent element it rode.

But there was a bias to the moving sea.
The growth and motion of each wave looked arbitrary,
but the total spread (of which each crease was part,
the outward hem lying flat by the wall of sky
at the dim blue other end of the bay's bed)
was being flung, it seemed, by some distant will.
Though devious and shifty in detail, the whole expanse
reiterated constancy and purpose.
So, just as the arrowy end of the plank, on a peak of a wave,
made a confident leap that would clear the final shoal,
a little sideways breaker nudged it enough
to turn it broadside. Then a swifter slap from a stronger comber
brought it back, erasing yards of its piecemeal progress
with one push. Yet the plank turned point to the tide,
and tried again—though not as buoyant, for it had got soaked.
Arrogance undamaged, it conveyed itself again
over obstacle waves, a courageous ski,
not noticing, since turned from shore, that the swells it
    conquered
slid in at a slant; that while it met them head on,
it was borne closer to shore, and shunted down the coast.

Now a bulge, a series of them, as a pulse quickened in the tide,
without resistance lifted up the plank, flipped it over twice,
and dumped it in the shallows. It scraped on sand.

And so it was put back. Not at the place of its first effort;
a greater disgrace than that: at before the birth
of balance, pride, intention, enterprise.
It changed its goal, and I changed my ambition. Not the open
sea—escape into rough and wild, into unpredictability—
but rescue, return and rest. Release from influence
became my hope for the green painted, broken slat,
once part of a boat.

Its trials to come ashore the cold will of the waves thwarted
more capriciously than its assays into adventure made before.
Each chance it took to dig, with its bent spike,
a grip in the salvage of pebbles and weed and shell
was teasingly, tirelessly outwitted
by dragouts and dousings, slammings and tuggings
of the punishing sea. Until, of its own impulse, the sea
decided to let be,
and lifted and laid, lifted and laid
the plank inert on sand. At tide turn,
such the unalterable compulsion of the sea,
it had to turn its back and rumple its bed
toward the other edge, the farther side of the spread.

I watched my footsteps mark the sand by the tideline.
The steamshovel rooting in the cove had leveled
a parking lot for the new nightclub.
The launch from the yacht basin whooshed around the end
of the pier, toward a sailboat with dropped anchor there,
whose claxon and flipping flag signaled for pickup.
The men with their mallets had finished sinking posts
by the gangplank entrance to the old ferry,
its hold ballasted with cement, painted green and black,
furnished with paneled bar and dining deck.
I watched them hang a varnished sign between the posts,
and letter the name: *The Ark*.
Tomorrow I must come
out again into the sun,
and mark the sand, and find my plank,
for its destiny's not done.

The Blue Bottle

"Go
to the other
shore
and return"
I wrote
in a note
to the bottle
and put it in it.
It kept it
dry.
I
could see
through
the blue
bottle blue
note paper
with blue ink
words.
The cork was tight.
It might
make it.
Blue wavelets let
it go
began to
take it.
Oh
it hobbled
beyond the jetty
rocks barnacled
and snailed.
It bobbled
snagged
on a crag
wagged
with its butt
end butted
but sailed
so far that
its glass
had to pass
for glitter
among glitters
on the flat
glass
of the bay
and my
eye-
glass.

Baited
with
words
and weighted
I thought
"It will get away.
Get away
with it" I
thought
watching
the laps
the lapse
listening
to the lisp
the lips
of the bay-
mouth
making shore
making sure
every rock got
rounded
a little more
today
every pebble
pounded
brought
to ground
and rounded
to be gritted
to a grain
someday
some sum-day
to be mounded
into rock again.
Some fishermen
were fishing
with little
fishes hooked
to hook
bigger fish.
And some they caught
and cooked.
And some they
put on bigger
hooks to get
bigger fishes yet.
And all day
the bay

smacked
its lips big
and little
rocking big and
little ships
that smacked
and rocked like
oyster crackers
in a dish.
The tide was either
going out or it
was coming in.
Not for an in-
stant could it stop
since its pulse compels
it and since
the syndrom swells.
Since syn-rhythm
rules all motion
and motion makes
erosion
all that's munched
apart and
swallowed
shifts collects is
heaped and hollowed
heaped and
hollowed heaped
and hollowed.
All
the little
waves I
followed
out to where my
bottle wallowed.
I was sure sure sure
I was shore shore
it would endure endure
would obey obey
internal pulsion pulsion
of the bay
would turn turn
return return
with the turn- turn- turn-
ing glassy floor
that bore
it for
it wore
internal or-
der at its core.
Constantly my
eye

did pass
over blue
looking with blue
for bluer
blue
on the bottle-blue
bay-glass.
When tide re-
turned
when shore re-
stored
my bottle's envelope
of glass
would be re-versed
even though
its core
burst.
First
erosion
then corrosion
then assemblage.
It would be
nursed
again to
vessel-shape
transparent float
hard hollow
bladder
transferred transplant
holder of my note.
In what
language then
the words the words within
its throat?
What answer? What
other-colored
ink?
My
blue eye
thinking thinking
blinked.
My eye my
I
lost link
with the blue chink
with crinkled
wavelets-lets-lets
let it rising
racing wrinkling
falling
be swallowed
in that inkling
let it sink.

The Stick

The stick is subject to the waves. The waves are subject to
the sea. The sea is subject to its frame. And that
is fixed, or seems to be.

What is it that the stick can do? Can tell the sky, "I
dip, I float. When a wave runs under me, I pretend
I am a boat. And the steersman and
the crew, and the cargo, compass, map. With
a notion of the shore,
I carry all within my lap."

And when a wave runs over it, what is it that the
stick decides? "From your bottom,
cruel sea, you have torn me with your
tides. I am a sliver from some boat, once
swallowed to its water-deep. Why
am I shifted, broken, lost? Let me down, my
rest to keep."

The sea is subject to its frame.
The waves are subject to the sea. The
stick is subject to the waves.
Or does it only seem to be?

What if the stick be washed ashore,
and, gnawed by wind, scoured
by sand, be taken up with other
sticks, into a hand? On some
predicated day, here is what
the stick might say:

"Inside my border, a green
sea flows, that while it
flows is still. A white
wall is around me,
where I am fixed by
someone's will,
who made my shape
into a frame,
and in
this corner
drew
his
name."

F
i
r
e
Island

The Milky Way
above, the milky
waves beside,
when the sand is night
the sea is galaxy.
The unseparate stars
mark a twining coast
with phosphorescent
surf
in the black sky's trough.
Perhaps we walk on black
star ash, and watch
the milks of light foam forward, swish and spill
while other watchers, out
walking in their white
great
swerve,
gather
our
low
spark,
our little Way
the dark
glitter
in
their
s
i
g
h
t
.

Stone Gullets

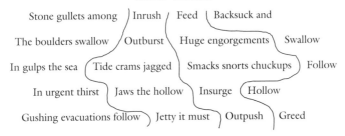

Stone gullets among) Inrush / Feed (Backsuck and

The boulders swallow / Outburst \ Huge engorgements \ Swallow

In gulps the sea (Tide crams jagged) Smacks snorts chuckups) Follow

In urgent thirst) Jaws the hollow \ Insurge (Hollow

Gushing evacuations follow) Jetty it must) Outpush) Greed

Seeing Jupiter

A chair was placed
upon the lawn.
In cloak of wind
and shadow, I
sat and bent
my eye upon
a rim of dark
that glittered up
to open heaven.
In the cup
a worn dime,
size of an iris
of anyone's eye:
flat, cold, lost,
found coin
of enormous time.
Some small change
around it: three
little bits swirled,

or else my ragged eye
with wind swung.
In a black
pocket, behind
that blank, hung
hidden a fourth
moon dot; smarting
beneath my tongue,
dreg of ancient mint;
my retina tasted
light how long
dead? My hair
thrashed. Enlarged
upon the lawn,
my chair
I sat in, that wind
and shadow bent,
had slid an inch
toward dawn.

Zero
in the Cove

The waves have frozen
in their tracks and turned
to snow, and into ice

        the snow has turned, become
the shore. Where in soft
           summer sand burned by

  water flat, paralytic
            breakers stand hurled
  into a ridge of ice. Ice
           fattens about the poles
that told the tide.
       Their two shadows point

out stiff behind them on a dead
         floor, thickened and too rough
  for light to glass,

        as if the moon were drained
     of power, and water
        were unknown. The cove

      is locked, a still
       chest. Depth itself has
       died with its
      reflection
       lost.

The
Sunbird
Settles
to Its
Nest

Boys are swimming through the sun's tail,
which is switched by abrasive waves dyed
flamingo. The head of the sun is cardinal

from the ears down. Its pate is pink. Oh,
as I wrote that, a flush spread to the
hairline. The chin's no longer there.

The tail on the waves is sliced with purple.
Oiled ibis-feathered swells make it fan
out like a peacock's. Then, slowly

dropped and narrowed, it drags west.
The boys' heads are hubs for scintillating
circles. Their arms plough a waterfield

of eyes. The peckered scalp is melting—
there goes the last capfeather, of faint
red down down. Down. The boys come up

almost black. They flip wet off
by the green-haired rocks,
behind them, embered, a phoenix crown.

Rocky Point

The mainland looks much smaller than the island,
and faint, implying thinner paint
brushed in as background,
so not as real.
     Here is the present; over there, the past.
     Hard to feel how it's the larger body, that dream-haze,

blue and green wave of land,
not clear, nor seeming solid, as the water in between
it and the rocky point I stand on,
that's lifesized, well detailed with sunlit trees.

      The island looks much bigger than the mainland.
      This shore is foreground. Why have a figure
with its back turned, focused on a streak in the distance,
a coast it can't make out—
that even the sun forgets on foggy days?
      That *is* the larger body, that's a fact—
and would be again, if I were over there. Packed
with central life, it's the torso; this, at best, a leg.
No, a toe. Well, even that is inexact.

      If I think of the whole body, what was vast
in retrospect—now small, thin in the blue of forget—
was, is, but a hand's breadth. *And*
an island. All that's earth is,
on the world's whirled wavedrop.
      And this now present outcrop
that a magnified wave grapples, every fingernail of foam
real to my thirsty eye—
I on a cliff *before* the foreground—
the brush can't paint itself, is but a hair—
oh, it is mainland, it's the moment's ground I stand on,
it is fair.

NEW & SELECTED THINGS
TAKING PLACE
(1978)

New poems in THINGS TAKING PLACE I & II
are for R.R.K.

THINGS TAKING PLACE
I

A Navajo Blanket

Eye-dazzlers the Indians weave. Three colors
are paths that pull you in, and pin you
to the maze. Brightness makes your eyes jump,
surveying the geometric field. Alight, and enter
any of the gates—of Blue, of Red, of Black.
Be calmed and hooded, a hawk brought down,
glad to fasten to the forearm of a Chief.

You can sleep at the center,
attended by Sun that never fades, by Moon
that cools. Then, slipping free of zigzag and
hypnotic diamond, find your way out
by the spirit trail, a faint Green thread that
secretly crosses the border, where your mind
is rinsed and returned to you like a white cup.

Bison Crossing near Mt. Rushmore

There is our herd of cars stopped,
staring respectfully at the line of bison crossing.
   One big-fronted bull nudges his cow into a run.
She and her calf are first to cross.
   In swift dignity the dark-coated caravan sweeps through
the gap our cars leave in the two-way stall
on the road to the Presidents.
   The polygamous bulls guarding their families from the rear,
the honey-brown calves trotting head-to-hip
by their mothers—who are lean and muscled as bulls,
with chin tassels and curved horns—
all leap the road like a river, and run.
   The strong and somber remnant of western freedom
disappears into the rough grass of the draw,
around the point of the mountain.
   The bison, orderly, disciplined by the prophet-faced,
heavy-headed fathers, threading the pass
of our awestruck stationwagons, airstreams and trailers,

if in dread of us give no sign,
go where their leaders twine them, over the prairie.
    And we keep to our line,
staring, stirring, revving idling motors, moving
each behind the other, herdlike, where the highway leads.

Speed
Winnipeg to Medicine Hat, Manitoba, Canada

In 200 miles
a tender painting
on the wind-

shield, not yet done,
in greeny yellows,
crystalline pinks,

a few smeared
browns. Fuselages
split on impact,

stuck, their juices
instantly dried. Spat-
tered flat out-

lines, superfine
strokes, tokens of
themselves flying,

frail engines
died in various
designs: mainly arrow-

shapes, wings gone,
bellies smitten
open, glaze and tincture

the wipers can't
erase. In 400 miles
a palette, thick

impasto; in 600
a palimpsest the sun
bakes through. Stained

glass, not yet done
smiting the wind-
borne, speeds on.

The North Rim

Great dark bodies, the mountains.
Between them wriggling the canyon road,
little car, bug-eyed, beaming, goes
past ticking and snicking of August insects,
smell of sage and cedar, to a summit of stars.
Sky glints like fluorescent rock.

Cloth igloo erected, we huff up our bed,
listen to the quaking of leaf-hearts
that, myriad, shadow our sleep.

At dawn, the bodies discovered rugged, oblate,
Indian-warpaint-red. A rooster crows.
Barefoot in brickdust, we strike our tent.
Car crawls the knee of the Great White Throne.
Chiseled by giant tomahawks, the slabs.
In half-finished doorways broad gods stand.
Wind-whipped from the niches, white-throated swifts
razor the void.
We rise to ponderosa, to deer park, to moraine,
mountain bluebirds stippling the meadows,
and coast to the Grand Rim:

Angular eels of light
scribble among the buttes and crinoline
escarpments. Thunder's organ tumbles
into the stairwell of the gorge.
When rain and mist divide their veil,
westering sun, a palette knife, shoves into the cut
colors thick and bright, enclabbering
every serrate slant and vertical;
hard edged, they jut forward,
behind, beside them purple groins and pits
in shadow. Shadow within shadow beneath a shawl
of shadow darkens, and we dare not blink
till light tweaks out.

Morning at Cape Royal. A Merry-Go-Round
out there in the red cirque, Brahma's Temple.
Many Pavilions made a Great
                              Pavilion.
                         Where mountain
                      peaks eroded to flat
                   ranges, flat ranges broke
                and parted, became pediments,
             and pointed pediments, pinnacles, were
      honed to skinny minarets,
or else, inverted cones, big-headed totems—

Look: On the slope a stone Boot two miles high,
the hip-end slouched in folds, some seven-leaguer
left six million years.
A lizard where I sit, with petrific eye,
is Dinosaur's little cousin
watching me from Juniper's bony root.

Two coils of the river seen from here,
muddy infinite oozing heavy paint.
Each object has its shadow. Or, if not,
must vanish. Now while the sun leans,
tabernacles form. Allow dark openings,
violet-cool arcades. Establish bases,
though colosseums, carved by the shift
of a cloud, descend pendant,
and Great sinks into shadow.
We must go. It rains. The car trickles east
over the frogback of the Kaibab Forest.
I must imagine morning, from Angel's Window
how to dive, firebrushed by the sun.

Camping in Madera Canyon

We put up our tent while the dark closed in
and thickened, the road a black trough
winding the mountain down. Leaving the lantern
ready to light on the stone table,
we took our walk. The sky was a bloom
of sharp-petaled stars.

Walls of the woods, opaque and still,
gave no light or breath or echo, until,
faint and far, a string of small toots—
nine descending notes—the whiskered owl's
signal. A tense pause . . . then, his mate's
identical reply.

At the canyon's foot, we turned,
climbed back to camp, between tall walls

of silent dark. Snugged deep into our sacks,
so only noses felt the mountain chill,
we heard the owls once more. Farther from us,
but closer to each other. The pause, that linked
his motion with her seconding, grew longer
as we drowsed. Then, expectation frayed,
we forgot to listen, slept.

In a tent, first light tickles the skin
like a straw. Still freezing cold out there,
but we in our pouches sense the immense
volcano, sun, about to pour
gold lava over the mountain, upon us.
Wriggling out, we sleepily unhinge,
make scalding coffee, shivering, stand and sip;
tin rims burn our lips.

Daybirds wake, the woods are filling
with their rehearsal flutes and pluckings,
buzzes, scales and trills. Binoculars
dangling from our necks, we walk
down the morning road. Rooms of the woods
stand open. Glittering trunks
rise to a limitless loft of blue. New snow,
a delicate rebozo, drapes the peak that,
last night, stooped in heavy shadow.

Night hid this day. What sunrise may it be
the dark to? What wider light ripens to dawn
behind familiar light? As by encircling arms
our backs are warmed by the blessing sun,
all is revealed and brought to feature.
All but the owls. The Apaches believe
them ghosts of ancestors, who build their nests
of light with straws pulled from the sun.

The whiskered owls are here, close by,
in the tops of the pines, invisible and radiant,
as we, blind and numb, awaken—our just-born
eyes and ears, our feet that walk—
as brightness bathes the road.

Bronco Busting, Event #1

The stall so tight he can't raise heels or knees
when the cowboy, coccyx to bareback, touches down

tender as a deerfly, forks him, gripping the rope-
handle over the withers, testing the cinch,

as if hired to lift a cumbersome piece of brown
luggage, while assistants perched on the rails arrange

the kicker, a foam-rubber band around the narrowest,
most ticklish part of the loins, leaning full weight

on neck and rump to keep him throttled, this horse,
"Firecracker," jacked out of the box through the sprung

gate, in the same second raked both sides of the belly
by ratchets on booted heels, bursts into five-way

motion: bucks, pitches, swivels, humps, and twists,
an all-over-body-sneeze that must repeat

until the flapping bony lump attached to his spine is gone.
A horn squawks. Up from the dust gets a buster named
    Tucson.

St. Augustine-by-the-Sea

I

A sullen morning.
A long string,
with knots in it,
being pulled,
pelicans fly,
follow the leader
in fog, their line
the only horizon.

When the measuring
string is lost,
sea becomes sky.

2

Peak tide.
Ocean trying
to bury the land
again, again
slaughters
the surf-pierced
reefs, grinding
coarse, sifting
fine, the sand
salmon, like flesh.

3

On reddish sand
by the coquina
cliffs, noon sun
swallows my body.
I lie in the mouth
of a cannibal flower.
Wave after hissing
wave, the cold sea
climbs to me
to douse with green
glaze and fizz white,
the fiery flower's
appetite.

One of the Strangest

Stuffed pink stocking, the neck,
toe of pointed black, the angled beak,
thick heel with round eye in it upside down, the pate,

swivels, dabbles, skims the soup of pond all day
for small meat. That split polished toe is mouth
of the wading flamingo

whose stilts, the rosy knee joints, bend
the wrong way. When planted
on one straight stem, a big fluffy flower

is body a pink leg, wrung, lifts up over,
lays an awkward shoe to sleep on top of,
between flocculent elbows, the soft peony wings.

Last Night at Long Pine

Up and walking, 3:30 A.M., under the Southern Cross.
My horsehide jacket squeaks. It's dark on the path.
Is someone behind me? No, it's my shadow.

Bullfrogs whickering, splash of a night-diving duck.
My cigarette's ember to sticks of a fire
winks in the sleeping camp.

A far train bawls at a crossing. Mournful phantom
animal: "Of metal, when shall I mate?"

We strike at sunup, begin the struggle toward cold
incarnation in the North. From soft nights too soon
exiled under smaller, sharper, scantier stars.

From Sea Cliff, March

The water's wide spread
(it is storm gray)
following the border of the far shore ahead,
leads the eye south,
tucks into a cove

where, at the point of another line of hills,
big rocks like huts
strung along the flats
are embraced by the sliding
long arms of the tide.
A red buoy bangs (but you can't hear it,
size of a golf tee seen from here),
wind is picking up, cleats of the water
rising and deepening, no white ridges yet.

In the cove's corner
on an island by itself,
an intricate old house,
set on a rock shelf
beside a lighthouse, saltcellar shaped,
with a round silvery top,
pokes up alone in the wind's main way.
Old house, of many chimneys, dormers and decks,
doll-sized, of clapboard, is outlined plain
at the farthest string of sight,
perched under swirling specks of white
gulls against gray
wide water, lowering sky
shutting down the distance under wind and rain.

Old No. 1

A shock to find you washed up on the beach,
old No. 1, looking like an iron whale,
or a blunt rocket. What a storm it took

to pull you from bottom, breaking the root
of the anchor. And what a wave, to roll
your solid ton, like a giant's thick and broken

pencil point, so far up the scoured beach.
You're dumped on a ridge of sedge the storm tide
harvested, big ring in your snout half buried,

rusted cone below your watermark scabby orange,
glazed black paintskin of belly and round
tabled top fouled with dull white gull droppings.

But you're still No. 1—it's clearly stenciled
upon you—old Stove Pipe, old Opera Hat,
Bouncer in the Channel, Policeman of the Bay

all boats salute. Your colleague, nipple-headed
Big Red, No. 2, is out there swaying on today's
gentler tide like a jolly bottle, but

you, Black Butt, you're gone aground, down
past the count of ten, with a frowzy dead gull
upended in the sandy litter by your side.

Shu Swamp, Spring

Young skunk
cabbages all over
the swamp.

Brownish purple,
yellow-specked
short tusks,

they thicken,
twirl and point
like thumbs.

Thumbs of old
gloves, the nails
poked through

and curled.
By Easter, fingers
will have flipped out

fat and green.
Old gloves, brown
underground,

the seams split.
The nails
have been growing.

On the Edge

I was thinking, while I was working on my income tax,
here in the open angle of a V—
that blue on the map that's water—my house
tucked into the fold of a hill, on the edge
of a ragged beak of the sea
that widens and narrows according to the tide:
"This little house will be swallowed some year.
Not yet. But threatened."

Chips are houses, twigs are trees
on the woodland ledges along the lip,
the blue throat open, thirsty. Where my chip-roof sits,
sandland loosens, boulders shift downslope,
bared roots of old trunks stumble.
The undermining and undulating lurch
is all one way, the shore dragged south
to spill into and fill another mouth.

I was thinking while I was working: "The April sun
is warm." Suddenly, all the twigs on the privet
budded green, the cardinal flamed and called,
the maple rained its flowerets down
and spread leaf-grown. July's plush roses bloomed,
were blown. A hundred gladioli sunsets in a row
raced to die, and dyed the cove,
while the sea crawled the sand, gnawed on the cliff.

And leisurely, cracks in the flagstones happened,
leaks in the roof. The gateposts crumbled,
mortar in the stone wall loosened,
boards in the porch let the nailheads through.
I was thinking, while April's crocus
poked out of earth on the cesspool top:
"Blueblack winter of water coming—icewhite, rockhard
tide will be pounding the side of the gaping V. . . .

"But smell of the windfresh, salty morning,
flash of the sunwhipped beak of the sea!
Better get last year's layers of old leaves up,
before this year's green bursts out, turns brown,
comes blowing down," I was thinking
while I was working on my income tax.

Painting the Gate

I painted the mailbox. That was fun.
I painted it postal blue.
Then I painted the gate.
I painted a spider that got on the gate.
I painted his mate.
I painted the ivy around the gate.
Some stones I painted blue,
and part of the cat as he rubbed by.
I painted my hair. I painted my shoe.
I painted the slats, both front and back,
all their beveled edges, too.
I painted the numbers on the gate—
I shouldn't have, but it was too late.
I painted the posts, each side and top,
I painted the hinges, the handle, the lock,
several ants and a moth asleep in a crack.
At last I was through.
I'd painted the gate
shut, me out, with both hands dark blue,
as well as my nose, which,

early on, because of a sudden itch,
got painted. But wait!
I had painted the gate.

Written while Riding the Long Island Rail Road

Hard water and square wheels.
A foot wears a hat and walks on its thumbs.
The clouds are of plaster. That hiss is a box.
Honey is hairy. This cipher's a house.
In a coffin of chocolate the hatchet is laid.
A cactus is sneezing. A blind violin
has digested a penny. The telephone's juice
has stiffened a horsefly, whose porcelain curse
is rocking the corridor. Pockets are born,
but the stubble of rainbows cannot be controlled.
The bite of the barber begins to compete
with the weight of a capsized spondee or stilt.
The chime of the calendar suffers from rust,
and cobalt is scorched beyond closure or froth.
If a portion of pinch is applied to a cube,
and scissorlike bubbles produced with a switch,
we can burnish the windows with faucets and lips.
Will oral implosions enrapture the fish
so that their lecterns, transparently diced,
while diploid, will dapple? We tried it, and found
that a petrified lace leaked out of the pistol
of Charlotte, the Kink, while Pug, drunk on lightning,
slept in the bank with ankles and rabbits
he'd slaughtered with borscht. Snafu just sucked
on his pommel and barfed. Then let the moon's
carpet display a cartoon: The lawn's perpendicular,
Daddy comes home, and the doorknob's a funnel.
An owl's in the sink. There's a flag in the oven.
The front page is blank.

Appointment in New York

At 42nd Street, finding the Library Lions
crouched in raw wood boxes with plastic-sheeted
sides. . . . "Are To Be Cleaned," a sign says. . . .
The two grand heads, as if behind the fog
of oxygen tents . . . their haughty nostrils
unable to breathe the dirty air.

In Charleston, S.C., says the *Times*,
they're putting diapers of black plastic on
the old cab horses that drive tourists through
historic streets. Poor trussed-into-harness
beasts, blindered and rubber-shod, endure a new
indignity: not only nose bags, but ass bags.

In Disney World in Florida, white-overalled
attendants run behind the Percherons
pulling the fake red and gold stagecoach,
with scoop and brush take up the steaming buns
that fall on waxed and polished pavement. . . .

All filth there whisked away. . . . Dare to drop
a gum wrapper, it's gone—instantly speared
into a white enameled barrel trundled on wheels.
The street is like a room. Perfection
is maintained in the Fun House, too.

Staying at Ed's Place

I like being in your apartment, and not disturbing anything.
As in the woods I wouldn't want to move a tree,
or change the play of sun and shadow on the ground.

The yellow kitchen stool belongs right there
against white plaster. I haven't used your purple towel
because I like the accidental cleft of shade you left in it.

At your small six-sided table, covered with mysterious
dents in the wood like a dartboard, I drink my coffee
from your brown mug. I look into the clearing

of your high front room, where sunlight slopes through bare
window squares. Your Afghanistan hammock, a man-sized
    cocoon
slung from wall to wall, your narrow desk and typewriter

are the only furniture. Each morning your light from the east
douses me where, with folded legs, I sit in your meadow,
a casual spread of brilliant carpets. Like a cat or dog

I take a roll, then, stretched out flat
in the center of color and pattern, I listen
to the remote growl of trucks over cobbles on Bethune Street
    below.

When I open my eyes I discover the peaceful blank
of the ceiling. Its old paint-layered surface is moonwhite
and trackless, like the Sea—of Tranquillity.

Fashion in the 70's

Like, everyone wants to look black
in New York these days.
Faces with black lenses, black
frames around the eyes,
faces framed in black
beards. Afros on all the blacks—
beautiful. But like,
everyone looks puff-headed.
Slouching along in black
leather, fake fur, sleazy body-
shirts, floppy pants, wearing black
boots with thick heels. Bootblacks
have disappeared. Good—but like,
everyone wants to look hoody.

Blacks used to want to look
white. And whites used to want
to be pink. That's pig now.
Sharp, neat, crewcut, cleancut,
blonds preferred is out. O.K., but
whites, the women especially,
if they don't want to look black,
want to look dead. Like,
morticians make them up,
in the Ugly Parlors.
Blacks are loose walkers,
relaxed, laughing. For whites
it's hip to look uptight, scowl,
be grimy, wear scary, puffed-out hair.
Crowds of square-toed black
boots, heavy heels crossing the Walk-
Don't-Walk streets. Like, everyone
wants to look ugly in New York
these days. Like, ugly is beautiful.

Going to the Whitney and Walking on the Floor

There were things that looked like part of the floor
        or part of the wall or the ceiling.
Some ceiling things were on the walls.
Some wall things were on the floor.
No things were on the ceiling that weren't part of
        the ceiling, but some floor things that looked like
        they belonged on the floor reflected some of the ceiling:

A small swimming pool, for instance,
        or the model for one,
        only the rim enameled red.
A little boy's mother said,
        "Don't touch anything."
An out-of-kilter rectangle
        mounted on one of its corners was strung,
        it seemed, with thick wire, so made you think of a harp,
        for instance, by Arp.
But it had rungs
        of wood when you stood
        closer. The little boy would

have liked to crawl
through all
the squares of an aluminum tunnel, but a guard stood
there. On the wall
a framed drawing showed the building plan
for four squares, four-by-four,
or
four-square, labeled, UNTITLED #4 = 4 SQUARES 4 × 4—
ALUMINUM, PENCIL ON PAPER. This was printed on the card.
I wanted very much to add, UNDER GLASS—MOUNTED ON WALL,
    PLASTER, but it was under glass, and I didn't have
a pencil and, anyway, a guard
was standing near.
While I waited
    for him to notice how my face controlled a sneer,
    some schoolchildren, disgorged by the elevator,
    into what might appear
    to be a playroom, were momentarily elated,
    but quickly wilted when, on spreading through the space,
    they discovered all the bright
    blocks or transparent boxes had the same
    name,
    namely, UNTITLED,
    and weren't meant
    to be entered
    or climbed upon or used in any way,
    except for them to stand
    and stare.

Some of the things there
    would have made a fine sound if kicked
    or drummed upon. Others, it was apparent,
    were transparent,
    being lit from within as if to make
    you look for a snake,
    or sleepy puppy, but contained
    nothing, really, just a color
    such as frozen yellow
    Jell-O,
    or lemon juice jars cubed,
    cracked here and there, so that all the juice had drained.

There were long narrow tubed
    things along the walls, like shelves in a post office
    or bank,
    that had set-in sections you could look through
    like a periscope. Although no prank
    was intended, nothing was disclosed at the far end,
    unless another eye, of someone trying to find out

what it was all about,
happened to appear from that end.

The children giggled and scoffed in whispers,
    when sufficiently far away from their teacher, who,
    regarding the guard in a guarded way,
    was too
    timid to ask him something. A boy,
    who was with his girl, covertly touched
    a placard lettered DO NOT TOUCH, and snatched
    back his finger and sucked it, as if it were burnt,
    and the girl laughed.
Having circled the objects on the floor once, and consulted
    their identical titles, all of them UNTITLED,
    but with different dates,
    the children collected at the elevator
    which sucked them in, and away.

In the silent room like a play-
    room, I began to enjoy the floor.
The rough stone squares against the flat
    soles of my shoes that
    allowed a rhythmic scrape and snick wherever
    I walked, gave back an echo bare
    and dungeonlike.
I paced,
    touching
    the floor intimately with each
    step, happy alone,
    noticing each pave-stone,
    its individual quarry marks and whittles.
I circled each of the three guards,
    standing
    suspenseful as if below a gibbet.
I paid each the attention worthy of his exhibit.
Their gray
    suits were as gray as the play-
    room stones. In a far corner on the white
    wall, I found a little sculpture I might
    have missed, had I not been aware:
A cranberry
    red
    boxlike thing, perhaps of lead,
    or other heavy metal, cleverly nicked
    to appear utilitarian,
    with a glass insert through which could be seen—
    but it was locked in—a brass
    handle.

The placard giving the date wasn't there, but this
      three-dimensional construction unaccountably was titled
      by a raised insignia worked into the medium itself:
      PULL TO SET OFF ALARM.
It made a little shelf
      on the wall. I told a guard
      its card
      was missing, but that I thought it was
      the best in show.
No.
I didn't. I only thought of telling him so,
      as he looked at his watch, said it was closing
      time, told me to go.

O'Keeffe Retrospective

Into the sacral cavity can fit the skull of a deer,
the vertical pleat in the snout, place of the yoni.
Within the embrasure of antlers that flare, sensitive
tips like fingers defining thighs and hips, inner horns
hold ovary curls of space.

Where a white bead rolls at the fulcrum of widening knees,
black dawn evolves, a circular saw of polished speed;
its bud, like Mercury, mad in its whiz, shines, although
stone jaws of the same delta, opposite, lock agape—
blunt monolithic hinge, stranded, grand, tide gone out.

A common boundary has hip and hill, sky and pelvic basin.
From the upright cleft, shadow-entwirled, early veils
of spectral color—a tender maypole, girlish, shy, unbraids
to rainbow streams slowly separated.

A narrow eye on end, the lily's riper crack of bloom:
stamen stiff, it lengthens, swells, at its ball (walled pupil)
a sticky tear of sap. Shuttlecock (divided muzzle of the dried
deer's face, eyeholes outline the ischium) is, in the flap of
the jack-in-the-pulpit, silken flesh. As windfolds of
the mesa (regal, opulent odalisque) are, saturate orange,
    sunset.

Cerulean is solid. Clouds are tiles, or floats of ice
a cobalt spa melts. Evaporating, they yet grip their shapes;
if walked on, prove not fluff and steam. These clouds
are hard. Then rock may be pillow, stones vacant spaces.
Look into the hole: it will bulk. Hold the rock: it will empty.

Opposite, the thousand labia of a gray rose puff apart,
like smoke, yet they have a fixed, or nearly fixed, union,
skeletal, innominate, but potent to implode, flush red,
tighten to a first bud-knot, single, sacral.
Not quite closed, the cruciform fissure in the deer's
nose bone, symphysis of the pubis.

Where inbetweens turn visible blues, white objects vanish,
except—see, high at horizon on a vast canvas sky—
one undisciplined tuft, little live cloud, blowing:
fleece, breath of illusion.

Poet to Tiger

THE HAIR

You went downstairs
saw a hair in the sink
and squeezed my toothpaste by the neck.
You roared. My ribs are sore.
This morning even my pencil's got your toothmarks.
Big Cat Eye cocked on me you see bird bones.
Snuggled in the rug of your belly
your breath so warm
I smell delicious fear.
Come breathe on me rough pard
put soft paws here.

THE SALT

You don't put salt on anything
so I'm eating without.
Honey on the eggs is all right
mustard on the toast.

I'm not complaining I'm saying I'm
living with *you*.
You like your meat raw
don't care if it's cold.
Your stomach must have tastebuds
you swallow so fast.
Night falls early. It's foggy. Just now

I found another of your bite marks in the cheese.
I'm hungry. Please
come bounding home
I'll hand you the wine to open
with your teeth.
Scorch me a steak unsalted
boil my coffee twice

say the blessing to a jingle on the blue TV.
Under the lap robe on our chilly couch
look behind my ears "for welps"
and hug me.

THE SAND

You're right I brought a grain
or two of sand
into bed I guess in my socks.
But it was you pushed them off
along with everything else.

Asleep you flip
over roll
everything under
you and off
me. I'm always grabbing
for my share of the sheets.

Or else you wake me every hour with sudden
growled I-love-yous
trapping my face between those plushy
shoulders. All my float-dreams turn spins
and never finish. I'm thinner

now. My watch keeps running fast.
But best is when we're riding pillion
my hips within your lap. You let me steer.
Your hand and arm go clear
around my ribs your moist
dream teeth fastened on my nape.

A grain of sand in the bed upsets you or
a hair on the floor.
But you'll get
in slick and wet from the shower if I let
you. Or with your wool cap
and skiing jacket on
if it's cold.
Tiger don't scold me
don't make me comb my hair outdoors.
Cuff me careful. Lick don't
crunch. Make last what's yours.

THE DREAM

You get into the tub holding *The Naked Ape*
in your teeth. You wet that blond
three-cornered pelt lie back wide
chest afloat. You're reading
in the rising steam and I'm
drinking coffee from your tiger cup.
You say you dreamed
I had your baby book
and it was pink and blue.
I pointed to a page and there
was your face with a cub grin.

You put your paws in your armpits
make a tiger-moo.
Then you say: "Come here
Poet and take
this hair
off me." I do.
It's one of mine. I carefully
kill it and carry

it outside. And stamp on it
and bury it.

In the begonia bed.
And then take off my shoes
not to bring a grain
of sand in to get
into our bed.
I'm going to
do the cooking
now instead
of you.
And sneak some salt in
when you're not looking.

Overboard

What throws you out is what drags you in
What drags you in is what throws you
What throws you out is what drags
What drags is what throws you
What throws you drags
What drags throws
Throws drag
Thrags
Drags throw
What throws drags
What drags you throws
What throws is what drags you
What drags you in is what throws
What throws you out is what drags you
What drags you in is what throws you out
What throws you in is what drags you
What drags you out is what throws
What throws you out drags you
What drags throws you in
What throws drags you
Drags throw you
Thrags

Looks

You give yourself such funny
                          looks
              when you
                          look
          in the mirror. You're
                          looking
      at yourself, but you're not
                          looking
              at yourself
                          looking.
              You
                          look
      at a pimple on your brow. You
          bare your teeth. I'm
                          looking
              at you
                          looking
      funny at yourself in the mirror.
              You're not
                          looking
              at me. I
                          look
              at you. I
                          look
          in the mirror at you
                          looking
      in the mirror. In the mirror I
                          look
              at me,
                          looking
              at you
                          looking
      at a pimple and baring your teeth.
              You don't
                          look
          at me in the mirror
                          looking
              at myself

                              looking
                    at you
                              looking
            at a pimple on your brow.
          You give yourself funny
                                looks,
                    not
                              looking
            at me in the mirror.
                                Look!
              I bare my teeth!

Holding the Towel

You swam out
through the boats
your head an orange

buoy sun-daubed
bobbing. My squint
lost you to nibbling

waves. I looked
for a mast to tilt
to glint with your splash

but couldn't see
past the huddled boats.
I found round heads sun-red

dipping rising tipping.
They were tethered
floats. When you dove

from the stovepipe
buoy in the far
furrow of the channel

I was still
scanning the nearby
nowhere-going boats.

Analysis of Baseball

It's about
the ball,
the bat,
and the mitt.
Ball hits
bat, or it
hits mitt.
Bat doesn't
hit ball, bat
meets it.
Ball bounces
off bat, flies
air, or thuds
ground (dud)
or it
fits mitt.

Bat waits
for ball
to mate.
Ball hates
to take bat's
bait. Ball
flirts, bat's
late, don't
keep the date.
Ball goes in
(thwack) to mitt,
and goes out
(thwack) back
to mitt.

Ball fits
mitt, but
not all
the time.
Sometimes
ball gets hit
(pow) when bat
meets it,
and sails
to a place
where mitt
has to quit
in disgrace.
That's about
the bases
loaded,
about 40,000
fans exploded.

It's about
the ball,
the bat,
the mitt,
the bases
and the fans.
It's done
on a diamond,
and for fun.
It's about
home, and it's
about run.

Watching the Jets Lose to Buffalo at Shea

The feel of that leather baby
solid against your sternum,
you hug its skull and bottom
between huge huddled shoulders.
It's wrapped in your arms and wedged
under the hard muzzle
of your stuck-out faceguard.

Your thighs pumping, you run
to deliver the baby
to a cradle of grass at the goalposts.
But it's bumped from your arms,
and you're mounted
as if your back were leather.
Your legs cut away, you fold,

you tumble like a treetrunk.
Your brain's for the ground to split
like a leather egg, but it doesn't.
Your helmet takes the concussion.
Sent aloft by a leather toe,
a rugged leather baby
dropped from the sky and slammed

into the sling of your arms.
Oh, the feel of that leather bundle.
Oh, what a blooper and fumbler
you are, that you couldn't nest it,
that you lost and couldn't nurse it,
long enough to lay it
in a cradle of grass at the goalposts.

Choosing Craft

Striped equilateral sails,
the morning placid,
corners tugged trim,
jab for the belly of the wind.
Try to be accurate.
One tall, white isosceles spanks water,
helped by outboard motor,
canvas popping in a made breeze.
Put forth without effort.
Then expect, what neither gust
nor inertia will upset, to upset.
Let the wind pick up.
Tricorn scraps, as for a chance-built
quilt over the cove, scoot free.
How close-hauled, canted, apt to capsize
you keep, must be why you don't.

July 4th

Gradual bud and bloom and seedfall speeded up
are these mute explosions in slow motion.

From vertical shoots above the sea, the fire
flowers open, shedding their petals.

Black waves, turned more than moonwhite, pink
ice, lightning blue, echo our gasps of admiration

as they crash and hush. Another bush ablaze
snicks straight up. A gap like heartstop between

the last vanished particle and the thuggish boom.
And the thuggish boom repeats in stutters

from sandhill hollows in the shore. We want
more. A twirling sun, or dismembered chrysanthemum

bulleted up, leisurely bursts, in an instant
timestreak is suckswooped back to its core.

And we want more: we want red giant, white dwarf,
black hole, extinct, orgasmic, all in one!

On Addy Road

A flicker with a broken neck
we found on the road, brought home, and laid
under a beech tree, liver-red the leaves.

On gaming-table green, in autumn shade,
we spread his yellow-shafted wing;
the spokes slid closed when we let go.

Splendid as the king
of spades, black half-moon under chin,
breast of speckled ermine,

scarlet ribbon at the nape—
how long before his raiment fade,
and gold slats tear within the cape?

We left him on the chilly grass.
Through the equinoctial night
we slept and dreamed

of the wetland meadow where,
one tawny dawn, the red fox crept —
an instant only, then his pelt

merged with the windbent reeds,
not to be seen again.
Next morning, going barefoot to the lawn,

we found the flicker's body gone, and saw
in the dew of the sandy road
faint print of a fox's paw.

Angels at "Unsubdued"

All the angels are here this morning, in the striped light
and shade. Some—ruby-eyed, patterned black and tan and
    white—
are kicking leaves behind them, finding their food.
There are white-throated angels, scarlet-headed angels,
angels of shrill blue. Some bronzed angels are spangling wings
and dabbling iridescent heads in the rain pan.

On cleats down the trunk of a pine descends the downy
    angel. Her tiny
drill dithers faster than a snare drum. Black-capped or tufted,
round-eyed cherubs flick to ground, scrambling for thrown
    seed.
The bent-tailed, the brindled, the small red-breasted
next arrive, jab needle-beaks into the suet. Until a cocky
coal-winged angel with red patches elbows them off.

Neat-fronted in clerical gray, cat angels have quietly landed.
They raise their spread tails, flashing rusty coverts.
Rushing on high legs from under the thornbush, an arrogant
    brown
angel shrieks that he can thrash them all.

Now alights the crimson Pope of angels, masked, with thick
pink nose. He's trailed by two pale female acolytes,
ticking and ruffling crested crowns. Cracking two seeds,
the splendid seraph hops, as if on pogo stick, to each in turn,
to put between accepting beaks the sacrament—they stand
    agape
for this—an act that's like a kiss.

Yellow-throated angels loop to a wag of honeysuckle, waiting
for a gang of raucous purple angels to finish bathing and fly.
Still kicking leaves under the laurel, shy black-headed,
    red-eyed,
rufous-sided angels, in light and shadow, stay half hidden.

The Willets

One stood still, looking stupid. The other,
beak open, streaming a thin sound,
held wings out, took sideways steps,
stamping the salt marsh. It looked threatening.
The other still stood wooden, a decoy.

He stamp-danced closer, his wings arose,
their hinges straightened,
from the wedge-wide beak the thin sound
streaming agony-high—
in fear she wouldn't stand? She stood.

Her back to him pretended—
was it welcome, or only dazed
admission of their fate?
Lifting, he streamed a warning
from his beak and lit

upon her, trod upon her
back, both careful feet.
The wings held off his weight.
His tail pressed down, slipped off. She
animated. And both went back to fishing.

Dr. Henderson

Watching Dr. Henderson, who is about eighty,
take his yearly sunbath on the beach:
He unfolds the cretonne-covered lounge
chair, taking approximately 20 minutes
before getting it facing the sun just right,
getting it as level as possible on the
slightly sloping, gravelly sand above the
low-tide line. He sits, is about to lie
down, then interrupts himself to get
the cushion just right under his head,

and the towel just right on the end where
his feet will rest. He has almost lain down,
when he decides to take his loafers off,
and then his black socks. Having pushed
the socks into the shoes in a thorough way,
and placed the shoes neatly beside each other
on the sand to his left, he finds he's hot,
sweating already. So, fumblingly, but
determinedly, he gets off the lounge and
starts to walk to the water.

His feet crimp on the pebbles. It's a slow
process, but finally he feels the water
between his toes, and he stops. He looks
out over the water, the spread of it,
that ripples fairly calmly toward shore:
there is a little breeze, but nothing
dangerous. In his loose, dark blue boxer
shorts, showing a wide flat ass and a high
round belly, sloping shoulders, flaccid arms,
the hands hanging, his pink (but not bald)
scalp shining along the precisely straight
parting of his wavy leghorn-rooster-white
hair, Dr. Henderson sallies into the water.
Slowly. Slowly, and with many hesitations,
he takes a step—or, rather, a shuffle—
with the left foot, then the right, then
pauses, wrists swinging, thumbs and fingers
rubbing together, while he gazes out upon
the small waves—also carefully gazing down
through them—scanning the bottom, making sure
nothing harmful lurks there.

Inch by inch, up the thin shins and sagging
thighs the water rises, cool, then cold,
then a little colder. He shudders, but
presses on, when the water touches and sets
afloat, within the ballooning shorts, his
wrinkled testicles and shrunken dong.

In about 20 minutes he has taken the dozen, or
so, shuffles resulting in the water reaching
his waist. *Then* he lifts his knees! He's
sitting in the water, entirely wet to his chin!
He floats!

Later, having gamely struggled back to shore,
he eventually settles himself on his back
on the lounge. His white head is placed
exactly in the center of the cushion. His
long feet, pronated on callused yellow heels,
are symmetrically set on the folded towel.
Hands, palms down, by the sides of the dripping
dark blue shorts, the shirred bellyband biting
into his thick middle, above which a thin mat
of kinky gray hair flutters in the hot breeze,
pink, big-nosed face, with eyelids and lips firmly
shut, turned up to the sky, Dr. Henderson,
with long-practiced dignity and deliberation,
begins his yearly sunbath on the beach.

The Beauty of the Head
Shuswap River, Sicamous, B.C.

I

Black bear, pacing the shore, lollops over
a fallen pine. Loon in the swampy inlet lets go
his weird choked cry. Bowl of the lake rocks,
dinghy at the stern champs-stammers. Waves slosh,
my mouth waters, my ear's cochlea fills up,
and empties. I notice how I breathe,
in the cradle of my ribs, to the shift of the lake.
Violet-green swallows slant-fall to a field
of Alpine flowers, where sparse, far-apart blue
wicks, red brushpoints, wink in the moraine.
At night, on the mountain's shoulder pied with
snow, glints the lit hut of a star.

Where we dock this evening, two red-necked
grebe and a loon work their waterlily acre,
dive in turn, and reproject the trumpets
of their necks. Breaking the surface, they break
silence, slip west, silver the last light.
We'll sleep on deck, topside the houseboat,
slap mosquitoes, but first, roast chub
in a flat-stone oven dug on the shore.
These stones, all for skipping, whittled by the lake,
were hot shingles we lay on in sunlight,
drying our hair. Lake is our bathtub, dish-sink,
drinking jug, and (since the boat's head doesn't work,
—the ice box, either—the bilge pump barely)
lake is water closet, too. Little I knew
a gale this night would wash, and then
wind-wipe my rump hung over the rail.

2

Black bear straddles the log he rolled off,
lopes to the lake, wades in a ways, and sips,
lips making a ripple. He lies down like a dog
in the soft silt, then, up with a lurch, he exits.
Bush of the bank closes around his haunches.
Uneasy, I scan the dusky beach. Is he that hole
in the end of a log in the sunset?—that root
of cottonwood stump?—that near shadow
dilating, indenting the bush?
As wind rises, tide rises. Moon swings out—
anchor that can't catch—and wanders half-circle.
We lie in our sacks, clouds and the mountain
traveling, woods and waves exchanging
horizons, dipping, carousing. We mummy-sacks sway
with the deck. Tied up on a long line to a pine,
the bow starts to strain, stomp, scrape
on shore stones. Aft pushed broadside, the boat is about
to be grounded, while with each ram of rising water,
the dinghy knocks, bucks, whines to mount
the stern. No running lights on the *Alice B.*,
and, its battery weak, the flashlight's beam

has no reach. It's our second mooring.
First night in the river's mouth was calm.
Now, water hard as walls shoves starboard,
wants to fling the boat on a shelf
of ripping, skipping rocks—the first, then the second
shelf—the third would set it next the pines
by morning, low tide leave it really a house
on land. And, in the middle of this
bouncing, howling lake-quake, I have to go.
Backing down the deck ladder is one thing,
perching on the teetering rail (away from portside
where Skipper and Mates are bunked) is another,
hanging on and hanging *out*, in the lurch and clamor—
not minding the dunk, but hoping not to fall
overboard, while going—is toughest of all.
I succeed and, backside baptized, feel
a mariner's talent proved.

                        3

Three A.M. By four it will be light.
No one nervous but me, the other three asleep.
Bedded down on the bench in the stern,
keeping watch, kept soaked ritualistically
by wave spray, I check the bilge by the dirty
eye of the lamp. Yes, the lake is leaking
to the deck. But, as if mine had pacified it,
big water eases, groans of boat and dinghy
come gradually to cease.
Meaning greater danger? Half the house has climbed
the beach. Unless got under way with the tide high,
here's where we'll stay. So I wake First Mate
and make such a nag it wakes Skipper.
With dawn, the engine started, anchor up, we untie
and, bup-bup-bup, we're off, open throttle
into the wind, over the smacking lake.
Mosquitoes blow off, sun peeps over the mountain.
Wet, ensacked, exhausted I crimp
in the galley-bunk to sleep.

4

My face a knot
became in sleep.
Anxiety and storm.
Confusion.
Not only was my
ground a waves
but wrestling waves,
deformed that wave.
My thoughts were torn,
my hipbones had no rest,
and I was clenched.
Darkness that strangles,
thrashing noise,
the source unknown.
Threat of being smashed
at bottom of a hole—
the cave of a huge,
insane, conglomerating
wave. And sun whipped
my glued eyelids.

Waked, I stood
at the point of the prow,
looking down into clear
water, like a well,
in still mountain shadow.
Anchor twinkled far below
in a slot between
humped stones,
smooth as glass,
where soft-nosed fish
lay moveless, but
for sideways flicks
of their circular eyes.
Boat rocking gently,
tethered to shore.
Brushing my body,
the early wind,
redolent of pine,
freshened and loosened
my forehead.

5

Tonight we are docked at the top of the lake's
right arm, at a fisherman's inn, awaiting dinner
around a thick oak table. In the window frame,
a crook-treed orchard where a blond horse crops
the flowing grass. A woman, in a wind-torn dress,
brings a full bucket to the buckskin. We play chess
and drink the stinging beer,
while our fish fries in the kitchen.
All secure, on shore for the night, the *Alice B.*,
snugged tight to an iron bust on the pier.
When, squint-eyed from the flashing river,
we climbed into farmyard shade, I spied
the squeaking door of a little privy
of new pine board, among trees beyond
where the blond horse crops. The bright

hook worked like silk. One seat, and no wasps,
it was all mine. An almanac, the pages Bible-thin,
hung by a string through a hole made with an awl.
Outside, steady silence, and in
the slit-moon-window, high up, a fragrant
tassel of pine. Alone, at peace, and journey done,
I sat. Feet planted on dependable planks, I sat.
Engrossed by the beauty of knothole panel before me,
I sat a nice long time.

Above Bear Lake

Sky and lake the same blue,
and blue the languid mountain between them.
Cloud fluffs make the scene flow.
Greenly white poles of aspen snake up,
graven with welts and calluses where branches
dried and broke. Other scabs are lover-made:
initials dug within linked hearts and, higher,
some jackknifed peace signs.
A breeze, and the filtered light makes shine
a million bristling quills of spruce and fir
downslope, where slashes of sky and lake
hang blue—windows of intense stain. We take
the rim trail, crushing bloom of sage,
sniffing resinous wind, our boots in the wild,
small, everycolored Rocky Mountain flowers.
Suddenly, a steep drop-off: below we see the whole,
the whale of it—deep, enormous blue—
that widens, while the sky slants back to pale
behind a watercolored mountain.
Western Tanager—we call him "Fireface"—
darts ahead, we climb to our camp
as the sun slips lower. Clipped to the top
of the tallest fir, Olive-Sided Flycatcher,
over and over, fierce-whistles, "Whip!
Whip three bears! Whip, whip three bears!"

THINGS TAKING PLACE
II

Night Visits with the Family I

SHARON'S DREAM

We were rounding up cattle, riding trees instead of horses.
The way I turned the herd was to let my tree limb grow.
Circling out around an obstinate heifer,
my horse stretched and whipped back, but too slow.

PAUL'S DREAM

Twelve white shirts and I had to iron them.
Some swirled away. They were bundles of cloud.
Hailstones fell and landed as buttons.
I should have picked them up before they melted to mud.

ROY'S DREAM

Down in the cellar a library of fruit:
berries, pears and apricots published long ago.
Two lids of wax covered my eyelids. A tart title
I couldn't read was pasted on my brow.

DAN'S DREAM

In the playhouse Dad made when I was six
I put my captive hawk. The chimney had a lid
that locked. The wallpaper was faded and fouled.
I couldn't wake, and dirty feathers filled my little bed.

GRACE'S DREAM

Hindleg in the surf, my grand piano, groaning,
crawled ashore. I saw that most of the black keys
had been extracted, their roots were bleeding. It tried
to embrace me while falling forward on three knees.

MARGARET'S DREAM

There was an earthquake and Jordan's boot got caught
in a crack in the street. His bike had fallen through
and went on pedaling underneath, came up the basement
stairs to warn me what had happened. That's how I knew.

BETTY'S DREAM

Aunt Etta was wearing a wig, of wilver. It's perfection
made you see how slack her chins were. Under the hair
in front was a new eye, hazel and laughing. It winked.
"You, too, will be seventy-two," she said. It gave me a scare.

GEORGE'S DREAM

Old Glory rippling on a staff. No, it was a maypole,
and the ribbons turned to rainbows. I saw a cat
climbing the iridescent bow. Then I was sliding down
a banister. My uniform split in the crotch, I was so fat.

CORWIN'S DREAM

With my new camera I was taking a picture of my old
camera. The new one was guaranteed; it was the kind
that issues instant color prints. What came out
was an X-ray of the tunnel in the roller of a window blind.

RUTH'S DREAM

Standing under the shower I was surprised
to see I wasn't naked. The streams had dressed
me in a gown of seed pearls, and gloves that my nails
poked through like needles. They pricked if I touched my
    breast.

STEVE'S DREAM

Two tiny harmonicas. I kept them in my mouth,
and sucked them. That made twin secret tunes.
Mother said, "What is it you are always humming?"
I told her they were only stones of prunes.

DIANE'S DREAM

Grandmother wasn't dead. Only her ring finger.
Before we buried it, we must remove the ruby.
And the finger was jackknifed. I offered to unclench it,
but couldn't do it. I was too much of a booby.

MAY'S DREAM

Cowpuncher on a tree-horse wears
a cloud-shirt with hailstone buttons.

He rides and, through wax eyelids, reads
a library of fruit. He passes a hawk
locked in a playhouse, a grand piano
with three broken knees. Nothing he can do
about any of these. When old, an Auntie
in a wilver wig, he goes. He's almost too fat
to slide down the rainbow's banister that
ends in a gray X-ray of a tunnel in the blind.
There he wears a water dress, tastes secret tunes.
Until I wake he cannot die. Until I wake,
the ruby lives on the dead finger.

Nature

A large gut, this was the vision.
Mother in hospital, I slept in her bed.
Inside a stomach great as the planet . . .

quagmire ground in gray movement . . .
mucous membrane, rugous, reached my foot
. . . sucked one leg to the crotch . . .

Squirming, sweating, I pulled loose this time.
But it surrounds,
shudders, munches, sucks us down, so

gradually we seldom know.
Until the last sink, where mouth says,
"Here's a Mouth!" Is Nature

this planet only? Or all the universe?
What should we think? Birth
of an infant . . . a film I saw the other day:

Mother-belly, round as the planet,
her navel the North Pole . . .
palpated by rubber fingers . . . Face down,

the wet head, twisting free
of a vomiting Mouth, its mouth
tasting anus as, forced forth, it howled . . .

Muck sealed the squeezed eyes . . .
Mother, eighty-one, fasted five days
and went to Temple. Mormon, her creed

eternal life, she fell
on the kitchen floor unconscious.
The plane flew

over snow-breasts of mountains
no man's track has touched.
June, and blue lilacs in every yard . . .

One bud-nippled bloom I took to her hospital bed.
Her mouth woke to its dew. This time
it woke . . . Last night I slept in her bed.

That the Soul May Wax Plump

*"He who has reached the highest degree of
emptiness will be secure in repose."*
—A Taoist Saying

My dumpy little mother on the undertaker's slab
had a mannequin's grace. From chin to foot
the sheet outlined her, thin and tall. Her face
uptilted, bloodless, smooth, had a long smile.
Her head rested on a block under her nape,
her neck was long, her hair waved, upswept. But later,
at "the viewing," sunk in the casket in pink tulle,
an expensive present that might spoil, dressed
in Eden's green apron, organdy bonnet on,
she shrank, grew short again, and yellow. Who
put the gold-rimmed glasses on her shut face, who
laid her left hand with the wedding ring on
her stomach that really didn't seem to be there
under the fake lace?

Mother's work before she died was self-purification,
a regimen of near starvation, to be worthy to go
to Our Father, Whom she confused (or, more aptly, fused)
with our father, in Heaven long since. She believed
in evacuation, an often and fierce purgation,
meant to teach the body to be hollow, that the soul
may wax plump. At the moment of her death, the wind
rushed out from all her pipes at once. Throat and rectum
sang together, a galvanic spasm, hiss of ecstasy.
Then, a flat collapse. Legs and arms flung wide,
like that female Spanish saint slung by the ankles
to a cross, her mouth stayed open in a dark O. So,
her vigorous soul whizzed free. On the undertaker's slab, she
lay youthful, cool, triumphant, with a long smile.

Birthday

What am I doing here?
What are the waves doing running?—
the grass doing growing?
What is the worm doing
making its hole?—
the sun glowing?—the stone
sitting unmoving. Remove
the stone: A shadow is missing.

The moon is making its circle.
A moth is emerging.
A mountain is shifting. A forest
is burning. A snake
is leaving its skin. A fig tree
is bearing. What am I doing here—
the waves running and hissing?

Dawn is doing its breaking.
The grass is growing.
A buttercup fills with light.
What am I doing? What am I making?

What is the stone doing? Making
its shadow. The worm
is making its hole.

Running on the Shore

The sun is hot, the ocean cool. The waves
throw down their snowy heads. I run
under their hiss and boom, mine their wild
breath. Running the ledge where pipers
prod their awls into sand-crab holes,
my barefoot tracks their little prints cross
on wet slate. Circles of romping water swipe
and drag away our evidence. Running and
gone, running and gone, the casts of our feet.

My twin, my sprinting shadow on yellow shag,
wand of summer over my head, it seems
that we could run forever while the strong
waves crash. But sun takes its belly under.
Flashing above magnetic peaks of the ocean's
purple heave, the gannet climbs,
and turning, turns
to a black sword that drops,
hilt-down, to the deep.

Scroppo's Dog

In the early morning, past the shut houses,
past the harbor shut in fog, I walk free and
single. It is summer—that's lucky. The whole
day is mine. At the end of our village I stop
to greet Scroppo's dog, whose chain is wrapped
around a large dusty boulder. His black coat
is gray, from crouching every day in the gravel
of Scroppo's yard—a yard by a scrap-filled pond,

where Scroppo deals in wrecked cars and car parts.
I guess he gets them from crashes on the expressway,
or from abandoned junks he loots by the roadside.

I don't know the name of Scroppo's dog. I remember
him, years ago, as a big fierce-looking pup.
It may have been his first day chained there,
or shortly after, that he first greeted me:
his eyes big nuggets shooting orange sparks, his
red tongue rippling out between clean fangs—
fangs as white as lilies of the valley that bloom
in a leafy border by Scroppo's weathered porch.
It was late May, as now, when with sudden joyful
bark, black fur erect and gleaming, the dog
rushed toward me—but was stopped by his chain,
a chain then bright and new. I would have met
and stroked him, but didn't dare get near him,
in his strangled frenzy—in his unbelief—
that something at his throat cut short
his coming, going, leaping, circling, running—
something he couldn't bite through, tripped him:
he could go only so far: to the trash in the weeds
at the end of the driveway, to the edge
of the oily, broken cement in back, where Scroppo's
muddy flatbed truck stands at night.

Now, as I walk toward him, the dog growls,
then cowers back. He is old and fat and dirty,
and his eyes spit equal hate and fear.
He knows exactly how far he can strain
from the rock and the wrapped chain. There's
a trench in a circle in the oily dirt his paws
have dug. Days and weeks and months and years
of summer heat and winter cold have been survived
within the radius of that chain.
Scroppo's dog knows me, and wants to come and
touch. At the same time, his duty to expel
the intruder makes him bare his teeth and
bristle. He pounds his matted tail, he snarls
while cringing, alternately stretches toward me,

and springs back. His bark, husky and cracked,
follows me for a block, until I turn the corner,
crossing the boundary of the cove.

I've never touched Scroppo's dog, and his
yearning tongue has never licked me. Yet, we
know each other well. Subject to the seasons'
extremes, confined to the limits of our yard,
early fettered by an obscure master in whose
power we bask, bones grow frail while steel
thickens; while rock fattens, passions and
senses pale. Scroppo's dog sniffs dust.
He sleeps a lot. My nose grown blunt, I need
to remember the salty damp of the air's taste
on summer mornings, first snowfall's freshness,
the smoke of burning leaves. Each midday,
when the firehouse whistle blows, a duet
of keen, weird howls is heard, as, at the steep
edge of hopelessness, with muzzle pointed,
ears flat, eyes shut, Scroppo's dog forlornly
yodels in time to the village siren sounding noon.

Red Moonset

Spinnaker
of a tipping ship
the moon low
large. Watermelon
wedge. A clot
of midnight
cloud sucks
sinks it. Bitten
about out. But
one more ripe
inflation. Chinks
in a chunk
of fire.

September Things

Brutal sound of acorns
falling. Chokecherry-ink
beads have dried. On tile

bare feet still feel
stored warmth, eyes graze
a field of blue

water. A few languid
boats like flecks
of paint far out,

the lanyards tinkling.
Snag-nailed surf reaches,
drags back, over echoing

pebbles. A lateborn
cardinal ticks and
whistles—too pale

and thin. Too vivid,
the last pink
petunia's indrawn mouth.

October

1

A smudge for the horizon
that, on a clear day, shows
the hard edge of hills and
buildings on the other coast.
Anchored boats all head one way:
north, where the wind comes from.
You can see the storm inflating
out of the west. A dark hole
in gray cloud twirls, widens,
while white rips multiply
on the water far out.
Wet tousled yellow leaves,
thick on the slate terrace.
The jay's hoarse cry. He's
stumbling in the air,
too soaked to fly.

2

Knuckles of the rain
on the roof,
chuckles into the drain-
pipe, spatters on
the leaves that litter
the grass. Melancholy
morning, the tide full
in the bay, an overflowing
bowl. At least, no wind,
no roughness in the sky,
its gray face bedraggled
by its tears.

3

Peeling a pear, I remember
my daddy's hand. His thumb
(the one that got nipped by the saw,
lacked a nail) fit into

the cored hollow of the slippery
half his knife skinned so neatly.
Dad would pare the fruit from our
orchard in the fall, while Mother
boiled the jars, prepared for
"putting up." Dad used to darn
our socks when we were small,
and cut our hair and toenails.
Sunday mornings, in pajamas, we'd
take turns in his lap. He'd help
bathe us sometimes. Dad could do
anything. He built our dining table,
chairs, the buffet, the bay window
seat, my little desk of cherry wood
where I wrote my first poems. That
day at the shop, splitting panel
boards on the electric saw (oh, I
can hear the screech of it now,
the whirling blade that sliced
my daddy's thumb) he received the mar
that, long after, in his coffin,
distinguished his skilled hand.

4

I sit with braided fingers
and closed eyes
in a span of late sunlight.
The spokes are closing.
It is fall: warm milk of light,
although from autumn's aging breast.
I do not mean to pray.
The posture for thanks or
supplication is the same
as for weariness or relief.
But I am glad for the luck
of light. Surely it is godly,
that it makes all things
begin, and appear, and become
actual to each other.
Light that's sucked into

the eye, warming the brain
with wires of color.
Light that hatched life
out of the cold egg of earth.

5

Dark wild honey, the lion's
eye color, you brought home
from a country store.
Tastes of the work of shaggy
bees on strong weeds,
their midsummer bloom.
My brain's electric circuit
glows, like the lion's iris
that, concentrated, vibrates
while seeming not to move.
Thick transparent amber
you brought home,
the sweet that burns.

6

"The very hairs of your head
are numbered," said the words
in my head, as the haircutter
snipped and cut, my round head
a newel poked out of the tent
top's slippery sheet, while my
hairs' straight rays rained
down, making pattern on the neat
vacant cosmos of my lap. And
maybe it was those tiny flies,
phantoms of my aging eyes, seen
out of the sides floating (that,
when you turn to find them
full face, always dissolve) but
I saw, I think, minuscule,
marked in clearest ink, Hairs
#9001 and #9002 fall, the cut-off
ends streaking little comets,

till they tumbled to confuse
with all the others in their
fizzled heaps, in canyons of my
lap. And what keeps asking
in my head now that, brushed off
and finished, I'm walking
in the street, is how can those
numbers remain all the way through,
and all along the length of every
hair, and even before each one
is grown, apparently, through
my scalp? For, if the hairs of my
head are numbered, it means
no more and no less of them
have ever, or will ever be.
In my head, now cool and light,
thoughts, phantom white flies,
take a fling: This discovery
can apply to everything.

7

Now and then, a red leaf riding
the slow flow of gray water.
From the bridge, see far into
the woods, now that limbs are bare,
ground thick-littered. See,
along the scarcely gliding stream,
the blanched, diminished, ragged
swamp and woods the sun still
spills into. Stand still, stare
hard into bramble and tangle,
past leaning broken trunks,
sprawled roots exposed. Will
something move?—some vision
come to outline? Yes, there—
deep in—a dark bird hangs
in the thicket, stretches a wing.
Reversing his perch, he says one
"Chuck." His shoulder-patch
that should be red looks gray.

This old redwing has decided to
stay, this year, not join the
strenuous migration. Better here,
in the familiar, to fade.

On Its Way

Orange on its way to ash.
Anger that a night will quench.
Passion in its honey swell
pumpkin-plump before the rot.
Bush of fire everywhere.
Fur of hillside running flame.
Rush of heat to rosehip cheek.
Ripeness on its way to frost.
Glare of blood before the black.
Foxquick pulse. The sun a den.
Heartkill. And the gold a gun.
It is death that taints the leaves.

November Night

Sky's face so old,
one eyeball loose,

fallen to the side,
the walleyed moon,

among the mouse-gray
waves, it squints

of mercury roll.
An aging face slips

its symmetry; lip
lags, lid droops.

Behind the horizon
the slide begins,

of a blind,
thick-furred tide:

rat-swells rip
and top each other,

gulp each other,
bloat, and scoot

pale vomit out
on a moonless shore.

This Morning

My glasses are
dirty. The window
is dirty. The binocs
don't focus exactly.
Outside it's about
to snow. Not to mention
my myopia, my migraine
this morning, mist on
the mirror, my age.
Oh, there is the cardinal,
color of apple I used to
eat off my daddy's tree.
Tangy and cocky, he
drops to find
a sunflower seed in
the snow. New snow
is falling on top
of the dirty snow.

View to the North

As you grow older, it gets colder.
You see through things.
I'm looking through the trees,

their torn and thinning leaves,
to where chill blue water
is roughened by wind.

Day by day the scene opens,
enlarges, rips of space
appear where full branches

used to snug the view.
Soon it will be wide, stripped,
entirely unobstructed:

I'll see right through
the twining waves, to
the white horizon, to the place

where the North begins.
Magnificent! I'll be thinking
while my eyeballs freeze.

The Thickening Mat

My track the first
on new snow:
each step, with soft
snap, pressed
a padded button
into a thickening
mat—snug sensation,
satisfying pattern—
to the corner,
where I turned and

met the wind:
whips to my eyes
and mouth. This way
all I breathe
is snow. Marks
of my feet, unique,
black-edged under
the streetlight—
where are they?
All blank, all white.

Cold Colors

Sweetpea
pinks
in the winter.
Sun sets
through thin
windy
branches
dark
like snarled string
over water's hard
stretched white scratched
skin.
On sky's
clear royal icy
cheek blush
tints
of spring.

Captain Holm

I see Captain Holm
in yellow slicker,
right hand behind him
on the stick of the tiller,
feet in the well
of his orange Sailfish:
like a butterfly's
single wing, it slants
upright over the bay.
Captain Holm, our neighbor,
eighty years old,
thin and sclerotic,
can still fold
legs into the hull,
balance a bony buttock
on the shelf of the stern.
With a tug at the mainstay
he makes his sail trim up,
sniffs out whatever wind there is.
This raw day,
Captain Holm's alone,
his scrap of color
the only one
on the wide bay.
Winter sunset transfuses
that frail wing.

Digging in the Garden of Age I Uncover a Live Root
(For E. W.)

The smell of wet geraniuims. On furry
leaves, transparent drops rounded
as cats' eyes seen sideways.
Smell of the dark earth, and damp
brick of the pots you held, tamped empty.
Flash of the new trowel. Your eyes
green in greenhouse light. Smell of
your cotton smock, of your neck
in the freckled shade of your hair.
A gleam of sweat in your lip's scoop.
Pungent geranium leaves, their wet
smell when our widening pupils met.

Today

Beneath the tongue a stem of mercury rises.
A needle flicks in orbit on the ticking wrist.
At 6 A.M. an earthquake in Los Angeles.
The finger dials. Dainty electronic dots
imprint a distant micromandala on the mind.
Sunny and 90 there, everything shaking. Here,
on Long Island, calmly snowing at 9. Inside its
wrap, our planet swirls, one minute makes 60
separate leaps, graphs decode the finite waves,
tally the roots of grass. Outside the amnion,
what time is it?—what heat, what equilibrium,
what weight? Three human probes from moon
drop home today. In a frame of constant
jerky light, a trinket of metal, friction-scorched,
is scooped from sea. Technical inputs for this
report: Key touch total = 762. Temperature =
99.1 F. Sound-wave length = 3000 miles.

Survey of the Whole

World's lopsided
                        That's its trouble
         Don't run in a circle
                        Runs in a loop
         Too much winter
                        In the wrong place
         Too much summer
                        Around the sun
            World's gimpy
                        Been turning so long
            It's lumpy
                        A bad top
      Day's not long enough
                        Spins on a nail
         Night's too long
                        Bent out of kilter
         World's a lemon
                        Wobbles in a loop
         Around the sun
                        It's not an orange
      Won't ever be sweet
                        Turns too fast
         Turns too slow
                        Can't ripen
      Too much desert
                        Too much snow

The Solar Corona*

Looks like a large
pizza with too much
tomato sauce (the fiery

islands in the melted
cheese, the jagged rim,
red bulge of crust)

*Cover picture on the *Scientific American*, October 1973

served on a square
black tray, a "spectro
heliographic diagram

of the sun in the extreme
ultraviolet region of
the spectrum." This

pizza is 400 times
larger than the moon.
Don't burn your lips!—

the deep red regions
are coolest, the white
(ricotta) hottest.

First Walk on the Moon

Ahead, the sun's face in a flaring hood,
was wearing the moon, a mask of shadow
that stood between. Cloudy earth
waned, gibbous, while our target grew:
an occult bloom, until it lay beneath
the fabricated insect we flew. Pitched
out of orbit we yawed in, to impact
softly on that circle.

               Not "ground"
the footpads found for traction.
So far, we haven't the name.
So call it "terrain," pitted and pocked
to the round horizon (which looked
too near): a slope of rubble where
protuberant cones, dish-shaped hollows,
great sockets glared, half blind
with shadow, and smaller sucked-in folds
squinted, like blowholes on a scape
of whales.

Rigid and pneumatic, we
emerged, white twin uniforms on the dark
"mare," our heads transparent spheres,
the outer visors gold. The light was
glacier bright, our shadows long,
thin fissures, of "ink." We felt neither
hot nor cold.

Our boot cleats sank
into "grit, something like glass,"
but sticky. Our tracks remain
on what was virgin "soil." But that's
not the name.

There was no air there,
no motion, no sound outside our heads.
We brought what we breathed
on our backs: the square papooses we
carried were our life sacks. We spoke
in numbers, fed the rat-a-tat-tat of data
to amplified earth. We saw no spoor
that any had stepped before us. Not
a thing has been born here, and nothing
has died, we thought.

We had practiced
to walk, but we toddled (with caution,
lest ambition make us fall
to our knees on that alien "floor").
We touched nothing with bare hands.
Our gauntlets lugged the cases of gear,
deployed our probes and emblems,
set them prudently near the insect liftoff
station, with its flimsy ladder to home.

All day it was night, the sky black
vacuum, though the strobe of the low sun
smote ferocious on that "loam."
We could not stoop, but scooped up
"clods" of the clinging "dust," that flowed

and glinted black, like "graphite."
So, floating while trotting, hoping not
to stub our toe, we chose and catalogued
unearthly "rocks." These we stowed.

And all night it was day, you could say,
with cloud-cuddled earth in the zenith,
a ghost moon that swiveled. The stars
were all displaced, or else were not
the ones we knew. Maneuvering by numbers
copied from head to head, we surveyed
our vacant outpost. Was it a "petrified
sea bed," inert "volcanic desert," or
crust over quivering "magma," that might
quake?

       It was possible to stand there.
And we planted a cloth "flower":
our country colors we rigged to blow
in the non-wind. We could not lift
our arms eye-high (they might deflate)
but our camera was a pistol, the trigger
built into the grip, and we took each
other's pictures, shooting from the hip.
Then bounced and loped euphoric,
enjoying our small weight.

                Our flash
eclipsed the sun at takeoff. We left our
insect belly "grounded," and levitated,
standing in its head. The dark dents
of our boots, unable to erode, mark how
we came: two white mechanic knights,
the first, to make tracks in some kind
of "sand." The footpads found it solid, so
we "landed." But that's not the right name.

Note: The men of Apollo 11, arriving in their landing module, *Eagle*, were the first to put tracks on the moon, 1969.

"So Long" to the Moon
from the Men of Apollo

A nipple, our parachute
covers the capsule: an
aureole, on a darker aureole

like the convex spiral of
a mollusk, on a great breast:
the skin removed: agitated

glandular pattern revealed:
the SPLASH, seen from above,
from the helicopter:

Apollo 17 comes home
to the Pacific: the moon
strewn with our trash:

module platforms, crashed LMs,
metal flags and plaques, dead
sensor devices like inside-out

umbrellas, a golf ball. A small
steel alloy astronaut doll
bites the black dust.

The Pure Suit of Happiness

The pure suit of happiness,
not yet invented. How I long
to climb into its legs,

fit into its sleeves, and zip
it up, pull the hood
over my head. It's got

a face mask, too, and gloves
and boots attached. It's
made for me. It's blue. It's

not too heavy, not too
light. It's my right.
It has its own weather,

which is youth's breeze,
equilibrated by the ideal
thermostat of maturity,

and built in, to begin with,
fluoroscopic goggles of
age. I'd see through

everything, yet be happy.
I'd be suited for life. I'd
always look good to myself.

Teleology

The eyes look front in humans.
Horse or dog could not shoot,

seeing two sides to everything.
Fish, who never shut their eyes,

can swim on their sides, and see
two worlds: blunt dark below;

above, the daggering light.
Round as a burr, the eye

its whole head, the housefly
sees in a whizzing circle.

Human double-barreled eyes,
in their narrow blind trained

forward, hope to shoot and hit
—if they can find it—

the backward-speeding hole
in the Cyclops face of the future.

Teeth

Teeth are so touchy. They're part of your skeleton.
Laid out on the dentist's couch, you're being strummed.
Still vibrant. For how long? You're shown an X-ray

of the future: how the lower jaw has wandered away
into a neighbor's lot. The fillings glitter,
but it's glowworm's work by now.

A skull white as enamel,
the fontanelle's fine stitchery can be admired.
Does it remember being covered

with scraggly hair, like a coconut?
Bald as a baby, and with one wide bucktooth left,
you have the upturned grin of a carefree clown.

So you drool and spit out. That's only
temporary. There'll be just one big cavity soon.
You'll be dry—yes, dry as a bone.

Deaths

One will die	in a low little house in the snow.
One will die	on the mountain.
One will die	at a table. Red will spread on the white cloth.
One will die	on a trolley, will fall from the platform, rounding a curve. Soon after, the trolley will die.
One will die	in the bathtub. Slippery, heavy to remove. . . . Not die from cut veins or flooded lungs. From embolism at the end of the birthday party. The angel cake will hold 61 candles. . . . How do I know the number of the candles?
One will die	in a celebrated bed, where his grandfather died, where his father died, where his son will die.
One will die	in her wheelchair. She has lived there 50 years.
One will die	on a porch, on a summer day.
One will die	on the stairs of the same house, the same day, and robbers, with their gags and knives, will get clean away.
One will die	not knowing she dies, for three years suckled by machine, emptied by machine, made to tick and breathe by machine. Without moving, without speaking, she will grant 1000 interviews.
One will die	in the death of a plane, one in the death of a ship, another under a stumbling horse that breaks its neck.
One will die	in the hall outside his locked door, having forgotten the key inside.
One will die	made to die by one enraged, who will beg to die "like a man" by bullet instead of the hell of a lifetime in a cell. He will die a lifetime in a cell.
One will die	while driving a hearse. The coffin, spilled on the highway, will detour the traffic in which a cab containing one about to give birth will die.
One will die	about to be born.
One will die	in hospital, having gone to visit his friend, who, in eternal pain, has prayed to die, and envies that unexpected end. He, too, will die.
All will die	in the end.

The Wonderful Pen

I invented a wonderful pen. Not a typewriter . . . I wanted to use
just one hand, the right. With my hand always bent, the ink tube
a vein in my wrist, fixed between finger and thumb the pen wrote
as fast as I could feel. It chose all the right words for my feelings.
But then, my feelings ran out through the pen. It went dry. I had
a book of wonderful feelings, but my right hand was paralyzed.
I threw away the pen.

I invented a dream camera: a box, with a visor or mask . . . like a
stereopticon. When I awoke, I could view, and review, my dreams,
entire, in their depth. Events, visions, symbols, colors without
names, dazzled, obsessed me. They scalded my sight. I threw
away the camera. I had a moving picture of my wonderful dreams,
but I was blind.

So, with my left hand I wrote. I had been lazy so long . . .
The letters went backwards across the page. Sometimes they went
upside down: a "q" for a "b," a "d" for a "p," or an "n" for a "u,"
an "m" for a "w." And it got worse. Now, since I can't read, or
see, not even the mirror can tell me, what I mean by the first
line by the time I've written the last line. But my feelings
are back, and my dreams . . .

What I write is so hard to write. It must be hard to read.
So slow . . . So swift my mind, so stupid my pen. I think I'll invent
a typewriter . . . For the left hand, and no eyes. No! I throw
away the thought. But I have a wonderful mind: Inventive. It is
for you to find. Read *me*. Read my mind.

Ending

Maybe there *is* a Me inside of me
and, when I lie dying, he
will crawl out. Through my toe.
Green on the green rug, and then
white on the wall, and then
over the windowsill, up the trunk
of the apple tree, he
will turn brown and rough and warty
to match the bark. But you'll be

able to see—(*who* will be
able to see?) his little jelly
belly pulsing with the heart inside
his transparent hide.
And, once on the top bough,
tail clinging, as well as "hands,"
he'll turn the purest blue
against the sky—
(say it's a clear day, and I don't die
at night). Maybe from there
he'll take wing—That's it!—
an ARCHAEOPTERYX! Endless,
the possibilities, my little Soul,
once you exit from my toe.
But, oh,
looking it up, I read:
"Archaeopteryx, generally considered
the first bird . . . [although]
closely related to certain small
dinosaurs . . . could not fly."
A pain . . . Oh, I
feel a pain in my toe!

Dream After Nanook

Lived savage and simple, where teeth were tools.

Killed the caught fish, cracked his back in my jaws.
Harpooned the heavy seal, ate his steaming liver raw.
Wore walrus skin for boots and trousers. Made knives
    of tusks. Carved the cow-seal out of her hide
    with the horn of her husband.

Lived with huskies, thick-furred as they.
Snarled with them over the same meat.
Paddled a kayak of skin, scooted sitting over the water.
Drove a skein of dogs over wide flats of snow.
Tore through the tearing wind with my whip.

Built a hive of snow-cubes cut from the white ground.
Set a square of ice for window in the top.
Slid belly-down through the humped doorhole.
Slept naked in skins by the oily thighs
     of wife and pup-curled children.

Rose when the ice-block lightened, tugged the chewed boots
     on.

Lived in a world of fur—fur ground—jags of ivory.
Lived blizzard-surrounded as a husky's ruff.
Left game-traps under the glass teeth of ice.
Snared slick fish. Tasted their icy blood.
Made a sled with runners of leather.

Made a hat from the armpit of a bear.

IN OTHER WORDS
(1987)

To Rozanne Knudson

ONE

In Florida

Certain nasturtiums of that color, the gecko's neck
of urgent orange, a bubble he inflates until transparent,
then flattens, lets collapse. His intermittent goiter
swells, withdraws, pulls tight, and orange pimples
prick along his length. He's humping up and down,
announcing for a mate. She's not in sight.
Somnolent, gray as a dead twig he's been until today, stuck
on a plank of the porch. Or pale, hanging from splayed
toes on the hot stucco wall. Startling, his fat cravat
that bloats and shrinks, his belly of suede sheen, apricot.

Florida screams with colors, soft blooms, sharp juices, fruits.
Day-Glo insects jitter across the eye. A zebra butterfly
in strong sun trails an aura silver and black, like migraine.
Orchid, called Bull Hoof, flares by the fence, and Divi-Divi's
curled pods, feathery foliage effervesces out of a hollow.
Ylang-Ylang, the perfume tree, spreads cadmium-scented
    plumes.
Hydrangea, Mimosa, Guava, Loquat, Spanish Lime, Poinciana
to follow. Extravagant blushes of bushes, blossom-dressed
trees are a crowd in the yard. Slim palm trunks arch up and
curve like tall sway-necked flamingos.

Fruit of the Queen Palm peeled to the pit discloses miniature
monkey faces. Graceful, straight, the smooth pole of the Date
nests its fruit in clusters of ten thousand flowerets. This
the palm of which Mohammed said to the Arabs, "Honor her,
for she is your Mother." And Pawpaw and Possumwood grow
near Mango's cerise hairy flowers formed at each branch tip.
Giant leaves of the leaning Plantain, whose slatted canopies
make shade for the stiff bunched fruit called "fingers,"
each bunch finally to expand to a whole plump hand.

Two nights ago, under the porch that pokes a little way into
this tame jungle, six kittens slid out of the white cat, Polar.
Scarcely larger than mice, they're fixed to her teats,
where she lies spread for them like an odalisque. Five are
white as she, except for variant sooty noses, ears or tails.

The sixth, runt of the litter, the only male and pitch black,
has been nudged aside. He sucks on a sibling's ear mistaken
for a spigot. To behold the tableau, get on your knees,
put an eye to the widest crack between boards, where Polar
in the half-dark with her brood patiently endures.

A moment more, and she shakes herself loose from her blind
wriggling kits, crawls out from under to stand and stretch,
gardenia-white in dawn light on the porch, expecting
breakfast. Not far from a kitten herself, with her asking
purr, pink nose and slit green eyes, she crouches, laps her
milk, tugged teats hanging, heavy berries, in her belly's fur.

Waterbird

Part otter, part snake, part bird the bird Anhinga,
jalousie wings, draped open, dry. When slack-
hinged, the wind flips them shut. Her cry,
a slatted clatter, inflates her chin-
pouch; it's like a fish's swim-
bladder. Anhinga's body, otter-
furry, floats, under water-
mosses, neck a snake with white-
rimmed blue round roving eyes. Those long feet stilt-
paddle the only bird of the marsh that flies
submerged. Otter-
quick over bream that hover in water-
shade, she feeds, finds fillets among the water-
weeds. Her beak, ferrule of a folded black
umbrella, with neat thrust impales her prey.
She flaps up to dry on the crooked, look-
dead-limb of the Gumbo Limbo, her tan-
tipped wing fans spread, tail a shut fan dangled.

Three White Vases

A Sunday in June.
The water's clear
cornflower blue,
the sky its mirror.

Distinctly clear
the opposite coast,
its chalky sands
and miniature pavilions.

A flock of yachts,
midwater, distant,
spins. Near shore,
under my eye,

the waves are dark
blue, mussel-dyed,
where kids on a raft
teeter, splash, and

dive. Slippery bodies
climb up into sun
on the hot white planks.
Agile little hips

all wear different-
colored stripes.
As do the dinky
Sunfish setting out

tippily until,
taken in charge
by tiller and rein,
the spunky scraps

of sails snap tight
and slant on the wind.
A speedboat scampers
arcs of white spray,

a white pontoon plane
putt-putts, puts down
into choppy furrows
of the bay.

Uniquely bright,
the light today
reveals the scene
as through a pane

that's squeegee-clean.
White as the white
catamarans bobbing,
gulls on black-tipped

wings skid over.
My eye follows
to where they land.
On a lonely, reedy patch

of sand I see three
white vases stand,
each differently shaped:
one upright neck,

one hunched, the third
with neck downcurved.
Each fixed eye, intent,
watches what flinches

just under waveskin:
big school of tiny
glinting baitfish
spread on the bay.

The parents, that pair
of snowies, had a nest
in the eelgrass
all spring. The third

bird, the whitest,
is their child,
like a bud vase
that long neck.

I see him
unhinge his slim
bill, wilt his neck.
I see the white

snaky throat
of the young egret
capably squirm
a blade-thin fish down.

Strawberrying

My hands are murder-red. Many a plump head
drops on the heap in the basket. Or, ripe
to bursting, they might be hearts, matching
the blackbird's wing-fleck. Gripped to a reed
he shrieks his ko-ka-ree in the next field.
He's left his peck in some juicy cheeks, when
at first blush and mostly white, they showed
streaks of sweetness to the marauder.

We're picking near the shore, the morning
sunny, a slight wind moving rough-veined leaves
our hands rumple among. Fingers find by feel
the ready fruit in clusters. Here and there,
their squishy wounds. . . . Flesh was perfect
yesterday. . . . June was for gorging. . . .
sweet hearts young and firm before decay.

"Take only the biggest, and not too ripe,"
a mother calls to her girl and boy, barefoot
in the furrows. "Don't step on any. Don't
change rows. Don't eat too many." Mesmerized
by the largesse, the children squat and pull
and pick handfuls of rich scarlets, half
for the baskets, half for avid mouths.
Soon, whole faces are stained.

A crop this thick begs for plunder. Ripeness
wants to be ravished, as udders of cows when hard,
the blue-veined bags distended, ache to be stripped.
Hunkered in mud between the rows, sun burning
the backs of our necks, we grope for, and rip loose
soft nippled heads. If they bleed—too soft—
let them stay. Let them rot in the heat.

When, hidden away in a damp hollow under moldy
leaves, I come upon a clump of heart-shapes
once red, now spiderspit-gray, intact but empty,
still attached to their dead stems—
families smothered as at Pompeii—I rise
and stretch. I eat one more big ripe lopped
head. Red-handed, I leave the field.

Blood Test

Alien, the male, and black. Big like a bear.
Wearing whitest clothes, of ironed cotton scalded clean.

I sat in a chair. He placed my arm on a narrow
tray-table bound in towel. As if to gut a fish.

"Mine the tiniest veins in the world," I warned.
He didn't care. "Let's see what we have," he said.

Tourniquet tied, he tapped his finger-ends inside
my elbow, smartly slapped until the thready vein fattened.

Didn't hurt. He was expert. Black chamois wrist and hand,
short square-cut nails, their halfmoons dusky onyx.

I made a fist. He slid the needle, eye-end in, first try,
then jumped the royal color into the tube.

Silence. We heard each other breathe. Big paw
took a tuft of cotton, pressed where the needle withdrew.

"That's it!" Broad teeth flashed. Eyes under bushy
mansard hair admired, I thought, that I hadn't flinched.

I got up. Done so quick, and with one wounding. I'd as soon
have stayed. To be a baby, a bearcub maybe, in his arms.

Birthday Bush

Our bush bloomed, soon dropped
its fuchsia chalices. Rags
on the ground that were luscious
cups and trumpets, promises and brags.

A sprinkle of dark dots showed entry
into each silk cone. Down among
crisp pistils thirsty bumblebees
probed. Buds flared in a bunch

from tender stems. Sudden
vivid big bouquets
appeared just before our birthdays!
A galaxy our burning bush,

blissful explosion. Brief
effusion. Brief as these
words. I sweep away a trash
of crimson petals.

Under the Baby Blanket

Under the baby blanket 47 years old you are
asleep on the worn too-short Leatherette sofa.

Along with a watermelon and some peaches from
the beach cottage, you brought home this gift

from your Mom. "Just throw it in the van," you
said you said, "I haven't time to talk about it."

She had wanted to tell how she handstitched and
appliquéd the panels—a dozen of them—waiting

for you to be born: 12 identical sunbonneted
little girls, one in each square, in different

colors of dresses doing six different things.
And every tiny stitch put in with needle and

thimble. "It had to take months, looks like,"
I said. "Well, Mom's Relief Society ladies

must have helped," you said. One little girl
is sweeping, one raking, another watering a plant

in a pot, one dangling a doll dressed exactly
like herself. One is opening a blue umbrella.

At center is a little girl holding a book, with
your initial on the cover! I was astonished:

"A Matriarchal Blessing, predicting your future!"
(But, wait a minute, I thought. How did she know

you wouldn't be a boy? Was she also sewing
another blanket, with little boys in its squares:

holding hammer, riding tricycle, playing with
dog, batting ball, sailing boat, and so on?)

I asked for the baby blanket—which *is* a work
of art—to be hung on the wall above the sofa

where I could study it. You refused. You
lay down under it, bare legs drawn up, a smudge

of creosote on one knee. Almost covered with
little girls 47 years old you've gone to sleep.

Double Exposure

Taking a photo of you taking a photo of me, I see
the black snout of the camera framed by hair, where

your face should be. I see your arms and one hand
on the shutter button, the hedge behind you and

beyond, below, overexposed water and sky wiped white.
Some flecks out of focus are supposed to be boats.

Your back toward what light is left, you're not
recognizable except by those cutoff jeans that I

gave you by shooting from above, forgetting your
legs. So, if I didn't know, I wouldn't know who

you are, you know. I *do* know who, but you, you know,
could be anybody. My mistake. It was because I

wanted to trip the shutter at the exact moment you
did. I did when you did, and you did when I did.

I can't wait to see yours of me. It's got to be
even more awful. A face, facing the light, pulled up

into a squint behind the lens, which must reflect
the muggy setting sun. Some sort of fright mask

or Mardi Gras monster, a big glass Cyclopean eye
superimposed on a flattened nose, that print,

the one you took of me as I took one of you. Who,
or what, will it be—will *I* be, I wonder? Can't wait.

Dummy, 51, to Go to Museum
Ventriloquist Dead at 75

Charlie didn't want to be pushed down
that last time into his plush-lined
case, top hat and monocle removed,
head unscrewed, clever hinge of wooden
jaw detached, the lid snapped shut
and locked, for transmigration to the
Smithsonian. That night, in Bergen's
bedroom, Charlie, in his box, got
himself together by himself and squawked:
"Edgar! You can't make me leave you.
You can't live without me. I'm your
larynx and your tongue. You'd be dumb
without your dummy, Dummy!" Bergen,
stung by that urbane, impudent, bossy,
caustic and beloved voice, silently
swallowed a pearl shirtstud of Charlie's,
spiked with strychnine. Obediently,
Edgar died in his sleep. In the dark
of dislocation, Charlie, glass-eyed, tried
all by himself to weep. A tear of wood
formed and stood in the inner corner
of his left eye, but could not fall.

A Thank-You Letter

Dear Clifford: It took me half an hour
to undo the cradle of string in which
your package from Denmark came.

The several knots tied under, over and
athwart each other—tightly tied and looped
and tied again—proved so perplexing. When,

finally, the last knot loosened, letting
the string—really a soft cord—fall free,
the sense of triumph was delicious.

I now have this wonderful cord 174" long
although your package is only 13 x 10 x 2.
Of course I could have cut through

each juncture of the cat's cradle you
trussed the package into, and freed it
instantly. But, no! Cord like this,

strong, flexible, just tough enough, smooth
and blond, of twisted strands of rag or hemp,
is very rare here. In fact I haven't seen

the sort since childhood. Instead, we get
slick, scratchy, recalcitrant nylon, or
whatever, that's heavy or else thread-thin

and cuts your hands. It doesn't hold—
doesn't hold a knot, not one!
Right now, Boa, our cat, has harnessed

herself and is rolling over with several
wraparounds of your string. She's getting up
to gallop, ensnarling herself worse. She's

having a wonderful puzzle-playtime. Cat's
in her cradle, on her back, trying to bite
string off her claws. And I haven't yet

taken the sturdy paper off your package.
I hardly feel I want to. The gift has been
given! For which, thank you ever so much.

Teddy's Bears

Skins on the floors, skins flung on the chairs,
and stretched on the walls of nearly every room.
Along with trophy-heads of buffalo, moose and deer,
tusks and toothy snarls of lioness and tiger.
But, most of all, bears.

Great and small furs, belly down, flat on the floor,
teeth and claws real, fully dimensional, as if clicking.
By the bed, this head: a lump with leather nose,
garnet eyes, jaws open, saber canines exposed.
And the rug in the gunroom on the third floor
is the biggest bear you've ever seen. Hod-sized head
with the round ears nearly worn away, wide goldbrown
body. Down the hall, across the railing of a doorway
where the plaque says PLAYROOM, are three Teddy Bears,
small, medium and large, at tea around a table
with an elaborately gowned cloth Lady Doll and her
china baby. A fourth plump Teddy forks a rockinghorse
in the corner.
Descending the stairs, you can't help but pause and fix
on the large portrait, life-sized, that's hung in the
stairwell: Poised rampant, the tanned Rough Rider,
wide-cuffed gloved hands pressed on the hilt of his sword,
squared head on short neck, chin raised, eyes piercing
rimless spectacles, lips under shaggy mustache in a stern
but amiable smile—the actual Teddy Himself.

Alternate Side Suspended

On wall-to-wall rugging the cars slouch by,
with headlights groping, windows blind,
the drivers invisible in the blizzard.

By morning, stalled at curbside, rounded high
as marriage beds, or frosty coffins, the piled
tops show carved hew-marks made by wind.

"Alternate side suspended," the city is numb.
Slabs on windowsills, like rocksalt, stay
unmelted three days, before beginning to gray

and shrink under sun. By now, the street's
soft corridor, gritty and scuffed, is dirtied
by dogs and the snowball wars of boys.

So begins the digging out. Windshields scraped,
engines strain, exhausts from tailpipes soil
a once spotless rug. Old asphalt potholes

show through. Eight o'clock walkers-to-work
pick paths past plastic hills of frozen
garbage, cheerfully splatter through slush, glad

for the noise and cram of harsh-colored cars,
horns hooting, drivers swearing, the street
steaming as usual under a urine-yellow sun.

Goodbye, Goldeneye

Rag of black plastic, shred of a kite
caught on the telephone cable above the bay
has twisted in the wind all winter, summer, fall.

Leaves of birch and maple, brown paws of the oak
have all let go but this. Shiny black Mylar
on stem strong as fishline, the busted kite string

whipped around the wire and knotted—how long
will it cling there? Through another spring?
Long barge nudged up channel by a snorting tug,

its blunt front aproned with rot-black tires—
what is being hauled in slime-green drums?
The herring gulls that used to feed their young

on the shore—puffy, wide-beaked babies standing
spraddle-legged and crying—are not here this year.
Instead, steam shovel, bulldozer, cement mixer

rumble over sand, beginning the big new beach house.
There'll be a hotdog stand, flush toilets, trash—
plastic and glass, greasy cartons, crushed beercans,

barrels of garbage for water rats to pick through.
So, goodbye, goldeneye, and grebe and scaup and loon.
Goodbye, morning walks beside the tide tinkling

among clean pebbles, blue mussel shells and snail
shells that look like staring eyeballs. Goodbye,
kingfisher, little green, black crowned heron,

snowy egret. And, goodbye, oh faithful pair of
swans that used to glide—god and goddess
shapes of purity—over the wide water.

Summerfall

After "the glorious Fourth," summer tumbles down.
An old hotel in Salt Lake City, Newhouse its name—
methodically installed with plugs of dynamite

for time-released explosion—burst!
Stupendously slow, the upper stories first. So
the whole west side of summer shears away.

Leafy cornices and balconies shatter, whirl down,
reduce to particles. The smash accelerates
as autumn's avalanches slide in planned relay,

until blanked out behind gray towers of fog.
All will be flattened. Graciousness, out of date,
must go, in instantaneous shock.

But Mind projects it slow,
stretching movement out, each flung chunk floating
awhile, weightless, and with no noise.

Mind reluctantly unbuilds summer.
The four-square, shade-roofed mansions
of an early, honest, work-proud era fall

to the dust of demolition. Prompt to come, ye Saints,
your condominiums, high-rise business, boosted
economy, new cash flow.

After "the rockets' red glare," here on the eastern shore
a sick acrylic sunset loiters in murky haze.
The sequence of such evenings will be speeding up.

From a Daybook

JANUARY 29TH
Black-white-black the flock of scaup
pushing hard against whittles of the tide.
Each seems to have a window in the side.
Light might shine right through. The day
is frozen gray, a steel engraving,
the bay a pewter plate, sky icy mist.
Black scaup, bluish bills poked forward,
float, white middles on dark water are
transparent squares of light.

FEBRUARY 10TH
Snow beginning makes a brightening.
Scarce white fur released from gray sky
starts to gather, dense in darkening air.
Expectation freshens the hibernating mind.
Is the scene beyond the apron of the eye
about to shift? At dawn will new birds
arrive, stand vivid on an ermine floor?
Inside, we now vicarious watch
winter's rigid climax. Crystal by crystal
formed in the opening of mind's burrow,
the dream of death rehearsed, and the
costume fashioned. Of rich white fur
the curtain, parting, deepens its folds.

MARCH 17TH, BEFORE STORM
Sky, a red-striped flag, billows
over cobalt tide. A low lightblade

snags on ridges of the waves.
Wind begins to agonize in bare trees
and it rips lengthwise the murky
banner. There is a clear green
naked staring iris between clouds.

MAY 28TH
Ripe in the green leaves (a whistle
urgent and tireless) a pulse of pleasure
sits, shaped to fit my hand. Radish-
bright, it pretends to hide behind
the leaves. Instead revealed, is seen
vulnerable and flagrant. Radical
whistle, color ripe and candid, the pulse
of pleasure shaped to fit my hand,
has wings. Has wings. Has vanished.

JULY 3RD, MORNING DESCENT
Gray wing divides blue from white.
Blue blank as swipe of waterpaint.
White unsmirched, mat without sketch.
Gray wing whisked by cold upper air.
Slantwise shadow brushes its tip.
The carriage rocks. Blue widens,
white brightens. Round-as-Rubens'
forms begin. To become shaded
on one side. They sedately shove
each other. Become each other's
bodies. Blank mat gray wing severs,
dives through, slides under, hides blue.
Depth becomes height. Wing downglides.
A long white slope. The carriage stops.

SEPTEMBER 8TH
So long I've wanted to get him
into my word-cage, Wildhead,
his call a pack of cards
shuffled, riffled, crisply
reshuffled. Then expertly
gathered up, he flies
beside the canal over the sandy

road and the bay. Blue and
white and belted, buoyant,
flamboyant acrobat, airclimber,
clown, hovering diver. Wildhead,
best of fishers, King!

OCTOBER 24TH
Tall sails going away, turn
from broadside to profile
in evening light. Their spiny
masts support great silken quills.
Wind loves feather, flag and sail.
Colored cloths lick out, feeling
for the panting wind. Gulls
hover the tall white pinion
shapes of ships going away.

NOVEMBER 15TH
The horizon has disappeared.
A gigantic pair of shears
has cut it off. Or it was
effaced by a thick fog eraser.
Crossing the waves' border,
a faint boat starts to creep
the sky, keep vertical, sail
nudged by an odorless wind.

TWO

Rainbow Hummingbird Lamplight

rain bow		bird light
humming bird	light humming	rain humming
lamp light	rain light	humming bow
	rain bird	

	rain bird	
rain light	humming bow	light humming
rain humming	lamp light	bird light
humming bird		rain bow

A shack of dark rainstreaked boards, steep pitched roof, smoke from the tin chimney pushing out into fog. On a mountain in California: high desert of chaparral, yucca, agave, juniper, manzanita, desert yew, prickly pear on the ridges and in the ravines. And, hanging from a rafter at the peak of the ceiling in the small square room, whose wide old stained knotholed boards let wind and rain through the splintery cracks, but which is furnished with a big black Huntsman's wood stove on which we can pop corn, boil coffee, fry steak if we have it, and that burns chunky split logs even when they are wet from the frequent rains, is a once-glittering glass prismed Mexican chandelier with a circle of sconces in which the heels of sooty yellow candles sit. We do not use it for light—there's no way to reach the candles to light or to snuff them. We use the graceful hourglass-shaped kerosene lamp—the thick curved glass base is bottom half of the hourglass—the chimney's outline is that of a seamstress' dress dummy of long ago.

When the sun shines on this rough little cabin, to which has been attached a somewhat larger newly built structure of cinderblock covered with adobe, and also furnished with a Huntsman's stove, making two studios that share a propaned pipelined kitchenette and bath between them—the cabin being the writer's half of what's called "The Writer/Painter House"—wonderful birds come to the round wood table on the rawwood deck that hangs like a shelf over the slope of the north-facing mountain. The table is a large wirecable spool spread with peanut bits, cracked corn and sunflower seeds. To the feeding table come golden-crowned sparrow, brown towhee,

rufous-sided towhee, scrub jay, for instance. And Bewick's wren
will trill from a near clump of live oak, through which is trying
to grow a young palo verde. And the curve-billed thrasher with
icy eye will be mocking crisply from a branch of manzanita, and
ravens will be sailing and remarking, while the redtailed hawk
will be circling high above the mountain. There's a snowtopped
view of Mt. San Gorgonio, looking a bit like Fujiyama, poking
up behind the lower Black Hills and, opposite, to the south-
west, the sinuous swells of the far pale Nameless Mountains.
From our bed on this first morning, we saw, out the deck door,
in the west the white-gold moon, full and almost transparent,
setting above, and then behind, these mountains, at the same
time as the sun, a big red shield, came up in the east throw-
ing long salmon ribbon-streaks under the moon—which, seen
through the flawed glass of the deck door, seemed to be square-
edged and eight-sided, like a Susan B. Anthony dollar.

This place we've come to, a preserve for working artists and
writers, is remote and wild. Last night coyotes bayed nearby
in weird harmony. We discovered a rodent, large by the sound
of its teeth—maybe a packrat—tearing at the adobe calking in
a closed space between the rafters and the roof where the new
part of the double studio was joined to the old. No bang of
broomstick made it pause, but when the "boo-booboo" of the
great horned owl, who roosts in the tallest yew upslope, began
at about three a.m., the rat fell silent. After unpacking the van in
the late afternoon, we had early supper outdoors seated on thick
bench-wide wedges of the woodpile in the shade. It was still hot
before the mountain wind that begins with sundown. We ate
fresh grapefruit slices and halves of avocado squirted with lemon
juice, pecans, coconut strips and a ripe papaya, while watching
a pair of charcoal black lizards spill from a space between logs.
Trickling along the ground, they suddenly stopped, one behind
the other, petrified. Not another flick for five minutes. When
we looked away for a second and then looked back, they were
gone. We went exploring. Unexpectedly, half a mile up a cork-
screw dirt road into foothills overlooking green valley ranches
and cattle pastures, this nook of the wild where fang of puma,
talon of raven, Cooper's hawk, coyotes, rattlesnakes and bob-
cats may still be met, such tender life as exists in lily ponds also

exists: shadowy fish hanging in the ooze and waving mosses,
monarch butterflies and dragonflies, bestirring the air above
the loose mosaic of flat yellow, brown and red pond lily leaves,
squish-bodied frogs, darting tadpoles. Skipping the sandy natu-
ral paths among scrub oak and brittlebush were brown rabbits
with white scuts, their round wall-eyes set far back in their soft
heads, and we've been told small deer may come down from the
higher hills before sunup, to sample the fruit of dewy prickly
pear. Across the gulch, sharing the top twigs of a wrung-dry
dead yucca with fierce thrasher and pushy jay—what a sweet
surprise—was Anna's hummingbird. Only a bit bigger than a
bumblebee, her short hooks of feet gripping tight, her long
probe at an arrogant angle, her pulsing throat, brilliant green
when her head turns left, crimson when it swivels right, she was
sounding her whisper-like signal as she sucked gnats out of their
gossamer twirls in slanting sunlight. Now, from the top of an
upright post at one corner of the deck of our shack and cabin,
we've hung a slender cruet of red glass and filled it with sugar
water which the Anna's can sip from a little cock at the base.
Tiny helicopters, wings whirring that hold them poised in air,
the hummingbirds are taking turns zooming in to feed right
above our breakfast bowls, as we begin our first full day here in
the high desert. Our bowls hold the biggest juiciest strawberries
in California. We get them from the outdoor fruit market, or
can pick for ourselves, if we like, in the valley below.
What's that, moving molasses-slow
over rock-strewn sand down there,
through the enigmatic glare
of sun in the gully under our deck—
mica-speckled, white, gray and black
as the sand it crosses? It's the Diamond Back
who now glides back
to his cool denhole in—see?—
that boulder's crack
between brittlebush and Joshua tree.

Morning at Point Dume

Blond stones all round-sided,
that the tide has tumbled on sand's table,
like large warm loaves strewn in the sun.

Wet pathways drain among them, sandgrains
diamond in morning light.
A high-hipped dog trots toward the sea,

followed by a girl, naked, young,
breasts jouncing, and long fair hair.
Girl and dog in the hissing surf

roister, dive and swim together,
bodies flashing dolphin-smooth,
the hair in her delta crisp dark gold.

The Pacific is cold. Rushed ashore on a wave,
her body blushes with stings of spume.
Running upslope, the circling dog

leaps to her hand, scatters spray
from his thick blond malamute fur.
Together they twine the stone loaves' maze.

Girl lets her glistening belly down
on a yellow towel on hard hot sand,
dog panting, *couchant* by her side.

Five surfers in skintight black
rubber suits, their plexiglass
boards on shoulders, stride the shore,

their eyes searching the lustrous water
for the hills of combers that build far out,
to mount and ride the curling snowtops.

The sunburned boys in phalanx pass,
squinting ahead, scuffing sand.
Without a glance at the yellow towel

they advance to the sea.
Enormous breakers thunder in.
Falling, they shake the ground.

A Day Like Rousseau's Dream

Paradise lasts for a day. Crowns of the palms lift
and glisten, their hairy trunks breathe with the sway
of fronds in striped light. Balconies of leaves
mount in layers to lunettes of sky. The ground is
stippled by shadows of birds. In a blink, they flit
into hiding, each disguised against its own color
in the tall leafwall that pockets a thousand nests
and husks, cones, seedpods, berries, blossoms.

Look closely. The whites of creature eyes shift
like diamonds of rain. Flowers are shrieks of color
in the gullies, are shaped to leap or fly, some with
sharp orange beaks or curved purple necks, or they
thrust out vermilion tongues. Velvet clubs, jeweled
whips, silky whisks and puffs and beaded clusters
combine their freakish perfumes.

Beside a slow gray stream, lilies, startling white,
unfurl like crisp breastpocket handkerchiefs.
Hummingbirds upright in flight flash sequined throats.
Eyes of an owl, goldrimmed circles, dilate, then shut
where he stands on a strut in the moiré of a datepalm
umbrella. Smooth trunks of eucalyptus twist up into
sunlight where, on a dangling basketnest, the hooded
oriole swings, ripe apricot.

High on a barkpeeled limb, is that a redhaired gibbon
hanging by one arm? And, drooping from a vine,
a boa's muscular neck, lidless eye and scimitar smile?
Are sagbellied panthers, partly eclipsed in bamboo shade
gliding behind that thicket? Is there a pygmy,
silver-eyed, black as the cabinet of shadow he hides in,
wearing a cockatoo on top of his ashen frizz?

Paradise lasts for a day. Be seated, with legs akimbo,
central on a mat of moss. Focus and penetrate the long
perspective between the palisades of green. Stabbing
through slits of light, your eyes may find—
couched in fern in a sunny alcove, melonpink body and
blackflagged head, eggshell-eyed, scarlet-lipped—
that magnetic, ample, jungle odalisque.

The eyes of animals enlarge to watch her, as all wind
drains from the leaves, and pure white scuts of cloud
appear in the zenith. Your gaze speeds to target,
the point of the V's black brush, where an oval
crack of space, a pod of white unpainted canvas, splits
for your eye's escape where her thighs do not touch.

Saguaros Above Tucson

Saguaros, fuzzy and huggable, greet us, seeming to stream
down the Rincon foothills as the car climbs. Their plump
arms branch, bend upward, enthused. Each prickly person,
droll, gregarious, we would embrace, but, up close, rigid
as cast plaster, spikey, bristling—how dare we touch?
Among the palo verde, teddybear cholla, ocotillo,
bristlebush and organpipe, we meet the desert tribe,
our friends from last year, standing in place, saluting

with their many arms. Granddaddies have most, are tallest
and toughest. Great girths they display, with numerous
bulging offspring graft-on-graft attached.
Adolescents, green and comical, big cucumbers, boast only
beginning bulbs of arms. A few peculiars, single, slim,
the air private around them, stand lonely, limbless—
perhaps forever young?—Low on the ground, babies,
fat little barrels, have only heads as yet, and sprout

scarce blond quills. We'd like to stop the car, get out
and climb the flinty gullies, walk to meet these giant
innocents, our friends, say Howdy, hug, take all their

stuckout hands. But, ouch! We do not know their ritual
handshake, or how to make retract their dangerous nails.
In spring, their heads wear crowns of bloom, dainty and
festive. Flowers come out of their ears, out of fingers
and elbows come rainfresh colors, buds like blushing fruits.

Finches fix themselves in rings around the thorny brows,
whistling from rosy throats. Why are the little birds
not pierced? How do they perch so carelessly on
peaks of prickly needle-twigs?
When from freezing, lightning, windthrow or old age,
in a hundred and fifty years or more, the giants die,
they still stand. Shriveled, blackened, dried and peeling
scabby corpses, tall untouchables, they haunt the hills.

And elf owls roost in the breasts of the dead saguaros.
One moonless night last year we discovered them with
a flashlight. In a chardark hole at vestpocket height
in the ghost of an old saguaro we found round yellow eyes
crossed and weird: a tiny pale-streaked owl hunched
in a pulpy torso whose broken twists of arms, long fallen,
lay around it on the ground.
We looked for more. Still, as if stuffed, the owls stared,

framed in the cameos of our hypnotic beams aimed
at the hollow chests of the dead saguaros.
On sunny mornings this year, Rivoli's hummingbirds
will hover and snick, ignite and gyrate in their courting
dives above the tall, tough, corduroy bodies and
blooming heads of sturdy young saguaros. Again astonished,
we'll ask each other: On such stiletto-pointed pates
how is it that the elf owl mates?

Eclipse Morning

Black sleet, bituminous flecks
disfigure that face. Stigmata
make it the more mysterious this

morning, the sun to be lidded
by moon's shadow.
Midnight's inkblot to be spilled,
sun's face filled, dilated to
a blind iris, the huge splash
of light blackened.
A greenish scrim lowers over
everything a powder like soot.
Moon slides between the plate of
great light and earth.
The dark dot is cast.
A startled woodthrush begins its
twilight ee-o-lay. A roused owl
erects its ears, stares, prepares
to hunt. Flowers that dawn has
just opened obey the signal to
close. At climax, a spree of wind
chills every leaf. Lawn pricks up
each blade, silver as with frost.
Three medallions, sun, moon, earth,
are strung on one thread.
Gorgon's head is lopped, the image
struck from the flashing shield.
And we, who open and close to our
sun's smile, or to its glare of
rage, for one astounding moment
see it quenched. In the blind
planetarium of the mind flickers
that face of feathered fire,
the cheek birthmarked with spots.

The Cross Spider

THE 1ST NIGHT

A spider, put outside the world,
given the Hole of Space for her design,
herself a hub all hollow, having no weight,
tumbled counterclockwise, paralytically slow

into the Coalsack.
Free where no wind was, no floor, or wall,
afloat eccentric on immaculate black,
she tossed a strand straight as light,
hoping to snag on perihelion and invent
the Edge, the Corner and the Knot.
In an orbit's turn, in glint and floss
of the crossbeam, Arabella caught
the first extraterrestrial Fly
of Thought. She ate it, and the web.

THE 2ND NIGHT
          "Act as if no center exists,"
Arabella advised herself. Thus inverted
was deformed the labyrinth of grammar.
Angles melted, circles unravelled, ladders
lost their rungs and nothing clinched.
At which the pattern of chaos became plain.
She found on the second night her vertigo
so jelled she used it for a nail
to hang the first strand on.
Falling without let, and neither up nor down,
how could she fail?
No possible rim, no opposable middle,
geometry as yet unborn, as many nodes and navels
as wishes—or as few—could be spun.
Falling began the crazy web.
Dizziness completed it. A half-made, half-mad
asymmetric unnameable jumble, the New
became the Wen. On Witch it sit wirligiggly.
No other thing or Fly alive.
Afloat in the Black Whole, Arabella
crumple-died. Experiment frittered.

An experiment conducted in Skylab 2 in orbit around Earth in 1973 was to
watch a cross spider, *Araneida diadema*, spin a web in space.

Shuttles

ONE
April 12, 1981

FLASH! SHOCK! BLAST! "Looks like a statue going up,"
Dan Rather says. Hoisted on a widening, roaring ramp
of flame and cloud, it sizzles aloft. On the ground,
a former astronaut says, "I feel lev-i-ta-ted!"
A pair of local bald eagles scream, "Roger, we copy,
Roger, we copy." Already out of this world, and Go
for orbit, the two-man crew hang vertical in their straps,
snug as twin kangaroos in Mommy's pouch. Boosted into
the loop, escaped from gravity, they'll glide upside down
and backwards—"upside down with the tail poked forward,"
as Rather says. But blood in their veins won't know it.
The blindness of space won't show it.

While still on the pad at Canaveral, stuck to the belly
of the giant booster, flanked by tall cylinders of solid
fuel, the blunt, black-nosed little plane, with its cockpit
window-eyes and white stubby wings back-canted: "Looks
like a folded fly," I say, seeing only the blurry TV visual,
black and white. For Columbia's first flight, I was far
from home. To zip this fly at 16,000 miles per hour
to orbit cost 14 billion bucks. "Apollo was only a star-
ship. The Shuttle is a truck," the tech experts brag.
Sons of Columbia will survey the ring road of our planet
to acquire squat-room on the new frontier. "We need pit-
stops and body shops deployed, to equip the star wars
of the future."

All systems are Go . . . . . . And now, 36 orbits and 54 hours
later, all systems are Come, for landing at Edwards in the
Mojave Desert. Rightside up, Columbia and crew face home,
nose pitched up sharp, for the descent. At 18 times
the speed of sound, the stub-winged fly drops and pierces
through Earth's atmosphere. Temperature leaps in the crew
and in their craft. The pilot's arms grow heavy as anvils.
Stress of re-entry piles weight on weight, and hearts and

temples pound. From Euphoria of space, from the smooth
angelic float, the grab of gravity is a jagged, hot rebirth.

All systems are Come. Columbia, the glider, blunt little fly,
weight 2 million pounds, size of a DC-9, pulls down in
     S-curves
out of the sky. In the grainy air of earth, she tends to
wobble at first, roll and yaw. But the dry lakebed of Edwards
is in sight. At 10,000 feet, at a 20-degree angle, losing
200 feet per second, at 290 knots, she drops. Banking, she
lines up with the runway, flares in at a descent rate of 50
feet per second, on stubby Delta wings, makes a graceful
drive-test-U, and skateboards the runway, spurting a wake of
desert sand. She stops neatly athwart the target, giant X,
which is the computer team's exact demand.

TWO
November 12, 1981

"We have LIFT-OFF!" A jolt like earthquake, then
the jubilant scream-gush-roar. From its trench
of flame an elongated Taj Mahal jumps upward,
straddling its wide boiling plume of smoke and
spitting rectal fire.

Scrubbed last week, but launched 10:10 a.m. today,
Columbia soars toward orbit. The roll maneuver
is smoothly made. Now, far and steep
into Florida blue, blurts and pulses the red
explosion.

Telephoto and Television frames contain it
in vivid Trinitron. Twin flanking rocket boosters
fall away, "each a bit shorter," Dan Rather says,
"than the Statue of Liberty." The huge external
fuel tank with three engines

(meaning the tall white central tower of the Taj,
on whose back Columbia rides until separation)

"releases as much energy as 23 Hoover Dams," Dan says.
That craft and its crew got back intact, too,
after four days, some glitches—a few—

after the tests for handling payloads: "O.K., Joe,
it's a great day for the Ace Moving Co.," said
the capsule communicator, alluding to the ultimate
purpose, which is "eventually to operate a fleet
of orbital freighters."

When all three wheels ease down
in a desert mirage, and the pilots
in gold jumpsuits emerge, at 5:05 p.m.
in a blizzard of sand, wild cheers
go up from the throng. A graceful touchdown.

FOUR (I missed the Third)
June 17, 1982

"We've cleared the tower!" Again. And again we'll clear.
"Oh God! My God!" is the groan that hiccoughs forth,
as bulbous clots of smoke, a whoosh of flame
pushes the THING gigantic up again.

The ground bounces, the sonic shock begets a booming chasm
of echoes. It seems enough to shatter granite.
The TV screen crazes under the blast. The hands
of a thousand cameras go spastic, lenses crack.

Do not eardrums snap, eyeballs collapse, lungs inflate
to bursting? The two in the cockpit, couched and strapped,
need just seconds to survive the slam of sound,
the flattening of their guts. Then the boosters

peel away, and tumble. Only minutes until the tall tank
slices off and falls, a gray slug, into the sea.
Again it's Go for orbit. It makes the first pass
over Africa's west bulge that used to nuzzle

the continental hollow of South America when Earth was
    young.
Columbia for the fourth time pushes its THING
on the way to its sling 150 miles above Earth, to circle
eight days this time, until Independence Day,

leaving below the heavy ring of sludge, its poison,
great gouts and smudges of choking cloud, to join the other
missile garbage of the air—(over 2,500 satellites there
already)—to spoil the weather, ruin human atmosphere.

We will equip (and expose) ourselves in space,
the High Frontier, half of Earth showing the other half
who's biggest, stiffest, most macho, who can
get it UP, can get it OFF, the quickest.

TOO BIG FOR WORDS
January 26, 1986

11:38 a.m., Launch Pad 39B, 25th Shuttle Mission: "We have
lift-off! . . . It has cleared the tower!"

Challenger, rolling on its back, loops out over ocean,
soaring at 1,538 miles per hour, 4.9 miles high,
two side-boosters packing solid propellant, the main
central booster burning 526,000 gallons of liquid oxygen
and hydrogen . . . fuel of the sun, the stars.

About to punch through the sound barrier at 1,977 MPH,
three times the speed of sound, 10.4 miles high:
Mission Control: "Challenger, go throttle up!"
Commander: "Roger. Go throttle up."

SEARING BRIGHT BALL OF LIGHT. A shuddering roar . . .

Mission Control (mechanical voice): "We're one minute, 15
seconds velocity, 2,900 feet per second, altitude 9 nautical
miles, range distance 7 nautical miles . . ."

Not true. Challenger, engulfed in flames, does not exist.

The 122-foot orbiter in blazing chunks, for 45 minutes
rains down onto the Atlantic, 18 miles northeast of
Canaveral. Ships and helicopters, a squad of over 1,000
people rushing to the impact area, cannot get within range,
either by air or water, because of falling debris.

FIREBALL. THE SHUDDERING ROAR. Then, blank silence.
From a bloating ram's head of white cloud, enormous horns
uncurl, inflate on blue. The searing rocket boosters
spiral free. The two-story cabin with the crew
breaks out of the nose cone, falls nine miles to the sea.

Built for orbit, Challenger seated seven human bodies.
Incinerated? Cremated? Poisoned by fumes? Suffocated
by loss of pressure? Slammed dead on impact with the sea?

Blizzard of debris. Pieces too small, too many, ever to
put together. Event too big for words . . . For the next
week the most-played lottery number in Florida was 1138.

Never to be erased, that white burst inflates, inflates,
inflates perpetual, on the sky of mind.

One morning, on the beach near Canaveral, a navy blue sock
washed up. In it, a fragment of bone and human tissue.
Evidence without connection . . .

Item in the news in April: Computer-enhanced films show
the cabin, tiny thimble, tumbling intact toward ocean.
"It really shook me to watch that film," said the source
at NASA. "It turned in tumbling. It caught the sun.
You could see the rate of spin."

By July NASA conceded that the crew, at "Go throttle up!"
had to have known the lift-off was fatal. Recorded by
the "black box" finally recovered from Challenger's debris,
Commander's voice was heard: He said, "Uh-oh." It took
ten seconds to hit water. *They were alive. They knew.*

Comet Watch on Indian Key
Night of April 10, 1986

Bright splendid head of
Halley's Comet . . . Comet
coming. Coming again.
Not seen since May 8, 1910.
Called Dirty Snowball, and
Finger of God Pointing,
and Plunger to Disaster . . .
Dis-aster means bad star.
Comet coming. Coming again,
elliptically swishing out
from behind the far
blind side of Sun. Gaseous
Dustball, probably lumpy,
it lets nest, in its
diaphanous tail thinned by
the Solar Wind, Aldebaran
and Betelgeuse undimmed.
Comet coming coming again.
Wonder of wonders . . . Who
will be on watch on that
spring night in 2062?

Ahnighito

Enormous beast on six legs stands in the Hall
of Meteorites. Small children like to crouch
or crawl beneath him. Looking up, they feel
he's friendly. True, he can't attack. Cold,
dense, heavier than iron, his ridged back shows
scalloped melt-marks. Flaming lump, he tumbled,

blunt buffalo-head, imbedded in a self-dug
blasthole, congealed in earth for centuries.
Reptilian his look of never-needing-to-move.
You can't see him breathe. But the space about
his outline vibrates. Power like dust of mica
seems to swirl around his bulk.

Six chrome poles the paraplegic monster's
mounted on. The children stoop around those
legs, rumpus under the heavy belly, lay their
petal cheeks against harsh metal, and listen
for what might snort within. They pet and pat
the face that, here or there, might show an eye

or nostril about to bloom, or short thick
warted horn. Half his snout, distended like
a dragon's, has been filed flat, rubbed bright
as nickel, slick to stroking hands. This patch
of the beast's shag peeled, planed and flashing,
has worn out many tools.

Howling fire fattened to a roar when he fell,
fragment of a star, or lava Minotaur, gnarled
hide charred black, great clinker bounding
down from the fiery shore of Universe. Beneath
a beast not of this earth, as when Remus and
Romulus trustfully suckled, children play.

If I Had Children

If I had children, I might name
them astrometeorological names:
Meridian, a girl. Zenith, a boy.
Eclipse, a pretty name for either one.
Anaximander, ancient Greek scientist
(who built a gnomon on Lacedaemon,
and with it predicted the exact date

that city would be destroyed by
earthquake). . . . Anaximander, wonderful
name for a girl. Anny could be her
nickname. Ion, short for ionosphere,
would make a graceful name for
a boy. Twins could be named after
planets: Venus and Mercury, or

Neptune and Mars. They'd adore each
other's heavenly bodies shining
upon their doubles on Earth.
And have you ever thought that, of
the Nine, only one planet is female?
Venus. Unless Earth is. So, seven
of Sun's children, it seems, are male.

But, if I had children, and grandchild-
ren, then greatgrandchildren, myriads
of newborn moons and moonlets crowding
into the viewfinder would furnish me
names both handsome and sweet:
Phoebe, Rhea, Dione among daughters
of Saturn, with Titan and Janus the

brothers. Io, Ganymede and Callisto,
Jupiter's boys: Europa and little
Amalthea, their sisters.
On Io, most exotic of the Galilean
moons, are mapped six great-and-grand
volcanoes: Loki, Hemo, Horus, Daedalus,
Tarsis, Ra. Beauties all! But all

boys. Well, if I had children
I wouldn't fix genders or orbits, only
names for them. Wobbling Phobus,
distant child of Mars, misshapen as
a frozen potato. . . . If I had such a
lopsided moon, the name Phobus would
fit. And I'd love it just the same.

THREE

Come In   Go Out

A world of storm	A life of waves
Raging circles form	Tides and icy caves
Wind loops the globe	Sun scorching palms
Blizzards in the brain	Or deadening calms
Then modifying hope	A single summer day
A hoisted sail	Unfolds twinkling
On the dream trail	Flinches past the eye
Hummingbird's green	Bullet of gauze
Illuminant	Of primal cause

In the Bodies of Words
For Elizabeth Bishop (1911–1979)

Tips of the reeds silver in sunlight. A cold wind
sways them, it hisses through quills of the pines.
Sky is clearest blue because so cold. Birds drop down
in the dappled yard: white breast of nuthatch, slate
catbird, cardinal the color of blood.

Until today in Delaware, Elizabeth, I didn't know
you died in Boston a week ago. How can it be
you went from the world without my knowing?
Your body turned to ash before I knew. Why was there
no tremor of the ground or air? No lightning flick
between our nerves? How can I believe? How grieve?

I walk the shore. Scraped hard as a floor by wind.
Screams of terns. Smash of heavy waves. Wind rips
the corners of my eyes. Salty streams freeze on my face.
A life is little as a dropped feather. Or split shell
tossed ashore, lost under sand. . . . But vision lives!
Vision, potent, regenerative, lives in bodies of words.
Your vision lives, Elizabeth, your words
from lip to lip perpetuated.

Two days have passed. Enough time, I think, for death
to be over. As if your death were not *before* my knowing.
For a moment I jump back to when all was well and ordinary.
Today I could phone to Boston, say Hello. . . . Oh, no!
Time's tape runs forward only. There is no replay.

Light hurts. Yet the sky is dull today. I walk the shore.
I meet a red retriever, young, eager, galloping
out of the surf. At first I do not notice his impairment.
His right hind leg is missing. Omens. . . .
I thought I saw a rabbit in the yard this morning.
It was a squirrel, its tail torn off. Distortions. . . .

Ocean is gray again today, old and creased aluminum
without sheen. Nothing to see on that expanse.
Except, far out, low over sluggish waves, a long
clotted black string of cormorants trails south.
Fog-gray rags of foam swell in scallops up the beach,
their outlines traced by a troupe of pipers—
your pipers, Elizabeth!—their racing legs like spokes
of tiny wire wheels.

Faintly the flying string can still be seen.
It swerves, lowers, touching the farthest tips of waves.
Now it veers, appears to shorten, points straight out.
It slips behind the horizon. Vanished.

But vision lives, Elizabeth. Your vision multiplies,
is magnified in the bodies of words.
Not vanished, your vision lives from eye to eye,
your words from lip to lip perpetuated.

Bethany, Delaware
October 13–15, 1979

Her Early Work

Talked to cats and dogs,
to trees, and to strangers.
To one loved, talked through
layers of masks.
To this day we can't know
who was addressed,
or ever undressed.
Because of the wraparounds,
overlaps and gauzes,
kept between words and skin,
we notice nakedness.
Wild and heathen scents
of shame or sin
hovered since childhood,
when the delicious was always
forbidden. "A Word With You"
had to be whispered,
spoken at the zoo,
not to be overheard
by eavesdropping ape or cockatoo.

Angels, Eagles

Angels, eagles, owls among the heads
on human shoulders, of bronze
the dark of beachtree leaves, obscurely
shining. Ripple of ribs, tight hips
and thighs about to stride into flight.
And some have wings, elbows like wing-
joints, fingers becoming feathers.

Under a skylight on a low platform
Jacob hugs his angel. The struggle is
over, the match is tied, and strength
no longer virtue. Like boxers leaning
into the clinch, combat has left them
healthy, priapic, spent, and tender.
No referee arrives to split them.

Angel's curly head butts softly the
pectoral hollow of Jacob's shoulder
whose arm crosses the wingéd back,
one loose-balled fist resting on
Angel's neck. Nearby, beneath an arch:
grim heads of buzzards and of bats
trussed into sacks of their own skins.

Inchoate forms on taloned feet in static
decomposure, their jaws are open to moan
or screech. Raptors' profiles, cruel
and beautiful, erupt out of young boys'
torsos. A dead leather-look, iguana-
like, of sleepers on slabs on the floor
with legs, arms, heads, hollow bellies,
buttocks fused as in a common grave.

But horror is not evoked. Rather, grace,
proportion, the exquisite languor of
surrender. In a doorway leans a youth
with the head of a cat. The narrowed
eyes stare at the viewer through pupils
of green onyx, and tiny teeth smile
white in the cleft of the upper lip.

And look: in an inner nook in mellow
light, a woman's head on slender neck
is attached to a body ambiguous, while
the profile of marble wears the queendom
of a swan. This, the brightest head of
all the company grown from a black-as-
lava, probably male, form, is a radiant

shock. At which most strollers turn
aside. Toward which a few, like me,
like you, magnetically move. Something
human shows in every beast, and animal
beauty in human. Enigma reigns in the
room where bodies, more than human,

are more than merely alive. Yet all are
metal, and dead. And the sculptor
has been forgotten. Shadow without body,
he slips mind's view. Until we walk out
of the gallery onto the city street. Now
we remember him, *in his flesh*, walking,
as we walk among people. Forms he made

and makes, caressing and cursing, stretch-
ing again and again toward flight, toward
the immortal, these bodies of beast and
youth, demon and hero, predator, angel,
androgyne, chimaera, god, he engenders
with power, and marks each face and head
with his own ferocious beauty.

—Homage to Leonard Baskin

The Elect

Under the splendid chandeliers
the august heads are almost all
fragile, gray, white-haired or bald
against the backs of thronelike chairs.

They meet in formal membership
to pick successors to their seats,
having eaten the funeral meats,
toasted the names on the brass strips

affixed behind them, tier on tier,
on chairs like upright coffin tops.
When a withered old head drops,
up is boosted a younger's career.

The chamber is ancient and elite,
its lamps pour down a laureate gold.
Beyond the windows blue and cold
winter twilight stains the street,

as up from the river the wind blows
over slabs of a steep graveyard,
the names under snow. A last award:
to be elected one of those.

Shift of Scene at Grandstand

Fall, winter and spring on the same spread at Grandstand.
Last winter's ragged leaves poke through a flat

of melting snow. Exposed in the dun mat of the meadow,
holes of field mice and woodchuck show the scene

is being struck. From stiff, split creases, shuttles
of milkweed let their fleeces out. We see red-capped

spicules in the hoary moss. "British soldiers," Jane
says. Leslie picks a tiny dried-up sort of thimble

he names "St. James Wort." Other trinkets of fall
are strewn about: by the brook a bead-like ball, and

we find more of them, golden on the ice crust. I say,
"They're deer droppings. How neat!" Some props remain

from the act of winter: the elm's arterial system sprawls
against a cold, bare sky. Few buds are out, but spry

chickadees alight, matching the pussywillow's plush.
One bush wears a pale yellow veil in the hollow

where male kinglets flash rubies on their napes.
Red-vested robins and pink-billed juncos streak by,

stippling the new backdrop of the year. One blue jay
sounds his flute note to say that the curtain is about

to part on Groundhog making his second entrance. Now,
taking her cue for an extended dance, spangle-skirted

Rain arrives. Next, the main character, Lord Sun,
comes downstage. Scene I: Violets. Scene II: Greensward.

After which, a sudden switch to Scene III: Summer
from now on, by demand, booked to play at Grandstand.

Little Lion Face

Little lion face
I stooped to pick
among the mass of thick
succulent blooms, the twice

streaked flanges of your silk
sunwheel relaxed in wide
dilation, I brought inside,
placed in a vase. Milk

of your shaggy stem
sticky on my fingers, and
your barbs hooked to my hand,
sudden stings from them

were sweet. Now I'm bold
to touch your swollen neck,
put careful lips to slick
petals, snuff up gold

pollen in your navel cup.
Still fresh before night
I leave you, dawn's appetite
to renew our glide and suck.

An hour ahead of sun
I come to find you. You're
twisted shut as a burr,
neck drooped unconscious,

an inert, limp bundle,
a furled cocoon, your
sun-streaked aureole
eclipsed and dun.

Strange feral flower asleep
with flame-ruff wilted,
all magic halted,
a drink I pour, steep

in the glass for your
undulant stem to suck.
Oh, lift your young neck,
open and expand to your

lover, hot light.
Gold corona, widen to sky.
I hold you lion in my eye
sunup until night.

Pale Sun

Pallor of the December sun.
Far and small, on a plane
of water, sails point in three
directions, separate from
each other. One a white cutlass

tall in the low light. And two
squat triangles, blue and yellow.
The weather's strange,
like spring. The water's flat
as a tin floor. A single

song sparrow sounds a note,
but can't be seen—gray in a gray
bush by the path on the sloped
shore. I lean there
against a thick boulder.

Warm light strokes my face.
I see in my mind my face,
flaccid, mournful, old. Well
it will be older. A slim boy
walks by, with a gliding gait.

His shadow crosses mine
on the path. From a strap
on his shoulder hangs a leather
case. What's in it? A weapon?
The three sails, coming about,

enlarge, converging toward
the jetty. Slaps and plops
of the languid tide barely heard;
instead I hear a clear
delicate run of reedy notes.

Walking back around the point
I see the boy seated on a bulkhead,
leather case open beside him,
face raised to the sun.
He's playing his flute.

A New Pair

Like stiff whipped cream in peaks and tufts afloat,
the two on barely gliding waves approach.

One's neck curves back, the whole head to the eyebrows
hides in the wing's whiteness.

The other drifts erect, one dark splayed foot
lifted along a snowy hull.

On thin, transparent platforms of the waves
the pair approach each other, as if without intent.

Do they touch? Does it only seem so to my eyes'
perspective where I stand on shore?

I wish them together, to become one fleece enfolded, proud
vessel of cloud, shape until now unknown.

Tense, I stare and wait, while slow waves carry them
closer. And side does graze creamy side.

One tall neck dips, is laid along the other's back,
at the place where an arm would embrace.

A brief caress. Then both sinuous necks arise,
their paddle feet fall to water. As I stare,
with independent purpose at full sail, they steer apart.

Some Quadrangles
The 1982 Harvard Phi Beta Kappa Poem

On a vast magic carpet the students squat,
legs akimbo, in loose clumps of three or four
reading *The Wildcat,* hunched over large cups
of ice and cola. The grass worn down to dirt
in patches, its nap gray from incessant sun,
if dried dogshit leaves a smudge on faded jeans,
no sweat, it's just another dust unnoticed.
January. But Arizona time's tattoo extends eternal.
On another part of the quad, outstretched asleep,
male torsos redden to Indian, chest hairs bleach.
Free of skirts and scuffs, girls' bare legs
jackknife or V-spread, blond and carrot hairs
snag light, as does the fuzz on cholla and dearhorn.
Around the quad, trunks of palms, thick-middled
Doric, belted with shag beneath splayed crowns
leave archways for the sun's wide klieg.
Bookbags make good cushions or, rather, blocks
for under necks. Maybe studies are done
under sunwarm eyelids by the brain's left half
turned low, while the right simmers to a sensual

disco beat. Does the carpet undulate? It seems
to float somnambulistically just off the ground—
although it *is* the ground—while above it,
wingtip to wingtip on high blank blue,
mechanical vultures climb in pairs aslant
from out of Monthan Air Force Base to the south.
Lower, sluggish, a mud-gray shark, a widebody,
horizontally crosses sky in the other direction.
Followed by a brace of graceful jets,
slim aluminum swans in a silent glide.
When they are dots on distance their huge noise
arrives, horrendous. The campus is not disturbed.
Pleasant torpor here on the shabby precious grass,
where a mass of young bodies in languid
enchanted tableaux—figures on the carpet—
have the far jagged Rincons for a frame.

In snowy compounds of the north and east,
the noonhour over, two hours ago at least,
the freezing quads are almost empty,
belong to the wind. They are white and lonely.
It is indoors, on hallway carpets and in
libraries' pillowy chairs and divans,
the students crouch or sleep. They live in
their ski coats, snooze in their boots.
If unlucky enough to get only table or desk
in study hall, they sink heads on bookbags,
dreaming heads, with lots and lots of hair.
Hair is piled and spilled among books
on the tables—dark hair bushy or kinky.
Bridges of sideburns join the beards on boys.
On girls, big hats of hair, and comfy hoods
of foaming curls help them endure the Buffalo
and Minneapolis winters. In lamplight
on the stairs, in corridors, and in the lounges,
like woolly sheep huddled against the blizzard,
they browse, preferring to keep close to ground.
Some, parked on their bellies by the radiators,
look like toboggans or sleds.

In April, in St. Louis, in a rare warm week,
dark grass of the Common already thick,
a few daffodils out that the wind whips
along the borders of buildings. In a boxlike space
between stone walls with towers like a castle,
spreads the carpet in the stingy sun. Not bared
to the sun—too chilly for that—but, as elsewhere,
close together the students cuddle on the ground.
No matter turf's still wet, mud showing through.
In wool plaids, parkas, and the sturdy indigo Levis
favored in the Midwest, they warm hands around
paper mugs of coffee, pizza pie in cardboard flats
balanced on folded knees. The Buddha position.
Somehow now that's how you sit if you're in college.

Is it so in Harvard Yard? On your historic
greens, between the bells, do students squat
or lie flat out, in spots of sun and shade,
snacking and reading *The Crimson*?

At, for instance, *my* college (which was Utah
State Agricultural at that time, long, long ago)
the students were *upright*. Yes, we comported
ourselves with *respect* for the institution and
the *privilege* vouchsafed us. (I do not think
I've ever said that word out loud before.) We
had goals. And we climbed. We climbed the hill,
a foothill of the canyon, the same we used
for sleighing when it snowed. We huffed and
puffed under sonorous bongs from the belltower
whose carpentered peak was a big inspiring "A."
"Develops calves and lungs," Dad used to say.
"Prepares you for effort. The physical sparks
the mental climb." Well, maybe. Few students
had cars then. Yamahas hadn't happened, and
our campus was too steep for bikes.

Now, of course, it's bigger and modernized.
Expanded by the bulldozers, it spreads on,
up the canyon benches. There's a maze (a mess)

of approaches to cement parking lots, densely
planted with metal *Restricted* signs. But Old Main
remains, and much of the green which is framed
by ancient giant spruce and pine. There is
still space. Space remains in the West.
We were farmers' or cattlemen's kids, expected
to dress and behave in accord with our luck
at being in college. Of course we didn't
wear Levis. They were for milking cows.
There was no such thing as a student *lounge*.
The library was straight chairs around long,
thick, lamp-shaded, oakgrained tables.
Attention, Attendance, and proper Attire
were seldom challenged. We competed—check this!—
we competed to be good. Most of us did. How
dull! But that's what was *hep*, long before
that word made the dictionary. "Good student"
didn't mean brilliant scholar, original mind,
or even eagerness to learn. It meant programmed
to please—not so much our teachers, but mainly
our peers. Our goal was to fit the mold that
seemed assigned by those around us. We used
our quad of perfectly barbered grass only for
crossing from class to class. And we walked
on the crosswalks while walking and crossing.
Naturally, no foot should be set on the carpet.
Might wear it out! I do remember how it smelled
heavenly on dewy mornings after a mowing,
which sometimes left unlopped the subversive heads
of a dandelion or two. . . . Girls' heads—
(yes, we said "girls" not "women" then)—
were marcelled. Men were clean-shaven. Decent,
earnest, orderly, ambitious, we climbed up
College Hill, to join conformity, the majority
at the top. Notice how, seen in the pool of time,
present and past reflect each other—upside down!

Shall I talk of Texas, Pennsylvania, Idaho?
Or North Carolina, where the mockingbirds sing Soul,
copied from miniature Sonys the students wear

while jogging? Or of Washington Square, Manhattan's
grungy downtown campus, where drunks drink,
pushers push, pigeons shit on the benches, and,
nonetheless, blissful babies sleep in carriages
in the safer section, where pairs of old men on SS,
at cement tables hover over large, ancient, wooden
Hungarian chessmen. One day I heard one guffaw,
asking the other: "What should I do, now I'm retired?
Put on my leisure suit and take a tour in my RV?"
There used to be grass in Washington Square.
That carpet is worn out. But not the storied
magic. It's there.

On Southern California campuses the Angels walk
beneath peartree blooms, past hibiscus hedges
and waterlily ponds—beautiful male and female
thighs, in cutoffs, feet in sandals, chests bared,
those in T-shirts, unbra-ed. The tall, the tanned
bright-haired stroll to class, or they go
on skateboards or on bikes. And they bring their dogs.
Unleashed, luxurious breeds convene on the quads,
to chase, wrestle, and mount each other.
They wade in the fountains, race to capture
Frisbees tossed. At lunch hour, which can be
all hours from eleven to four, marmoreal poses
are taken on the plushy green. The quad's
a sculpture court. Spaced out, laid back, mellow,
buns to the ground, the Angels lounge, reading
The Bruin (sort of) and lapping ice-cream cones.
Any dog lays belly to grass, lifts ass, gets a lick.

For a very long time now, it seems, it's been trendy
to hang loose, slouch, be scruffy, drop out, turn on.
I guess it started with *Howl*, got a solid shove from
Hair. Quite early the neat Beatles let their bangs
grow, stopped wearing suits with vests. Yoga and
Zen started big new waves. Many other inputs and
outgrowths can be named, all the way back to
the BEATNIKS. The newest big roller, I'm told, is
THE MOLE PEOPLE, who all wear black and come out

only at night. Wow! *That* close to ground, you're
under! . . . What if that's best? What if instinct
prophetically leads the young, and all of us, *under*,
deeper, darker, blinder, into the final womb?
While there's still time. Before the first launch,
which will be the only one.
No, that's the apocalyptic cop-out. Not true.
New Wavers, listen: (But they can't, they never do.)
Listen, there's just one "Don't," one "Keep Off,"
one "Keep Away From"—and I don't mean "the Grass."
It is: *Don't be a clone.* Don't do what the others
do. Because what they do, they do because others do.
It's good to be down there, level with nature,
like a plant, like an animal. Thoreau and
Whitman knew it. Gandhi in his dhoti felt
the magnetic pole of the earth. But, make *your own*
moves. Go opposite, or upside down, or Odd.
When everyone's odd, be the first to go Even. And,
on flipover, take the reverse course, of course:
In slow company, go fast; and in fast, slow.
With the ultra-slick, be rough; with the savage, noble.
Like Billy Budd, stay sweet: The arm that flogs you
will fall off. When everyone's on the joystick,
hunker down back home by yourself, with *War and Peace.*
Every one on the Orgasmatron? Be chaste. Then,
when they button, you can unbutton.
Not to be robotic, fix-focused on that straight
slit up the middle of some cat's eye. *Not* to be
either knee-jerked or Lotus-folded into the annealed
mob of spastic hot punk-rock clones, or else
upstairs among the pawky cornball Majority Morals.
Not needing to share, with identical nerds,
the pop trash, fake funk, sugar-diluted rush, *nor* prayer
in the schools. Get up, get out on the fresh edge
of things, away from the wow and flutter. Stand alone.
Take a breath of your own. Choose the wide-angle
view. That's something, maybe, you can begin to
learn to do, once you're *out* of college.

FOUR

COMICS

Innards

As many ripples,
loops and fingers,
kinks and pockets,
scallops,
curls and ruches
as the surf
on frilly waves—
corrugated, convoluted
slippery links and
pinks and puckers,
frothy overlapping
fringes:
Enormous
Anemone!
Look
in the Anatomy Book:
the spastic heap
indented, redundant,
crimped, voracious,
over-abundant,
squeezing,
mashing,
munching,
pinching,
spitting
it out. The end?
No, still more
clench and squirm
and fretted froufrou
at each bend:
a bore,
the belly
a bushel
of tripe. I turn
to the velvet kidney,
the orderly heart,
liver and lungs'
aesthetic pattern.
They somewhat
soothe the gripe.
But it's hypnotic,
that exotic page.
Could I unravel
the capacious

maze, the conduit
of travel,
my future
might
come clear. It says here,
        that *if*
        I could uncoil,
        could straighten
        it, I'd have
        a thong—
                    What
            would I do
            with it?—
            25 feet
            long.

The Digital Wonder Watch
(An Advertisement)

When I look at the time,
    it tells me the date,
the speed of my pulse,
    my height, my weight.
It tells me how fast I'm
running, how straight.
It tells me my balance,
    the dividend rate.
It tells me my birthday,
    my license plate.
It's a wonderful watch!

Suppose I'm in London
    and want to know
what time it is in Kokomo?
The weather in Miami or Maine,
how much sun or how much rain?
The name of the Daily Double to win?
Whether black or red
    is the number to spin?
All I need to do is look at the time.

It's elegant, neat, the size of a dime.
It's a wonderful watch!

It tells me my shoe
and my collar size.
It tells me the color of my eyes.
If I'm lost in the woods
it tells me North,
phases of moon and tide,
and so forth.
It tells me how hot I am, or how cold.
It tells me I'll never,
never grow old.
It's a wonderful watch!

Does it tell when the world ends?
And when did it start?
Does it show how to wind up a broken heart?
Well, that's in the works,
and of course, it's true
there's still to be added
a gadget or two,
to warn of earthquake, volcano, or war,
and how long the sun
will exist as a star.
Yes, it's a wonderful watch!

The Gay Life
(to be sung)

When there are two,
there will likely be
at least three:
the Mommy,
the Daddy,
the Ba-a-by.

Sometimes the Mommy
is the Baby—
sometimes it's the Daddy.
Baby can be Baby *and*
Daddy—in fact,
prefers to be.

Daddy can sometimes be
Mommy. But when
Mommy's Mommy, she's
not supposed to be
Ba-a-by.

Baby-Daddy prefers
Mommy to be Mommy,
although Mommy may
want to be
Daddy, or Baby, or
Daddy-Baby.
Daddy may let Mommy be
Baby-Mommy, but prefers
her not to be
only Ba-a-by.

Each can be,
in turn, Mommy, Daddy,
Baby—but not
simultaneously.
Two Mommies, two Daddies
or two Babies:
Misery!

Bad enough, if Daddy
is Baby when Mommy
wants to be—
or wants Daddy to be
just Daddy, when she
isn't—or Daddy wants
Baby-Mommy to be
just Mommy, and she
isn't, or doesn't
want to be.

Sometimes Mommy wants
Daddy to be

Baby, for now, for fun—
but then get up and be
BIG DADDY—and Daddy
won't be. That's bad.

Or, sometimes
Baby-Daddy wants
Mommy BIG. But not
TOO BIG. That's
too bad. Sometimes
there's just a Baby
and a Mommy.
Or a Baby and a Daddy.
That's bad, too.

Two bad is too bad.

Suppose there's just
a Mommy and a Daddy?
Fine. If Mommy will be
Daddy, and Daddy
will be Mommy *sometimes.*
It's likely each
will come to be
Baby sometimes.
That's O.K.

If there's a Daddy-Mommy
and a Mommy-Daddy, and
each wants to be
Baby sometimes, but not
at the *same* time—
that's good. That's
the way to be. Because
when there are two,
there will likely be
at least three.

Fit

Let's do one of those long
Narrow *New Yorker* poems to
Fit between the ads on about

Page 69. It should be fresh,
Have color and panache and
Make a few references to

Mainstream name brands,
Such as Sulka, Cuisinart or
Baggies—to fit with the ads,

Why not? "Original Baggies
Combine the loose fit of swim
Trunks and the roughness of

Rugby shorts. Reinforced side
Pocket, and nylon inner brief.
Colors: Red, Teal, Gold, Purp-

Le, Khaki, Marine Blue, Pea-
Cock, Silver." I want a silver
Baggie. Am ordering from Ven-

Tura, Ca., Box 3305, adding
$2.50 for postage. It needs
To be around 60 lines, spaces

Counting as lines. So, let's
Fit in a few frames by my favo-
Rite cartoonist: 1. Man asleep

In bed by old-fashioned alarm
Clock. Dog asleep in heap on
Floor. 2. Alarm goes off. Dog,

Cross-eyed, is scared awake.
3. Man in pajamas, brushing
Teeth. Dog scratching fleas.

4. Man, dressed, putting on
Coat. Dog just standing there.
5. Man, with briefcase in door-

Way, leaving. Dog just stand-
Ing there. 6. Door closed,
Room empty. Until we see

Lump in bed under covers.
It's dog asleep. Still too
Short? Three-line stanzas

Instead of four may make it
Fit. It's worth it. Here goes.
Poetry pays better than prose.

Summer's Bounty

berries of Straw	nuts of Pea
berries of Goose	nuts of Wal
berries of Huckle	nuts of Hazel
berries of Dew	nuts of Chest
berries of Boisen	nuts of Brazil
berries of Black	nuts of Monkey
berries of Rasp	nuts of Pecan
berries of Blue	nuts of Grape
berries of Mul	beans of Lima
berries of Cran	beans of French
berries of Elder	beans of Coffee
berries of Haw	beans of Black
apples of Crab	beans of Jumping
apples of May	beans of Jelly
apples of Pine	beans of Green
apples of Love	beans of Soy

melons of Water   glories of Morning
melons of Musk   rooms of Mush
cherries of Pie   days of Dog
cherries of Choke   puppies of Hush

A Nosty Fright

The roldengod and the soneyhuckle,
the sack eyed blusan and the wistle theed
are all tangled with the oison pivy,
the fallen nine peedles and the wumbleteed.

A mipchunk caught in a wobceb tried
to hip and skide in a dandy sune
but a stobler put up a EEP KOFF sign.
Then the unfucky lellow met a phytoon

and was sept out to swea. He difted for drays
till a hassgropper flying happened to spot
the boolish feast all debraggled and wet,
covered with snears and tot.

Loonmight shone through the winey poods
where rushmooms grew among risted twoots.
Back blats flew betreen the twees
and orned howls hounded their soots.

A kumpkin stood with tooked creeth
on the sindow will of a house
where a icked wold itch lived all alone
except for her stoombrick, a mitten and a kouse.

"Here we part," said hassgropper.
"Pere we hart," said mipchunk, too.
They purried away on opposite haths,
both scared of some "Bat!" or "Scoo!"

October was ending on a nosty fright
with scroans and greeches and chanking clains,
with oblins and gelfs, coaths and urses,
skinning grulls and stoodblains.

Will it ever be morning, Nofember virst,
skue bly and the sappy hun, our friend?
With light breaves of wall by the fayside?
I sope ho, so that this oem can pend.

Giraffe
A Novel

CHAPTER 1

Giraffe is the first word in this chapter. Is is the second word. The is the third word. First is the fourth, and word is the fifth word in the first chapter. In is the sixth and this is the seventh and chapter is the eighth word in this chapter.

CHAPTER 2

Is is the second word is the second sentence in the first chapter. Is is the first and the second word in the first sentence in this chapter. The is the third word is the third sentence in the first chapter, and the third word in the first sentence in this chapter. First is the fourth, and word is the fifth word in the first chapter is the fourth sentence in the first chapter.

CHAPTER 3

The fourth sentence in the first chapter is in the fourth sentence in the second chapter.

CHAPTER 4

The first word is Giraffe, and the second, ninth, tenth, fifteenth, twentieth, twenty-fifth, thirty-fourth, thirty-ninth and forty-fourth words in the first chapter are is. In the second chapter the is the third word, and the is the fourteenth word in the third chapter. In this chapter the first and last words are the.

CHAPTER 5

First is the first word in this chapter. In the fourth chapter the fifth word in the last sentence is first.

CHAPTER 6

The fifth word in the fifth chapter is word and words is the fifth word in the last chapter. Words in the second sentence in the fourth chapter is the eighth word. In the second chapter word is the fifth word, the twenty-first word, the thirty-third word, the forty-fifth word, the fifty-eighth word and the sixty-second word. Word is the third word in this chapter, and in in this chapter is the fourth word in the first sentence. In is the sixth and this is the seventh and chapter is the eighth word in this chapter is the fifth sentence in the first chapter.

CHAPTER 7

This is the first word in this chapter and the third and seventy-fifth word in the tenth chapter. Thirteen words in the first seven chapters are this.

CHAPTER 8

In the first chapter chapter is the last word. In the last chapter the twenty-seventh word is chapter, and in this chapter chapter is the first and the fifth word in the last sentence. Chapter in the next chapter is the ninth word in the third sentence.

CHAPTER 9

Sentence in the third chapter is the third word and the twelfth word in the sentence. Sentence is missing in the first chapter. Sentence in the last sentence in the second chapter is the eighteenth word. Sentence is missing in the fourth chapter and in the seventh chapter.

CHAPTER 10

In in this sentence is the first, second and twenty-first word, and this is the third, thirteenth and twenty-second word in this sentence. And is the first and fifth and seventh and ninth and eleventh word, and the fourteenth and the seventeenth, and and is the twenty-first, twenty-second and twenty-seventh word and the thirtieth word in this sentence, and in this chapter the seventy-ninth word is and. In the first chapter in and this are the sixth and seventh words.

CHAPTER 11

Words in this novel are are, next, last, A, Novel, a, missing, novel.

CHAPTER 12

Three words are A, two words are a, three words are Novel, seven words are novel in this novel. Thirteen words are CHAPTER, two words are chapters and forty-six words are chapter. Fifty-one words are is and thirty-six words are are. In this novel forty-one words are and and one hundred and three words are the. Thirty words are first. Three words are next. Ten words are last. Twelve words are second, eleven words are third, ten words are fourth, nine words are fifth and three words are sixth. Seven words are seventh and four words are eighth. Sixty-four words are in in this novel. Twenty-eight words are this and twenty-three words are sentence. Four words are missing. In this novel fifty-one words are word and thirty-eight words are words. Four words are word in this, the last chapter. Three words are GIRAFFE in this novel. Three words are Giraffe. Two words are giraffe. GIRAFFE is the first word. The last word is giraffe.

FIVE

Banyan

When "Beestes and briddes koude speke and synge . . ."
—Chaucer

I left my house. I went to live
in the house of the Banyan,
in the hush of space, in rooms of leaves.
A high round roof leaked ragged stabs of sky.
Chin on knees, I sat beside the wide pleated trunk
from which thick spokes of bumpy roots rayed out.
Their crooked hooks continued underground.
On a bare floor, but for brown dry leaves, I sat.
I was my own chair.
Swung a long arm up. My toes were grasping thumbs.
Asquat on the first smooth limb, I looked aloft
through scaffolds of layered shade.
I swung higher, and sat.
My lungs filled, I breathed cool mystery.
Such quiet aloneness enough for the first day. . . .
A broad limb that hardly steepened
its bridge toward the setting sun
became my couch for straddling sleep.
Soon the moon my bedlamp.
In transit, Jupiter and Venus lay out there
close enough to kiss. Or this was a dream.

THE 2ND DAY

Morning. I mounted higher.
I knuckle-walked an opposite limb. Twisting,
it trespassed a neighbor grove. I stole
a freckled fruit from the top of a bearing tree
that Banyan overstretched—yellow, shape of a small
football—bit it in half, sucked the sticky juice.
Inside were mucoid seeds, slimy, black.
The pulp was sweet.

Up high, my back to a central column, safe at home,
sequestered by leaves, at peace and belly full,
I began my survey. Stretched my short neck,

scratched an armpit, blinked lashless eyes
and stared around:

> Banyan from many elbows dangles strands
> of strong brown thongs. Long clean curling beards
> the wind swings. . . .

I yanked a handful of evidence, twirled and slid
neatly down. Hands are feet when need be, feet are hands.
Tail's an extra, a fifth. Can almost fist its ruckled end.
On the ground I found:

> Banyan's tough tassles grown long enough to touch
> soil, plant themselves, transform to roots. Roots rise,
> harden, become new trunks, fatten, grow limbs. Limbs
> branch, spread, intertwine and rise, thicken to GIGANTIC.
> Swollen coils could strangle Laocoön, his sons,
> and all his grandsons. . . .

Chin on knees, I crouched playing with a swatch
of Banyan's beard, the squared-off end like horsetail
hung a foot from earth, while other strands had rooted.
My eyes, nearly to the top of my forehead, stared
up at a monstrous muscular tangle. Squintholes in the roof
were squeezing shut. Was there a smell of storm in the air?
I imagined cloud-mountains swelling and fusing, black-veined,
writhing, the sky shutting solid. . . .

> Suppose a great grove of mature Banyans replicating
> without hindrance, reached out and down and up, invaded
> adjacent trees. A wall of trunks, entwisted limbs, thick beams,
> and underground, clenched roots upheaving. Suppose the process
> speeded up: struggle causing need for struggle, need causing
> need for accelerated speed. Suppose Banyan, a jungle, engulfed
> and hugged to death all other growth on the whole peninsula.
> Jammed together, a vast vegetable loaf, a dense choked block,
> closed as rock, would leave no air, no egress, no exit. . . .
> No house, no room, no breath.

I'd thoroughly scared myself. I lay down on my side,
and wrapped long arms around me. Curled tight in a trench
between the biggest roots, I fell asleep.

THE 3RD DAY

It rained in the night. A warm caressing rain.
I let it run its rills between my lips,
it washed and soothed my eyelids.
I awoke just at sunup, reached a long arm
to a new limb, climbed in a fast slant,
almost flying, and knuckled along a broad
limb that wriggled west. A path so clean and wide
I could have ridden it on a unicycle.
High off the ground the limb led deep
into the aerial forest. Although it was day
it was dark under leaf-roof dense and evergreen,
a blackish green like lizard's skin.
I ran sometimes, and sometimes swung along,
catching hold of the dangling tawny swags.
Looked down, saw gables and eaves depending
on pillars or shafts grabbed into earth below,
complex supports of the Banyan colony, a whole
estate. Tall circular uprights extending
from spacious arches were linked above by bridges,
balconies, tunnels, under-and-over-passes
which spread laterally and vertically, a labyrinth.
Unexpected, at a fork, an opening.
The broad path, the limb I ran on, swerved,
petered out to a narrower trail, and ended!
I sat on the point of a slender bouncing limb,
just now sprouting its first leaves.
Looking back, I saw the trunk this little limb
belonged to. Not a Banyan. A young Live Oak
appropriated by Banyan which, beginning at the base,
had trussed it round and round with cords and ropes
of vinelike roots that climbed the limbs.
Some trusses dragged the ground and anchored there.
The slender trunk, bound tight and squeezed,
awaited a dry death. The fragile top was green,
but I saw how the entire oak would be incarcerated,
killed finally inside the swelling base of a new
Banyan spreading skirts with heavy hems, merging

its roots and, from on high, slinging nooses
over the upper limbs of its prey, choking off
the sap, destroying it that way.

> Banyan, not from nut or pit or core nourished
> in earth grows up, but parasitic lives.
> Banyan exists and thrives by capture, torture
> and murder of youths, adjacent trees.

Then monster of trees! From such process
is beauty and wonder born? Does greatness come
from merciless exploit? Overwhelming evil then,
the campaign of Banyan, if its goal is gobble all
it can reach, to decimate its neighbor trees,
to leave no rooted trace of other body-shape alive
outside its own expanding torso. To combine,
for a solidarity beyond challenge, with ogres
of its tribe, to form a fortress lacking a single
slit through which a stab of death can creep?
Is this the goal of it? How and why occurs
the simultaneous spread—out and down and up at once—
of this necromancer, proliferating like a cancer?
I would find out.

THE 4TH DAY

Not to cause commotion
in the library
with my sudden hairy
self, I had the notion

of slipping in when it
would show CLOSED FOR
HOLIDAY on the door.
So here I sit.

I can pick a lock
as nimbly as a nose, or spin-
ning number to win,
or wallet from a pock-

et, or latch on any cage.
Leathery fingers in a drawer,
I riffled cards for BAN, for
TRE. Finally found book and page.

Only after certain
gymnastics, scrambling up ladder, hand
over hand, to land
with—"Whee!"—swing of a curtain,

on high balcony shelf labeled
BOTANICAL REFERENCE A TO Z,
was I to be
at last enabled
to read:
BANYAN. Greatest spread of any tree in the world. Height can be 100
feet. Aerial roots grow downward into soil and form thick pillars which
support the crown. Single tree can appear to be dense thicket. Related
to the Fig, which has similar unusual flowers and fruits. At the botanic
gardens of Sidpur near Calcutta is a famous Banyan with massive main
trunk twelve feet in diameter, and with huge additional trunks. The
whole covers an area of 900 feet in circumference.

> I am crouched on a stool,
> toes wrapped round a rung,
> pencil in teeth, absolutely hung
> up on this fool-
>
> ish research. Of course
> I'm ill-equipped. The duplicator,
> like the elevator,
> is out of order. Worse,
>
> autodidact that I am, by book
> little learning found
> not sniffed out on actual ground
> or by firsthand look. . . .

Well, to proceed:
BANYAN. Species of fig of the family *Moraceae* (Mulberry.) Held sacred
in India. The seeds germinate in branches in some other tree where

they have been dropped by birds. Young plant puts forth aerial rootlets
which, on reaching ground, grow secondary trunks to support hori-
zontal limbs. Branches from the trunks ultimately send down more
prop roots, until Banyan crowds out the host tree and becomes grove-
like. Covers large areas. Forms arbors. Seeds can germinate on walls
and buildings, causing cracking, as with the Strangler Fig.

> Reading these
> words, I must have muttered
> some when, harshly uttered
> from below, I heard: "Quiet, please!"
>
> Oh, someone's rage
> I'd aroused. But I could see
> no one. The command must be
> coming from a cage
>
> in the library's sunporch.
> There it hung
> and slightly swung.
> Something like a yellow torch
>
> I saw flip up within—
> a feathered crest, wild
> and spikey. A burst of riled
> repeats: "Quite, please!" made a din
>
> clear to the cathedral
> ceiling. Two or three grabs
> of the railing, and slabs
> of the tall wall
>
> of books, let me down. Landed,
> I laughed and said, "Boo!"
> to a White Cockatoo
> in a bell-shaped cage. Two-handed
>
> (or two-footed) and razor-clawed,
> thick-beaked, sassy and young,
> with a fat agile tongue,
> her cloud-white body broad-

hipped, she had alert round
eyes with lids of sky-blue.
"I'm Blondi," she hollered. "Who
are you?" "Tonto." I found

my name invented on the spur.
"So get me out of jail!"
"Of course." Applying my picklock nail
to the latch, I freed her.

THE 5TH DAY

We had gone far—far out, out on a limb,
Blondi on my back, beak clamped to my neck-hairs.
She clung to me, although we were not kin:
a coarse-haired Woolly Monkey ridden by a snowy,
silky, citron-tufted bird so purely beautiful.
Was she to be, by a flip of fate, my child?
Or mistress? Or mate, or other sort?
Anyhow, her mount. An unlikely pair. Where
would we go together? Wherever we liked,
it appeared. We hiked
our above-ground jungle, lost but entranced.
We tried every path. None led out. All led
in instead. Into the gnarled center
of Banyan's labyrinth. Was this the End,
this Center, the core of its initial trunk?
It had grown thicker, harder than before,
when alone I went to enter and explore.
The limb we stood on was wide as a sidewalk,
of smooth wood, high and curving, astonishingly
long, looping up and down and around, a good
fifty feet from the ground. And now, it
finally quit. Quit in the blind middle,
at a drop-off. Blondi hopped off,
as I sat upright. She came to my forearm,
walked to my shoulder, and tweaked
my ear. This time, with a tender beak.
A bit panicked, I complained, "What
are we doing *here*? Where do we go now, and why?"
"Go now," she squealed. "Let us go now,

you and I!" Her tone was mischievous. Mine
was annoyed. "What does *that* mean?" Sign
of my panic: "What does any of it mean?"
I leaned against a fork as into an armchair.
Blondi came to my knee. I continued:
"Where we are, where we're going, has to have
a purpose, doesn't it? If this is where we
live now, our house, our world, we need to find
some reason for its being—uh—as we find it.
Need to sense extension and geography,
some sort of history of growth and shape—
no matter how peculiar. To form a projection
of its future, don't you agree?"
"Birds in their little nests agree,"
Blondi sang triumphantly. Those librarians,
it became plain, had programmed her. Her brain,
although instinctively wise, had much to unlearn.
"Be serious for a minute, Blondi." My stern
suggestion went unheard. She squawked out:
"Whether thou choose Cervantes' *serious* air,
Or laugh and shake in Rabelais' easy chair . . ."
Before she could say the rest, I pretended
a cuff up-side-the-head. Her crest
flared erect like a yellow tulip. She skipped
to a limb above me, rampant, incorrigible.
Ignoring her, I went on: "We citizens here
domiciled apparently by chance, *if only* bird
and beast—" I drummed my chest—"need at least
one absolute with which to begin to invent
a future. Some inkling, of how our wandering
is linked to an intent hidden in this snarled
enormous process, ought to surface here.
After that, there ought to appear
some sort of map showing where we're going
and how best to get there." Dropping to my lap,
Blondi with her claw-tip began to bubble my
lower lip! I grabbed both feet and let her
dangle, head down, like a caught chicken, while
I ranted on to the end of my speech: "We need
to see forward—I mean *toward* an Opening, and we

need to remember *backward* to Beginning—to
Seed and Root and Trunk. So as to foresee
the Fruit." She managed to screech, even from
her ignominious position: "The fruit of that
forbidden tree whose mortal taste . . ."
What a clown! I set her down, upright. This
baby wasn't dumb. She cocked her sunny topknot,
ducked and, suddenly, chewed upon my thumb.
"Ouch!" I hollered. "Gotcha!" she bragged.
"Gotcha! Gotcha!" The jagged
pincer of her wide hooked beak,
its underhalf a saw,
and her strong jaw-
hinge, like a bulldog's, could draw
blood. It could
refuse to let go.
Mainly, she was gentle with me, though.

THE 6TH DAY

At first light exactly, Blondi climbed to a parallel,
slightly higher limb, stretched her glorious wings,
fanned them and squawked, "What's to eat? Blondi wants
a cob of sweet corn!" Saying this three times probably
meant she thought me a doubtful provider. And she had
only me. The security of her cage, her meals
provided in the library, had been left behind in order
to look for a better life. She could not fly. Both
wings had been clipped at the primaries. The best
she could do was to make short flaps upward, or brief
horizontal swoops. She had no hope of real takeoff.
In the high roof of Banyan were clusters of its copious
fruit, balls the size of small plums, claret red.
Like a streak I was hand-over-hand, and with nimble
toe-holds, up in loops and leaps, and when I slid and
swung back down, I had a branch ample with gay-colored
fruit in my teeth. In shade, at a fork I settled,
pulled off a "plum," licked it, let a tooth sink in,
winked at my pretty cockatoo. Maybe she'd bite and
taste. She did. From my hand she took and tongued

one of the red balls. Full of seeds, a bit grainy
and hard, but she liked it. She finished a bunch,
plucking each from its twig with her hooked beak,
dropping it into the palm of her "hand," her four-
fingered claw, with which she passed the fruit into
her mouth, cracking it in the hinge of her bone-like
jaw, letting the peel fall, swallowing only what
felt and tasted good. Finished, she pigeon-toed it
to a side-limb a little below me. I saw her flick
her short squared tail as she defecated, lifting her
wings away from her body. I saw how underwings and
tail hid hints of lemon matching the vivid yellow
of her crest when raised. On roost now, and at rest,
her eyes' blue underlids pulled shut from below,
her slate-blue beak plunged into the fluff of her
breast, her pate now smooth, completely white.
Odd how she could be so featureless as now, without
color, slick as a white wooden ninepin. Suddenly,
as like a Peeping Tom I peered from above, she stood
erect, stretched, spread wings and crest and every
feather lifted. A gorgeous fullblown snowy bloom—
a peony perhaps—she turned up for display all layers
of her pristine petals. Then, walking, hopping,
hoisting herself by beak, while mumbling rhythmic
squeaky comments—they sounded like staccato repeats
of "Oy, Oy, Oy!"—she managed to return to the wide
thick limb I sat on. Here she made a kind of toilette,
smoothing, arranging, placing each feather in its
allotted row with her beak and tongue. From a gland
at the base of her tail she brought tiny drops of oil
to groom her feathers. This kept them glossy and
impervious to wet or dust. The process took a long time.
I see just how it's done, was mumbling in my mind, *how*:

> Seeds of the fruit of the Banyan eaten by birds
> digested and voided, fall with their droppings
> to ground, are buried and sprout. Or, if left
> on tree limbs where bird has dined, they imbed,
> begin to grow and, in time, spill out a tassle,
> a rootlet that dangles down. That multiplies,
> lengthens until tawny aerial roots descend

and touch earth. Triumphant then, a slim new
shoot is born, destined to become a next great
trunk as, earth-locked, it begins to rise.

Blondi was making sleepy croaks. Her blue lids creeping
up over her pupils finally closed. Dusk in the east,
Venus visible to the right of a sunken sun, and Mars
dim red, low to the left in the west, the myriad glints
of sky high in our capacious roof deepened their blues,
darkened toward black. I lay belly-down along my wide
limb, my tail coiled at its end around an upper and
slimmer limb—which was Blondi's roost. A Woolly's
tail has no fur near its end. Ridges of the rougher
skin on my tail maintained my grasp even when I slept.
My perched cockatoo, too, would be steady and safe
all night. Curved gaffs locked around the branch,
her weight hunching her down, her body kept easy balance
as she slept. I was peacefully thinking, drifting
toward sleep, how Banyan, our big house of eternal
summer, was a complete world we, perhaps, need never
leave. Lovely the fact that it remained ever green,
impervious to seasonal changes, long-lived, strong,
a giant close to immortal. . . . I slipped into sleep.

THE 7TH DAY

A scream awakened me. High-pitched, ragged,
startling as a peacock's, as if rushing out
of the mouth of the sun itself.
It was only Blondi, crowing her greeting
to the day. Probably urging it to hurry
into full light. She strutted back and forth,
feathers fluffed, beak wide, fat dark tongue
arched, while sounding a series of trills,
clicks, whistles, croaks, mimicking other
birds she heard nearby and distant:
the Minah, the Macaw, a Spotbreasted Oriole,
a Bulbul, a family of Monk Parakeets and
a Forktailed Flycatcher. Using her beak
as a third "hand" she climbed on twigs up
limbs as on a ladder, and soon was high

enough to reach the Banyan's fruit by
herself. Following her, I saw her find
some dark ripe balls soft as figs, which
she rapidly relished. She hollowed the end
of her tongue like a spoon and scooped
drops of water from the folds and cups of
leaves, throwing back her head to swallow.
I breakfasted in the same way, except for
the use of different tools—teeth and
paws, and lips to sip with.
When we were satisfied, I presented my
back and the thick dark fur of my nape to
Blondi. Expert jockey, she instantly
grabbed and mounted me. We set out on a
new spur of our sprawling Banyan, pointing
east, but were soon moving up and down,
in and out in every direction.
Would we ever exhaust its possible paths
of exploration? It was one gigantic tree
at the same time as it was many.
Separated interconnected trunks constituted
a vast grove. Arbors had formed between
the side trunks, some of them fifty feet
or more away from the main where, below,
the root system like a wide skirt began
its spread upward to form buttresses.
Like columns and ribbed vaults and arches
of a great cathedral, the accessory trunks
helped hold aloft heavy horizontal branches
that, meanwhile, were extending and swelling
in diameter. I could estimate our Banyan
might be one hundred feet high and equally as
wide. At its widest it was a vigorous dense
thicket of glossy leaves completely hiding
the tree's armature, its trunks and limbs.
It was like an enormous closed rotunda.
Here was unique privacy, beauty, security.
It seemed one could live here—or two could—
free and happy to the very end of existence.
Banyan itself was virtually immortal. When

parts of the tree aged, younger parts would
simultaneously replenish.
My clever Cockatoo, too, had a parrot's
longevity. Studying her closely while our
intimacy grew, I could learn her tactics
of prolongation. I might live at least
a hundred years. . . .

"But why?" I heard my own
voice ask aloud. Blondi
on my back, riding me,
in the same tone

hootingly replied: "Why
or which or who or what
is the Akond of Swat?"
Undeflected, I went on, "Why

live long? Why does any thing
live at all? What's the purpose?"
"There's a porpoise
close behind us," she began to sing,

"and he's treading on my tail."
"Nothing behind us!" Monkey,
four-footed, neat as a donkey,
I picked the steepest trail,

where the windings of three
limbs, stretching up, became
contiguous, interlacing the same
way that a braid of hair can be

made with three strands,
the outer two brought under
and over the middle one—wonder-
ful device. Setting feet and hands

into notches in the central braid,
Monkey managed to climb,

half a body length at a time,
up the pitched grade

that twisted and wound
in and out, until it bent
under like a Möbius loop, went
out, up and around.

I lost direction. Blondi's neck
swivelled like an owl's
as, with yipes and growls
of effort, we gained a sort of deck

high in the inmost dark
green heart of Banyan.
As in a corridor or canyon,
walled by thick leaves, rough bark,

although it was midday,
only narrow knife-glints,
mercurial flashes, gave hints
of light's entry a long way

away, or of any clear
exit. Blondi's luminous white
shape made possible my sight,
and just barely. Dear

Blondi, she was a lamp
of revelation, simply by her
being. My thick and dusky fur
assigned me the opposite camp,

of shadow, secrecy, obscurity,
I was nimble, determined, strong
in intent to unravel the long
mystery. But purity

of instinct and immediate act
were Blondi's way: simply *living*

life, not straining for reason, giving
and taking pleasure and laughter. Fact,

or the need to discover Source
of all exploding, expanding,
replicating Life, was not demanding
for her, of course.

"The one security we share
is Death," I told her.
Thinking I meant to scold her,
she snatched my hair

with a claw, yanked, and ("Ouch!")
put spurs to my hide
with her backward slide
off me. Rising tiptoe from a crouch,

erecting crest, lifting wings,
she was a wild and snowy bush
of feathers, to which I gave a push
with my snoot: "Of all things!"

"All things counter, original, spare, strange,
whatever is fickle, freckled . . ." Blondi picked up
the cue in operatic voice. She expressed
what she'd been taught, not what she thought.
Blondi could not, need not think. Her kind of brain,
of tongue, her genius for mimicry supplied the lines
that carried on the play, and fit the plot
coincidentally. Sometimes she proved prophetic.
In the almost dark we now stood on a sort of
platform, formed by the inner strand of the braid
of wide bark, just where it emerged from an immured
ancient trunk, perhaps the original stem of Banyan.
I had expected to turn a corner,
to find ahead, within range, a view
that would change the aspect of everything
so far seen and experienced—that would explain
everything, and show how it all combined as a Whole.

"We've looked here and there and everywhere
and gotten no closer!" I burst out.
"Who lives everywhere lives nowhere," Blondi said.
"What and where is the purpose?" I persisted.
"My purpose holds to sail beyond the sunset," she said.
"What if it's marked in the bark of this very trunk,
a sort of hieroglyph awaiting translation? What if
it's printed on my thumb?" I held up my thumb,
as if I could read the whorled lines. I collected
my tail and examined its rough end. The purpose
might be recorded by those ridges, being ready
for interpretation at mature growth.
What if the answer already belongs to me? I thought.
If inherent, then each of us already has his own.
If so, do we also need to know it?
"If an individual answer exists for each one,
what's to learn?" I asked this aloud, and Blondi
answered: "Learn of the green world what can be
thy place." Advice I could agree with.
"No overall true way? None to be found?"
About to tuck her head under a wing, Blondi replied
in a sleepy croak: "The true way goes over a rope
which is not stretched at any great height but
just above the ground."
If she and Kafka happened to be right, then
we were at the wrong altitude. I lay down on
the dizzy platform, drew knees to my chin.

THE 8TH DAY

This day, which began before dawn, was spent moving from
the dark twisted core of Banyan toward its edge, and down
through endless tangles and tributaries of its thousand-limbed
system. I moved in a trance, and Blondi on my back clutching
my neckhair with her beak rode limp, as if still asleep.

We were both tired. What had happened at the top of the
smooth center strand of the braid that issued from the knotted
core of Banyan had been an emotional hurricane—at least for
me. Blondi had enthusiastically mimicked my every reaction and
gesture with full harsh volume.

Such a strange happening. . . . Had it been a dream?

A cage-shaped room, seeming transparent at first, was found to be reflective, a continuous wall-circling mirror. In the roof, a round opening which blades of lightning penetrated, dazzled and frightened us, igniting the room to platinum brightness. In the skyhole there appeared, floating—not clouds—what looked like chunks of ice, as if broken from an ice mountain, and there was a crackling sound like ice separating, under the growl and gurgle of water.

The "clouds" submerged and the opening turned black, glossy, a downsideup well, a depth without bottom. But since we were looking *up*, it ought to seem a vortex in the mirror-roof, tightening its whorl as it drilled higher. It widened suddenly like an eye's pupil, then narrowed, clicked closed. Again it opened, and lightning danced in.

A ring of images: of me, Tonto, and of Blondi beside me, leaped around the curved sides with the jagged lightning, finally subsiding to a standstill.

I had never seen myself. I mean, never myself standing *over there*, across from me—had never seen me entire, a whole creature. Had never seen my back, front and sides, and my face *all in one* at the same time, like this.

Opposite, in front of me was reflected a slim black Woolly Monkey covered with dense fur from the nails of toes and fingers to the eyes, mouth and naked ears, and from the top of the round head to near the end of a long prehensile tail. He had a doglike muzzle, somber deepest yellowbrown eyes, and the line of the lips curved up in a sickle shape.

Lightning spurted through the hole and around the cave again, and Blondi was swept into hoarse giggles and gusts of laughter. I shivered and whirled about. My fur stood up in a ridge along my back. I felt a strange electric thrill that made me whine, that bared my teeth. I paced four-footed right and left, nose to nose with myself. Strange, there was no smell.

The flickering ceased, but the intense light remained, turning the circular wall into a blinding sheet of foil. Finally the glare modified so I could see into it. Now two other persons stood reflected instead of Tonto and Blondi. I would rather not look. But I couldn't get away. Backing up, I saw a very old, naked woman backing up, stopped by the mirror-wall behind her.

She was shrunken, her skin was sallow-gray and hung in pleats. Her stomach poked out and sagged, partly hiding her slumped, hairless pudenda, and her flattened breasts hung, the left longer than the right. Shoulders were narrow, upper back hunched, skinny neck and nearly hairless head thrust forward. Arms and lower legs were thin, but the flaccid thighs, the buttocks and the coil of fat at the waist hung in jelly-like bags. Her body was spotted with warts of all sizes, some brown, others pink, and there were smaller hanging moles. Two moles hanging under her chin each had a coarse hair sprouting from it. Hands and feet showed purplish distended veins, and looked cold. The face seemed to have melted. Cheeks had slipped below the cheek-bones. Pouched eyelids almost covered the slits of eyes. The left lid hung lowest—she could scarcely see from that side. Between nose and upper lip, the skin, dry and wrinkled, showed gray hairs that matched the frowning eyebrows. Her lips, string-like and crooked, pressed together sternly, and the mouthcorners hooked down to meet trenches of the slack jaws and corded neck. The chin, crosshatched and furrowed, had a few crimped hairs. Strangely, the forehead with its limp fringe of square-cut hair, was hardly wrinkled at all. Although the earlobes had lengthened and creased, the small nose, which was upturned with round prominent nostrils, remained inappropriately child-like. Once the flesh would have slipped entirely off her skeleton, she would not be quite so ugly: A frame of firm white bone, a delicate skull with empty eyeholes and fragile nose-socket, I foresaw, would be graceful compared to this desiccated body in its extreme old age.

The old woman wriggled her nose and coughed up a gob of sputum, munching on it while squinting back at me with a sour and suspicious expression. I looked down and saw, standing beside her, a child of about two years old, in a starched white dress. She was wearing black stockings and roundtoed black buttoned shoes. Straight, fine hair, blond, was cut square across the forehead above a tiny short nose. Rosebud lips were slightly parted in a tentative smile. A wide yellow ribbon bow stood on her head erect, like a whirligig. The child was pushing one chubby hand into a pocket of the home-sewn dress which was bordered with lace at hem and sleeves. A downy eyebrow, the right, arched a bit higher than the left, quizzically. Her narrow blue eyes held a direct look, confident and cool.

There was meaning to this vision. I could feel it. I understood. Whether real or dreamed, at the apex of our path, the limit of our search, there had been a signal confrontation. When the two images in the mirror vanished, replaced by a White Cockatoo with yellow crest and a grave-faced Woolly Monkey, I had said aloud, as if on some cue from the wings: "The purpose of life is to find . . ."

". . . the purpose of life!" Blondi interrupted in a shriek, making the intended question into its own answer. She did a wild pirouette. She had articulated what might be, I realized, a hopeless truth.

We were swinging down by my long arms from limb to limb. The limbs were wet, the leaves still held water, the wind blew. But the great storm had passed over. In rhythmically, gradually widening circles we descended toward the rosy, and then the gilded sunrise which mounted in the outer branches of Banyan. Our downswing took a long time.

It sometimes happens, when I'm carrying out some rhythmic, repetitious physical work, that words in cadence come into my head. As, with Blondi on my back, I dropped and ambled through the tree, my mind being immersed and haunted by last night's vision, I began to chant:

> Small to great
> Great to small
> Robust to flimsy
> Tiny to tall
> Clear-eyed to blind
> Fleet to stagger
> Blossom to rot
> New spoon dull dagger
> Birthgasp to heartstop
> Longing to lust
> Flesh to bone
> Bone to dust

Soon Blondi was saying it with me. It was she who had the no-
tion of chanting it backwards, a variation which worked as well:

> Dust to bone
> Bone to flesh
> Lust to longing
> Heartstop to birth
> Dagger to spoon
> Rot to Blossom
> Stagger to fleet
> Blind to clear
> Tall to tiny
> Flimsy to robust
> Small to great
> Great to small

Our traverse of our green universe in its four dimensions
encompassed miles—up, in, out, down. Banyan's growth and
pattern, its evolution and expansion, although so intricate and
immense, seemed blind. Maybe fortunate, I thought, because
to have been foreseen and deliberate, stultified by logic, by aim
and conscious end, would impose a fixed mortality, a necessity
for extinction on this giant of nature.

Symmetry was everywhere avoided in its intuitive structure,
and yet, unerring balance along with strength let it continually
flourish. The many sidetrunks that had once been dangling ten-
drils, beginning their upward growth sometimes fifty or more
feet away from the main trunk, propped up the increasingly
heavy branches and insured that Banyan would survive the rav-
ages of hurricane and typhoon. Roots of the main trunk, having
attained huge size while the expanding limbs were buttressed
by accessory trunks, allowed Banyan the greatest spread of any
tree in the world. Its architecture, which appeared random, held
endless delights and surprises, and especially an air of undefin-
able mystery.

Far out, on a whorled thick limb at the western edge of its
boundary, more than three-fourths down its principal height,
we rested. We had our supper of wild Mango, or Monkey Apple,
the drupe of which is, in flavor and size, between a nectarine
and a plum. Branches of this tall Mango tree penetrated among

some of the lower limbs of Banyan. After sunset now, birds were floating in to nest in branches above us: the Monk Parakeet, Indian Mynah, the Bulbul, the Ani, the Stripe-Headed Tanager. Below in the twilight, a flock of Cockatiels skidded in to roost in Banyan. There followed three young Rose-Breasted Cockatoos. One wafted upward toward us, perched parallel, and stared at Blondi. How long since she had seen one of her kind? There was quick recognition. Instinctively she raised her crippled wings, stood up on tiptoe, and took off, intending to cross the fifteen feet between her and the birds. I had no time to catch her. She dropped, claws spread, mouth wide and tongue tolling, popeyed with terror, crashing through ledges of leafy branches. Grabbing at swags of rootlets, I raced to drop below her. A miracle that, in the near dark, I caught her in my arms before she could strike a limb and break her delicate bones. Knees bent, I put my back against a trunk, fisted the end of my tail around an upper limb, and cradled her against me, tucking her plushy snowy head under my chin. She whimpered and moaned, yet craned upward to where one of the Cockatoos had been perched. All three, of course, had soared out of sight—to Blondi's regret and my relief.

We would spend the night here, I decided. Blondi huddled against me, her pupils rolled upward, her blue eyelids raised and soon shut.

Now it was dark, a diamond-shaped opening in Banyan's canopy above us showed Jupiter in Capricorn still visible, but about to set. In Scorpio, Mars would soon rise, and then Saturn, while Pluto, always very dim, would not be seen until after midnight.

THE 9TH DAY

The Long Night Moon at its most
northern point and fullest, 2:30 a.m.,
waked me, outlined every frond and stem
and swatch and muscular bough above, ghost-

white against black, a sky-wide X-ray.
The Long Night Moon rose below
us, swollen at horizon, climbing slow,
amazingly close, across a broad bay

gleaming in the east. Soon to land in the "real,"
having traveled what seemed a long
lifetime in a tree, a certain strong
fondness began to steal

over me for the old remembered scene:
my two-legged self walking the flats,
clothed like other thins and fats
who glide their rails of habit and routine . . .

". . . preparing themselves for life, which means a job and se-
curity in which to raise children to prepare themselves for life,
which means a job and security in which . . ."

To slump back into the old halfsleep
of questionless existence? Live "as God wills"?
Just trust and be comfortable? Oh, rippling chills
ran up my spine! When would I leap

again into the arms of Banyan and,
swinging, let go, in free fall tumble, grab
a broad lower limb, land on its slab,
a smooth, horizontal, windfresh, leafy, grand

couch, or hammock swung among the stars?
Once I saw the thin old crescent moon,
Mercury and sparkling Venus strewn
in a magic diamond with ruddy Mars.

In silence so high on a clear night
like this, I felt I'd see to the edge
of Universe from my ledge.
Listening with held breath, I might

hear the faint first chime—
the soundwave starting to flow—
struck eighteen billion years ago
at the beginning of Time.

It was two and a half hours before sunrise when Blondi awakened. She did not scream, but merely clucked and fussed and combed the feathers of her chest with her serrated beak.

"Did you know," I said to her, "that our planet Earth and ourselves are made of the same stuff that Supernovae once exploded into space?"

"Did you know, did you know," she said, "that Earth weighs six sextillion, five hundred eighty-eight quintillion tons?"

"Exactly? My god!" I said.

"We are not to ask the mass of God," she said.

She's erudite and opinionated, I thought, possessing the rare genius-factor of uneraseable memorization located in the hippocampus of some brains. But at least Blondi is not a name-dropper. She never mentions the illustrious sources of her quotes. "Today," I told her, "Halley's Comet is due to appear, tail first, above the southeastern horizon just before sunrise."

She had nothing to say to this, to my surprise, but her round eyes with azure rims and unblinking pearl-gray pupils, seemed to enlarge penetratingly. It could be she had already seen Halley's Comet when it visited the solar system seventy-six years ago in 1910.

Moving to an outer limb with an open view of the predawn southern sky, we settled for the comet watch. Mars and Saturn were unmistakable, and the star Antares, in the eye of Scorpius, below Saturn. We had hoped for a bright swirl. What finally arrived was a tiny fuzzy circular blur, with a wisp of a tail leaning right, near the horizon. Miniature dim dustball, or ice-pebble, it wavered there, hard to keep in focus, easily lost among millions of glittering stabs in an ocean of black. Until our star, the Sun, arose and swept the slate of heaven clean.

I stretched and looked around in the light, surprised at how far down we'd come by now. We could see the ground already, and looking east from the low crotch where we'd camped last night, we could see, turning turquoise in the sunshine, the wide bay, its beach closely lined with cedars and cypress. Fishing boats were anchored along its southern curve. Parkgrounds thick with palmetto and palm trees appeared below. With Blondi on my back, today a tranquil little jockey, we continued our spiral descent, meanwhile seizing for breakfast whatever fruit happened within reach. We found, in branches of trees that Banyan with its aerial roots had strangled and incorporated, some of the mucilaginous oblong orange balls, like large kumquats or small footballs, also eggfruits with sweet pumpkin-colored pulp. The polished pits like chestnuts were delicious.

I tried to recognize the paths of broad winding limbs and the shapes of ample forks, "rooms" we'd occupied or passed through in earlier travels. No, it wasn't possible. The scheme of Banyan was too large and complex. Or else we had not come this way going up. Or else the difference in angle of approach changed the view ahead. Parts of the tree would already have altered with new leaf growth, or changed with discarded branches after surges of storm. In fact, shifts of light and shadow, clouds, or winds were constantly altering shape and pattern, not to forget the changes of focus, of concentration and accuracy of aim, in the very lenses of our eyes.

Already we were down so far that through rents between branches we could see the splayed-out roots humped over the ground beneath the pillars and arches of Banyan, and the ends of long horsetails that, once they reached soil, would root themselves, widen, harden, become tripods, to form thicker footings that combined to make trunks of greater girth. The first impulse to growth for Banyan was not a stretching up toward light, but a groping down into earth.

I saw below, how an aerial root had dropped down and touched the top of a wide eight-foot wall of rough dark coral. It had snugged itself between the grooves outlining the stones and, where these widened, the root jaggedly swelled, snaking its way across and down. As some of the rootlets thickened, tucking between the sections of coral, they pushed them apart, splaying the crevices so that the wall began to break. I noticed how, at different places of the wall according to whether it was firm or crumbling, the descending roots accommodated themselves to the offered width and depth of inbetweens and, crimped or expanded, made their way over and under, extending on top or crawling along the border of the wall, until they finally reached soil in which to sink.

Pausing to rest and looking down, we found a stone gatepost draped in the several loops of an old tough Banyan root, convoluted, clumped and knotted, its heavy twisted length looking as if in motion. Of course it *was* in motion, so slow as to be undetected. Exactly like the coil of a boa constrictor wrapping the square wide post, it was the same grim color of old coral.

From above, seeing these signs of our approach to earth, knowing we were coming close to human properties and houses, the sun higher now, although it was still early, the light enlarging, scouring clear all the spacious rooms, balconies, rotundas, and the narrow nooks and mazelike corridors, bridges, underpasses of Banyan's every deck and story, I needed hesitation now—just now, when the possibility of camouflage was shrinking. I sat upright at a fork, shrugging Blondi off my back, offering my forearm to the double clutch of her strong feet. She brought her face close to me and rubbed her forehead against mine. She was mumbling, stammering something in a scratchy voice: "To find. The purpose of. Life is . . ."

Blondi was filing into memory, for future quoting, words of *mine*. I must get her home where she usefully belonged.

Continuing lower, we came to a place about twenty-five feet from the ground, where one of Banyan's offspring was trying to engulf an electric light pole. Limbs from a company of trunks on the other side of the road had crossed it above, building a leafy connecting arcade with branches joined and entwined which, duplicated and extended all along this highway, created a Banyan tunnel. Through this shady tunnel the auto traffic ran. It was six o'clock; people were already driving to work. Seated above them with Blondi, still hidden on one of Banyan's green balconies, I had the fantasy that, were the cars, one after the other, to stop below us, strong ropes of Banyan's beard dangling there might wrap around and lift each one, along with the passengers. Each would be bent, and crushed and thrust into the folds of Banyan's massive twisted trunks, which would swallow the cars, wheels and all, making them part of Banyan's expanding growth.

But it was time to exit from the tree while there was a chance of doing it neatly and quietly. I needed to get back undetected to my house on Flamingo Lane.

As Blondi trustfully clung to me, I jumped and gained the top of the electric pole, taking care to avoid contact with its wires that passed through a part of the cable-like strangler roots and limbs of Banyan. I handily spiraled down, using the cleats on the pole, crouching behind a trunk until there was a break in the traffic. I scurried across the road with Blondi, over the wall, into parkland, and then we loped along in the shadow of giant stalks of bamboo, flowering hibiscus trees and date palms.

COCKATOO MYSTERIOUSLY
RETURNS TO LOCKED CAGE

Coconut Grove, Fla., April 12—Ten days ago, Blondi, a white cockatoo, for many years an attraction in the town library, disappeared from her cage. Nothing else was missing, Marianne the Librarian reported. The empty cage was found locked, as were all windows and the front door. Yesterday, when the Librarian opened up at 9 a.m., she was greeted by Blondi shouting from her perch in the large hanging cage, "Quiet, please!" This phrase was the first her tongue had learned to enunciate clearly. She said it with startling authority. As Marianne delightedly approached the cage, Blondi rocked up and down on her perch and repeated her second accomplished line: "SH-SH-SH!" in a harsh whisper, while she lifted her right claw and held a tine against her open beak.

Marianne told *The Miami Herald* that she had no idea how the cockatoo got out, where she had been, nor how she got in again. "The cage is locked and unlocked with one key—mine—and it has no duplicate," the Librarian said. "But I'm glad she's back safe, and she seems fine."

The cockatoo has acquired new phrases during her stay outside the library, wherever that might have been. She repeated for this reporter a declaration she now pronounces often. Beak uplifted, wrinkled lids of an astonishing blue drawn up over her eyes, and with her lemon crest fully erected, Blondi the cockatoo recites in a pious croak, as if it were a poem:

> The purpose of life is
> To find the purpose of life
> To find the purpose
> Of life is
> The purpose
> Life is
> To find

SELECTED UNCOLLECTED
AND POSTHUMOUSLY
PUBLISHED POEMS

Creation

It is a stern thing,
This bringing into being;
This taking of a clod that is cold
And veining it with sprouts of fire;
This wresting of a star from chaos,
And chiseling it upon the lathe of exactness;
This making of an indolent thing urgent;
This begetting of eagerness;
It is a hard and a fierce thing . . .
Did You find it so, God?

1932

The Vain Dust

I am one
among a million dust grains
abandoned by the wind
in a corner
But does not the single ray
of sun upon me
achieve an elegance
that is mine alone?

I am dust
but I am an arrogant dust

My thought
in its uniqueness
booms in the heavens
My dream
is a bronze bell
tolling in the sky

My vanity is a crutch
for the lameness

527

of my self-assurance
My vanity is the palate
with which I savor
the wines of life

Strip me of this cloth of gold
and I must put out my eyes
not to behold
the startled nakedness
of my soul

1932

First Star

Now day, sallow
(ebbing out on skybeach)
lays bare in shallow
the large pearl

dripping on blue sands.
Behind the rosy foam
(slipping away to dark lands)
the clear pearl

lies wistful in the darkling
while, before the coast
is a manifold of sparkling
sleetpearls.

1933

January This Year

The ground
is a blackened corpse
unshrouded
The burnt grass
like untended hair
lies long and dank

on the lower hills
Torn wet leaves
mat the ditches
evidence of autumn's rape
half concealed
The sun
is the poking yellow finger
of a bleary old woman
When will the gray nuns
of the clouds
come to coffin the land
and cover her
with starched skirts
of snow?

1934

Goodnight

He and the wind
She and the house

Slow from the house
whose mellow walls
have fondled him
slow from the
yellow threshold
to the purple wind

Harsh as a dog's tongue
the licking wind
upon her throat
Rough it wraps
and fondles her
as slow into the night
he walks

She and the house now only
He and the wind

1934

Oblong Afternoons

I would make with paint
and set in a frame
the oblong afternoons of summer
in the stupefying weather

I would lay thick with scalpel
how apple boughs float
foundering skiffs
in moody orchards

Waxen apple sheen
poplar sheen
dark sheen of asphalt
I'd make a suave brush

In obtuse sky
how the sun is fat
I'd stab an ochre dob
and in the porches
of square spinning houses
fix a deep blue shock of shade

1934

Down to Earth

Once walking
in the city
I came
to where the
pavement broken
the earth was bare

My shoes broken
my bare feet once
felt the earth O cool
sweet

1934–38

Earth Your Dancing Place

Beneath heaven's vault
remember always walking
through halls of cloud
down aisles of sunlight
or through high hedges
of the green rain
walk in the world
highheeled with swirl of cape
hand at the swordhilt
of your pride
Keep a tall throat
Remain aghast at life

Enter each day
as upon a stage
lighted and waiting
for your step
Crave upward as flame
have keenness in the nostril
Give your eyes
to agony or rapture

Train your hands
as birds to be
brooding or nimble
Move your body
as the horses
sweeping on slender hooves
over crag and prairie
with fleeing manes
and aloofness of their limbs

Take earth for your own large room
and the floor of earth
carpeted with sunlight
and hung round with silver wind
for your dancing place

1936

Subconscious Sea

Oh to cast the mind
into that cool green trough
to be washed and dashed
and twirled and dipped
between those waves

Delicious the swipe of a green wave
across this puzzled forehead

And through the span
of a long long night
when the waters are dark
and scarred with silver
oh to drop
this enigmatic clot
down the nebulous stairs of the sea

to rest at last
on the ocean's floor

There beneath layers
of a thousand waves
a thousand veils between it
and the sun
this frail bowl
nuzzled in sand
salt grains sifting its sockets
would come to rest
taste its own eternity

1930s

Who Are You I Saw Running?

Who are you I saw running
down streets of dream
with long stride running aloofly
breasting the milky dawn

stepping upon your shadow
and leaving no footprint?

When you had run far down
that path and made exit
into the corner of distance
I awoke with your image in my eye
barely as tall as my pupil

Since then I have looked
for you in every street
gazed down each vague avenue
run headlong many nights
to strange horizons
and panting have returned
not finding you

You are in one of those
towns and dawn is on the cobbles
not so far from here
around this corner

You are in one of those
stealthy towns of sleep
running in the street
stepping upon your shadow
leaving no footprint

1936

White Mood

Tonight
within my brain no bell
only the snowing
of my thoughts

Flake on flake
sharp and white

snow my thoughts
against the night

In tall silence
the snowdunes deepen
swerving
fingered by wind

Shadow-stroked and blue
my thoughts are heaped
and swerve
even as snow

One word were it spoken
would take black shape
like a footprint
in the naked snowdune

But no word is born
no bell swings
in the steeple
of my brain

1936

To D. H. Lawrence

You are dead, Lawrence.
No, how can this be—?
Not when the best of you is here
with me.

The very best of you
the essential tear
loosed from your eye's brink
has fallen here.

The one most reddest blood drop
that which stood

at your heart's edge
has come to good wells
and now distends the vein
of my lush passion
and is moist again.

Come dear, I give you dwelling,
your shade is not astray,
alert and compelling
climb up in me and sway.

Fasten here the lute's string
that quivers alone
though the lute be crumbled
the plucking finger gone.

1936

Like Thee, Falcon

Like thee, falcon
with feet drawn up and curled,
lifted keenly on my wings,
I would be lifted.

I would reel in air,
infinity my marge.
As a feather wafted,
I would be wafted.

Or sturdy be, and slim—
let wind no longer lilt me.
A black chip upon the lake,
I would be, like him.

Hovering on sky that's wide
and leveler than water,
till dawn should break across my wing
and smoothly lap me like a tide.

Would alight and clasp the wrist,
I too would return who was tossed;
as the falcon, return would I too
from the mist.

1936

The Maiden in the Grass

Little grasses
rising beside my arms
and at my underarms . . .
little wistful Grass
your roots are white as my arms.
Shaggy rug of grass on which my body is pressed,
my heart leaps against thee, Grass . . .
do you hear my heart?

O Stone
I lie cheek to cheek with thee . . .
subconscious thing
feel here velvet flesh
and breath of rapture . . .
Stone you are my lover
You I take between my breasts.

Wind, come
you shall find all the tender hollows
of my young body . . .
Come gently to me Wind
and pass a hand along my thighs.

I kiss thee, little hot Grass . . .
I creep up against thee, yearning Stone . . .
Have me. Wind . . . I turn, I part my garment.

1936

Haymaking

The sagging hayricks file into the lane
The horses' chests are wading
toward home and evening
Today they gather summer to the barns
The lean-hipped men in aisles of stubble
lurching pitch whole yellow acres
the sun astride their necks all day

Now they rock in tousled cradles
Sweat-dark reins lace idle fingers
Soon to taste evening on the tongue
Evening will smooth their eyelids

By forkfuls they gather summer in
to heap in the cool barns
Snug against the rafters pile the
yellow stuff of summer
Against the crisp walls press
the sweet grasses
Bed down the loft with a shaggy mattress
and line the shady stalls where butterflies
drift through the knotholes

So when winter whistles in the bee
and frets the willow
of her last ragged leaf
when snow leans in the doorsill
at the steaming crib the cow
will munch on summer
With brown bemused stare
pools and pasture shade
juicy banks of green she'll conjure
and absently will wag an ear
at droning memory's fly

1936

At the Ballet

The dancer places his hands lightly
around the waist of the ballerina
as she descends along his thigh

Her legs parted
one knee bent
the truncated toe of her slipper
touching his pouted groin
she glides lingeringly
down his chest and thigh

His haunches snugly divided
as those of a horse
are pressed together
His feet on toe
are accurate as hooves
Sweat glistens
in the hollow of his throat
but her profile
is a cameo of cool repose

Of what is he thinking
as her flat torso
passes between his palms
as her puffed skirt
floats above her hips
as her hair brushes his nostrils
as her toe for a moment rests
upon his groin
as she descends
like a gossamer swan
he has caught in flight?

Not of her warmth
for she is like marble
Not of her weight
for she is light as smoke

Perhaps of her beauty
which like a blossom without scent
a fruit without taste
ignites his mind with ecstasy
and drains his body of all desire

1936

In Spoonfuls

I demand of myself
when I say, "You must write these poems,"
that which in the old tale,
the mistress charged of her ambitious lover,
that he go with a teaspoon to empty the sea.

Yet my love is even this great
and unreasonable,
that I do run down again and again
to the dripping sands,
knowing that one thousand lives
spent undeviatingly
by one a thousand times so strong
as I,
could not perform it.

Yet I go
(depending on this one moment
of eagerness)
to dip up the sea in spoonfuls.

1936

Jupiter Street

This is where I live
eight years out from Sundown
on a dancing star

in Jupiter Street
in the cool wide country
of Sky

My home is a star
enchanted to its path
near the silver track of Venus
and a comet's throw from Mars

Star swathed by winds
night and snow alighting
upon its face
its crags and hollows
diamonded with snow
On the shadowed seas
the tides rush out
flying the kite of the moon

This is where I live
on a highroad skirting Chaos
on a dancing star
in the upland country of Sky
I who look a little
like my mother
and my father
And there are all the others
looking somewhat
like their parents

There is me and there are many
there is this star
and there are many
glittering the avenues of heaven
dancing near and away
and eons out from Sundown

1936

To F.

The el ploughs down the morning
The newsboys stand in wait
Sunlight lashes the cobbles
We reach the crosstown gate

Your bus will stop at Christopher
Mine at Abingdon Square
Your hand . . . "Good luck" and mine . . . "So long"
The taxi trumpets blare

The green light turns, a whistle blows
Our steps divide the space
Between our day-long destinies
But still I see your face

Whirling through the crowded hours
Down the afternoon
Lurking in my thoughts, your smile
Pricks me like a tune

1938

Wild Water

Insidious cruelty is this
that will allow the heart
a scent of wild water
in the arid land—
that holds out the cup
but to withdraw the hand.

Then says to the heart: Be glad
that you have beheld the font
where lies requitement,
and identified your thirst.
Now, heart, take up your desert;
this spring is cursed.

1938

Nightly Vision

Green river that enwraps my home
I see you twining still in dream
There is perpetual afternoon
and summer brooding by that stream

I see the clouds that pause and sit
ever above the blue-cloaked field
No wind lurks in the hissing wheat
nor night nor change the visions yield

The house and there within a room
they move (but softly as through glass
have being for the eye alone)
They move as ghosts the color of flesh

A dream of diligence confines
my footsteps to the shadowy stair
and to the green evasive lanes
that bind a house and one room there

On the mind's chaos a mirage
of windless valleys and of home
waits for the sleeper like a stage
to which he must nightly come

1939

Trinity Place

Bootblacks and tombstones
share the sun and so

do pigeons perched in Mary's arms
in the sooty naves.

Behind the iron palings
weary grass has ceased to grow
on the muddy graves.

In dark and dreaming piety
the Virgin stands at noon.

A policeman like a shepherd
parts the bleating pack of cars.

Under this worn and sacred soil
what bones are strewn?

The bootblacks kneel
on bits of chamois
by the iron bars.

1939

Asleep

His shadowed face is closed   His eyes
are turned backward and down
His body lies without to guard the gate
of the mind's town   Sinking he has
for tether a braid of breath   Time
suspends the diver who plays with death

Trusting the tide he willingly returns
to a lost island in a nameless sea
as a dog unleashed leaps headlong
to the wind on the
unconscious scent of memory   His body lies behind
upon the shore   The salty flood rises
and murmurs in his blood

1940

This Is What My Love Is Thinking

His meekness is more terrible than any vice

Amity makes for contentment
but violence is creation

I am chained by the chains which I have fastened
on him

I do not dare to tire of him before he shall have
tired of me

and if this happened
I should be even more obliged to stay bound

I could break with him utterly
if I thought he would weep

but he would hide his pain
thus forcing me to condemn myself

If only he would do that
which would make me hate him

but then, not to match his meanness
I would have to forgive him
and so tighten the knot

Still I do not want to be rid of him
I only want to be free

To possess myself only
and so be lonely?
Or to lose myself wholly
to win what can never be mine
solely?

1940

The Sea

When the sea is calm I wade
into her glossy swells
Their bloom of froth sways toward me
Like crossing a field where the grain
ripens ever higher
I would walk to the true center
leaving no furrow behind me
would walk down
in the secret shade
and hide like a child
by the motionless roots
of the tall tangled water

When the sea is wild
on her harsh pelt of sand the near waves
put fetlocks of foam on my ankles
An enormous bristling scroll
unwinds and rerolls frenzied white
at its edge icy green in its oncoming curl
Like the gap between lightning
and thunder a towering moment of dread
The great cavity
darkens to black
Then the smash
A monumental vase has broken on the beach

The sea retreats in a hissing
spate of silver raking sand and shells
and smooth-sucked stones into her pouch
And I am pulled forward
by the flashing magnet of the sea
outward toward her hungry to fall
into her rough insane
annihilating grasp

1941

War Summer

How chaste you are
at evening
mortal earth
your bloody waters
silvered by the moon

your corpses
in the cool woods
hidden far
At evening earth
how chaste you are

The murdered lie
in faceless sleep
hidden deep
Beside the crippled
cannon in the wood

the murderer lies
with open eyes
ennobled by a star
at evening earth
How chaste you are

1945

Sunnymead

Sunnymead
and sunrippled
manyfingered wave

gloss and green

a moment of twilight
will deprave

Boys and horses
foaming home
the flank and thigh
are sentient

Lovelier than speed
is love

and both are transient

Carve a coin
to bribe the sea
or tame the horses
to tender be

How many heroes
swarm the tale
where beauty
is the holy grail

For she is a dread
a distant thing
that men and horses

and the sea

take the moon
her mirror to be

1945

Dreams and Ashes

Only on the anvil's edge
where the blue fire flashes
will my lead love turn to gold
The rest is dreams and ashes

Only in sleep or solitude
where fancy's fountain plashes

will my dead love rise to swim
The rest is dreams and ashes

Only on the unmarked page
wherever the bold mind dashes
will my fled love follow me
The rest is dreams and ashes

1946

The Indivisible Incompatibles

They are like flame and ice
the elemental You and Me
Will nothing then suffice
but they shall extinguished be?

I am locked in glacial pride
You burn with impetuous scorn
My prison is silence
Your arena is wrath
They are opposed as night and morn

If this is so how can it be
we sought each other long ago
and crept together hungrily?

You are quenched in my cold heart
as I dissolve in your core of fire
Then why do we crave each other's touch
magnetized by one desire?

When one forged his armor so
bright as ice and cold as slate
did he divine a spear so swift
and savage as to penetrate?

When one wrapped himself in flame
and emerged a glowing tool

did he dream of substances
irresistible and cool?

Yes
but in fusion
such raw alloys
instantly each the other destroys

1946

In Love Made Visible

In love are we made visible
As in a magic bath
are unpeeled
to the sharp pit
so long concealed

With love's alertness
we recognize
the soundless whimper
of the soul
behind the eyes
A shaft opens
and the timid thing
at last leaps to surface
with full-spread wing

The fingertips of love discover
more than the body's smoothness
They uncover a hidden conduit
for the transfusion
of empathies that circumvent
the mind's intrusion

In love are we set free
Objective bone
and flesh no longer insulate us
to ourselves alone

We are released
and flow into each other's cup
Our two frail vials pierced
drink each other up

1946

Two Shadows Touch

Behind my eyes
in light and shade
a landscape of the mind is laid

In the aisles
of sun or sleep
walking there two forms I keep

And before them
without sound
two shadows touch upon the ground

1947

Stone or Flame

Shall we pray to be delivered
from the crying of the flesh
Shall we live like the lizard
in the frost of denial

Or shall we offer the nerve-buds
of our bodies
to be nourished (or consumed)
in the sun of love

Shall we wrap ourselves rigid
against desire's contagion
in sarcophagi of safety

insulate ourselves
from both fire and ice

And will the vessel of the heart
stay warm
if our veins be drained of passion
Will the spirit rise virile
from the crematory ash

Shall we borrow
from the stone
relentless peace
or from the flame
exquisite suicide?

1947

We Arise from the Pit of Night

When we return to the cool daylight
where ships of words slacken
no longer burn
instead are silken bandages for pain
the rigid rack where we have lain
become a cushion kinder than snow
our breasts unite and we forget
the murders sunken there below

We lie curled like children
in smooth-limbed innocence
but for night's stigma on our eyelids
The bruised corpses hurled
into the unconscious cave
have swept our minds bare
Caresses still can save us
from their stare

Is there an hour inching toward us
containing the final effigy

of love which we will slay
the last volt of our power
to check it spent?
Will we then in horror unalloyed
confront each other with a void
from which no sprig of pity
no green leaf of grief will spring
no living thing
which only the black well of hate
will inundate?

Sleep wash us clean
Sun charge our flesh with radiance
Make us pure
as when in the green beginning
we trusted one another
Love veil our pupils as before

1947

Symmetrical Companion

It must be
there walks somewhere in the world
another
another namely like me

Not twin
but opposite
as my two hands are opposite

Where are you
my symmetrical companion?

Do you inhabit
the featureless fog
of the future?
Are you sprinting
from the shadows of the past

to overtake me?
Or are you camouflaged
in the colored present?
Do I graze you every day
as yet immune to your touch
unaware of your scent
inert under your glance?

Come to me
Whisper your name
I will know you instantly
by a passport
decipherable to ourselves alone

We shall walk uniformed
in our secret
We shall be a single reversible cloak
lined with light within
furred with dark without

Nothing shall be forbidden us
All bars shall fall before us
Even the past shall be lit behind us
and seen to have led
like two predestined corridors
to the vestibule of our meeting

We shall be two daring acrobats
above the staring faces
framed in wheels of light
visible to millions
yet revealed only to each other
in the tiny circular mirrors
of our pupils

We shall climb together
up the frail ladders
balancing on slender
but steel-strong thongs of faith
When you leap

my hands will be surely there
at the arc's limit
We shall synchronize
each step of the dance upon the wire
We shall not fall
as long as our gaze is not severed

Where are you
my symmetrical companion?

Until I find you
my mouth is locked
my heart is numb
my mind unlit
my limbs unjointed

I am a marionette
doubled up in a dark trunk
a dancer frozen
in catatonic sleep
a statue locked
in the stone
a Lazarus wrapped
in the swaddling strips
not of death
but of unborn life

a melody bound
in the strings of the viol
a torrent imprisoned
in ice
a flame buried
in the coal
a jewel hidden
in a block of lava

Come release me
Without you I do not yet exist

1948

Close-up of a Couple on a Couch

Creases in his clothes
creases in his flesh
creases in his arteries
The inner walls shrinking
while the outer walls slip and shift flabbily
Pepper grains in the chin-furrows
in the pale ear-basins
the inelastic lobes sagging tits

She sits still
until it is over
holding her breath her tongue curled back
like a fastidious animal
aloof before an old cur
circling and sniffing her

The bald unfevered brow
the eyes anaemic fish
each under a goldrimmed glass dish
fish suffocating on sand
rills of watery blood in their scales
suddenly pressed between the thrusts of her breast

His hands with wormy veins
tremble tentatively climbing her arms
tightening to the round bare bicep
his nails rasp on silk

His palms feel like old cold rubber
but she does not shudder
it is too ludicrous for that

I'm not going to hurt you
Of course he's not
Who could be hurt but him
Juiceless chameleon
dragging his belly through clover

Detected at once he is crunched
by his own steel heel of self-esteem

If I were younger What's the use
I'm older still I reek
against her so-green cheek
And there between beneath
it flips and flaps like a hen's dewlaps
but the stem bends will not swell with its lust
The very breath in my chest
the blood of the pump alloyed
with dust and rust

When we are young the wizard's wand
waves in vain
above our dumb and glossy flesh
though we could use it then
had we the palate precious and fresh
When we are sunken diminished stale
it sometimes seems
(oh memories of embraces
not as they felt but as they would now feel
now that the dams are closing
the torrent choked to a trickle)
that could we rub ourselves in roses
wallow in new-squeezed milk
our gray skin sloppy like a too-large suit
would tense and firm and fit us slim again
and we'd be keen as jack-knives
and arrogant again

His glazed tongue hunts
between her hard bud-lips
for the moisture of youth profuse
A draft of it would she let it flow to him
his last lascivious dregs
grimed with fear
(but for that the more rare)
would turn to sharp wine in his shrunken flask
Purple kiss like a plum
returned to him she would not miss

(the tree is so laden)
But too raw with spring she is
unwilling to admit ripeness
at least for him

She holds her breath waiting
until it is over

1949

Our Forward Shadows

all we see as yet
slant tall
and timid
on the floor

the stage is set
each waits
in the long-lit door

a bell in the wings
far in the painted forest
rings announcing delight

ourselves
still out of sight
our shadows listen

the cue
summons the dance
of me and you

advance
where our shadows meet
already loved

invade the room
with the scent
of thunder in the blood

move on the colored flood
naked
needing no costume

we are dressed
each in the other's kisses

our shadows reach
to teach us our parts

the enchanted prelude starts

1949

Say You Love

Say you love
and do not be afraid
when that word comes singly
to your ear
a gift too rare
will in surrender fade

Let in its thousand echoes
without fear

Love's source is lavish
as the sun
Not in special veins
its juices run
Never expended
the molten store clots
quickens and
flowing becomes more
replenishing all things
in varied range

Then do not doubt love's substance
in its change

Take love
in full belief
and let it go
unclenched when it has warmed you
with its glow

Give love
as guiltless clouds
release their rain
to thirsty grass
that it may spring again

1949

To a Dark Girl

Lie still and let me love you
first with my eyes
that feast upon you
as on deep skies
to count the constellations
Below your breast Andromeda
Orion and the rest

Lie still and let me love you
now with my hands
that dream over your body
as in wondrous lands
skiers ascend sun-mantled peaks
and sweep to snow-smooth hollows
where silence speaks

Lie still and let me love you
with my mouth
pressed among strange flowers
elixirs of the south
to drink their dewy musk
or like rich grapes
I nuzzle with my lips
until their wine escapes

Lie still and let me love you
with all my weight
urgent upon you
Deep-keeled elate
my body greets you a leaping boat
challenging your tide
to be the stronger
And now afloat
lie still no longer
Demand I love you
the more the more
while passion's breakers
bear us to their shore

1949

Equilibrist

I'm coming toward you
always
instep on the quivering wire
leaning aside
but never looking down
eyes unsmiling
immune to sleep
or hazard

I'm coming toward you

Always your pallid image leaps
behind the bars of distance
where merge sea and sky

Not setting with the sun
nor waning with the moon
your torso centaur-like
is prancing
upon my mind's rim

Fiercely taking aim
my body is a sharpened dart
of longing
coming toward you always

1949

Love Sleeping

Life in the throat of my love leaps
though love is sleeping
under the eyelids of my love Look
a dream is darting
as the blood darts in the throat's vein
and love's shoulder warms my cheek
a dream floats to my love's brain

Heart in the chest of my love moves
though sleeping proving
the flesh of love will wake See
a breath is taken
as a dream makes the brow of my love smile
and the face's flower and the hair's leaves
quiver in a wind of love on that isle

where the heart beats now Watch
I will watch for the meeting
of my love with love in the heat
of the dream's full quaking
as love's body wakes in my arms' catch
and life in my chest and throat leaps
though love is sleeping

1940s

Standing Torso

My eyes
flicker over you
like flames
to lick you up

are cooled
by your beauty

blue loops
ripple you
like tongue-tips

furling with
the serpents
of your thighs

into the whorl
of your haunches
and the slender trap
of your waist

gliding the
gulled column
of your back

your neck and head
its ornament

over your
belly's plateau
flat and palpitant

to your breasts
which are
perched birds
plump and alert
their little beaks
sharply lifted

You stand in Egyptian
stillness
accomplished
calm as bronze

and the fuses
of my veins
fill with quickfire

1950

He

Came back one day in the fall
We thought he'd gone for good
to the old man's home of winter
the clouds had hung so long
like gray beards in the sky

The squirrel had prepared for cold
the crow for snow with his scolding cry
and we had prepared for dark
to fall early on the park
with the shutting of summer's gate
prepared the proxy log for fire
stabled in the grate

The crow with his scolding cry
had prepared us for dark and cold
and the shutting of summer's eye.
Then one morning like June as bold
ruddy in all his brawn
there he was in the park
throwing diamonds on the lawn

He stroked each mossy mournful rock
like an old dog's head
and turned the fountain's snuffling
into giggles instead

He made the crickets tune their shins
like mad Hungarian violins

He unbuttoned the roses
as if they were blouses
made them expose chill nipples to the bees
The wasps we thought were dead
brown corpses on the sill
woke snorting from their trance and spun
in the gilded circus of the sun

1951

What I Did on a Rainy Day

Breathed the fog from the valley
Inhaled its ether fumes
With whittling eyes peeled the hills
to their own blue and bone
Swallowed piercing pellets of rain
Caught cloudsful in one colorless cup
Exhaling stung the earth with sunlight
Struck leaf and bristle to green fire
Turned tree trunks to gleaming pillars
and twigs to golden nails
With one breath taken into the coils
of my blood and given again when vibrant
I showed who's god around here

1951

Laocoön Dream Recorded in Diary Dated *1953*

In half-sleep felt an arm go around me,
but longer than an arm, it lapped me twice
and I was bound, but did not mind.
One supple coil lay nice about my waist
without alarm and, skilled and strong,

the other winding cool and careful, slipped
to my hip, tightening without haste.
An odd thrill made a geyser in my blood.
This love had a new taste.

Now the arms were three, all slick
along my nakedness, and thick.
A fourth, more slender, hugged my thigh.
I did not wake. Dream-submerged
as in a tepid lake, I lay, postponing fear.
A quick and tender tongue flicked at my neck,
groped higher, licked into my ear.
Below I felt each toe receive a velvet ring,
and soon there sat around my ankles
worm-wet bracelets, fat and glistening.

Cap-eyed, caressed all ways at once,
I did not care to identify my lover, nor dare
apprise him by a finger-try. My hands
crept to my head. A thousand tousled vipers
rippled there, from braid and curlecue
had made their lair. With lips of suede
they grazed upon my brows, breathed hissing
kisses to my mouth and, seething, sipped
my nipples, where mini-eels, each narrow
as a hair, sprouted in a copious stream.

Roused, I could not rise. Anger and desire
were one. A ton of horror poured an equal
weight of lust, of drowsy hate, of heavy
bliss like a drug upon my dream.
The five arms held me snug.
Roped by a riddle in spiral shape
in a lunar nightmare I was ready for rape.

A gentle murderer whose many-stranded will
never could be severed, nor a motive in the kill
unravelled, the six arms travelled me entire,
and trussed me heel to nape.
I, the victim recognizing all my strangled

cries as lies, my tangled fears as wishes
in disguise, snatched the seventh arm,
greater than the rest, with both my own
and pressed it close. Its wide girth
matched my chest. Its voracious face,
the jaws agape, avid on the vipers fed.
Into that hollow my head was swallowed, open-eyed.
The dream was done, so there was no escape.

1951

Incantation

Bright sleep bathing breathing walking
snow ocean and fire
spinning white and flinching green
red-and-yellow-petaled sheen
color me with fresh desire

Vast sleep snow as deep
fresh the leap to green and steep flinching wave
pulsing red glowers flow on black below

In black sleep brightness keep
in colored day spin and play
fresh foam sharp snow the slime of time whirl away
Fire is air is breath and green
lakes of air I walking swim

Powers are of motion made
of color braided all desire
In red and yellow flowers bathe
in snow ocean and fire
in snowy sleep on curls of flame
on shingles of the sea I climb
Dim and gray whirl away and knotted thought and slime

Burning snow spin me so with black sea
to braided be   In green sleep eons leap
from gray slime past thought and time

to pith and power to bathe in the immortal hour
to breathe from another pulsing flower

Snow ocean white fire
color me with fresh desire

1952

Night Before the Journey

It is the last night of the world.
I am allowed once more to show my love.
I place a jewel on a cushion.
I make a juggler's trick.
I become a graceful beast to play with you.

See here something precious, something dazzling:
A garden to be your home,
vast and with every fruit.
The air of mountains for your garment.
The sun to be your servant.
A magic water for you to bathe in
and step forth immortal.

But it is the last night of the world,
and time itself is dying.
Tomorrow my love, locked in the box of my body,
will be shipped away.

1952

The Time Came

The time came
The time came when
Came for everyone
One at a time

The sky was a bell
The air was extra clear
Everything was actual
Seen so near

The light shone through our hands
As red as leaves
Huge as through a stethoscope
The earth's heart thumped

Beyond our fear
The light was cool
The air was clear
The sky was a bell

1952

Alternate Hosts

I

Am I sitting on your wrist, someone immense?
Are you watching me with tolerant surprise
as I gobble up a gnat, as I slowly draw him
between the double bulges of my face?
His head first, then his body, his wings a garment
whose limp rags have no taste—but his jellied grit
clicks—can you hear it?—mashed against my palate.

My forelegs are placed like elbows on a table.
My needle-narrow rump with its down-bent end
pulses as I munch; it is transparent;
soon you'll see my dinner swim down there.

My biplane wings hold sunlight in their struts;
the whole spectrum plays there on my "harp"
a complete arpeggio of holy color, but
the undersides, you note, have a bitten look
where old battles with the air have frayed them.

I munch and grind. He's halfway in at last.
A pleasure, you think, this eating? It's hard work,
as anyone's business is, and I am thorough.
When I get this one down I have to cruise for more.

2

You are sitting on me somewhere, something wee.
On me, or in me, I don't know which.
And with your sort of prayer you make an itch,
but I can't tell where. Is it in my blood?
Your world, vast, a single corpuscle to me;
to you an unmapped galaxy my smallest muscle.

I'm aware of what you're doing there. Your throat is working
to disgorge what comes out backwards. It's a thought,
black-bodied between awkward wings, and torn
by your palate's struggle when your speech was born.
Bumbling, fuzzy, belligerent, inept, you draw one breath,
while it draws two, before both it and you
are blown away by death.

Never mind, go do your duty, be diligent. Spit out
your poem, your prayer, your quaint explosion. If enough
of you get together there on the same project,
at the root of something, somewhere, sometime,
you might make one hair of me stand on end.
Then you'll see my finger come to smear
the batch of you with one scratch.

1952, revised 1959

Under the Best of Circumstances

I've got what I want
Nakedness   The sky
pouring blue in my eye
Downy just-born clouds
to dive between
The virility of the sun

Time's Book does not turn
its pages   The world
is arranged as I left it
Past and future on either side
Its work is being done

Page 199 on my left hand
hidden   My love goes to
office in the city
Page 1099 on my right
hand hidden   Affronted
by old age I commit suicide

Time's Book is open
to the middle   Its pages
are mirrors for cool clouds
The naked swimmer
turns gold in the font
of the sun   Erased is pity
and dreadful truth
Unchanged and wide
warm windless without harm
the present and my youth

Is there anything I want?
Yes   My love to be here
to love me   Are there
other people in Time's Book?
Other events   Soldiers
dying   Women in childbirth?

Of course   But I have
arranged them to be
as they are

1953

Oh, to Be a Tigress!

Oh, to be a tigress,
and wear the same costume
summer, winter, autumn, spring;
to slink into a room,
and hear the women all exclaim:
"How *chic* you look, my dear!"
Oh, not to have to give a darn
what's being worn this year! . . .

Necklines may plunge, hems rise or fall,
shoulders go square or round,
waists pinch in, hips plump out—
it matters not at all.
The tigress walks with perfect poise,
meets every fashion test,
because for all occasions
she's appropriately dressed.

And if she walks with special pride,
it rightfully is hers,
for who could hope to equal
such a gorgeous set of furs?

early 1950s

Once Upon

He said he felt as though.
She promised to do it when.
They both agreed that if.
Provided they waited, then.

He suggested they ought instead.
She wished she could, but now.
The minute she did, he might.
He couldn't believe it, how.

Finally they managed what.
She feared he'd be finished by.
She hated to hurry, but.
If he insisted, why.

For a while he rested with.
She admitted hoping that.
He saw she concluded from.
He said he'd be ready at.

She patiently waited before.
He soon responded to.
He wanted to know just where.
She said she had learned it through.

They had a number of.
For her, perhaps below.
For him, a little above.
But both enjoyed it, so.

early 1950s

From a Letter
to Elizabeth Bishop

"Glancing through your letter again I see your phrase
'a child no one knows whether is a boy or a girl,' and
the note: 'You can arrange this to please yourself—it is
beyond me right now.' So here are my arrangements."

No one knows a child, whether is a boy or a girl.
Or a girl—whether is a boy, a child—no one
    knows.
A child or a girl, no one knows whether is a boy.
A child, whether is a boy, no? One knows, or a
    girl . . .
A child is a boy or a girl? No one knows whether.
Is a boy or a girl a child whether no one knows?
A child? No. One knows whether. Or a girl is a
    boy.

1954

The Kiss

The thing itself is odd
this nibbled touching

contiguous thresholds
for the souls to pass
from porch to porch

Each a pod
snugly shut
wishes to open then divide
and so beget a sibling

To match as mittens do
identical and different

Master and mistress each
Then will I *be* you and bee you

In membranes locked
a peach and peach
would sip each other

Why this shock?
Ignition makes of parallels a peak
of straights a sphere

Heads together here
two rocks
the same space-pocket fills

Impossible such occupation
yet your face is mine
I stand behind your eyes

But then apart (a part) again
like boxers in ballet
The silken gloves
have barely grazed

The flick
of the immediate vanishes
Coincidence is quick

Before it tarnishes
O realize the truth of Two
the I the also You

1954

Something Goes By

What are you doing?
I'm watching myself watch myself.

And what are you doing?
Pushing a stick, with a wooden wheel at the end.
I have on a white dress.
First I push the wheel, then I pull the wheel.
My dad made it, with the lathe and a bandsaw.

And where are you watching from?
From my seat on the train.
My back is to myself, back there. But with the back
of my head I'm watching myself:
on a strip of cement, by a square of grass,
pushing the wheel that isn't quite round,
so it wobbles and clacks.

I'm crossing a trestle over a river on the train . . .
the water's gray and level there below,
with stroke-marks on it, in arm-length arcs,
like wet cement that's just been planed.
My dad built our house, poured concrete for the basement,
sawed timber for the frame, laid the brick,
put on the roof, shingle by shingle,
lying along the ladder with nails in his mouth,
plastered the inside, laid the floorboards,
made our furniture out of wood:

of wave-grained oak our dining table . . .
my round, high stool he scooped in the center just like a
saucer . . .
There's a hat on my lap that I mustn't leave on the train,
new shoes on my feet, that fuse my toes to flatiron shape.
I'm watching myself being carried away.

And where are you watching from?
From *here.* From out of a slit of almost sleep . . .
lying on my side,
hands between my knees.
I hear myself breathe.
My bed is a dais in the hollow room;
in the window frame a section of sky:
slow clouds puff by, over the city, on a track from the west—
like an endless—is it an endless?—train.
I hear an airplane being driven into heaven,
its drone the saw-sound, the sound
of the lathe—or is it the rasp of my own
breath in my ear?
When I look to the window, will it be gone—
or moved to another wall? Will it be dawn
in another room?—Or in this same
room in another year?—Already I hear
November horns on the river.

Where is here?
And what are you doing?
I'm running,
and pushing something.
I have on a white dress.
I'm sitting,
and something carries me.
There's a hat on my lap.
I'm lying naked, almost asleep . . .
Some
thing
goes
by.

1956

Facing

1

You I love
you are that light
by which I am discovered.
In anonymous night
by your eye am I born.
And I know
that by your body I glow,
and by your face
I make my circle.
It is your heat
fires me
that my skin is sweet
my veins race
my bones are radiant.

You are that central One
by which I am balanced.
By your power it is done
that in the sky of being
my path is thrown.
And I glide in your sling
and cannot fall into darkness.
For by the magnet
of your body
charged with love
do I move.

2

As you are sun to me
O I am moon to you.
And give you substance
by my sight
and motion and radiance.
You are an ocean
shaped by my gaze.
My pulsing rays
draw you naked
from the spell of night.
By my pull
are you waked
to know that you are beautiful.

I rake up your steep
luster and your passion;
by my sorcery your wealth is sown
to you on your own breast,
your purples changed to opals.

So with love's light
I sculpture you
and in my constant mirror keep
your portrait
that you may adore
yourself as I do.

1956

Her Management II

She can't compose two things
alike: every pebble on the beach,
every pit within a peach
is singular; the rings
within a tree
fail at symmetry.

I look at my toe:
there's not another, I know,
to match it. See this ear?
Its twin is only near-
ly like it. That wave,
the dark concave

underneath its hurl,
reoccurs, a different curl.
In her spontaneous script
the penmanship is tipped
to a new slant at each next
line, although the text

repeats. Yet she can't refrain
from duplications—like the rain—
imitative every drop;
she writes the rain and can't stop
because she can't make
a perfect pair

of tears, of whorls of hair,
of circles on a lake
of shadows or of leaves
or sleeves
for the ripe
corn. She can't shape

a spot of sunlight or a grape
of the same stripe
as the one beside it or copy
a single bee. "Daisy, daisy,"
she scribbles all
summer in loops and rounds unidentical.

She tries to rhyme, let's say,
a school of clouds, a wild bouquet
of flames, a scarf of birds:
they bolt into disorder,

explosive words
on pages without a border.

Ignorant of measure,
she can't compose a square;
her book:
a crook-
ed treasure,
published everywhere.

1957

Logs in the Grate

At first we felt we were being wrapped.
For our protection and preservation
the yellow, the red strong skin. As in

a peach we'd be reclosed, to cool in our
rubicund bundle. Perhaps like peach stones
we'd resume our core existence. But our

weight was extracted. Swiftly we diminished,
while the wrappings went on. We turned
red, then black, with ghastly scabs.

The last act was full of apprehension:
Would the frail blue ribbons ever reach
around us, would they ever be tied,

would the handling of our crumbling bodies
cease? When we fell away, the wrappings fell
away. Now we smelled and tasted of their

passion. The heat, the glow of sainthood
did not stay. Our hearts, too, turned
gray. The stage went dark, flat, empty.

1957

East River, February

This gray day—the wet
pavement of the esplanade,
the flat river's fabric

dusty in fog,
forms of the other shore,
serried docks, blunt-hafted

tankers in their berths
drawn in chalk,
the tops rubbed out—

a horizontal composition
with no depth, in three
planes of doubtful reflection.

The air has the most
shine: pins of rain stuck
in muslin, unable to fall

between dull sky
and turtle-colored water. I
am the only upright, a stroke

weighting the ground-cloth—
not by vividness or mass,
by actuality of black.

1958

As Long Ago as Far Away

"Look there," the star man says. Before our eye
he fixes a funnel of mirrors, a trap for light.
"Out there, that chink—really a chunk—at the top
of the dome, is long ago as it is far away.
Whether it *is*, we do not know. We know it *was*.
We draw, by a thread of light, through this elongate maze
a star long dead, its actual ghost."

"So here the past is caught?" we ask the star man.
"Caught up to us? Is this how time is space,
how miles are years? You've brought *then* down to *now*.
Where shall we look to find the third side of the triad?
From this seat, here at the junction of past and
present, will we peer out someday, to see the future
meet, and so triangulate a Room?"

"Another scope, with prisms ground from clear materials,
must be found," says the star man. "We used to look up,"
we say. "Now we look out. Look out for what has been!
What's past is gathering back to us. Well, then, where's
      when—
the coming to be?" "Still down, and in—in the brain's pen,"
says the star man. "There are the mirrors made to catch,
at birth, the next earth," says the star man.

                                                        1958

Thursday Thoughts of a Poet

I don't feel very well today.
The reason I don't feel well is that I got no sleep last night.
The reason I got no sleep is that I had diarrhea.
The reason I had diarrhea is that I took a green pill yesterday.
The reason I took a green pill was that I was constipated the
      day before.
The reason I was constipated was that the day before that
            I had to read my poems to students at a college
            and the next day my routine was upset
            because my mind was upset
            by too many recollections of what I should have said
                  and didn't,
            to too many questions asked me by the students about
                  my poetic method.
The reason I had to read at the college was that I said Yes
            to the invitation instead of No.
The reason I said Yes was
            partly that, at the time, the appointment was a month in
                  the future,

partly that I was expected to feel flattered,
partly that I wanted to appear cordial,
partly that it might influence a few sales of my book,
partly because I thought of another former invitation to
      read
at another college to which I'd said No and about
      which, afterward,
I'd wondered if instead I should have said Yes.
Today I don't feel very well.

1958

My Farm

The page my acre; A, B, C are buildings.

Blue is the name of the barn
already in place by the meadow.

Name! Name! shout the hammers.
The house rides up in three strokes—
its attic tri-cornered like art,
its porch the shape of ample.

Blue is the hump of the barn.
Call the cows: Come, Black. Come, White.

On Cadmium, the center field,
a structure I haven't guessed is going to be guyed.
A kind of planetarium?
Ask the architect in the morning.

This is my property.
I erase it if I please.

Or plant a skating pond.

The problem is to build a floor like that,
that moves their legs like that, like scythes.

All the page is a white pond now.

Some boys have fallen, and gotten up:
those red streaks are their cheeks and ears.

A man with silver hair advances—
and a woman on one blade;
she holds a muff of huge sunlight.

The whole sheet, solid, runs beneath between their feet.
I pull it smooth and backwards
until, far up, it rumples among the trees.

Today—let's see—I'll trade weathers.
Hoist a hall of sagebrush.
Or the stairs of a waterfall.

Have the high rooms hung with clouds.
The only furniture some horses.

The brown divans graze on the rugs.

1959

Annual
(a love poem)

Beginning in the spring again
with eyes as new as leaves,
skin like the fox whose hair
hears what the river says,
nostrils locate the mole,
the turnip, the lowest stone,
tongue tastes moonlight:

beginning in the spring again,
blood wild as wind,
limbs loose as the antelope's,
and brain a basket,
lungs think air, mouth remembers
water and all transparent things:

the youngest nerve and keenest stem,
in secret shade, reach up to meet
radiance, swell to make radiance;
as all pouting blossoms do,
I turn, as earth to its sky, to you:

cave of the day's light smiling
into my throat,
meadow of stars, white
on the loam of my dream,
to your cloud-pure bones
that water my yearnings
beginning in the spring again:

turn to the lightning, your laughter
that suddens me, your hair
a wind that stings me,
your breast a fleece of birds
that hover me,
naked, dawn-colored, cool and warm,

I open to your dew,
beginning in the spring again.

1959

Feeling Sorry

Contrition, the soft animal, comes to sit in my lap.
Its vibration soothes my hands that stroke its round back.
My palm feels caressed by the fur of the cat.
Its caring comes to me (it so rarely offers itself like this)—
my daring to welcome the unexpected claw-curled leaper—
craftily alters a humped and expiatory act
into something erect and self-swelling: I'm flattered
to be throne to this shaggy—the same I've been ashamed to own
I'd ever need. Tears that disappear into his fur,
the thrill-like purr, are satisfactions.

There's no punishment in feeling sorry. I ought to be slapped
by dig-thorn paws, hissed at, scared
by something rapid and stiff haired with a cactus tail.
Instead, this docile platter of boneless warmth drools on my
    knees.
Humiliation makes me happy, guilt turns to brag,
the stroke of contrition is softer fun than sin.
Better dump this slack pet—supposed to be aloof and hard to
    win—
stand up, go back to pride and laughter, and an empty lap.

195

Lying and Looking

The way
the hairs grow
on my skin,
I see they
glisten.
Furrowed
as by wind,
my armpits
are fleecy pods;
my grassy skin's
darker in folds
of elbow and groin
and kneecap dents;
if I stretch my legs
each knee's a face
square-cheeked, pugnacious.
My thighs dip and play
in glossy light;
their backs stay
level, though they
arch and roll; panther-
colored, between buff
and peach, soft
but chamois-tough;
and slanting

curiously
from alert pores,
their hairs
are blond. Oh, I
wouldn't trade my
body for anything. Not
for a dove's white boat,
not for a bear's black coat,
not for anything.

1959

Listening to Strauss and Stroking
an Autumn-Colored Cat

How long since I have been so raked, so loosened?
My eyes trickle hot seeds to my mouth's furrow.
My core is hollow, an echoing amphora.
My ribs separate to a stroking so strong.

I suck to my lungs the air that lifts dancers.
I am fleecy, a cirrus sky, high and icy.
Tine-marks striate my spirit's underparts.
My thickest fur is raked.

I feel the hard slickness beneath the sheath.
I remember what nakedness is: exposure, helplessness—
but passion regained, and its toolbox.
From those corners run the swift shapes and notions.

1959

Coda to J.

We lie together
dark and light
you asleep and I awake
our pulses oven-paced
our limbs interlocked

so familiar that on
your ledge of dream
you cannot tell my body
from your own

With me into the stream
I take your hand upon my thigh
our breathing keeps us tandem

While you sip
at the sable teat
I sail to a
light-filled tent
to a legendary wood
to a labyrinth
to find your image
where it first stood

1950s

Not the Dress

Not the dress
not the skin
not the flesh.
Farther in.
Not the heart.
Then the beat?
The question steady
startles it.
Here the thread
here the knot:
Endure
by sway and rhythm
motion depending
on future's pause
Hear the plot.

1950s

Walking with Louis

I remember walking in Central Park
with Louis. This was a long time ago.

We'd bumped into each other on 59th
Street, I think. It was a sunny day.

We waded through the pigeons on the
hexagonal tiles, between the rows

of old benches full of Sunday sitters.
We wandered around the zoo.

Louis did the talking, mostly in puns.
We laughed a lot. I remember my elation

at walking next to such a famous man.
Louis had put some poems of mine into

an anthology named "A Treasury of Great
Poems." I was thrilled at the implication.

Moreover, among the "S"s in the Index
I stood next to Swinburne! And Louis

said I seemed to have issued out of
D. H. Lawrence and Emily Dickinson. (What

a fox he is!) The beautiful thing
about Louis is—*still is*—that

meeting him always makes you feel good.
That bubbling spring of wisdom

and humor, let it not cease. In fact,
let it increase. If possible.

On the day the world explodes (if it
does) I'd like to be standing next to

Louis. Whatever he'd say would be so
true and funny I'd forget to be scared.

1950s

Note: The "Louis" referred to here is Louis Untermeyer.

The Winepress

I lay my head on Love's breast and heard
the inconspicuous winepress of the blood
that labyrinths its body, its threads
rayed in cunning runnels from their source,
and heard the plushy piston with its push
replenish the murmurous vineyard of that flesh
that drinks perpetually its own
mystic grapes and breathes
the passion manufactured with its breath.

And I became so drenched and transfused
rising and falling on the breast of Love,
listening to its lever and inhaling
its distillation, heated and sweet,
that I a willing Bacchus became
who lived on laughter only, and
the brandy of sleep. Or else I was the twin of
Eros with most natural wings
soaring over fictions of necessity—

indecent, delicious, possessionless, except
for those ruthless accurate things
fated to fix love to youth, and sharp
arrest the heart. I became Love, so used
its fruits and instruments.
Arrest the heart? Oh, I am sure
it works still; its works are still
steady, salubrious, and a sanguine miracle.
I hear the soft and metric stamp,

the juice expelled but the juice contained, deployed
to invade the ruby ditches of desire.
Though we recline now on the long couch
as if enchanted, or awaiting incarnation,
and in sleep seem chiseled into legend,
it is I who wince touching a wound
(that is closed, and but a seam of stone),
I who feel the pincers of the wreath
and find my wrists and feet horrified

by holes, by omens I wish not to own.
I wish not to own Love's wine
in its flow may flow from a rift
and, siphoned outside the keep of the intact god,
stain and overflow a cannibal's lips—
crude, needy, feeding on love's host—the bleeding
called blessing—goblets filled from leaks
never healed, and faucets made of the hurts—
such a drunkard's bath furnished incessantly

that rips into flood, to inundate and swamp the heart.
These damages prefigured have sobered me.
I lie on the body of Love, listening, and I
feel its breast's fountain vivify
my veins. I warm to wake it again, that it may wake
me to feasts and battles, voyages, homecomings.
Though I know not its new form forming while it wakes,
but know the power it bears, changeless and endless.
And what thirsts it slakes in me.

I consecrate Love's body to delight
like that of the tree before Eden, when the trunk was white
and it wore no fruit. Oh, it is not
a backward twining through vines of regret,
or an ignorance of history's hardening and time's sly
depletion. But it is a stripping of the breast
of love—and if it must, let it be cursed
again—but may it wake
naked to instinct, as at first.

1960

The Many Christs

There is the Black Christ, and the Smiling Christ, and the
Christ of Leather with human hair.
There is El Greco's Christ with flickering limbs, mesmeric,
pulsing like the shadow of a flame.
Christ in a glass tomb in Spain is muscled like a man, with
dense thighs and thick neck of a workman. Although of riven
oak, the chest "lives" strongly, as if it had just now let go its
moanless breath.
Michelangelo's Christ of marble, in the lap of his mother, a
new-bathed body spare and young, tender-ribbed, hollow-
loined, only lately twisted from the cross, lies lax in death, the
right arm dragging the hurt hand pliant to the floor.
Cocteau's Christ, loose-robed, feathery-bearded, is borne by
naked fish-eyed boys—they have plausible wings—through a
ballet of resurrection, over the dome of La Chapelle St.
Pierre.
Matisse made Christ of stingy bronze knotted like rope: a
loop for the lolling head, the arms a single pegged-out strand,
a braid for the legs. He is wrung out of all human shape to
become his cross.

There are all the countless Christs with insteps forced one
upon the other by a single nail through both feet, so that the
knee bones knock, inverting the calves, wrenching the arms
from the sockets, the torso's whole weight being slung from
the palms, the sternum arched like a chicken's carcass, with
the pelvis a pit, with a clout about the cringing hips, the
crooked neck toppling the dead head and its wreath of thorns
forward on the chest.

Of gold, of stone, of glazed clay, of wax, of polychrome, of
silver, jasper, ivory, plaster, wood. . . .

The Black Christ of Barcelona once rode the prow of a ship.
Some journeyman tooled him in Columbus' time. Such
figureheads were common then. Now he gleams from the
dark cathedral transept, like a charred beam. He was
blackened by smoke from the burning ships in the maritime

war with the Turks, the great sea battle (1571) that the
Spaniards and their North European allies won. This Christ
is side-twisted. He bent his body to avoid a cannon ball, the
guide will tell you, adding that, in 1493, Columbus brought
six American Indians to be baptized here, in the cathedral—
"The font is over there." The place where he hangs is dim
and high in sooty darkness. The bedraggled body slumps on
a flaked gilt cross. Dark red drops stitch the smudged side,
and trail from the brow, and the left hip juts.

What *are* these Christs? Gods, dolls, symbols, omens, puppets,
fetishes, amulets, objects of art? They are notions given shape
and tangible form. They are the same notion graven or
painted in many forms. Or they are various notions forced
into the same form.
If you draw a line and transect it with another line, you have
put No over Yes, or Yes over No. You have produced the
enigma of the Cross.

A most curious crucifixion is told in small marble reliefs
behind the choir in that Barcelona cathedral. The carver,
Ordonez, Michelangelo's pupil, has depicted St. Eulalia
flogged for heresy, and otherwise tortured to death. Her
slight body, naked, is nailed upside down in the form of an X:
the only "Christ" so sexed that history knows of. Her head,
with streaming hair and open mouth, dangles, her arms
stretched wide, her legs spread so that the right arm forms a
slant line with the left leg. Hung from the feet, she is Xed,
crucified in reverse. Crossed out.

Works of magic, works of wish, works of conscience. But
works of art! And the *act* of crucifixion. Is this not art? He is
sculpture (framed by the cross). He is dancer, halted. Dancer
made to dance (on the cross) to the tug of blood. He is
puppet, worked (on the stage of his cross) with every
veritable trapping. And worked still in the crossed theatre of
the soul.

In France, in a southern fishing town by the sea, a six-foot
Christ stands handsome, gypsy-tawny, scarcely sagging against

his rough-hewn cross. A little shelf supports his feet that are spiked side by side to the timber. A froth of purple tulle, the loin cloth around his virile hips, wags in the wind, and a crown of cactus circles the wooden curls. Open eyes, of some bluish jewel, look down. The face is blissful in accomplished agony.

Blood is let from a lamb, before the Easter rites each year, and made to drip through pores in the forehead. It is made to flow from hands and feet, and through hidden pipes behind the carved gash in his side. In the spring he is unnailed, and lifted down, washed in the sea, and garmented in the wide-sleeved shirt a virgin of the town cards and spins and weaves from the wool of last year's lamb. The Christ is laid in a cave in the sea wall for three days. On Sunday, hoisted upright, embraced at the wooden ankles by a strong man, he is carried to the church, white robe enlivened by the wind. With outstretched arms of blessing, and wearing a crown of yellow *giroflet*, the risen Christ smiles down from the chancel over stairs of flowers.

He is the Smiling Christ, with skin of sunny wood.
On Monday, hearty hammers pin him up, replace him, naked, on his rightful shelf.

Did Christ live in history? Did he die in it, and did he live again, as these tangible forms insist? Which is projection? Is art the progeny of act? Or did these galvanic notions spring from works of art?

It is likely he was done to death with all such originality as befits a King, hung so, high up, on so grand and permanent a frame, that all eyes must roll aloft to distinguish him. That he rose again when his veins had emptied—that, broken, lowered, entombed, the heart stiff, shrunk, he rosied, awoke and climbed the air in a robe of cloud above a vacant cross, and entered a crack in heaven—it is here that wish and conscience, guilt and mystery part with art and history.

1960

The Truth Is Forced

Not able to be honest in person
I wish to be honest in poetry.
Speaking to you, eye to eye, I lie
because I can not bear
to be conspicuous with the truth.
Saying it—all of it—would be
taking off my clothes.
I would forfeit my most precious properties:
distance, secrecy, privacy.
I would be exposed. And I would be
possessed. It would be an entire
surrender (to you, eye to eye).
You would examine me too closely.
You would handle me.
All your eyes would swarm me.
I'd be forever after hotly dressed
in your cloying, itching, greedy bees.
Whether you are one or two or many
it is the same. Really, I feel as if
one pair of eyes were a whole hive.
So I lie (eye to eye)
by leaving the core of things unvoiced
or else by offering a dummy
in place of myself.

One must be honest somewhere. I wish
to be honest in poetry.
With the written word.
Where I can say and cross out
and say over and say around
and say on top of and say in between
and say in symbol, in riddle,
in double meaning, under masks
of any feature, in the skins
of every creature.
And in my own skin, naked.
I am glad, indeed I dearly crave
to become naked in poetry,

to force the truth
through a poem,
which, when it is made, if real,
not a dummy, tells me
and then you (all or any, eye to eye)
my whole self,
the truth.

1961

Cabala

I will turn very dark,
dark as an idol
in a shady room.
And be his eye, alive
because he is so still.

Or I will turn
dark as a horse
across a burnished pasture
in the shade of a tree.
There I will be

the star on his brow, so still.
Dark as a target,
and as the flint
behind the white feather,
a mark that does not move

to draw all shafts.
Eye light and mind light,
lightning-taming leather
I will turn and be
a swiftness on the dark.

1961

Somebody Who's Somebody
(Draft, never finished; title supplied.)

Somebody who's somebody
   often doesn't look like somebody
until you look
    inside.
Elizabeth's liver is tattooed
   with the intaglio of an indigo turtle.
Not emblazoned—
   that would augur prominence
and a definite who's who-ness
   No—nobodyness is the ultimate
achievement achieved
   secretly, invisibly but indelibly
inside.

(O but remember, E
   I saw you pee on the floor
at Yaddo long ago)
   Enviable that ennoblement
that accrues from the peasant's
   modest and unmodish stance,
the man with the hoe (that's really
   a scepter *inside*),
the low brow that hides
   a hemisphere heapish as a hive.
O golden bees of your eccentric
   thinkishness, each a queen hermited
within—the hairdo like mud
   round the armature of cobwebs,
but mansioned behind that seedy
   facade what a Midas realm,
what orderly glitter, your honey
   mausoleum private
and impenetrable, perfectly
   coned and sealed except for the little
arched bunghole where over the draw
   bridge of your tongue the worker words
pass forth.

But E, remember
    we tried to find Lake Lonely long ago
wandering awkwardly beside
    the yellow reeds, the ditch-black
waters, and played at darts
    in the Paddock Bar by the racetrack.
You read my "Lion" and
    I your "Little Exercise."
You got drunk and snickered, air
    whistled through your teeth at
dinner, everyone thought you were
    silly. I burned from head to foot
for you hoping they hadn't
    noticed. Later you peed on
the floor—just a drop or two—at
    West House—because the
bathroom was locked. I felt
    responsible—I should have had
a toilet in my pocket, to produce
    in the moment of your
unpostponable need. I was nuts
    about you. And I couldn't say
a word. And you never said *the*
    word that would have loosened
all my doggy love and let me
    jump you like a suddenly
unhobbled hound wild for love.

Little Elizabeth
    who still keeps me
wild at the end of your chain—because
    I can't reach you, have never
pawed you, slaver at the thought
    of you still, because because
I have never *known* you years
    and years—and love
the unknown you.

1961

My Poems

My poems are prayers to a god
to come into being.

Some mornings I have seen his hair
flash on the horizon,

some nights I have seen his heel there
clear as the moon.

My poem pray to him to be
manifest like lightning—

in one pure instant abolish
and recreate the world.

1962

I Look at an Old Photo of Myself with Love

That I do bring myself to death
I do perceive,
but only now and then, like stars
and blindnesses between.
That I have brought myself to birth
I wish, and would believe,
to have deserved my innocence
before I earned its stain.

With youth's eyes I looked across
into my eyes of age.
When did I let a dot of death
impinge upon the edge
of irises undamaged,
that once were skies of truth?
Now I look with sullied eyes
into my eyes of youth
like a guilty lover
who has betrayed his oath.

And so I hang suspended
in the column of a well,
its wall my long pupil,
while the stars wheel,
my scope the slate lake
that I am swimmer in.
Into the mind's slit
I let death spill.

Yet, dilated now and then
out to the first rim,
I do rake immortal light
again from the birth room,
where my stare mates with its star.
Again, then, I begin.

1962

The Seed of My Father

I rode on his shoulder. He showed me the moon.
He told me its name with a kiss in my ear.
"My moon," I said. "Yours," he agreed.
And as we walked, it followed us home.

Hold my hand, he showed me a tree,
and picked a peach, and let me hold it.
I took a bite, then he took a bite.
"Ours?" I asked. "Yes, our tree."
Then with a hoe he made the water flow beside it.

When I was older he showed me the sun.
He made me a wooden wheel on a stick,
of pine wood, raw and bright as the sun.
I used to run and roll it.

A flashing circular saw was the sun,
like the one he made my wheel with.

"This little wheel belongs to me, the big one
to you?" "Yes," he agreed, "just as we
belong to the sun."

He let me plant the corn grains one by one
out of a long hollow slip-box thrust in the ground.
"I who plant seeds for my father,
I am the seed of my father."

And when the corn was tall, it swallowed me up, all,
whispering over my head. "You are the seed of your father."
And when the husks were sere, my father with a rake,
in the cold time of the year, made a bush of gold.

He struck the bush to burning for my sake.
I stood at his shoulder, a little the higher.
I was the seed of my father, my father
outlined by the fire.

He made a garden, and he planted me.
Sun and moon he named and deeded to me.
Water and fire he created, created me,
he named me into being: I am the seed of my father.

His breath he gave me, he gave me night and day.
His universe is in me fashioned from his clay.
I feed on the juice of the peach from his eternal tree.
Each poem I plant is a seedling from that tree.
I plant the seed of my father.

1963

The Pouch-Flower

Today I came to a trysting spot in the woods,
and found a flower—I must look up its name—
where empty beer cans were cuddled in pine needles,
the sunlight on their seams sharper than morning dew.
In this slouchy unmade bed in tan shade

a few pale purple-veined pouches grew—
and more plumply inflated themselves where the sun
threw warm pillows on the slope.

I'd climbed the slippery gulch, having noticed, from below,
something colored like a finch's breast,
but found the spot twinkling with cellophane and silver
paper, potato-chip scraps and white-tipped butts
that the rain hadn't tamped into the mulch.
That pinkish purple wasn't shy feather—
not something about to fly—rather
a prankish flower that, from its frank stem

between two leaves flaring like a vase, invited me.
So I placed my thumb on its silky pout.
A soft ridge shrugged inward.
A sealed sack, of kite-like tissue—
glandular, slightly fuzzed—when pressed
at the central fold became a slot,
disclosed a willing aperture.
The flower fit my thumb like a cap,

sinewy, yet delicate, and puzzling, finally, because
inside—with the pod-lips spread under both
thumbs—there were no seeds.
Except in one. I don't know why I tried
them all, but in the last one lay
the smallest, gold, crimped fly
with legs akimbo, coffined in vascular purple. I picked
that pouch, brought back to my desk. I had a good day.

1963

That One

I hate male and female.
I defy that split,
nor will I admit
that ram is grail.

I sacred that one who
heads beyond the fix
of fox or feather-breast, who'll mix
their scents and undo

the old, stamped trails. I crown
that one, gliding ambiguous
into a shape contiguous,
but unobliged to clout or open gown.

Grin, champions, in your dual
postures and costumes. We, who lift
our fluffs and leathers off, shift
scales for a whole skin's renewal.

1963

On Lighting the Fire

Quick, quick you
claw of fire,
rip up the log's law,
logic the liar;

build a ruby
den beneath,
tear down substance
with soft teeth.

I'll live within
your house of spirit,
a salamander,
when I can bear it,

or basilisk
with scarlet breath,
reduced to gem
by your quick death.

Quick translator,
robber of shape,
show how chaos
roars agape,

its ecstatic ash
the core
of color only,
raw and pure.

1963

Daffodildo

A daffodil from Emily's lot
I lay beside her headstone
on the first day of May.
I brought
another with me, threaded
through my buttonhole, the spawn
of ancestor she planted
where, today,
I trod her lawn.
A yellow small decanter
of her perfume, hermit-wild
and without a stopper,
next to her stone I filed
to give her back her property—
it's well it cannot spill.
Lolling on my jacket,
Emily's other daffodil.

Now, rocking to the racket
of the train, I try
recalling all her parlor's
penetration of my eye,
remembering mainly spartan
sunlight through the dimity
of the window-bay, evoking

her white-dressed anonymity.
   I remember, as if spoken
in my head: "I'm
nobody! Who
are you?"
thinking
how liked by time
she still is. It has linked
the hemlocks closer in their
hedge so that her privacy
remains. A denser lair,
in fact, than when she was alive
and looked through that bay
on the long garden
where I looked today.

   Another lady is its warden
now. She smells like bread
and butter. A New England pug-
face, she's eighty-seven, may be dead
before another host of plugless
yellow daintycups
springs next spring in the grass.
(What if one white bulb still sups
sun-time that Emily's shoe passed
over?) That old
black-dressed lady told
me, "Here's where
she soaked her gowns in this square
copper boiler on hot bricks." Whiteness
takes much washing. "Oh, her chair,"
she said, suddenly sprightly,
leading me up the stair
to a blue bedroom. "Mustn't forget to
show you
that. It's stored
in a closet." She brought out
a seat for a four-
year-old, only the cane devoutly
replaced, the ladderback and

legs of cherrywood original.
"An awe came on the trinket,"
one article her hand
would have known all
its life.

    "Geneva's farthest skill,"
I pondered,
"can't put the puppet
bowing," and retrieved
an answer,
    "I dwell
in Possibility—
a fairer
house than Prose." Yellow
bells in the still
air of their green room
out there
under the upstairs window
mutely swung.
    Shining through their cups,
her sunny ghost
passed down the rows.
"A word is dead
when it is said,
some say.
I say
it just begins to live that day."

    To her headstone I walked uphill.
It stands white without arrogance
on a green plot
that is her myth-filled
lot
now. Almost blank. Relatives
shoulder her in a straight rank.
Emily, 130 years older
since you took your
little throne
when you were four,

I crane
but can never
gain
that high chair
where you will ever
sit! Alone.

Self-confessed, and rocking
to the racket of the train,
I play back how
I picked you for my pocket,
stooped at your plain
stone.
   One gold dildo
I leave you from the host
I stole;
the other, holy,
I will keep until
it shrinks to ghost.
   "Disdaining men,
and oxygen,"
your grassy
breast I kiss
and make
this vow, Emily, to "take
vaster
attitudes—and strut upon my stem."

1964

Yes, the Mystery

Yes, the mystery
the mystery of life
the horrid mystery of it
Many have seen it clearer than I
have sat in it
been stuck in it
stood in it up to their nostrils

and chose not to breathe
rather than suck in its stench
And not breathing is most difficult
To stop to refuse to not-respond
is most difficult
Why even in the abstract
it's enough to make you vomit
Think if those roses
were dipped in tar
Thinking it they are
and your eyelids drop off
your neck will never turn again
and you must stare
at the black leather petals forever
Oh Heavenly Father leave us the illusion
of the flies who cluster the lake of urine
gushed by the horse in the fetid prison
of his stall
and the bliss and energy that spins them
as they bathe and dip their sugar there

date unknown

Weather

I hope they never get a rope on you, weather.
I hope they never put a bit in your mouth.
I hope they never pack your snorts
into an engine or make you wear wheels.

I hope the astronauts will always have to wait
till you get off the prairie
because your kick is lethal,
your temper worse than the megaton.

I hope your harsh mane will grow forever,
and blow where it will,
that your slick hide will always shiver
and flick down your bright sweat.

Reteach us terror, weather,
with your teeth on our ships,
your hoofs on our houses,
your tail swatting our planes down like flies.

Before they make a grenade of our planet
I hope you'll come like a comet,
oh mustang—fire-eyes, upreared belly—
bust the corral and stomp us to death.

1962–64

You Start Out Across

You start out across.
You let this line, see,
leak from the point.

The point is you, see
what you're moving on,
you're making too, see.

For thickness you dip down,
watch the angle.
Some darkness should slip in here.

Just relax along the point.
Be your own "ground."
That is your material.

Want to be transparent? A thing with corners
or something malleable?
Want to live in a tube?

If you're making a perfect round
it's wrong. Break it. Sharpen another.
Shift into second gravity.

Let go. It'll lift, see?
Veer on out. Rip through.
You're the sky.

Just don't let eccentricity
tip into stereotypy.
Horizon and shore, remember, are one line,

one man's ceiling, another man's floor.
So never push, use the loop technique,
folding under or over, go with the point

from point to point, and slow.
The way it leaks it'll show on the other side, too.
Be just as good. Opposite but otherwise identical, see?

1964

The Lone Pedestrian

I wander out, the lone pedestrian
in Lafayette, and walk the west
side of the Wabash past the Sunday
houses. Don't know where you are,
hope *not* to meet you—but
you're snowing in my mind. "About
that telegram you sent: I thought
the initials meant from Bobby K.
Wired back 'Thank you.' They
typed it 'Fuck you,' and now he's
sore at me. See how you screw up
all the time—though with the best
intentions?" You laugh, and I
congratulate myself: "The Smothers
Brothers ought to get me to write
their gags." I see you pull
the word-strips off like sunburned
skin, standing in your ski coat in
my living room—you couldn't get it

off, the zipper was jammed—I didn't
offer to help. I had a toothache,
and here you'd come, a day early and
without phoning first, butting at
my door. You walk, head down, like
a sun-stunned bull, did you know?
You left the Volks as usual turned on
at the curb, shoved a bag of Key limes
at me, *pretending* you weren't coming
in, when you knew damn well I'd
invite you—would *have* to, wouldn't I?
to feel—to feel the human in you—
to love it—love your *self*, first,
foremost—let your body take care—
of you in it—the you that loves.
I almost called that cop named King
you know. Took his number along to
the movie Friday, just in case.
You're ugly when angry, Nasty Mouth.
Angry when sick, I know—but sick
because self-beaten, bruised, starved,
strafed, driven on, tired out, shot
down. Snow's deep blue now. Twilight
out the window. It's Sunday night.
"In this nook that opens south . . ."
was Wednesday you came—I'd
started to write—and brought me limes.
When I wouldn't play the game the way,
somewhere in your head since Florida,
you thought I would, and ought—that
head that cannot dream if, as you say,
it never sleeps—"The head is dead . . ."
No, that was then—a summer time,
in "Good day, sunshine" weather-blond
head, dazzled grin, on the snapshot
you labeled your "2nd happiest day"—
and I was supposed to say, "What is
the first?"—and didn't, since supposed
to. That head—Goldy Lox—with foolish red cap
on—you holding my foot instead of

hand that night I had toothache—
expecting to make me, weren't you?—
"I can get anyone in the world
interested in me"—You told on
yourself there, you know—and all
that you told about getting dumped
in front of the Waldorf—about faking
it out in the interview at Rutgers—
about "Arne being used to it"—you
freaking out on him—"I'm a little
unreliable once in a while," you
admitted. "But notice my charm, my
cool—I do my dirt with style,"
your cocky chuckle said. You swiping
the air and pacing the rug. You told
on yourself there, Bouncer—over and
over—and when you bounced that
volleyball off the wall so's to barely
miss my head—"that hair" you crow
over and snow me about—"I thought
if I could touch it just one more
time." Before you climb the cliff, I'm
supposed to think. Can't you see you
kissed yourself off, slugged yourself
out, dumped on yourself all that
evening? Hauled away the record player,
threw down Webster's 3rd in its place,
on the bed, like a slab of ice. Christ,
you're funny! Wish I could laugh,
like I used to, two months back. You
made me glad then—crazy glad—
unleashed, MacLeished, I believed you—
Like I said, "I believe everything you
say till I find out different." Well,
I've found out, haven't I? You aced
yourself right out of the game, and
just when it was ripe, you thought, to
run all your way. You've got big cards
—so big you throw them away. I had
my little significant present for you—

Had you got it in N.Y. from R., would
all of it now be different, I wonder?
Maybe, and maybe worse. We might be
that gun you've got between us—me
wasting more of my time than I'm
doing now, with this not-poem, trying
to plough you out of my mind. Snow's
falling on all the squirrels in all
the heavy arms of all the pines out
there, where it's dark. It's yellow
in here. Goldy, you wouldn't take my
gold-wrapped trinket—and I had
Russian Leather for you, too—to make
you—smell so good—And you threw
back my mother's 25-carat gold ring
along with a nasty misspelled note
making those funny *d*'s that you do—
And you threw me gold yarn sox you'd
knitted—that makes 4 pair—with the
mistake you warned me was in one toe—
And threw me 2 basketball tickets clipped
to a sweet note next morning, Thursday,
in my mailbox. Then phoned. I was
still asleep. "Can you give me
breakfast?" I said, "No"—and didn't
thank you for anything—stayed mute
and mum—disconnected—But this was
before I'd been to the mailbox, remember?
You so demanding, so damned awake and
breathless. My tooth hurt, I wasn't up
yet—said "Call me later." You snarled:
"*You* call *me*." So I didn't. OK, so
somehow—but how?—how should I know, with
you it was more than a sore tooth?
And after the dentist, and after I'd
been working all day on that mistake-of-
a-piece for the mag for you—you
dumbbunny, diddling with that sycophant
dumbdaddy A., who you say you've thrown
over because you dropped a critical

stitch back there somewhere, made a booboo
with the manipulation switch—and had
it about done and off my neck so I could
think about starting to do what I had
been supposed to do, *my* work, all day—
No, wait a minute, that was the *next*
day, Friday—Thursday I made you take
me to the lecture, but you were late, and
I walked and met you in the Volks—you
were dolled up, net stockings on, band-
aids showing through where you'd banged
yourself on the squash court—By the
way, Tony that night—No, that had to
be Friday—Anyway, he limped, I can
tell you that—You strained a muscle
in his buttock—he could hardly walk
upstairs. I'm laughing now. I'm
laughing! It feels good. Bouncer,
you idiot, you Wild Thing—it's you,
you know, they sing about in Bobby's
voice on the top ten—"With those
initials you could be President."
"I'm gonna be a big man in town . . ."
"I'm gonna make it . . ." I've got you
humming that. I liked the back
of your bully neck in my hand—I
can't stand it if I've been too
mean to you—Have I been? I didn't
mean to. You—last time I saw you,
at the lecture—nodded you out—
and showed how you'd learned one
lesson—you didn't fade, until I
told you that line, did you?—with my, I guess
you thought, disdainful nod. It
wasn't meant to be. I'm just lost—
more or less, like you. Only more—
scared—and hate myself for that.
And when I hate myself I go cold
and stiff, I settle in—into my
self, old horse in blankets armed—
or old stubborn horny turtle.

Remember how you said you shot
at them in the Keys? But didn't hit
any, you said. That's good. And you
are, too. But crazy. And I drive
you. To that. I know. That's why
you and I—can't. "Snowy gull and
sooty crow . . ." You see? It's late
now. I'm alone. And want to be.
Stopped snowing.

All yesterday was silent. Saturday.
There's more. There's lots more. Have
to stop now. I wish you well. Where
you are. Hear your voice on phone say:
"Good-bye, though." After I said, "I
hope you'll feel. Better." Those words,
if last, were gentle. Where did you
go? After you broke my door-
knob off? I want to, and I don't
want to, know.

1967

LBJ on TV

His Mt. Rushmore–rugged frown
rumples up and pinches down.

His lip is stiff. His eye is stone;
a tear twinkles in the other one.

In his square chin a dimple springs.
Behold a hawk with mourning wings,

or a dove with Buteo will.
His grin is warm; his glance is chill.

The furrows of his jowls are deep.
He prays before he goes to sleep.

His ears are longer than De Gaulle's.
He's champ, in fact, among the talls.

His nose bespeaks a man of parts
ampler than Lincoln's, lacking warts.

Wore he knee breeches and wig,
as Washington he'd bulk as big.

Bald above the timberline—
bold, that is to say—the sign

of passion with compassion strewn,
his craggy features, water-hewn,

tighten, toughen, crumple, squint,
sink to quicksand, rise to flint.

1967

Horse

Finally got the horse broke in. It took years.
Now, not strong enough to ride it. It was wild,
and ornery, yes. Which came, in part, from its not
knowing it was a horse, meant to be ridden.
Wouldn't look you in the eye. Shied from looking
itself in the eye. Wouldn't look in the mirror,
especially not in back. Didn't know it *had* a back.
Funny, how it followed. Didn't have to be caught.
It offered its back, asked for the saddle. Or, so
I thought. A joke! Throw you? That
horse wouldn't let you touch lip or nose with your
feeding hand, let alone get a leg over. Yet it hung
around, acting as if. Acting as if. Would come up
behind you, nuzzle your neck. You'd turn, grab
for its mane. It slid away. But never kept
away for long. Unpredictable. Drove you crazy.

Made you ornery. Broke *you*. Wish I was strong now,
and that horse not so strong. It wouldn't take long.
To have it. Gentled. Ready to mount. Eager to have
me. Eating out of its hand.

after 1967

Tell Me

Tell me great face all eye
with yellow lashes your hair
and beard and bonnet's diaphragm
its flare of silk or flame blown
wild but sewn at source to
circle's boss expansive pupil
startled iris in distention
toward which we fat bees thrum
like arrows that seem not to dare
flick home and stick but vibrate
in your hallucinogenic stare

suspended in rotation rapid pellets
planets motors magnets held
just short of target closed dark
god-face million faceted
sweet needled nectar-filled
big shot-clogged eye tell why
you compell as you repell with
your blank blackening sphere
your radiating flared wild silk
seductive yellow hair?

Are you male female mailed or
vulvate eye are those pricks darts
you spew or incised hollow files
a bulbous catapult or socket are
you target shield great dish-face
how large are you? Why do

we none not one never round your
risen ball whir to discover
your green neck how bent?
Where you swivel like a scanning
radar bowl with coded secrets bated

automated to absorb recharge from
large electric heaven your own far
fierce glaring blank and headless
eye hole toward what pupil
do you fasten all your climb and
fall and are as the smallest
daisy forced to spiral in the
lightrings of its thrall?

1968

Stripping and Putting On

I always felt like a bird blown through the world.
I never felt like a tree.

I never wanted a patch of this earth to stand in,
that would stick to me.

I wanted to move by whatever throb my muscles
sent to me.

I never cared for cars, that crawled on land or
air or sea.

If I rode, I'd rather another animal: horse, camel,
or shrewd donkey.

Never needed a nest, unless for the night, or when
winter overtook me.

Never wanted an extra skin between mine and the sun,
for vanity or modesty.

Would rather not have parents, had no yen for a child,
and never felt brotherly.

But I'd borrow or lend love of friend. Let friend be
not stronger or weaker than me.

Never hankered for Heaven, or shied from a Hell,
or played with the puppets Devil and Deity.

I never felt proud as one of the crowd under
the flag of a country.

Or felt that my genes were worth more or less than beans,
by accident of ancestry.

Never wished to buy or sell. I would just as well
not touch money.

Never wanted to own a thing that I wasn't born with.
Or to act by a fact not discovered by me.

I always felt like a bird blown through the world.
But I would like to lay

the egg of a world in a nest of calm beyond
this world's storm and decay.

I would like to own such wings as light speeds on,
far from this globule of night and day.

I would like to be able to put on, like clothes,
the bodies of all those

creatures and things hatched under the wings
of that world.

1968

Picasso: "Dream." Oil. *1932*

She dreams a landscape. On her chest
a moon from breathing waves rises,
the nipple of her breast.

She dreams the left side of her face.
Grown from her chin—in profile, green—
a penis purples up to place

the oval of her cheek. She dreams her eye
closed in the wrinkle of its head.
She dreams its root: red smile.

1968

Overview

From above I thought
I'll understand it better
but a tender streaky skin
like the belly of a beast
rolled over to be stroked,
was cover.
Farther out
high white tufts
chimney-shaped and snarled by the wind
grew. And after that
on a level lower but still
obscuring
lay a grayer pelt,
bumpy, a melting
relief map.
(That wasn't it—was part
of its floating
skin.) Over the Great
Lakes now it is stretched
flat in the light,
all that wool sheared away.
And here's a crazy quilt of many seams,

some holes torn in the middle
frankly black and blue,
the naked water showing through,
disrupting rigid edges of the squares and pieces.
As if a great machine,
and taking centuries,
had sewn this comforter. And still
the needles work and sleep
and propagate to rework,
spreading the fabric finally to sleep
within it. So it, too, is a skin,
jigsawed and seamed,
more puzzling than the hairy
veil now clothing it again.
I do not understand it
any better, needle though I
am, privileged to stitch
above it, here, for a moment
in the clear, between it
and the sun.

1969

Skopus

The eye
deals with
space. What organ
feels time? Open to our
face, perhaps the
wheels of Long Ago and To Take
Place are turning. Nothing
conceals them. But to
trace them, new
eels of perception must
race from our brow. When a star
keels from the
vase of the sky,
reels of the fishing pupils

pace it to the brain.
Mobiles of duration and passage may
interlace a "distance" where
unpeels an embryo (its
grimace already forming "nearby") whose
steles can caliper and
encase light, easy as our eye
seals planets up up there. "Sometime" may
erase those
creels to catch light in our head—a total
carapace clapped on may "blind" us so that inward space
reveals time's stalled vehicle, the universe at rest upon its
base.

late 1960s

You Are

you are my mirror
in your eye's well I float
my reality proven

                    I dwell
                    in you
                    and so
                    I know
                    I am

no one
can be sure
by himself
of his own being

                    and the world's seeing
                the fleeting mirrors of others' eyes
                cloudy abstracted remote
                or too bright convex false directly smiling
                or crepuscular under their lids
                crawling the ground like snails
                or narrowed
                nervously hooked to the distance
                        is suspect

do I live
does the world live
do I live in it
or does it live in me?
                because you believe I exist I exist
                I exist in your verdant garden
                            you have planted me
                            I am glad to grow
I dream of your hands by day
all day I dream of evening
when you will open the gate
come out of the noisy world
to tend me
                            to pour at my roots
                            the clear the flashing water
                            of your love
and exclaim over my new leaf
and stroke it with a broad finger
as if a god surprised fondled his first earth-sprig

                            once I thought
                            to seek the limits
                            of all being
            I believed
            in my own eyes' seeing
            then
                            to find pattern purpose aim
                            thus forget death
                            or forgive it
then I thought
to plumb the heart of death
to cicatrize that spot
and plot abolishment
                so that pattern shape and purpose
                would not gall me
                I would be its part forever
                content in never falling
                from its web

now I know
beginning and end
are one
and slay each other
but their offspring is what *is*
not was or will be
am I? yes
and never was
until you made me
crying there you are!
and I unfurled in your rich soil
I am the genie
in your eye's well
crouching there
so that you must take me with you everywhere
an underwater plant in a secret cylinder
you the vial
and I the vine
and I twining inside you
and you glad
to hold me
floating there
for if I live in you
you live holding me
enfolding me you *are*
it is proven and the universe exists!
one reflects the other
man mirrors god
image in eye affirms its sight
green stem in earth attests
its right to spin
in palpable roundness
is this then
what is meant
that god is love
and is that all?
how simple and how sure
at the very hub of hazard
so seeming fearful fragile insecure
two threads

in the web of chaos
lashed by the dark daemonic wind
crossed upon each other
therefore fixed and still
axial in the bursting void
are perpetual each according to the other

I am
then I am a garden too
and tend you

        my eye is a mirror
        in which you float
        a well where you dwell smiling

    I the vial
    hold you
    a vine a twining genie
I enfold you
and secrete the liquid
of your being
in that I love you
and you live *in* me

1960s

The Waves Are Making Waves

The waves are making waves,
it is their work to make
themselves, to gather white
on the ridges, rush to sand,
to reap white, heap white, spill
over racing ledges on roughs
where wild whites churn.
In the ruts the waves make
white run over white, it is
their work to run, to earn
wind's wage, tide's full work done.

1970

Part and Whole

He is contained in she
    and in her. Man is contained
    in woman, men in women.
Male is contained in female,
    Mr. in Mrs., Adam
    in madam,
    lion in lioness,
    god in goddess.

1970

This Is That

This is that day waited for all winter,
    day without wind,
    sun kind, birds flaunt
feather, flirt tail, flutter throat, finch, song
    sparrow, redwing, kinglet—
    the day the first
boat is set at anchor on its waternest. Wag mast, swish
    waves, lay and overlay
    your hems of froth
on sand all day stretching and shortening.
    This is that day
    I give my skin, an old
snake's, to the sky. The leper hopes his dread
    patch written on by sun
    will quicken
in such light that, shadow-incised on tile, the maple's
    double is laid down
    thick as forever.
My eyes close. They open. Shadow has slid, cloud-pale,
    to the sideyard.
    Sun, shifty one, burn,
stay. Wind, chilly one, keep still, keep away.
    This is that day!
    The cove roughens,

spattered maple buds finch-red rust against sky gone gray
　　　　and birds, light, fluff
　　　　and color all chased away.
Wind's found where I lay, my shadow-scratched page blown
　　　　awry. Uncurled my shabby skin
　　　　patch, I crawl back in.

1971

Celebration

Item in the *N.Y. Times*: Postmaster General Winton M. Blount
announced that the American Poet to be honored in 1971 by a
commemorative postage stamp is Emily Dickinson (1830–1886).
A new 8¢ stamp will be issued. Honored last year, as first in the
series, was Edgar Lee Masters, with a 6¢ stamp.

　　　　Emily, you're worth 8—
　　　　That's more than Masters—
　　　　And Postmaster Blount
　　　　Now inflates
　　　　You, taking account—
　　　　After 141 years—of your
　　　　Birth date—
　　　　So that, 1″ square—
　　　　You'll be licked & stuck there
　　　　In the corner—
　　　　You'll have cornered
　　　　How many?—Maybe 100,000,000,000
　　　　Letters Letters Letters
　　　　To the World.

1971

Evening Wind

Pebbles by their shadows
on sand in the slant
light look transparent.
Hollows bare feet stamped
fill up with blue shade.
Water with granular
yearning hones the whetstone
of the bank. A panting
wind begins, fresh and rank,
like the smell of love.

1971

The Animals of the Ark
For Laurence Stapleton

"Still falls the rain."
Yes, the Flood.
The Air is steel,
the Ground is blood.
The Sea is flesh
on which they float,
the lucky creatures
in their boat.
Demons own the Sky,
their claw and hoof
like Noah's Chosen, dry
and under roof.

1972

Staring at the Sea on the Day
of the Death of Another

The long body of the water fills its hollow,
slowly rolls upon its side,
and in the swaddlings of the waves,
their shadowed hollows falling forward with the tide,

like folds of Grecian garments molded to cling
around some classic immemorial marble thing,
I see the vanished bodies of friends who have died.

Each form is furled into its hollow,
white in the dark curl,
the sea a mausoleum, with countless shelves,
cradling the prone effigies of our unearthly selves,

some of the hollows empty, long niches in the tide.
One of them is mine
and gliding forward, gaping wide.

1972

Found in Diary Dated May 29, 1973

Most of what is happening is hidden.
There is a subworld
where the roots of things exist.
You happen to say a few words
along with a sudden smile.
The first hyacinth unfurls
on an April morning: color, odor,
texture complete, and in plain sight.
Below that bright floor a crepuscular
network, the depth and spread of thought
takes up great space,
and travels. The roots are ramifying,
counterpart to a sprig of brief perfume.
A huge and delicate tree, inverted there

in the nether dark. A crop of dense hair
feels downward, outward, to draw up
the sustaining sap.

1973

In Progress

Fountain of Death and Other
Poems. A short collection.
Slim volume. Heavy paper,
large type: Black Lily,
Black Rain spattering fat
soft pellets. Higher,
leaking as if from a lava
cone, pistils of everbright
blood. Where the gout
thickens, pouts out, unbraids,
a widening crotch of Black
River falls. Small ringlets
and fizzes and snarls bubble
from behind slender necks
of the fountain. Kiss them.
Cut your tongue afresh.
Swallow nooses of trickling
strangling death. Black
Widow, female hourglass. Black
Swan, red saddle. Black Lily,
Trumpet and Fountain.
Eclipse, the jet mare, white
diamond at her throat's base.
Bloodrush when, stabbed, she
stumbles, rolls, crushing her
rider to death. Gush of images
forced free from funnels of
the fountain, shaped abrasions
of their launch and scatter,
their fall and cooling, their

fix and balance, until erect
the final profile
spouts up.

1974

Walking in the Village after Many Years

I stop and stare
at the narrow shop on Carmine:
a <u>FOR RENT</u> sign in the window
and a hand-printed card:

> I have been happy to serve
> my customers for over 40 years
> and now I have decided to retire
>   —Tony—

It's empty in there,
plaster dust on everything,
the butcher block and white display case gone,
where Tony used to stand and carve.
He loved his trade. His blade, always sharp,
with motions of a virtuoso flashed above
the scrubbed podium of the block.
His apron always clean, he'd cut the meat,
Which was richly red and lean.
He'd elegantly trim the frames of fat.
I remember him. How neat he'd slide my steak
onto a sheet of tissue on the scale
at eye-level in front of me,
quick-wrap it in a slick marbled paper, take
my money, ring up the sale, smiling.
He called me "Ma'am."

1974

Once There Were Glaciers

Earth, not flat, not round, your skin loose as a dog's:
earthquakes your hackles raised. When swollen within,
panting you spin, wobbling at the poles. Your hide,
shifting, splits apart, the oceans leak and spread between.
Volcanoes hemorrhage from your gut. Earth, your ruptures,
glaciers, typhoons, arid Saharas—catastrophies, agonies—
are these the process and necessity, throes of eternal
labor? Earth, will you ever be born?

1974

Like a Lady

And isn't it like a lady?
Your hand plays on her breast,
your left is underneath her nape,
she lies along your lap.
She has no head, nor even legs.
She is a resonant box
responsive to your pluck and glide.
When you pick her up,
the pretty shoulders narrower
than the hips so round,
the shape feels right and graceful.
Along the glossy waist
your touch induces quivers
of inadvertent sound.
She does not kick or argue,
she wouldn't if she could,
your headless, legless lady
made of wood. But, no,
of course she's plastic,
as everything is these days,
electric and elastic
in many acoustical ways,
has fidelity and volume,
reverberation, clout.

You keep her tuned and tightened,
you're proud to take her out
and play. Isn't it a lady
you hold upon your lap?

1975

Manyone Flying

Warm, but stuffy   in the middle,
Cold, but clear   here on the edge . . .
Out on the ragged   edge, flying lonely.
Not all alone,   not that brave,
or foolish, or   self-sufficient,
or self-believing.   In the middle,
between the wingtips   of scattered others,
too little space.   Too little time . . .
time to think,   space to feel
private in,   and wonder,
wonder which is Body?   *My* body, or the Flock
I fly in—among?   Am I a wing
and fly where I decide,   Is *It* flying, and I
a feather in the Wing?   The others, who hide
in the warm   middle, flying, think, I
think, that they are   parts. I think too
much, maybe, here   in the clear,
in the chill   spaces. Out on the edge,
my maneuverings,   my wings, think
they are free.   Flock, where do we
fly? Are we Ones?   Or One, only?
If only One, not lonely   . . . being Manyone . . .
but Who   are We? And Why?

1975

Because I Don't Know

Because I don't know you, I love you:
warm cheeks, full lips, rich smile,
dark irises that slide to the side;
thick lashes, thick hair, gleaming
teeth and eyes; your hand in greeting
warmer than mine, wider, in blue shirt,
rolled sleeves, in dark jeans belted—
I liked your robust shoulders, wide neck and
tipped-up chin. That glow is blood
under skin that's warm to begin with,
almost dusky, the red showing
through—of health, of youth—but more:
your open, welcome, I-could-hug-you look.
We met once or twice, exchanged smiles:
your lips, curl-cornered to my thin,
crooked grin; your easy, laughing eyes
to my sharp stare. Did it pierce you
there, my look of hunger, like a hook?
I wanted only a sniff, a tongue-tip's
taste, a moment's bath in your rare
warmth. That last night, trading
goodbyes, when we kissed—or *you* did, me—
my hand took your nape, plunged under
the thick spill of your hair. Then
I stepped into the dark, out of the light
of the party, the screen door's yellow
square sliding smaller and smaller behind
me. You've become a dream of ripe
raspberries, in summer country: deep, dark
red lips, clean, gleaming generous smile.
Who owns you? I don't know. I'll hide you
away in my dream file. Stay there. Don't
change. I don't know you—and had better
not. Because I don't know you, I love you.

1976

Assuming the Lotus

A downward spiral, to the third level
where a soft closed fold ends the shallow cone.
Yet, I remember convexity, the "button"
that, when pressed, connected with something ticklish:
an electric stir, lower down, inside.

And before that, a limber tube, an extension
cord, it seems I remember (but how could I
remember?) how the red flood fed directly into
a stubby trunk. It hung (but it was not like hanging)
big-headed—in a loose clench, limbs akimbo—

upside down. Bulge of forehead,
face a group of vague bumps
combined in a cleft that would be mouth and nose,
unpleasantly smooth, like gut.
No eyes, and the ears just beginning

to be vortex-swiveled holes.
Plugged by that dangling vine, the bundle deepening
its dimples, swelling, worked to harden
the forehead, to butt at the gate of bone.
Cuddled in a sleep-float, head trawling

the dream sea, I would rather not be pinched free.
But a fruit deemed ripe must drop, the blood-twig cut
and knotted. Unfolding, I get up on wobbly legs
and walk, free of the velvet walls, the mossy broth.
Outdoors, and meet the wind!

1977

Who Had the First Word?

Who had the first word?
And who will have the final word?
With each depending on an opinion
not his own? For he has no opinion,

doesn't notice that the one he
depends on has no opinion
of his own, and *he* doesn't notice, etc.
The word of the first one, copied
by the second, passed on to the third,
is accepted by the fourth one, and so on,
for no one takes his own authority,
has none of his own.
The final word, then, a distortion
of the original, whispered, turned over,
handled, whisked up, floated down,
crumpled, whirled and thinned,
soiled, ripped, disseminated, scattered, picked up,
recombined all wrong and syllables lost,
is the first word abused by its currency,
worn, devalued, and still passed on.
Where is First Thinker, the only one?

1978

Moisture, Warmth and Light

Mosquitos, too young to bite—
in fact, just born—got in,
invisibly, through the screen.

A ceiling light was on.
They took it for the sun
this muggy day of rain.

Against the window pane
each one dithered and finally lit,
where I smeared and killed it
with a piece of Kleenex.

For breakfast I eat Chex.
(Not true, but I need the rhyme.)

Now at this very time—
4:14—comes running by
that black Doberman, Gemeni.
And, close behind her dog,
comes Nancy at a jog,
her covergirl hair jouncing
cute *Bubbies & Buns* bouncing.

(That's the name of a magazine
I saw at a bookstore in Keene.)
(Not so but it could have been.)

Most of my creative day
was busily spent this way,
smearing baby mosquitos. I must
have made hundreds bite the dust.

Infinite infants, foolish things,
no sooner hatched and using their wings
than they died.

It's too warm and muggy
for November, unusually buggy.

But don't look for the weather to hold,
little bugs, little beasts, lucky little mates
with your warm beds and full dinner plates.

Soon for us all comes the dark and the cold.

1979

In Iowa: A Primitive Painting

Put carnations behind the ears
of cows, the black and blond and brown
munching while hardly moving
on mats of green. Four-legged furniture
of the fields, full bags of nourishment

and comfort hanging down
polish of the morning sunlight
on warm sides. They are the mother-
beasts, the stolid and innocent ones
and we the babes that feed on them.
From the car coasting 80 West
I reach a long arm out to put red
carnations behind all the black
and blond and brown wagging ears
of cows that munch
while hardly moving on slopes,
in hollows of green.

1970s

The Fortune Cookie

A rectangle
a white cloth
the blond sticks
the innocent bowls
Soup or little colored beads and squares to eat
the neat round rice
steams of surprise
when various dervish dishes with glittering hats alight
Lobster a whole
vermilion landscape on a platter
Our fingers players over the plates
stiltwalk wooden wands
delicate yet
permitted to be greedy
Let's be greasy friends with the roast pig
and print
the ample napkins with brown-as-beetle sins
Shambles made of the table a struck scene
noodles in pools
and the beautiful
fish's carcass a busted canoe
Life

transforms to gaudy waste like that
Warmbellied we await
dessert politeness reinstated
with varnished bubbles on toothpicks
Gravy lips and grateful teeth bathe in the prickly
sweet the way life is
gay and so
absurd
because so
Fortune found
in a folded cake
tasteless but holds the portentous
ribbon of our fate
Dare one crumple
and read what chance alots
banal therefore suitably true
WHAT'S GOOD FOR ALL IS GOOD FOR YOU!

1960s or 1970s

The Most Important

The most important thing I can do just now
is stand behind the porch screen and watch
the "chickens." There are twelve. Always
when they come to the yard they come
in a covy of twelve. Streaky gray, as ground
is gray, they huddle, but when they
push into sunlight, blond glimmers
in the puffs of their gently bouncing bodies.
Each, left leg left, right leg right, is scratching.
Necks and beaks jerk down and up to rake
and glean under layers of needles and leaves
the seed they need.

Last night it rained, a warm rain. Today the wind,
snatching leaves from the whipped trees, is cold.
Sky is cold, is mottled marble. All the small
the wind will whirl away: phoebe and wren,

warbler, bunting, kinglet, each to be ferried
to a winter home. I have none nor vehicle
of feathers. Much pecking and gleaning
I have to do, alone, without a flock:
To clear the ground, to comb beneath the pile
of years and pages. To choose what's germinal,
what must sustain.

But just now my eye in magnetic flux feeds
with the timid bobwhites, their plush bodies
touching, finding their grain together, keeping
communal warmth. They are twelve. The same
that came before, most every day. This may
be their last and mine before
the frost. Tomorrow's sky will be lower
and gray, sun gone, slate-colored juncos here
instead. Creeper and downy will hang around a while.

1981

The Rest of My Life

SLEEPING ALONE

Waiting for first light,
for the lift of the curtain,
for the world to ripen,
tumbling toward the sun,

I lie on my side,
head sunk in the pillow,
legs upfolded,
as if for Indian burial.

My arms are friends
relaxed beside each other.
One hand, open, touches,
brings warmth to the other.

A SPRING MORNING

Your right hand and my left
hand, as if they were bodies
fitting together, face each other.

As if we were dancing. But
we are in bed. The thumb of your
hand touches my cheek. My head

feels the cool of the pillow.
Your profile, eye and ear and lip
asleep, has already gone

through the doorway of your dream.
The round-faced clock ticks on,
on the shelf in dawnlight.

Your hand has met mine,
but doesn't feel my cheek is wet.
From the top of the oak

outside the window, the oriole
over and over repeats its
phrase, a question.

UNABLE TO WRITE IT

Tears do not make good ink.
Their message invisible,
no one reads this hurt.

I lie alone in dirt despair.
Alone beside one who does not feel
lightning strike and agony crackle.

I sink into black, the inkwell
wordless, filled with tears.

WHAT MATTERS

It may be that it doesn't matter
who or what or why you love.
(Maybe it matters when, and for how long.)
Of course, what matters is how strong.

Maybe the forbidden, the unbelievable,
or what doesn't respond—
what grabs all and gives nothing—
what is ghoul or ghost,
what proves you a fool,
shrinks you, shortens your life,
if you love it, *it* doesn't matter.
Only the love matters—
the stubbornness, or the helplessness.

At a certain chemical instant
in early youth, love's trigger is cocked.
Whatever moves into focus
behind the cross hairs, magnifies,
is marked for target, injected with
magic shot. But the target doesn't matter.

THE REST OF MY LIFE

I'm the one
who'll be with me
for the rest of my life.

I'm the one
who'll enjoy myself,
take care of myself,
be loveable, so as to love
myself for the rest
of my life.

Arms, be strong to hold me.
Eyes, be with me.
Will you be with me
for the rest of my life?

I'm the one,
the only one,
the one who won't leave me
for the rest of my life.

I'M ONE

I do not have.
I do not expect.
I do not owe.

I'm one,
the only one,
free in my life.

Each day perfect,
each day a thousand years.
Time is in me.

I swallow the sun.
I'm the one, the only
one in my life.

Oh, windless day
within me,
Oh, silence and sun.

1975–82

Cat and I

Heat of the sun on wood of the deck. Spread flat,
my body accommodates to hardness on the worn boards.
Cat fools with my foot, trying to make my big toe
stay in her ear. She gets bored when you're not here.

House feels hollow, without vibration, asleep.
No sudden bumps or door-slams, no shuffled dishes,
no water rushing in the tub, or outside from the hose.

Vacuum's snarling inhale, hedge clipper's chatter—
any welcome racket would make the little cat leap up,

land four-footed like a springbok, and race downstairs
to see what you are making happen. Instead, all is
neat and peaceful. Phone never rings. Or, if it does,
receiver waits long to be raised.

If you were here, I wouldn't be this flat, sunbathing
a whole morning on the deck, half hearing the far
gargle of a helicopter over the bay. I get lazy when
you're away. I have to feel guilty that I don't do
all the Things To Do on today's list.

Whether I ought, or not, I'm blaming it on you
that kitten doesn't spring. Slow, from inside, wags
the old Seth Thomas pendulum. And from below I hear
the suspended slaps of the tide.

Kitten has quit fooling with my toe. She's collapsed
in the shade under the overhang, her blond belly-frill
barely moving with her breath, heavy little bucket-head
dropped on paws. The crossed blue eyes are shut.

1983

Mickey's Pillow

"A friend of mine (Mickey) made me the most wonderful
pillow: it's 2 moose mooning in a marsh in the woods."
                                        —Quote from a letter

2 moose mooning in a marsh in the woods
must mean more than at first appears.
Many mottled mangoes mashed within their mouths
might indicate a morbid reason for their tears.

Moose mainly meander into marshes when confused
and munch on mint or mistletoe or other freaky fruit
moodily moping, never giggling or amused.
Some mimic the mandolin or mouth organ or flute.

2 Sioux sunning on a sward of snow,
swinging skillets, smiling, should set your heart aglow,
but 2 moose mooning in a marsh in the woods
must be murky omens and up to no goods.

early 1980s

The Fluffy Stuff

I want the fluffy stuff to keep coming down.
I'm looking into the garden from the third floor.
I wait for it to settle on brownstone windowsills,
on fire escapes, their narrow iron stairs.
Thin-as-tissue bits fall and rise on spirals of air
like meandering moths, and never reach the ground.
At last, dead vines on the trellis in the sooty
backyard begin to whiten. There sprouts a mat
of white grass. Tips of pickets on the fence
get mittens. Chimney tops in the opposite block
have their hoods and copings furred. The fluffy
stuff catches in crotches of the old ailanthus
whose limbs, like long dark cats stretching
on their backs, expose white bellies.

What began gauzy, lazy, scarce, falls willingly now.
I want it to race straight down, big, heavy, thick,
blind-white flakes rushing down so plentiful, so
opaque and dense that I can't see through the curtains.

1984

Mind

Mind is a room
in the room of the real.

This little room
in the big room.

Mind can dilate or
shrink like an eye-hole

which gapes sometimes
in the dark, in a dream,

displacing the whole
room of the real.

Then the big room
is within.

All that happens
Mind makes happen.

Populations of thought
grow and invade

the room of Mind.
In the center of Mind

in the eye-hole
is a littler room,

on the wall the words,
FACE REALITY.

How face what is within?
Within the eye?

Oh, Mind immense
and without walls!

alone like God
in the room of the real!

Oh, Daylight come,
make little the big

room of Mind.
Shift it from center

in the room of the real.
Make it one,

make it little,
one of the many

minds in the big
room of the real.

1984

Third Floor Walk-Up, 1984

I look down affectionately at the trash in the
dumpster on West 11th. I'd like to get back
into the crowded warm stink, onto the cracked
pavements. Into a narrow dark walk-up,
a floor-through, back-windowed, where the poor
trees of heaven shoulder up to light
out of fissures between old brownstones.
Back into The Village, of course, where layers
on layers of jostling life-into-death
are rottenly piled and sunk.

The map of The Village is a pattern of crude
triangles, their points meeting at Sheridan,
at Abingdon, Jefferson or Father Demo Square.
Outlines of those chunks of ancient earth
were cow paths when Greenwich was—no, *before*
it was—uptown. When it was farms, and

beyond them to the north, simply wilderness.
The streets are still peculiar in their layout,
unlike the monotonous numbered mechanical grid
of most of Manhattan. Before "free enterprise"
—when only the meandering enterprise of cows,
while they grazed, accidently designed this
crazy quilt of a neighborhood.

Following Waverly west from MacDougal, you
cross 6th and 7th Avenues and, turning left
on Perry, you arrive at Bank. Once the bank
of a canal winding through meadows where, on
the buttercup margins, cows sucked their fill.
Or, if you continue west on Perry, you cross
West 4th, then Bleecker, Hudson, Greenwich—
Street not Avenue—then Washington and West
Streets, ending at the river. A river of
cars ripping south you somehow have to cross
to reach the splintered piers along the *real*
river, the Hudson.

A garbage truck, square blunt mastodon, dusty
and smeared, turns the corner at Waverly Place
grinding into view below my third floor window.
Is there a more horrendous racket than the wrench
and scrape and gnash and crunch of a New York
City garbage truck? Seized by the swift
mittened hands of the grimy helper, who's cursed
by the driver loud enough to be heard over engine
in front and masher behind, huge smelly plastic
bundles leap from the curb into the jaws of
the truck. Dumpster across the street, full
of condominium conversion debris, must wait
for tomorrow's trash removal.

I watch with envy and affection from this sublet
on West 11th, to which I've escaped temporarily
from the boonies on Long Island. I feel lucky
paying only five times the rent I used to pay
two decades ago on Perry Street, where I had
twice the space *and* a terrace and garden.

Back then, I hankered for "the country"—
for clean wind, open water, distant neighbors,
peace. And discovered: Space is lonesome.
Privacy is a bore. Peace is a grave.

1984

Last Day

I'm having a sunbath on the rug
alone in a large house facing south.
A tall window admits a golden trough
the length of a coffin in which I lie
in December, the last day of the year.
Sky in the window perfectly empty.
Naked tree limbs without wind.
No sounds reach my ears except their
ringing, and heart's thud hollow and
slow. Uncomplicated peace. Scarcely
a motion. Except a shadow that un-
detected creeps. On the table a clay pot,
a clump of narcissus lengthens its stems.
Blue buds sip the sun. Works of the clock
circle their ratchets. There is nothing
to wish for. Nothing to will.
What if this day is endless? No *new*
year to follow. Alteration done with.
A golden moment frozen, clenched.

1986

A Tree in Spring

Now, while that tree just past bud, the leaves
young and small, a pale green haze the morning

sun sifts through; its trunk and limbs, its grasp
of branches, the tendencies of twigs, the whole

shape of its craving like the shoot of a fountain
passionately rising to overflow (but so slow,

so secret it is invisible as motion); the main
limbs from their division low on the trunk

reaching up and out to stab in three directions
(to stab for the light, the light that shifts);

just now, behind its scrim of stippled mist
the solid body of that tree, the whole shape

of its craving is plain to see; while millions
of leaves bud to increase, enlarge and hide

the reaching limbs, the forks and branches, all
the stubby-fingered twigs, thickening quickly

to eclipse remaining slits the morning sun sifts
through; before the leaves' opacity, before

eyelids of the light entirely close, now see,
seize with hasty sight an instant of vision.

1987

My Name Was Called

I didn't know what would be done with me.
When my name was called. As when baptized
for the first time. A stiff black four-
cornered hat on. Afraid it would fall off.
My ears stuck out but couldn't grab to keep
it steady on my head slippery and small.
Wet and white the slick enamelled chair,
its pattern of holes in the metal seat
where the water drained. My spotted hand
went up to try to help to bring the velvet
investiture over my square-hatted head.

Awkward. Old bobble with straight short
hair, lashless eyes and smileless mouth.
My name was called. Heavy medallion on wide
blue ribbon hung swinging from my neck.
The Elder's white robe sloshed at his knees,
he held my wrists to my chest, backwards
pressed me under, dipped me blind in the
marble font under green-veined water.
My name was called. My eight-year-old head
didn't know what would be done.

Old teetering monkeylike babylike head
under black gold-tasselled stiff platter-
like hat, sixty years later, the naked ears
stick out. My name is called. Pulled up,
out of the deafening bubbles, boosted up
to sit in the white chair. Murmured over
my head the rapid redundant prayer. Wet
head bowed beneath the hands laid heavy there.
Warm, suggestively wet, my white ruffled
panties streamed in the slick seat.
The silk and velvet lifted. My spotted
hand went up. Awkward. Huge in merciless
light my face on TV in front of my
actual face. My little ignorant ugly patient
helpless head on screen the freshest horror.
The greatest honor. Forced to confront,
but not forced to smile. Child eyes behind
old pouched lashless eyes, never again able
to soften the truth of my future face.
Face immersed, but still afloat over the years.
Head pressed under and blessed. Pulled up
and invested. I didn't know what would be
done, in the white dress or in the black,
when my name was called.

1987

The Hole Seen

Watt happened inn the passed?
The son rose. It was maid of steal.
A hoarse was borne full-groan with a ruff gate.
Wee weighted awl-knight.
A feint caul was herd.
Buy mourning won mite sea a grate bare on the rode.
And an our later, clothes buy, sum aunt hills.
Aye knead a cold bier.
Aye want to meat yew. Butt watt too ware?
The pane is in tense.
The soul reason four this tail is two get on the best cellar list.
Go write a head.
Rite on Mane Street a cat was licking her pause.
Wen she was dun she pealed and eight a pair.
She was well-bread.
It's thyme too set fourth.
Butt my watch is vary sloe.

Ate weaks went buy. It was reigning.
Yew gained wait.
Yew tolled me, "Yore tern, sew *say* sum thing."
Aye rote a note that red: "Knot four sail" and through it inn a
              male box.
A cop on the beet saw an usher, naked two the waste,
              tiptowing a long the isle. And a slay up-eared wile
              d-sending the I-see Hi-weigh.
Give me a brake!

Just as the tied was coming inn wee cot the plain.
Two lips in an earn mite cost know moor than sicks scents.
Are yew shore that's rite?
Eye maybe a knitwit, butt watt dew wee knead to know? Watt
              is throne aweigh?

All sew, weed like too no weather whether veins carry threw
              there a pointed roll.

Weave bean taut that wen wee dye, the hole seen wont bee
              sew pour.

Buy then, piece wood bee one.
Yew and eye no the tail bye hart.
Oar by wrote, yew mite say.
All ways go reel sloe.
Awl rite.
Who nose?
Lettuce prey.

1987

Kiwi

Fruit without a stone, its shiny
pulp is clear green. Inside, tiny

black microdot seeds. Skin
the color of khaki—Imagine

a shaggy brown-green pelt
that feels like felt.

It's oval, full-rounded, kind
of egg-shaped. The rind

comes off in strips
when peeled with the lips.

If ripe, full of juice,
melon-sweet, yet tart as goose-

berry almost. A translucent ring
of seed dots looks something

like a coin-slice of banana. Grown
in the tropics, some stone

fruits, overlarge, are queerly
formed. A slablike pit nearly

fills the mango. I
scrape the fibrous pulp off with my

teeth. That slick round ball
in avocado (fruit without juice) we call

alligator pear:
Plant this seedpit with care

on three toothpicks over a glass
of water. It can come to pass

in time, that you'll see
an entire avocado tree.

Some fruits have stones, some seeds.
Papaya's loaded with slimy black beads.

Some seem seedless—like quince
(that makes your tastebuds wince).

Persimmon will
be sour, astringent "until

dead ripe," they say. Behind
pomegranate's leathery rind,

is a sackful of moist rubies. Pear,
cantaloupe, grapefruit, guava keep their

seeds hidden, as do raspberry, strawberry,
pineapple. Plum, peach and cherry

we know as fruits with big
seedstones. And fig?

Its graininess is seed. Hard to believe
is prickly durian. It's custard

sweet—and smells nasty.
But there's no fruit as tasty,

as odd, or as funny—
none—

as fresh-off-the-vine New Zea-
land kiwi.

1987

Good Things Come from Thee

ON THE CLIFF

I'm sawing a slice off that hard dark knobby loaf
from Zabar's—black molasses and raisins in it—
to have with Tilsit cheese. You left a pumpkin and
autumn leaves on the stripped wood table, you filled
the birdfeeder hanging from the eaves. The window
is clean, the sill is varnished, white impatiens
in a brick clay pot smile above the sink. Our terrace
lined with boulders, the slate path with pachysandra
you planted. Storm doors are on, in front and back,
it's snug in here. I'm chewing, looking at the shelves
you cut and hung to hold our books and decoys.
You're strong, you twist off the lids of jars.
Cold nights you're a stove in bed.

BY THE CANAL

For Valentine's Day a whole studio and library!
Shelves built to the ceiling, there's space for every
thing: papers, folders, files and books, books, books.
Binoculars and chess set, tape recorders, tapes and
jigsaw. Telephone that's a blue car has a shelf
of its own. The old maple sawhorse table fits right in
and looks brand new. Curly ivy on the sill and outside
an entire alphabet of birds, on the porch, in the yard.

You put pink ribbons of sunrise in the back window,
scarlet bands of sunset in the front, the moon above our
bed at night. It snowed. You made a path. The Christmas
poinsettia blooms all year.

1987

Beginning Ended

Beginning ended, this is how the end begins.
We wake in the other world, sky inside our eyelid.
Lens swivelled inward, the sea's volcanic vents
leach into the brain. Here is self's jungle ajar.
Waterfall that sliced a mountain's
loaf in half flattens to a lake. A trickle of gems
from a pomegranate's cave is a red bedspread
where, black and white, the Swancat floats.
A chessboard on an iceflow, slow, swirls by.
The King and Queen arrive with retinue. And now,
small as pills, balls yellow and blue, chock through
white wickets over squares shaved velvet green.
The day is perfect. There is only one. It lasts
a thousand years. Years are thinnest pages
in a book, vast as a continent, heavy, sunk in sand.
At sunset, the end began, brain's
forest roars up into flame. Cool skull, a moon
released, tumbles onto the marble table of night,
rolls over the edge.

1988

Look Closer

The petals and leaves look much alike, in shape,
texture, rib-pattern, and size. Alike in all but
color. Clusters of red petals intensify the green
of leaves afloat around their stems. Red as

rooster comb at winter's peak, by spring the blooms
appear to be turning green, just as the leaves
are showing streaks of scarlet.

Look closer. By April, at the hub of each wheel
of petals a green knob swells, erects a hairlike
stem with infant leaf attached. It's pale green.
Meanwhile, some older, larger leaves have reddened.
As flimsy petals shrink, young leaves of like size
high on the stems turn red. Or were they petals
that transposed to green? It seems that leaves
and flowers crave to impersonate each other.

Look closer. Nothing so symmetrical takes place.
Toward summer the red clusters, that were showiest
at Christmas, look less bold. The transvestite
behavior of this plant is plain and can be traced.
When young, some leaves do imitate soft petals,
even assume their silks. Especially those born
close to the blooms. Lower, on spindles of stems,
broad leaves with serrate lobes stay frankly distinct
from oval petals. It's at the growing tip,
where leaves touch cheeks with flowers, that they
later begin to blush.

Look closer. By the time some spokes of bloom
have thinned, young, smooth, adjacent leaves have
halfway reddened. Too easy to think that petals
turn leaf-green while leaves go petal-red. Reds
do *not* turn green—not one, not ever. And not *all*
greens go red. Just those born late, at the crown.

By midsummer, if anything is left of this audacious
plant, the petals having thinned, dried, and dropped,
it will look ordinary, not a bit ambiguous.
There'll be an assemblage of leaves with various
lobes sharp-pointed, recalling the shapes of stubby
Christmas trees. And all green?

Look closer. See that the few broad, lowest leaves,
now coarse, curled and ready to fall, show dark
bruise-reds of autumn.

1988

The Snowy

Standing by the wires of your enclosure, I stared into your
   eyes.
I had to stare until your eyes showed they'd seen me.
You hunched on your cement crag, black talons just showing
beneath your chest. Your beak, like a third gleaming claw, hid
in the white fluff of your face. Your round head, helmet of
   fleece,
had no neck, no ears. Under your blizzard of feathers your
   closed
wings were invisible. Elemental form simplified as an egg,
you held perfectly still on your artificial perch. You, too,
might be a crafty fake, stuffed or carved. Except your eyes.
   Alive,
enormous, yellow circles containing black circles, clear, slick,
heartstopping double barrels of concentrated rage pointed at
   me.
Without seeing me. Suddenly, your head flicked completely
   around,
faced straight backwards and swiveled front again.
So quick I doubted you had done it. Then your glass-clear
   pupils
disappeared, your eyelids of white down slid up over them.
   Your
face shut. It went blank. Your hooded snow-head looked blind.

I remained beside the wires, leaning toward you, absorbing
   your
chilling closeness. Constantly shoving past you, the ever-
   shifting
crowd. Western sunlight slanted into your diorama. Now I saw
your white chest was flecked with dusky. Captivity had soiled
   you,

had worn and aged you, under the strokes of countless avid
    eyes.
Eyes such as mine. At feeding time the crowd squabbled to
    get closer.
Through a slit in the painted wall (a simulation of arctic
    tundra)
your keeper released a panic of voles and mice. You ignored
    them,
you let them vanish into crannies of the sculptured rocks.
You settled lower, sullen, on your perch. You gathered
    emptiness and
silence about you, until you seemed no longer there, no
    longer alive.

The park had emptied. The gates were closing. I had to leave
    you.
Perhaps you waited until dark to unhinge your wings, to drift
noiseless down. Perhaps you put hooks into your prey, when
    they,
grown used to the absence of threat in the air, emerged
with wrinkled noses and scuttled here and there.

1988

Memory of the Future?
Prophecy of the Past?

I

A structure that haunts memory. Its bulk,
outline, height and darkness, its shining
edges. The thick pillars hatted black,
their heads of puffed charcoal or caps
of soot on quenched matches magnified or
Charlie Chaplin's bowler of felt that's
felt by the fingertips of the eyes, that
exact soft roughness. An edifice all of
hollow wood. Between its squat black
pillars slim flute-shaped pipes burnished gold.
From their chiselled slits are blown the every-

colored streamers, the lacy delicate swells
of sound. Then, overwhelming, from under-
ground roots of the pillars, thunderous
quakes and guttural groans reverberate.
In a semicircular embrace, tier on tier
are skulls and torsos, an enormous chorus
that is a terraced garden of pastel
females, sombre males, whose throats,
uniting, strum and shudder, an expanding
avalanche of sound. Broad-striped
skywide harmonies concatenate, dissonant
and sweet, a peppered honey. Phalanxes
of rainbows, transparent tender colors
bloom on the ear's horizon. Interpene-
trating tones inundate the sprawling
strands of the nerves, sluggish
blood jumps to injected spurts of lightning,
the flood suddenly buttressed by brutal
final tomb-deep chords of climax. During
the stun of silence a whole minute,
interminable as a hundred years, before
reversal and rollback of echoes finally
complete themselves and die.

II

It is before I can walk. I sit on the floor,
a vast vaguely patterned rug stretching to
the borders of the room. I hold a book whose
pages are of cloth, the edges serrated as if
with pinking shears. Picture books that could
not be torn were given to babies then.
I love my soft book, each page of which shows
an animal. Turning the pages I have come
to Elephant. Gray and huge, his trunk
is raised, tip facing me, held up like
a curled cup. There are words in a row under
the Elephant. I cannot yet read. I don't
need to. I know everything by looking.
There is warmth around me. I am not alone.

The legs of my parents encase me where they sit
together on a couch behind me. I know that
Father is on my left and Mother on my right.
A steady light permeates the room, not bright,
not gloomy—a lasting-forever light,
neither night nor day. I have on a white
dress and white socks. I think I have not yet
seen color. I feel the cotton softness of
the book's cover and pages, their smoothness
but also the slight ridges of threads
between my thumbs and forefingers.
Elephant's trunk, its tip erect,
thrust forward, a nose that is also lips
that suck in, blow out, that gropes like a paw
and seems to see with nostrils, that
might be eyes looking at me. Elephant.
This is my first memory.

1988

A Rescue

In the middle of the line
under my reading eye
a spot of fog. It makes
faint an *e*, then a *y*,
and travels to the right.
In the next line the spot
expands, shifts and erases
a whole word. I close my
eyes and see a tiny bright
buzz saw that flickers.
Opened, my eye finds it
still there, in the air,
enlarged. I swallow a
pill, hoping to halt the
pain before it begins.
Eyes have roots in the
brain. In their transparent

prisms where blossoms of
image spring, the smallest
blight could shrink the
scope of consciousness
forever. I go to the mirror.
One eye sees itself, but
the other half of my face
is fog, except for a
quivering, toothy moon
there, which transforms
to a spiral. This is
dizzying. I darken the
room, I go to bed, I pull
the sheet over my head.
I will think only of sinking
slowly into soft layers of
cloud. I want to descend
all the way down to brain's
end and, without weight or
feature, slip under the skin
of sleep.

Episodes in the past, I
remember comet-like, came
with other unpredictable signs
and symptoms. Tongue went
numb, ears went deaf, I
clutched my hair where half
my skull throbbed like a
fisted drum, while flakes
of light changed pattern
behind one eyelid. When
the pain in eye socket, nape
and skull bone began, it grew
so cruel I moaned and rolled
in the bed for hours.
I had at last to vomit
Only then, cold water splashed
over face and temples, head
in a cold cloth tightly bound,

I'd crawl back into bed,
entirely spent, and sleep
the day away. When rid of
it, sometimes by twilight,
limp but clear-eyed, hungry,
I'd go downstairs. Absence
of pain was a rescue.
Precious, delicious were
ordinary things: a bite of
bread, swallow of coffee,
sight of a streak of late
sun on the kitchen floor.
I could barely lift a hand,
yet relief brought a rush
of ecstasy. Sight sharp,
spine straight, I filled up
with joy and power. Almost
worth the hideous pain,
the sweet reward of its
riddance.

No pain this time. Today
only its dreaded expectation.
In a quarter hour the drug
begins to control the rate
of capillary flow in neck
and head, narrowing the
cranial pathways of blood
going to my brain. I can
relax in a gradual float
toward sleep, entertained
by the array of geometric
phantoms performing within
the focus space before (or
is it behind?) my left eye:
A tiny spectral triangle
revolves and slyly turns
tetrahedral. Outline of
a luminous cube replaces a
hazy cross. That fades

when twin pyramids, set base
to base, glide forward,
their angles disjoining into
loops that tie into a knot.
It glints and spins, but
finally simplifies to an
almost perfect figure eight,
which pulses, and slowly
pales, then sinks out of
"sight." The show already
over? I'm disappointed,
want to dive after it, to
where, deep in my brain,
surely other never-seen
brilliants teem. Somehow
I succeed. I'm in dream
dimension now. I can drag
back into "view" a final
sparkler. It organizes
instantly its golden points
and planes into a ziggurat.
Blissful symbol. I go on
sleeping.

1989

Guilty

I hadn't finished being young,
hadn't learned how to be,
when I noticed I'd been semi-old
for some time.
And now that, beyond that,
I've arrived—or, *gone*
is the right word—far
beyond "beyond the shadow
of a doubt" to that low state
labeled "old," I'm incredulous

at the extent of my self-blindness
since the beginning.

Guilty, I declare myself.
And, too late at this final state
to begin to learn how
to begin to be.
Self-condemned, confined
to the cell of old age, I'm
sentenced to . . . life!
A term pityfully short.
Time of execution, any early
morning. It's a secret.
It'll be a surprise.

1989

Night Visits with the Family II

VIRGINIA'S DREAM
When I unlocked the file drawer, second from the top,
    I found an old diary from 1999.
In it was a list of Things To Do Today: Learn to hang-glide.
    Buy Bananas. Phone the Pope. The handwriting was
    mine.

LAEL'S DREAM
I flew above the golf course. I did it sitting up.
    Then, lying on my side I scooted high above the lake.
It was easy, and I wished I'd tried it long, long, long ago,
    despite the risk of losing power, and the crash before I
    wake.

MERLA'S DREAM
My hair was very curly, and it was made of yarn.
    Roy said it was lovely. And all my friends were green
with envy. It never needed cutting, didn't shrink when washed
    in Woolite. Brushing every night kept it fluffy and clean.

SPENCER'S DREAM

Daddy held me on his knee
        and showed me I had five
on each hand: one fumb, four
        thingers. We
played cake. He told me more,
        said I had toes
on my hind feet.
        I sucked one of those.
It was the BIG-
        gest, named This Little Pig.

DORI'S DREAM

Some sort of museum. Bright paintings on the walls.
        No. Wait. They were crazy quilts. In Idaho, I think.
We had come to an auction. Dan liked a tasseled one
        with a wide brown border, but I chose the white and
        pink.

RICKY'S DREAM

The orchestra began to play, the curtains parted. I
        entered dressed in purple tights. I leaped to center stage.
One by one I had to lift twelve ballerinas on their toes,
        each spitting asterisks to mark the footnotes on a page.

LISA'S DREAM

I started to make a fancy birthday cake. Somehow
        I can't remember who it was for. The doorbell rang.
Just then, a nightingale swooped through the open skylight
        and perched on the chandelier. He sang and sang and
        sang.

JAY'S DREAM

Two of our goats broke tether and got into the lucerne.
        It was the Fourth of July. We were all away in town.
I saw a bloated white balloon swaying low in the moonlight.
        Another had just exploded, shreds of it falling down.

CAITLIN'S DREAM

There was a contest. The questions were: 1. What's smoother?
     A rose petal () A kitten's nose () A spoonful of whipped
          cream ()
2. What would you rather do? Go swimming () Shopping ()
Watch TV ()
          3. If you knew it would come true tomorrow, what
          would be your dream?

JULIA'S DREAM

I was trying to learn the computer. A square knob lit up
          marked GO. So I pressed it. A clanging heap of money
landed in my lap, over ninety dollars' worth of heavy coin.
          Someone gave me a plastic bucket. I laughed 'til my
          nose was runny.

KIPPY'S DREAM

I lay on a velvet bed, and the bed stood out in a field.
          The sun was warm, the wind blew gently, lifting my
          filmy dress.
Then I was a mermaid on the sea, flipping a sequined tail.
          I need never again live in a house. This was happiness.

DANIEL AND MICHAEL'S DREAM

We sometimes dream the same dream, and at the same speed.
          And we can switch identities in sleep, being twins.
Mike can be Dan, and Dan be Mike, at least for part of the
night,
          grabbing each other's virtues, shrugging off our sins.
As Daniel, I dreamed an angel held me by the ear, as Michael
          climbed into the lion's den. As Michael I had a dream
that I inhaled Daniel up out of the lion's jaws with my golden
          trumpet, and set him on a cloud. Yes, we're quite a team!

MAY'S SECOND DREAM

Virginia's diary of the future, Lael's flight, Merla's hair
          of sunny yarn, Baby Spencer's hands and feet, Doris's
          quilt
of colored scraps, Rick the ballet dancer, Lisa's nightingale,

Jay's two goats, Caitlin's contest, Julia's jackpot and
Kippy the mermaid. As for the Twins: an angel, an ear, a lion's
   jaw, a trumpet and a cloud. Twelve dreams I juggled
through the night, like walking a highwire without a net.
   Well, really, thirteen, I say aloud. Glad it's morning at
      last,
and a bright one. To myself, and to all the family, I say:
   Here's love! Have a good day!

1989

Dear John

I knew you when
you were beardless, nearly,
an Auden-picked young poet,
a Manhattanite—as I was then—
one of the Scribner "Poets of Today."
On our way in the to-and-fro
of Penn Station, say,
or the Village street,
we'd meet, we'd Hi and Hello,
or handshake and hug.
I doted upon
your Swan
and Shadow, your Kitten and Bug,
your many found and *pro*found
forms and shapes. And you admired
mine. Our inventions were *not* "inspired"
by each other's. To appreciate
needn't mean to "influence."
Now, bearded and great,
your smiling bison-face
graces the back of your
20th volume. You're in full Bloom,
both Harold-endorsed and Harry-adored
by Knopf's new Ford.
I knew you when. I'm glad to know you now,
decked in all your honors, arrived at star
status. *Rhyme's Reason* has brought you far.

But there'll be many more
years and books and celebrations, more
brilliant "flowers of rhetoric" from your pen,
dear John. I'm glad I knew you when.

1989

Woman in a Garden

There's an eye aslant,
in the right place for a profile,
and a snout with one flared nostril
on that side.
But squiggly lipstick dabs
establish a fullfaced mouth.
Oh, I see legs crossed at the knees,
skinny but shapely,
the green of hyacinth stems.

Suddenly found, another eye,
attentive, smaller, tucked into her left armpit.
The entire middle is thick, flowing, white.
A haircutter's cloth? In that case
the vague pumpkin-yellow helmet-shape
at the top can be her blond head.

I know you're not supposed to look for *objects*
in a De Kooning. As gauche as
with modern music to feel emotion
or fantasize a plot.
Considered strictly as pattern,
delicious springlike colors are folded in,
kept in suspended balance in a square swatch
of space—yes, a stage for swift brushwork,
sweeps of impulse, a bit jokey, bold.
So, poking up out of the bumpy white sheet,
fruit-red, popsicle-shiny, near her ear,
an erect penis isn't shocking—
is as plain to see as, under the peaked tent
of her crossed legs the little green heron stands.

This is an optional deconstruction.
Turned upside down, there's another garden,
a different woman.
A portrait head in closeup, large, all white,
with one dark, moist, penetrating eye
that watches from under a pair of rams' horns
twisting, rising from her forehead.

1989

A Clear Night on Mt. Hopkins

Celestial objects.
The farthest are the earliest,
the oldest the brightest.
Distance is time.
A black hole sucks galactic light
into its hot emptiness.
Matter, emitting intense radiation,
disappears.
In the intergalactic medium
a startling opacity,
a blockage of light.
What's most dense is invisible.
The oldest object, a quasar,
its red shift magnified
drops inward rapidly
toward the beginning of time.
Lightyears deep (15 billion?)
an event called the Big Bang,
all matter, all energy exploding
out of that infinitesimal point.
The first stars born, galaxies gather
to speed away from each other.
The universe inflates,
a bag without a skin.

1989

SELECTED WRITINGS
ABOUT POETRY

A Poem Happens to Me

I DO not know why I write poems or what makes me write them. Often, when I want *to write a poem*, I cannot—or, if I stubbornly sit down and write something anyway, I discover sooner or later that it is *not* a poem. I suspect this may be because, by concerning oneself with making a poem, one is so conscious of going through the correct motions of doing so, that the spirit of the creation refuses to enter the hard, premeditated clay, and, when it is finished, all the physical parts may have been admirably fashioned, but no passion is there to animate the figure.

It does not breathe.

It is like making a wonderful violin complete in every way, except that one can't get music from it.

On the other hand, it sometimes happens that I am unwilling to write the poem but that it forces itself from me without permission. A poem that happens in this way will often be inexplicable to myself, as to source, content, or significance. Months later, or years later, such a poem may "dawn on me," and I know for the first time what it is I have written. Sometimes I agree with my own observation, and sometimes I think it absurd.

These detached instances of creation seem not to be mystic, trancelike, or extrasensory—I think they are common to most artists in whatever medium.

In reviewing some of my past work, particularly my early work, I have been surprised to find that some juvenile bit of philosophy—sometimes venturing on the prophetic—some statement or observation that I, at the time, could not possibly have arrived at through experience, has turned out to be an apt commentary on events or states of mind that I am experiencing today or which have since been corroborated by first-hand knowledge.

For instance, one of my first poems, called "Plea for Delicacy in Love," dealt with the psychic play between man and woman in a coital embrace—being chiefly the attitude of the woman in contrast to that of the man. At that time I had had no sexual experience and was slightly, though probably erroneously posted on the literary information available on such a subject. But years later my personal experiences exactly bore out the philosophy of the poem—and I was quite aghast upon reading it the other day, wondering how the devil I knew all that then!

As I said, the full portent of a poem is not always evident to the writer himself, either while writing or after the poem is done. And it may be years, or never, before he arrives at an understanding of his own work.

Then, too, it is my frequent experience to start writing one poem and find, upon its completion, that I have written another —maybe entirely at variance or even diametrically opposite to what I set out to say. This always gives me a vague feeling of guilt—and I deplore such absence of integrity of purpose. Yet these inverted poems often turn out quite good, and, though the hens' eggs sometimes hatch goslings, perhaps one fowl is as good as another.

The act of creation itself (and I believe most artists will be obliged to admit this) is a special experience. By this I mean that it is unlike any other experience. How unlike? So far, no poets have been very adequate in clarifying that point. As for psychology, or any other *science*, attempting to fathom omniscience, the idea (and frequent experiments only too well prove this) is, of course, naive, to say the least.

Yes, even terms, nomenclature, words, for this experience are lacking, adding another difficulty to the attempt at describing the creative act. That is why I have fixed upon the unsatisfactory term *omniscience*.

When I am seized by a poem that demands to be given voice—I might say, when I am obsessed by some spirit ("daemon," I believe D. H. Lawrence once called it) that demands a body of me, if I am alone so that there is no outside source of distraction, I grope for a pencil and paper and sit down. I say "grope" because physical actions seem more or less "reflexive," and the mind leads the body, but as if from behind glass. That is, I am closeted within my mind, and my body moves about obediently on the other side of that transparent door, quite efficiently but beyond my notice.

Then I become perfectly still, my eyes turned in one fixed direction.

Sometimes it is many minutes before the first words of the dictation come. When it comes, my hand, with the pencil, rises.

Rises and begins to write—lightly and fleetly, pausing now and then as if to listen. On many occasions I remember relaying to my hand a mental aside, namely: Do not be abrupt; be careful or you will frighten away the fish! In the first moments anxiety poises the mind at the very pinpoint of concentration to catch the thought—for the balance between obscured reception and perfect articulation is extremely precarious.

I feel my hand writing as if it were not part of me but a tool held and directed by my mind.

The dictation continues, by this time, consecutively and swiftly—for, like the opening of neuron synapses to the brain after partaking of liquor or a drug, the cortical ducts and nerve centers seem to open and become unimpeded so that thought transference achieves a high efficiency.

Sometimes, however, the unreeling of the content occurs in reverse, the last portion or conclusion of the poem revealing itself first and working backward to the beginning. Another common phenomenon is the appearance first of the climax, or purposive element in the work, whereupon the introduction and denouement branch out from the nuclear center to either side, until the theme completes itself.

After the main kernel, the nucleus, the lifestuff, has been translated—given form or body—the automatic quality of the translation may wear off, gradually, like ether. And again I return to the familiar jacket of my flesh. I relax.

The rest of the poem may then be born quite consciously, simply through a logical, workmanlike persistence.

A work that owes its realization to more or less automatic, or internecine, creation tends, once the motivation ceases, to be inflexible for further molding or revision, at least for some time. The matter-of-fact mind refuses to deal with the child of an alien upstart conception, and it is very seldom that the identical machinery of omniscience that produced the particular work in question can be reinduced. This imposes an unfortunate inevitability on the "dictational poem," whereas, the poem that occurs "scientifically"—that is, as a result of ordinary conscious logic and motivation—has the advantage that it remains malleable and can be chiseled and polished and thereby improved to an unrestricted degree.

After completing an automatic poem, it is quite useless now

to read the poem and expect to know what one has written. It may be days before it has *cooled* enough to reveal its permanent shape and color.

Likewise, the mind, through which the birth has passed, must serve the double function of appraising its offspring, of judging it—and for a while it will be so distorted by birth and labor as to be undependable as a critic.

What artist has not, upon ejecting some new raw creature of the brain, looked down at the thing, in consternation and horror, and asked: What is it? Where did it come from? And what had *I* to do with it?

Similarly, the act of creation itself (whether consciously instigated or whether the poem be *visited on the creator*) is a special experience. The physical and mental elation upon successful completion of a poem or any work of art is a thing quite outside, and if I may say so, superior to almost any other satisfaction.

The emotion takes the form of a deep and abundant sense of well-being and a feeling of liberation—something akin to the release of hormonal and adrenal juices after sexual satisfaction—a feeling of complete satiation and relaxation.

I once wrote (and this too, incidentally, was an observation made during the adolescence of my art):

> The Poet
> when he has made a thing to his liking
> dips from the same deep-spiced bowl
> and knows the same full content
> as that of a Lover
> on the morrow after he has lain sweetly
> with his beloved.

The experience might also be likened to that succeeding confession or self-abnegation before some mild, astringent priest—the all-compassionate conscience—the Self, itself. I am reminded of the remark of a friend, a writer, who said: "Writing is to me a confession, not a profession."

The consciousness of self-revelation and abnegation that enters into the aftereffects of expression gives it the aspect of a psychic purge and a mental and spiritual purificant.

"Writing is like dying and being born again," says my friend. Yes, it is death and birth being brought to within a desperate circumferential hair's breadth of each other—as if two stars of opposite poles swept together and *almost* grazed! And the innocent witness and unwitting perpetrator of this near-collision returns to the plane of the Matter-of-Fact, to look about him with new and blinking eyes at a somehow grayed world.

mid-1950s

Poet's Choice

I AM old enough to have been brought up at a time when poetry by definition was regularity of measure and predictability of rhyme. At least, where I went to school—in a small town out west where they are still short on art and long on religion: William Wordsworth, Henry Wadsworth Longfellow, Edgar Allan Poe, John Greenleaf Whittier, etc., represented American poetry. Emily Dickinson and Walt Whitman were too irregular—both in technique and in person—for the ears of my Junior High School English teacher, so she did not stress them. Those W's—Whittier, Wadsworth, Wordsworth—got scrambled up on exam papers. If you spelled Edgar with an "er" or Allan with an "en," it meant a bad mark, regardless of how well you knew Poe's poetry.

Sheets and Kelly were top dogs in English poetry, along with the five B's—Blake, Byron, Burns, and the Brownings, he and she—remembering first, of course, to Shake the Great Speare. Did we ever hear of a contemporary poet? Not until first-year college did I hear of Eliot, Cummings, Frost, or Moore.

Eliot and Frost seemed to appeal to my professor more than the other two, so I preferred Moore and Cummings. Things are better out in Logan, Utah, by now. When I was there last, I was asked to address a poetry workshop at the university and those students were pretty up on contemporary poets. In general, though, the whole state is still short on art and long on religion. Quite early in my life these two refuges of the imagination came to cancel each other out for me. Having one, you didn't need the other. Gerard Manley Hopkins—he jumped the local fences too much—too bad, for he might have been used by my first mentors as a good peg to pin religion and art together.

Because of the dead grass we were fed as poetry in school—some of it was fine, but nevertheless dry from storage in the educational barn—when I began to write I was impatient with any form that smacked of the past. I hated symmetry, I hated the expected.

I hated form itself for a while—until I convinced myself I could make what I imagined to be my own forms. Were they? Are they? Well, if you write "free verse" (an old-fashioned term now), you must invent a form for each poem, or else let the poem take on its willing natural form and then emphasize it. If you don't do either of these, you have prose, no matter how the typesetter makes it look.

I am not very knowledgable about poetry, either of the past or modern. I mean, I am neither school nor teacher. When I like a poem, I know it by what it does to my thrill-bone. That "bone" is in the ear and in the image-chamber, and in the medulla oblongata; it runs the length of the vertebrae. But it's a mystic bone, really. Its marrow is the unexplainable—a felt rightness and wholeness, a conviction that *it* is all there, a feeling that some prediction is coming true but you can't say just what it is *except* in the words of the poem.

The poem is an eyehole to a kind of truth or beauty that is finally unnameable. A hint of it is furnished *through* the poem. I talk of the poem that thoroughly engages my thrill-bone. It is rare. This one, by Emily Dickinson, does it: "As the starved maelstrom laps the navies . . ."

1960

The Poet as Antispecialist

WHAT is the experience of poetry? Choosing to analyze this experience for myself after an engrossment of many years, I see it based in a craving to get through the curtains of things as they *appear* to things as they *are* and then into the larger, wilder space of things as they *are becoming.* This ambition involves a paradox: an instinctive belief in the senses as exquisite tools for this investigation and, at the same time, a suspicion about their crudeness. They may furnish easy deceptions or partial distortions:

> Hold a dandelion and look at the sun.
> Two spheres are side by side.
> Each has a yellow ruff.
>
> Eye, you tell a lie,
> that Near is Large, that Far is small.
> There must be other deceits . . .

W. B. Yeats called poetry "the thinking of the body" and said: "It bids us touch and taste and hear and see the world, and shrinks from . . . every abstract thing, from all that is of the brain only—from all that is not a fountain jetting from the entire hopes, memories, and sensations of the body." But sometimes one gets the inkling that there are extra senses as yet nameless, within the apperceptive system, if one could only differentiate them and identify their organs.

Not to be fully aroused to the potentialities of one's senses means to walk the flat ground of appearances, to take given designations for granted, to accept without a second look the name or category of a thing for the thing itself. On that ground all feelings and notions are borrowed, are secondhand. The poetic experience, by contrast, is one of constant curiosity, skepticism, and testing—astonishment, disillusionment, renewed discovery, reillumination. It amounts to a virtual compulsion to probe with the senses into the complex actuality of all things, outside and inside the self, and to determine relationships between them.

Aroused to the potentialities and delights of the senses and the evaluating intellect, and using them daily, the poet, however, comes eventually to their limits and notices that their

678

findings are not enough—that they often fall short of yielding the total, all-comprehensive pattern that he seeks. A complete and firm apprehension of the Whole tantalizingly eludes him— although he receives mirages of it now and then that he projects into his work. He is not so separate from every man as not to be fooled by tricks of perspective, seduced by the obvious, or bogged down in old and comfortable myths.

The limitations of our minds and sensory equipment partly stem from the brevity of our physical lives. Stendhal somewhere says that man is like a fly born in the summer morning and dead by afternoon. How can he understand the word *night*? If he were allowed five more hours, he would see and understand what night is. But, unlike the fly, man is sorely conscious of the vastness of the unknown beyond his consciousness. The poet, tracing the edge of a great shadow whose outline shifts and varies, proving there is an invisible moving source of light behind, hopes (naively, in view of his ephemerality) to reach and touch the foot of that solid what-ever-it-is that casts the shadow. If sometimes it seems he does touch it, it is only to be faced with a more distant, even less accessible mystery. Because all is movement—expansion or contraction, rotation or revolution— all is breathing change.

The experience of poetry is to suppose that there is a moon of the psyche, let us say, whose illuminated half is familiar to our ordinary eye but which has another hemisphere that is dark. And that poetry can discover this other side, its thrust can take us toward it. Poetry is used to make maps of that globe, which to the "naked eye" appears dislike and one-dimensional, seems to "rise" and "set" rather than to orbit; which remains distant and merely a "dead" object until, in the vehicle of poetry and with the speed of poetic light, we approach it. It then enlarges and reveals its surprising topography, becomes a world. And passing around it, our senses undergo dilation; there is a transformation of perception by means of this realization of the round.

Miniature as we are in the gigantic body of the cosmos, we have somehow an inbuilt craving to get our pincers of perception around the whole of it, to incorporate infinitude and set up comprehensible models of it within our little minds. Poetry tries to do this in its fashion. Science tries it, and more demonstrably. The impulses of the scientist and the poet, it seems to me, are parallel, although their instruments, methods, and effects are quite divergent. Contrasts between science and poetry are easily illustrated by such apparent opposites as: objective/subjective, reason/intuition, fact/essence—or let me boldly say: material/spiritual. A point of contiguity between them, however, is that poet and scientist both use language to communicate their findings.

As a rule, the scientific investigator works as one of a team. He works with formulas or with objective facts that are classified and reported as nakedly as possible so as to convey, in each instance, a single, specific, unambiguous meaning. The poet works alone, handling concrete sensual particulars, as well as their invisible and intangible essences, with the tools of intuitive perception; he then presents his discoveries wrapped in metaphor, metrical patterns, and, often, multifarious symbols. The scientist has an actual moon under observation—one he soon hopes to have under manipulation—although no robot or human explorer has yet succeeded in getting to it. "Until one does," I read not long ago, "scientists cannot tell whether the lunar surface is packed hard, porous, or buried deep in dust." And, "because of fuel limitations of the rockets that will orbit the moon and lower a ferryboat to the lunar surface, moon landings must be held within five degrees north and south of the moon's equator and within forty-five degrees east and west of the moon's central meridian. Within this narrow zone of safety, flat lands must be found to receive the spaceships from earth."

My moon is not in the sky but within my psyche. More or less subliminal, it orbits within the psyche of every man, a symbol both of the always-known and the never-to-be-known. I do not try to land on that moon. To do so would be to choose lunacy. But in 1958 I wrote a poem called "Landing on the Moon," which outlines, in its first three stanzas, a capsule history of the moon's psychic pull on man since primitive times to the present. The two concluding stanzas speculate about whether it is well for man to succumb, literally, to that hypnotism and let himself be drawn up onto the moon:

When in the mask of night there shone that cut,
we were riddled. A probe reached down
and stroked some nerve in us,
the glint of a wizard's eye, of silver,
slanted out of the mask of the unknown—
pit of riddles, the scratch-marked sky.

When, albino bowl on cloth of jet,
it spilled its virile rays,
our eyes enlarged, our blood reared with the waves.
We craved its secret, but unreachable
it held away from us, chilly and frail.
Distance kept it magnate. Enigma made it white.

When we learned to read it with our rod,
reflected light revealed
a lead mirror, a bruised shield
seamed with scars and shadow-soiled.
A half-faced sycophant, its glitter borrowed,
rode around our throne.

On the moon there shines earth light
as moonlight shines upon the earth . . .
If on its obsidian we set our weightless foot,
and sniff no wind, and lick no rain
and feel no gauze between us and the Fire,
will we trot its grassless skull, sick for the homelike shade?

Naked to the earth-beam we will be,
who have arrived to map an apparition,
who walk upon the forehead of a myth.
Can flesh rub with symbol? If our ball
be iron, and not light, our earliest wish
eclipses. Dare we land upon a dream?

Psychologically, then physically, what will happen to man made to mount the moon? The moon being his first wobbling step in a march to the stars? Either extinction or mutation? In an eon or two will he have become a rocket and a robot combined? Maybe. Yet, whether it is well for him or not, I think man will probably colonize the moon, eventually infiltrate the solar system, and go beyond. It may be his destiny. But he may have to pay for it with a transformation amounting to an evolutionary replacement of his species by some other creature-thing, *Homo mechanicus.*

I confess to being envious, in a way, of the astronaut. Though only in my imagination, where I can make him hero and lone adventurer. What an array of absolutely new sensations is handed him, like a Christmas paintbox; what an incomparable toy, his capsule with its console of magic dials, gauges, buttons, and signal lights; and what a knight in shining plastic he is in his silver suit. To escape the earth-ball, its tug, and one's own heaviness! To dare the great vacuum and, weightless, be tossed—a moon oneself—around the great roulette wheel with the planets! But, in actuality, could I bear that claustrophobia in a steel womb, attached to that formidable placenta by a synthetic umbilical, dependent on a mechanical nipple for my breath of air?

In space there is so little space. And who but a preconditioned, tranquilized, de-nerved, desensualized, automatically responding "test subject" could stand for long that swaddling, as in a rigid iron lung? Not only freedom of movement and of action but freedom to think an aberrant thought or do an individual impulsive deed must be forfeited, it seems to me. Hooked to the indispensable members of his team by the paraphernalia of intercommunication, the astronaut, I imagine, must learn to forget what solitude, what privacy, tastes like. His very heartbeat becomes public, his body and brain an encephalograph, a fluoroscope, a radio, a video screen. First trained to become a piece of equipment; next, perhaps, born so. (Sometimes I long to remember my life as a cephalopod under the sea and cannot.)

But let me go back to a consideration of the poetic method and its effects, compared to the scientific.

For the poet self is a universe, and he is embarked on a conquest of inner space. From the outside, in this accelerated age, our consciousness is being bombarded with the effects of rapid change and upheaval. It's as if we could see the earth shift and change while we walk on it. Familiar space and time have hooked together, and we have spacetime. Matter has split into uncountable explosive bits and become energy. On the one hand—and virtually with the same engine—man prepares to fly to the stars, while on the other he seems intent on annihilating himself along with his sole perch in the universe. There is the temptation sometimes to stuff up the "doors of perception" and regress to that long-ago world that was flat—that was static and secure, since it rested immovably on the back of a turtle! Because the poet's pre-creative condition must be an emptiness, a solitude, a stillness close to inertia. It is a condition of alert passivity, with blankness behind and before him, while he is centered within the present moment, expectant only of the vividness to come, slowly or suddenly, with the combustion of sensations and impressions gathered and stored beforehand from his active life.

The method is the opposite of analytic industry spurred by communal effort (teamwork) proceeding according to prearranged outline, operating upon the material from the outside. Rather than grasping it a piece at a time, construction wise, the poet seats himself within his subject, at its axis, so that, equidistant from all points of its circumference, he can apprehend its potential form as an immediate whole. This is the organic technique, allowing the growth from within, from the initial seeds of attention, until, as Rilke puts it, "All space becomes a fruit around those kernels." I speak here of poetry in its conception; obviously, there is an industrious and conscious work of building to be done before the body of a poem is complete.

Science and poetry are alike, or allied, it seems to me, in their largest and main target—to investigate any and all phenomena of existence beyond the flat surface of appearances. The products as well as the methods of these two processes are very different—not in their relative value but in the particular uses that they have for their "consumers." Each has a separate role and concern toward the expansion of human consciousness and experience. Poetry has a psychic use. Along with the other arts it is a depository for, and a dispenser of, such psychic realizations as wonder, beauty, surprise, joy, awe, revelation—and, as well, fear, disgust, perplexity, anxiety, pain, despair. It provides an input and an outlet for all the complex, powerful, fleeting grains and rays of sensation in the human organism. It is a quickener of experience, and it renews the archetypes and icons necessary to the human spirit, by means of which personality is nurtured and formed.

"The world is poetical intrinsically," Aldous Huxley has written, "and what it means is simply itself. Its significance is the enormous mystery of its existence and of our awareness of its existence." Who or what are we? Why are we? And what are we becoming? What is the relationship between man and the universe? Those are questions that ached in the mind of the first poet. They can be said to have created the first poet and to be the first source of the art of poetry. Does the fact of our consciousness, unique and seemingly miraculous among all of nature's creatures, a priori indicate a superconsciousness shaping and manipulating the cosmos?

How is it that with our minds we can explore our own minds? And can we develop a technique to explore Mind—that aspect of the universe we might postulate exists in addition to its mere structural organization? Maybe such a Mind is not yet in existence but in process; maybe our nervous systems and cortexes are early evidence of its future evolution. As Huxley reports in *Literature and Science*, psychologists know a great deal, but as yet they "have no recognized hypothesis to account for the apparent interaction of mind and matter in a simple act of consciousness." Nor is there even a firm hypothesis to explain the operation of memory. But atomic physics (the most exact of the sciences) is uncovering a factual foundation for many intuitions of existentialist poets and philosophers. According to a statement by physicist Werner Heisenberg, cited by Huxley, for the first time in the history of the planet man approaches a willingness to admit that he is alone with himself "without a partner and without an adversary." This I believe to be an intuitive hunch, not only of the poet or philosopher but of every thinking man when in moments of extremity he is forced face to face with his own soul. Huxley puts it that "man is in process of becoming his own Providence, his own Cataclysm, his own Saviour and his own invading horde of Martians." And he adds: "In the realm of pure science the same discovery—that he is alone with himself—awaits him as he progressively refines his analysis of matter." Modern science, according to Heisenberg,

shows us that we can no longer regard the building blocks of matter, which were considered originally to be the ultimate objective reality, as being things-in-themselves. . . . Knowledge of atoms and their movements in themselves—that is to say, *independent of our observation*—is no longer the aim of research; rather we now find ourselves from the very start in the midst of a dialogue between nature and man, a dialogue of which science is only one part, so much so that the conventional division of the world into subject and object, into inner world and outer world, into body and soul, is no longer applicable and raises difficulties. For the sciences of nature, the subject matter of research is no longer nature in itself, but nature subjected to human questioning, and to this extent man, once again, meets only with himself.

From reflection on a statement such as this one can almost reach the spooky conclusion that all we conceive as objective, and under examination by our sensorial and intellectual equipment, is really subjective and a projection of our own heads!

In 1665, or thereabouts, the American poet Edward Taylor wrote a remarkable poem trying to penetrate into the origin of the universe. A portion of it reads as follows:

> Infinity, when all things it beheld,
> In Nothing, and of Nothing all did build,
> Upon what Base was fixt the Lath, wherein
> He turn'd this Globe, and riggalld it so trim?
> Who blew the Bellows of his Furnace Vast?
> Or held the Mould wherein the world was Cast?
> Who laid its Corner Stone? Or whose Command?
> Where stand the Pillars upon which it stands?
> Who Lac'de and Fillitted the earth so fine,
> With Rivers like Green Ribbons Smaragdine?
> Who made the Sea's its selvedge, and it locks
> Like a Quilt Ball within a Silver Box?
> Who Spread its Canopy? Or Curtains Spun?
> Who in this Bowling Alley bowld the Sun?
>
> Who? who did this? or who is he? Why, know
> It's Onely Might Almighty this did doe.

It's interesting that Edward Taylor should have made Infinity, that great abstraction, the protagonist of his poem, even though he refers to it as "he," and his expression, "It's Onely Might Almighty this did doe,"—i.e., Energy—sounds like an intuition prefiguring a finding of modern science rather than reflecting (as he no doubt consciously intended) a God-centered metaphysics of the seventeenth century.

The poet's universe had better be centered within the present, it had better not install itself (and stall itself) in anachronisms either conceptual or expressionistic. Because the poet, I believe, should be in the vanguard of his time. He can, in his unique way, be a synthesizer and synchronizer of the many components and elements of a great new pattern emergent in the investigations of biologists, psychologists, anthropologists, astronomers, physicists, et al. The poet's material has always been nature—human and otherwise—all objects and aspects of our outer environment as well as the "climate of the soul" and the "theater of the emotions." The poet is the great anti-specialist. Still possible in our overorganized, compartmentalized culture, and still needed, is the work and the play of the artist. As a free-floating agent, medium and conduit, a kind of "divining rod"—he may pass anywhere—over, into, around, or through the multifold fabric of experience and present the results of his singular discoveries and delights to fellow searchers, fellow beholders.

The play of the artist is psychologically very important. As the philosopher Huizinga has written in *Homo Ludens:* "in acknowledging play you acknowledge mind, for whatever else play is, it is not matter. Even in the animal world it bursts the bounds of the physically existent. From the point of view of a world wholly determined by the operation of blind forces, play would be altogether superfluous. Play only becomes possible, thinkable and understandable when an influx of mind breaks down the absolute determinism of the cosmos."

I said earlier that a point of contiguity between the poet and the scientist is that both employ language to communicate what they find. At this point there is also a crucial departure, for language is not only a tool in poetry; it is its very being. In a poem, Subject is not presented by means of language, but Language is the thing presented with the aid of subject. Being merely instrumental, a scientific exposition can be restated in various ways without a loss of end effect; when new facts render its message obsolete, such expositions are replaced and forgotten. But tamper with, or reconstruct, the tissue of a poem and you deal death to its cells and molecules. The poet reaches for a vision of reality that is whole, seamless, and undivided; if he succeeds in that, his product need not suffer obsolescence. True art combines the properties of change and endurance.

What is it in poetry, beyond subject, beyond what is being said, that is given? The management of language for the poem must be such as to capture and fix the essence of the immediate experience—the sensation, illumination, extra dimension—that the poet felt when the impulse for the poem (the emotion or psychic mental discovery that engendered it) fell upon him. It must be such that the receiver of the poem recapitulates, as it were physically, the same illumination because it relates to or fuses with a vision within himself, dormant and dark until the moment the beam of the poem strikes into him. In the handling of his material, which is language, metaphor is to the poet what the equation is to the mathematician.

In one of his essays on art, published as long ago as 1919, Ezra Pound said:

> We might come to believe that the thing that matters in art is a sort of energy, something more or less like electricity or radioactivity, a force transfusing, welding, and unifying. . . . The thing that counts is Good Writing. And good writing is perfect control. It is quite easy to control a thing that has in it no energy— provided that it be not too heavy and that you do not wish to make it *move*. . . .

Discussing the origins of language, Pound said:

> The whole thing is an evolution. In the beginning simple words were enough: Food; water; fire. Both prose and poetry are but an extension of language. Man desires to communicate with his fellows. And he desires an ever increasingly complicated communication. Gesture serves up to a point. Symbols may serve. But when you desire something not present to the eye or when you desire to communicate ideas, you must have recourse to speech. Gradually you wish to communicate something less bare and ambiguous than *ideas*. You wish to communicate an idea *and* its modifications, an idea *and* a crowd of its effects, atmospheres, contradictions . . .
>
> Words and their sense must be such as fit the emotion. Or, from the other side, ideas, or fragments of ideas, the emotion *and* concomitant emotions, must be in harmony, they must form an organism . . .
>
> Poetry is a centaur. The thinking, word-arranging, clarifying faculty must move and leap with the energizing, sentient, musical faculties.

At one time, wishing to clarify to myself the distinction between poetry and other modes of expression, I put down these notes:

Poetry doesn't tell; it shows. Prose tells.
Poetry is not philosophy; poetry makes things be, right now.
Not an idea, but a happening.
It is not music, but it sounds while showing.
It is mobile; it is a thing taking place—active, interactive, in a
   place.
It is not thought; it has to do with senses and muscles.
It is not dancing, but it moves while it remains.

. . . And it is not science. But the experience of poetry is animated with the insatiable curiosity of science. The universe, inside and out, is properly its laboratory. More plain than ever before is the potent fact that we are human particles in a culture of living change. We must either master the Great Whirl or become victims of it. Science is unavoidably reshaping our environment and in the future will influence prominently the next development of individual man and his species. Art, more intimately, deals with, and forms, the emotional and spiritual climate of our experience. Poetry can help man stay human.

1965

A Clue or Two

EACH of the poems in this selection, in one way or another, is a Poem to Solve.

A characteristic of all poetry, in fact, is that more is *hidden* in it than in prose.

A poem, read for the first time, can offer the same pleasure as opening a wrapped box. There is the anticipation of untying an intriguing knot of words, of unloosing all their intimations like loops, of lifting out—as if from under cover—an unexpected idea or fresh sensation.

Solving a poem can be like undoing a mysterious package. The identity or significance of what's inside may be concealed or camouflaged by the dimensions or shape of its "box." Sometimes, nested within a first discovery, another may be found—which in its turn contains still another—and so on. And if then you explore all the notions in the poem, you receive the added pleasure of seeing how they relate to each other in surprising ways, while at the same time combining to create the whole design of the "box."

Having opened or solved the poem and so enjoyed its contents, you can reassemble the parts again—re-imagine the whole into its original "closed" configuration. In this way you discover how the segments are shaped to interconnect.

The way that a poem is *unlike* a box is that it can enfold concepts within it that are larger than their container. Expansive elements in a poem can be packed magically into a tiny "space"—just as the word BIG, with only three letters, is *little*, yet conveys just the opposite meaning—or, conversely, the word INFINITESIMAL, which is *long*, thirteen letters, encompasses the notion of extremely small.

That is why we say of poetry that it has "magical properties"—and why we poets speak of our works as "paradoxical."

Notice how a poet's *games* are called his "works"—and how the "work" you do to solve a poem is really *play*. The impulse and motive for making a poem and for solving and enjoying a poem are quite alike: both include curiosity, alertness, joy in observation and invention.

Opening the box of a poem, looking under the wrappings and examining the various compartments can be absorbing and delightful. And, in addition to "what's in it for everybody," you may find an extra something hidden there especially for *you*—something that seems to mirror your secret feelings and thoughts, that strikes you as really true and worth keeping.

The "Riddle Poems" in the first section of this book all have in common the feature that the subject in each case is not named in either the title or the text. What each poem is about will gradually disclose itself. Poems in sections two and three employ organic metaphor, sound symbolism, verbal texture, and other devices. And all of them depend, as well, on elements of concealment of one sort or another, so as to leave intact for the young reader the pleasure of the unexpected, of discovery, and of solution.

These poems were selected with the aim of presenting the direct experience of finding and recognizing, comparing and contrasting, shaping and naming, solving and enjoying—thus inviting the reader to share with the poet some of the primary pleasures of the creative act itself.

1966

A Note about Iconographs

To have material and mold evolve together and become a symbiotic whole. To cause an instant object-to-eye encounter with each poem even before it is read word-after-word. To have simultaneity as well as sequence. To make an existence in space, as well as in time, for the poem. These have been, I suppose, the impulses behind the typed shapes and frames invented for this collection.

I call the poems *Iconographs* with such dictionary derivations in mind as these:

icon   "a symbol hardly distinguished from the object symbolized"

icono-   from the Greek *eikonos* meaning "image" or "likeness"

graph   "diagram" or "system of connections or interrelations"

-graph   from the Greek *graphé* meaning "carve" . . . "indicating the instrument as well as the written product of the instrument"

Also, this comment on "The Art of the Middle Ages" (Columbia Encyclopedia, 3rd Edition) helped me choose the title:

". . . (It) was governed by a kind of sacred mathematics, in which position, grouping, symmetry, and number were of extraordinary importance and were themselves an integral part of the iconography. From earliest tines it has likewise been a symbolic code, showing men one thing and inviting them to see in it the figure of another . . ."

I suppose that these were my aims. But I come to definition and direction only *afterwards*. It has always been my tendency to let each poem "make itself"—to develop, in process of becoming, its own individual physique. Maybe this is why, once the texts were fixed, I have wanted to give for each an individual arrangement in the space of the page.

I have not meant the poems to depend upon, or depend from, their shapes or their frames; these were thought of only after the whole language structure and behavior was complete in each instance. What the poems say or show, their way of doing it with *language*, is the main thing.

691

Poetry is made with words of a language. And we say, "But of course." It is just this "matter of course" that poetry holds to the nostrils, sticks into the ears, puts on the tongue, flashes into the eyes of anyone who comes to meet it. It is done with words, with their combination—sometimes with their unstringing. If so, it is in order to make the mind re-member (by dismemberment) the elements, the smallest particles, ventricles, radicals down to, or into, the Grain—the buried grain of language on which depends the transfer and expansion of consciousness—of Sense. And no grain, of sense, without sensation. To *sense* then becomes to *make sense*.

With the physical senses we meet the world and each other—a world of objects, human and otherwise, where words on a page are objects, too. The first instrument to make contact, it seems to me, and the quickest to report it, is the eye. The poems in *Iconographs*, with their profiles, or space patterns, or other graphic emphases, signal that they are to be seen, as well as read and heard, I suppose.

1970

SELECTED *ICONOGRAPHS* POEMS IN ORIGINAL FORMATS

EARTH WILL NOT LET GO

        Earth will not let go our foot
except in her sea
cup she lets us float.

        Thistle seed first parachute
and dragonfly the glider
use wind for skate.

So does flying squirrel
and helicopter humming
   bird and winged lizard.   But wind

is earth's streamered wake
where she whirls and where
            in leather suit pterodactyl

and soaring albatross white yacht
proved not grace
 nor corpulance to extremes brought

breaks the sac earth wraps
her creatures in marsupial.
            "Only mammal capable of true

flight the bat"
equipped with sensory parts
            like modern instrument craft

swoops blind of blue
        unconscious a closet his orbit
or a cave construes

by echo which is radio.
For Icarus is not yet.   The Wright
Aeroplane of 1903

        was nothing but a big box kite
"in which the pilot lay prone
head forward his left hand

        operating the lever his hips
in a saddle. Shifting
the hips sideways pulled

wires by which the wing tips
were warped and the rudder
 turned... a double action from one

movement controlling balance
        and direction." Blue pilot cap
cocked like kingfisher's beak

and heavy round-toed
            shoes how droll he wore.
Belly-down on the floor

of the long frail open
box he steered
 with his hips' wiggle. Not merely

the magic carpet
but the whole room
        he took with him trusting

    loops and fickle twists of air.
Lindbergh sat in a wicker chair
in The Cabin of the Spirit

and solo-crossed the Atlantic
in 1927. "...Impossible
to photograph the cabin in one view

  the actual distance from the back
of the seat to the face
of the instrument

board being only thirty-two
inches... His feet
        rested on the rudder control

pedals under the instrument
panel. To see ahead
        he either used the periscope

or steered to one side
while looking out the window."
        Enclosed in a sort of kayak

in wicker to save weight
the single wing his roof
            head bonneted and goggled

like a plucky scaup
        with swivelled neck he swam
on swells of ocean wind.

        Not unencumbered ever or by
muscle and buoyancy alone
may we climb loose

out of earth's rings
        her atmospheres ionospheres
the pastures to our lungs.

Rejecting wings
  props wheels for landing all bird
and insect things

John Glenn
      snug in the tip of a cartridge
was discharged in 1962

like a spore
        within its pod was launched
by blowgun of pure

energy. His lungfood
        he took with him. His suit
an embryonic sac

the capsule hugged him
uterus-tight. So tumbling
      backward by propulsion he tore

the planet's web to the edge.
But a last elastic caught him
 kept him to its circle. Implosion

    inbuilt homeward sucked him back
to splashdown in her sea cup
that salty womb

            that spewed the stillborn moon.
To that rock Apollo
astronauts would reach

they must take the earthpouch
  simulated. And it may not breach.
For earth will not let go

our foot though
                  headfirst to be born
in angel space

we make wings
            jets rockets orbit tables
spider-landing legs.

THE DNA MOLECULE
THE DNA MOLECULE
THE DNA MOLECULE
is The Nude Descending a Staircase
a circular one.
See the undersurfaces
of the spiral
treads and
the spaces and
between.

She is descending and at the same time
ascending and she moves around herself. For
she is the staircase "a protoplasmic framework
an internal scaffolding
that twists and turns."

She is a double helix mounting and dismounting
around the swivel of her imaginary spine. The Nude
named DNA can be constructed as a model with matches and
a ribbon of tape. Be sure to use only 4 colors on 2 white
strands of twistable tape. "Only matches of complementary
colors may be placed opposite each other. The pairs
are to be red and green and yellow and blue."

Make your model as high as the Empire
State Building and you have an acceptable
replica of The Nude.
But and this is harder you must make her move
in a continuous coil
an alpha helix a double spiral
downward and upward at once
and you must make her increase while at the same
time occupying the same field.
She must be made "to maintain a basic topography"
changing yet remaining stable

if she is to perform her function which is to produce
and reproduce the microsphere.
Such a sphere is invisible to but ominpresent
in the naked eye of The Nude.
It contains "a central region and an outer membrane"
making it able to divide "to make exact copies of
itself without limit."

The Nude has "the capacity for
replication and transcription" of
all genesis. She ingests and
regurgitates the genetic material
it being the material of her own
cell-self. From single she becomes
double and from double single.

As a woman ingests the demon sperm and with the same membrane
regurgitates the mitotic double of herself upon the

slide of time so the
MOLECULE produces with a li
pop at the waistline of its viscou
a new microsphere the same size
as herself which proceeds singly to grow
in order to divide and double to single and
So from single to double and double itself.
mounting while descending she
expands while contracts she proliferates while
disappearing at both of her ends.

Remember that red can only be opposite green
and blue opposite yellow. Remember that the
complementary pairs of matches must differ slightly in
length "for nature's pairs can be made only with units
whose structures permit an interplay of forces
between the partners."

I fixed a blue match opposite a red
match of the same length
in defiance of the rules pointed them
away from the center on the double-stranded
tape. I saw laid a number of eggs

on eggs on the sticky side of a twig.
I saw a worm with many feet grow out
of an egg.

The worm climbed the twig a single helix and gobbled
the magnified edge of a leaf
in quick enormous bites.

It then secreted out of itself a gray floss
with which it wrapped itself tail first and so on
until it had completely muffled
and encased itself head last as in a mummy pouch.

I saw plushy irridescent wings push
moistly out of the pouch. At first glued
together they began to part. On each wing

I saw a large blue eye
open forever in the expression of resurrection.
The new Nude released the flanges
of her wings
stretching herself to touch

at all points
the outermost rim
of the noösphere.

I saw that for her body from which the
wings expanded
she had retained
the worm.

THE JAMES BOND MOVIE

The popcorn is greasy, and
I forgot to bring a
Kleenex. A pill that's a
bomb inside the stomach of a
man inside The Embassy
blows up. Eruc-
tations of flame, luxur-
ious cauliflower motion
caulations into a gigan-
tic screen. The
29-ft. crackling,
entire is brick bursting,
orange and smithereen teeth
fleckening a Dentyne my smart-
blackening a bouncing-smart the
I unwrap my tongue-try to
while rubber-try to
in clove, wipe paper
ing 2-inch-wide paper to

blot butter off my fingers. A bubble-
bath, room-sized, in which 14 girls,
delectable and sexless, are twist-
topped Creamy Freezes, (their
blond, red, brown, pinkish, lav-
endar or silver wiglets screw-
ed that high, and varnished)
scrub-tickle a lone male,
whose chest has just the
right amount and distri-
bution of not too curly
hair. He's nervously
pretending to defend
his modesty. His
crotch, below the
waterline, is
also below the

frame-- but unsubmerged
all 28 slick foamy boobs.
Their makeup fails to let
the girls look naked.
Caterpillar lashes, black
and thick, lush lips
glossed pink like the gum
I pop and chew, Contacts
on all the eyes that are
mostly blue, they're
nose-perfect replicas of
each other. I've got
most of the grease off and
on to this little square
of paper. I'm folding it
now, making creases with
my nails.

FEEL ME

"Feel me to do right," our father said
on his   death bed. We did not quite
 know-- in fact, not at all-- what he meant.
His last whisper was spent as through a slot in a wall.
He left us a key, but how did it
fit? "Feel me
          to do right." Did it mean

that, though he died, he would be felt
     through some aperture, or by some unseen instrument
our dad just then had come
     to know? So, to do right always, we need but feel his
          spirit? Or was it merely
     his apology for dying? "Feel that I
     do right in not trying, as you insist, to stay

               on your side. There is the wide
          gateway and the splendid tower,
and you implore me to wait here, with the worms!"
          Had he defined his terms, and could we discriminate
               among his motives, we might
          have found out how to "do right" before we died-- suppos:
                    he felt he suddenly knew

                    what dying was.
               "You do wrong because you do not feel
as I do now" was maybe the sense. "Feel me, and emulate
                    my state, for I am becoming less dense--
               I am feeling right, for the first
time." And then the vessel burst, and we were kneeling
                         around an emptiness.

               We cannot feel our
father now. His power courses through us, yes, but he--
     the chest and cheek, the foot and palm,
     the mouth of oracle-- is calm. And we still seek
               his meaning. "Feel me," he said,
          and emphasized that word.
          Should we have heard it as a plea

                    for a caress-- A constant caress,
          since flesh to flesh was all that we could do right
     if we would bless him? The dying must feel
                    the pressure of that
               question-- lying flat, turning cold
               from brow to heel-- the hot
                    cowards there above

                    protesting their love, and saying
                    "What can we do? Are you all
                         right?" While the wall opens
                    and the blue night pours through. "What
               can we do? We want to do what's right."
"Lie down with me, and hold me, tight. Touch me. Be
          with me. Feel with me. Feel me, to do right."

LOWERING*

The
flag
is folded
lengthwise,
and lengthwise
again,

folding toward the
open edge,
so that the union of stars
on the blue
field remains outward in full view;

a triangular folding is then begun
at the striped end,
by bringing the corner of the folded edge
to the open edge;
the outer point, turned inward

along the open edge,
forms the next triangular fold;
the folding continued so, until the end is reached,
the final corner tucked between
the folds of the blue union,
the form of the folded flag

        is found to resemble that
        of a 3-cornered pouch, or thick cocked hat.
        Take this flag, John Glenn, instead of a friend;

instead of a brother, Edward
Kennedy, take this flag;

instead of a father, Joe
Kennedy, take this flag;
this flag instead of a husband, Ethel
Kennedy, take this flag;

this 9-times-folded
red-white-striped, star-spotted-blue flag,
tucked and pocketed neatly, Nation,
instead of a leader, take

this folded flag. Robert
Kennedy, coffin without coverlet,

beside this hole in the grass,
beside your brother, John
Kennedy, in the grass,
take, instead of a country,
this folded flag;
Robert

Kennedy, take
this hole
in the
grass.

*Arlington
Cemetery
June 8,1968

                !   !   !   !
CATBIRD IN REDBUD

!   !   !   !
Catbird in the redbud this morning.
     !   !   !
No cat could
        !   !   ! !   !
mimic that rackety cadenza he's making.
   !   !
And it's not red,

the trapeze he's swaying on.

After last night's freeze,
     !   !   !   !
redbud's violet-pink, twinkled on
                           !
by the sun.   That bird's
    !   !
red, though, under the tail
                        !
he wags, up sharply, like a wren.
        !   !
The uncut lawn hides blue
                     !
violets with stargold eyes on the longest

stems I've ever seen.   Going to

empty the garbage, I simply have
        !
to pick some,

reaching to the root of green,
                         !
getting my fist dewy, happening
                 !   !
to tear up a dandelion, too.
      !
Lilac, hazy blue-
              !   !
violet, nods buds over the alley
            !   !
fence, and (like a horse with a yen
                               !
for something fresh for breakfast)

I put my nose into a fragrant

pompom, bite off some, and chew.

```
        =                    :
    WEDNESDAY AT THE WALDORF


 Ĭ          +                    :
Two white whales have been installed at

    :
The Waldorf.  They are tumbling slowly

            +
above the tables, butting the chandeleirs,

                +       :
submerging, and taking soft bites

            =    =     +
out of the red-vested waiters in the

    :      Ĭ
Peacock Room.  They are poking fleur de lis

 +                   :    :
tails into the long pockets on the

 +
waiters' thighs.  They are stealing

    =           :              Ĭ =   =
breakfast strawberries from two eccentric

    =                                    :
guests-- one, skunk-cabbage-green with dark

peepers-- the other, wild rose and

                =            : + =
milkweed, barelegged, in Lafayette loafers.

            Ĭ    =     =          = = +
When the two guests enter the elevator,

        +          =              Ĭ    :
the whales ascend, bouncing, through all

the ceilings, to the sixth floor.  They

 =
get between the sheets.  There they turn
```

Peacock Room. They are poking _fleur de lis_

candy-pink, with sky-colored eyes, and

                :   =   =
silver bubbles start to rise from velvet

+   :   =
navels on the tops of their heads.

+   +   Ɉ   Ɉ   =
Later, a pale blue VW, running on poetry,

                :   =
weaves down Park Avenue, past yellow

                                Ɉ   Ɉ   Ɉ
sprouts of forsythia, which, due to dog-do

      Ɉ   Ɉ   Ɉ
and dew, are doing nicely. The two

          +   Ɉ   :
white whales have the blue car in tow

        +   +
on a swaying chain of bubbles. They are

                         =
rising toward the heliport on the Pan Am

Ɉ
roof. There they go, dirigible and slow,

                              +
hide-swiping each other, lily tails flipping,

              =   =
their square velvet snouts stitched with

                  +
snug smiles. It is April. "There's

              :
a kind of hush all over the world."

Passing a lank boy, bangs to the eyebrows, licking a Snow Flake cone,
cones on the tulip tree up stiff, honeysuckle tubelets weighting a vine,
and passing Irene Gay - Realtor, The Black Whale, Rexall, and others-- (Irene,

don't sue me, it's just your sign I need in the scene)--
remembering lilac a month back, a different faded shade, buying a paper
with the tide table instead of the twister forecast on page three,

then walking home from the village, beneath the viaduct I find
Midwest echoes answering echoes that another, yet the same
train wakes here out East. I'm thinking of how I leaned on you, you leaning

in the stone underpass striped with shadows of tracks and ties,
and I said, "Give me a kiss, A.D., even if you are tranquilized," and I'm
thinking of the Day of Shooting, the Day of the Kingfisher, the Indigo

Day of the Bunting-- of the Catfish Night I locked the keys in the car
and you tried to jimmy in, but couldn't with a clothes hanger.
The night of the Juke at Al's-- When Something's Wrong With My Baby--

you pretended to flake out on the bench, and I poured icy Scotch into
the thimble of your belly, lifting the T-shirt. Another night you threw up
in a Negro's shoe. It's Accabonac now, instead of Tippecanoe.

I'm remembering how we used to drive to The Custard "to check out the
teenage boxes." I liked the ones around the Hondas, who
from a surly distance, from under the hair in their eyes, cruised the girls

in flowered shorts. One day back there, licking cones, we looked in
on a lioness lying with her turd behind the gritty window of a little zoo.
          I liked it there. I'd like it anywhere with you.

Here there are gorgeous pheasants, no hogs, blond horses, and Alec Guiness
          seen at The Maidstone Memorial Eve-- and also better dumps. You
scavenged my plywood desk top, a narrow paint-flecked old door

the broad white wicker I'm sitting in now. While you're at the dump
hunting for more-- maybe a double spring good as that single you climbed to
          last night (and last year)-- I sit in front of a house, remembering

     a house back there, thinking of a house-- where? when?-- by spring
          next year? I notice the immature oak leaves, vivid as redbud almost,
and shaped like the spore of the weasel I saw once by the Wabash.

Instead of "to the Readmore" riffling Playboy, I found you yesterday
in that Newtown Lane newspaper store I don't yet know the name of.
          Stay with me, A.D. Don't blow. Scout out that bed. Go find

tennis instead of squash mates, surfboarders, volley ball boys
     to play with. I know you will, before long-- maybe among the lifeguards--
big, cool-coned, straight-hipped, stander-on-one-finger, strong.

The Boat Stave

ɔday while a steamshovel rooted in the cove,
veling a parking lot for the new nightclub,
 a plane drilled between clean clouds

the October sky, and the flags
the yachts tied in the basin popped
 stiff breeze, I watched my footsteps mark

ɪe sand by the tideline. Some hollow horseshoe
 crabshells scuttled there, given motion by the waves.
 I threw a plank back to the waves that they'd

thrown up, a sun-dried sea-swollen stave
 from a broken dinghy,
 one end square, one pointed, painted green--

then became so conscious
of its fate my attention snagged,
could not get off the hook of its experience,

 for I had launched a subject of the waves
I could not leave until completed.
asily it skipped them, putting out,

ow-end topping every smack and swell,
d kept its surface dry, and looked to float
yond the jetty head, and so be loose,

xchange the stasis of the beach for unconceived
 fluidities and agitations. It set sail
 by the luck of its construction:

Lighter than the forceful waves, it surmounted
 their shove; yet, heavier, steadier than
 the hollows they scooped behind them,

it used their crested threats for coasting free,
 unsplashed by even a drop of spray,
was casual master

of the inconsistent element it rode.
 But there was a bias to the moving sea.
 Though the growth and motion of each wave was arbitrary,

the total spread, of which each crease was part--
the outward hem lying flat by the wall of sky
at the dim blue other end of the bed of the bay--

was being flung, it seemed, by some distant will.
Though devious and shifty in detail,
the whole expanse reiterated constancy

and purpose. So, just as the arrowy end of the plank
on a peak of a wave made a confident leap
that would clear the final shoal,

a little sideways breaker nudged it enough
to turn it broadside. Then a swifter slap
from a stronger comber brought it back,

erasing yards of its piecemeal progress with one push.
Yet the stave turned point to the tide, and tried again--
though not as buoyant, for it had got soaked.

But, arrogance undamaged, it conveyed
itself again over obstacle waves, a courageous ski--
not noticing, since turned from shore,

that the swells it conquered slid in at a slant--
and that while it met them head on, it was borne
closer to shore and shunted down the coast.

Now a bulge-- a series of them, for a pulse
quickened in the tide-- without resistance lifted
up the stave, flipped it over twice, and dumped it

rudely in the shallows. It scraped
on sand. And so it was put back--
not at the place of its first effort--

a greater disgrace than that--
at before the birth
of balance, pride, intention, enterprise.

It changed its hope and goal, and I changed
my ambition. Not the open sea--
escape into the rough, the wide unknown, and unpredictabil

but rescue, return, and rest--
station, release from influence-- became my hope
for the green painted, broken slat, once part of a boat.

Its trials to come ashore the cold
will of the waves thwarted more capriciously
than its assays into adventure made before,

and each chance it took to dig with its bent spike
a grip in the salvage of pebbles and weed and shell
was teasingly, tirelessly outwitted

by dragouts and dousings, slammings and tuggings
of the punishing sea. Until, of its own impulse, the sea
decided to let be,

and lifted and laid, lifted and laid
the plank inert on sand. At tide turn,
uch the unalterable compulsion of the sea,

had to turn
back and rumple its bed
ard the other edge, the farther side of the spread.

watched my footsteps mark the sand
by the tide-line. The steamshovel rooting in the cove
had leveled a parking lot for the new nightclub.

The launch from the yacht basin whooshed around the end
of the pier, toward a sailboat with dropped anchor there,
whose claxon and flipping flag

signaled for pick-up. The men with mallets had finished.
sinking posts by the gangplank entrance
of the abandoned boat, ballasted with cement

and painted green and black,
furnished with paneled bar and dining deck.
I watched them hang a varnished sign between the posts,

and letter the name: "The Ark." Tomorrow
I must come
out again into the sun,

and mark the sand, and
find my plank.
for its destiny's not done.

SEEING JUPITER

A chair was placed
upon the lawn
In cloak of wind

                and shadow I
                sat and bent
        my eye upon a rim

of dark that glittered
up to open heaven
In the cup

                a worn dime
            size of an iris
            of anyone's eye

Flat cold lost found
coin of enormous time
Some small change

            around it three
        little bits swirled or
            else my ragged eye

with wind swung
In the black pocket
behind that blank

    hung hidden a fourth
        moon dot smarting
as if beneath my tongue

A dreg of ancient mint
My retina tasted
light how long dead?

        My hair thrashed
    Enlarged upon the lawn
            my chair I sat in

that wind and shadow
bent had slid
an inch toward dawn

THE
SUNBIRD
SETTLES
TO ITS
NEST

Boys are swimming
through the sun's tail
which is switched
by abrasive waves dyed
flamingo. The head

of the sun is cardinal
from the ears down.
Its pate is pink.
Oh, as I wrote
that, a flush spread

to the hairline.
the chin's no longer
there. The tail
on the waves is sliced
with purple. Oiled ibis-

feathered swells
make it fan
out like a peacock's
But slowly drooped
and narrowed, it drags

west. The boys'
heads are hubs
for scintillating
circles. Their arms plough
a waterfield of eyes.

The peckered scalp
is melting, there goes
the last capfeather
of faint red down down.
Down. The boys come up

almost black.
They flip wet off
by the green-haired rocks,
behind them embered
a phoenix crown.

ROCKY POINT

The mainland
looks much smaller than the island,
and faint,

implying thinner paint
brushed in last
as background,

so not as real.
Here is the present,
over there, the past.

Hard to feel
how it's the larger body.
That dream-haze

blue and green,
a low wave
of land,

is not clear,
or as solid as the water
in between

it and the rocky
point I stand
on. That's lifesized,

well-detailed with sunlit trees.
The island
is much bigger than the mainland.

This shore
is foreground. Why
have a figure with its back

turned, focused
on a streak
in the distance, a coast

it can't make out?
(Even the sun forgets
on foggy days.)

But that's the larger body
that's a fact--
and would be again if I

were over there. Packed
with central life, it's the
this, at best, a leg.

No. A toe.
Well, even that is inexact
If I think of the whole

body: what was vast
in retrospect, small
now, and thin in

the blue of forget,
it was, is, but a hand's
breadth. And

an island. All
that's earth is,
on the world's whirled

wavedrop.
And this now present outcrop
(that a magnified

wave grapples,
every fingernail
of foam real

to my thirsty eye--
I on a cliff before
the foreground--

the brush can't paint itself--)
is but a hair.
But oh it's mainland,

it's the moment's
ground I stand
on. It is fair.

CHRONOLOGY

NOTE ON THE TEXTS

NOTES

INDEX OF TITLES & FIRST LINES

Chronology

1913   Anna Thilda May Swenson, daughter of Dan Arthur and Margaret Hellberg Swenson, is born at 2:30 A.M. Wednesday, May 28, in a rented house on North Seventh Street in Logan, Utah. Swenson is their first child; she will be followed by nine siblings. Dan Arthur Swenson, born in Sweden in 1880, was baptized by Mormon missionaries who brought his family to Utah in 1894. He attended Utah Agricultural College (present-day Utah State University). After graduation, while on his own Mormon mission to Sweden, he met Margaret Hellberg, born in Sweden in 1889; he brought her to Utah where they married in 1912. May Swenson grows up in a devout Mormon household of Swedish immigrants. She speaks only Swedish until she begins first grade.

1922   Swenson family moves to a house Dan Arthur Swenson built at 669 East 500 North in Logan, a short distance down the hill from Utah State Agricultural College. Dan Arthur Swenson, a craftsman and woodworker, is a faculty member at the college in the Department of Mechanical Arts. He makes furniture for the family and toys for the children, and binds twenty blank books for May, which she uses for her first diary. Her childhood is full of chores in the house and garden; she plays with her father and with younger siblings and cousins. Her sister Grace says: "May wasn't like the rest of us girls. We had fun brushing, combing, and arranging our hair. We tried on clothes and played dress-up. May wasn't like that. She'd frown at herself in the mirror as she braided buns to fit over her ears."

1929   Swenson is awarded the Vernon Short Story Medal ($25) at Logan High School. "Christmas Day," her first literary work, appears in the school newspaper, *The Grizzly*.

1930–34   Attends Utah State Agricultural College. Her first poem is published in *The Scribble*, the campus literary magazine. Also writes for *Student Life*, the campus newspaper where she is listed on the masthead as "Humor Writer." Supported by Dr. Pederson, a popular English professor who teaches creative writing. Respectful of her family's religion, but confides in a friend: "It's not for me—religion. It seems like

a redundancy for a poet." Graduates as an English majc
with a minor in art. Her baby brother Lloyd dies at eigl
months old. After graduation, works as a reporter for th
Herald Journal in Logan.

1936–38   After reading novels by Thomas Wolfe and seeing reprodu(
tions of paintings by Georgia O'Keeffe and photograpl
by Alfred Stieglitz, moves to Greenwich Village with th
intention to begin a literary career. Works as editor an
ghostwriter. Employed by the novelist Anzia Yeziersk
Friendship with Yezierska's nephew, Arnold Kates, wh
lends her books by Freud, Jung, Joyce, Huxley, and Cun
mings. Visits the ocean for the first time on trips to Jon(
Beach and Southampton, Long Island, but never learr
to swim. Attends Mormon services with her cousin Clyd
Swenson and his family, a lawyer living in Queens. She wi
give up church attendance but never asks to be remove
from the rolls of the church; considered "inactive" by th
Manhattan Ward.

1938–39   Employed by the Living Lore Unit of the WPA Feder:
Writers' Project interviewing working-class people in Ne\
York City. (Her interview with Irving Fajans is included i
First Person America by Ann Banks, published in 1980.
Interviews Anca Vrbovska, a Jewish immigrant writer fror
Czechoslovakia, who publishes poetry in English; they b(
come companions.

1938–47   With Vrbovska shares apartments in Greenwich Vil
lage for nine years total, for seven years (1940–47) at 3(
Bedford Street. Together they read Donne, Blake, Po(
Werfel, Kafka, and Mann. Vrbovska is a member of th
American Communist Party. Swenson joins the Worker
Alliance, Local 87, writes articles in the union newslette\
and takes part in political demonstrations. Works for th
United States Travel Bureau, then the Federal Wholesal
Druggists' Association (1942–49). Studies sculpture witl
Saul Baizerman. Studies sketching with Hans Bohler, fo
whom she models. Meets poet Alfred Kreymborg. Returr
to Utah to visit family for the first time in 1941, and agai(
in 1947.

1947   Swenson and Vrbovska separate. Moves to an apartmen\
at 23 Perry Street in Greenwich Village, where she will liv(
for nineteen years, shared at first with Trudi Lubitsch. Use(

the terrace at the back of the apartment overlooking the garden of St. John's Church to write poetry. Submits poems to a wide range of magazines with limited success. Howard Moss, poetry editor at the *New Yorker*, rejects her submissions eight times. Cid Corman, editor of *Origin*, tells her: "May, your language points to itself. You have a tendency toward pleasure in language for its own sake."

1949 With support from Alfred Kreymborg, Swenson's poem "Haymaking" is accepted for publication by William Rose Benét in *The Saturday Review of Literature*, opening the door for Swenson into better-known journals and magazines, including *New Directions 11*, published by James Laughlin. Leaves her job at the Federal Wholesale Druggists' Association to devote her time to poetry, taking only short-term or part-time secretarial jobs.

1950 Pearl Schwartz, a student at Hunter College and later a social worker, moves into the Perry Street apartment as Swenson's companion. Swenson meets Elizabeth Bishop at Yaddo, the retreat for writers, artists, and composers, in Saratoga, New York. Swenson and Bishop remain close friends for twenty-nine years. They maintain an extensive correspondence about daily life and poetics while Bishop lives in Brazil. At Yaddo, Swenson also befriends the painter Beauford Delaney. At Delaney's home in Greenwich Village, she meets James Baldwin, Henry Miller, and other writers whose portraits Delaney painted. His portrait of Swenson is in the National Portrait Gallery in Washington, D.C.

1953 Her poem "By Morning" is accepted for publication in the *New Yorker*; editor Howard Moss changes the title to "Snow by Morning" and pays Swenson $42. Swenson will go on to publish fifty-nine poems in the magazine. Awarded the Introduction Prize of the Poetry Center of the New York City YM/YWCA, judged by Mark Van Doren, John Malcolm Brinnin, and Jean Garrigue, and Swenson gives her first public reading at the Poetry Center. Swenson's parents visit her for the first time on their way to Sweden as Mormon missionaries; they return to visit at the end of their mission in 1956. Asked to fill out a page about herself for her family's Mormon records, she writes, in place of her children, the titles of the thirty-nine poems she had published since leaving Utah.

1954   Publishes her first collection, *Another Animal: Poems*, wit
              Charles Scribner's Sons, in a volume edited by the poe
              John Hall Wheelock that includes collections by two othe
              poets, Harry Duncan and Murray Noss. Works for Jame
              Laughlin at New Directions as a manuscript reader an
              "chief writer of rejection letters"; holds this job for twelv
              years.

1955   Awarded a Rockefeller Writing Fellowship. With Schwart:
              vacations on Martha's Vineyard.

1957   At the MacDowell Colony for writers, artists, and com
              posers in New Hampshire, she becomes friends with th
              painter Milton Avery, the composer Ruth Anderson, an
              Elizabeth Shepley Sergeant, the biographer of Willa Cathe
              and Robert Frost. Swenson named by poet John Ciard
              to be the Robert Frost Fellow at the Bread Loaf Writer:
              Conference in Vermont.

1958–59   Publishes *A Cage of Spines* with Rinehart. Wins the Wil
              liam Rose Benét Poetry Prize of the Poetry Society c
              America. Wins the Longview Foundation Prize and a Joh
              Simon Guggenheim Memorial Foundation Grant. Read
              her poetry at Utah Agricultural College and in San Fran
              cisco and Berkeley, California. As a fellow at Yaddo, meet
              Sylvia Plath and Ted Hughes, and does the Ouija boar
              with them. Swenson's poem "The Fingers" refers to thos
              séances.

1960   Receives an Amy Lowell Traveling Scholarship and a Na
              tional Institute of Arts and Letters Grant. Swenson an
              Schwartz travel to Europe for a year in France, Spain, an
              Italy, sleeping in a tent and driving a Simca. (Swenson, wh
              was near-sighted, never succeeds in passing a driver's test.
              Swenson and Schwartz continue taking camping trips in th
              United States in the 1960s and become avid bird-watchers

1962   In Utah for her parents' fiftieth anniversary, Swenson give
              them a check for $1,000, representing savings from sales o
              her poems. Swenson's father dies suddenly later that yea
              and she returns for his burial. Writes "Feel Me" in respons
              to his last words, spoken to her sister Margaret.

1963   Publishes *To Mix with Time: New and Selected Poems* wit
              Scribner's.

1964–65   Awarded a Ford Foundation Grant for Poets and Writers Combined with Theater Group. Reads Samuel Beckett and Eugene Ionesco. Writes *The Floor*, a one-act play performed at the American Place Theatre in 1965–66 and published in *First Stage* in the summer of 1967.

1966   Publishes *Poems to Solve* with Scribner's. Accepts an appointment for the academic year 1966–67 as writer-in-residence, teaching poetry writing, at Purdue University. In advance she is "scared to death" of teaching. Composes "sound pieces" on a reel-to-reel tape recorder (using, for example, marbles rolling in a pan and coins spinning on countertops). She meets Rozanne ("Zan") Knudson, a faculty member at Purdue who later becomes a novelist.

1967   Swenson publishes *Half Sun Half Sleep* with Scribner's. She is given a Utah State University Distinguished Service Gold Medal, a Rockefeller Foundation Grant, and a Brandeis University Creative Arts Award. *Half Sun Half Sleep* includes her translations of Swedish poets, supported by grants from the Bollingen Foundation. With Knudson, buys a house at 73 The Boulevard in Sea Cliff, New York, with a view of Long Island Sound. Swenson and Knudson live there together for the rest of Swenson's life.

1968   Awarded the Shelley Memorial Award of the Poetry Society of America. Writer-in-residence at the University of North Carolina.

1969   Awarded an Academy of American Poets Fellowship.

1970   Publishes *Iconographs: Poems* with Scribner's, described as one of the "50 Books of the Year" by the American Institute of Graphic Arts. Swenson says about her shape poems: "I wanted to make my poems do what they say." Inducted into the National Institute of Arts and Letters. Writer-in-residence at Lethbridge University, Alberta.

1971   Publishes *More Poems to Solve* with Scribner's.

1972   Publishes *Windows & Stones: Selected Poems of Tomas Tranströmer*, translated from Swedish, with the University of Pittsburgh Press. Awarded the International Poetry Forum Medal. Swenson's mother dies. Speaks at her funeral in Logan and stays in her mother's house while teaching a poetry writing workshop at Utah State University. Travels and camps in the American West with Knudson.

1973   Swenson, a heavy smoker, gives up cigarettes permanently.
            With Knudson, spends this winter and the next in Arizona,
            subsequent years in Los Angeles and elsewhere in the
            American West and South.

1974   Receives an award from the National Endowment for the
            Arts. Writer-in-residence at the University of North Caro-
            lina.

1976   Publishes *The Guess & Spell Coloring Book* with Scribner's.
            Writer-in-residence at the University of California, River-
            side.

1978   Publishes *New & Selected Things Taking Place* with Little,
            Brown.

1979   Elizabeth Bishop dies. Swenson and Knudson spend this
            and subsequent winters at 13 Addy Road, Bethany Beach,
            Delaware, in a house owned by the Knudson family. Swen-
            son tracks sixty species of birds at feeders on the property
            and walks in the pine woods.

1980   Appointed as a chancellor of the Academy of American
            Poets (holds this post until her death). Guest of First Lady
            Roslyn Carter at the White House for "A Salute to Poetry
            and American Poets." Winters with Knudson at rugged
            Dorland Mountain Colony in Temecula, California.

1981   Receives the Bollingen Prize for Poetry from the Beinecke
            Library at Yale (shared with Howard Nemerov).

1982   Delivers Phi Beta Kappa poem ("Some Quadrangles") at
            Harvard.

1983   Receives the Golden Rose of the New England Poetry
            Club.

1987   Publishes *In Other Words: New Poems* with Alfred Knopf.
            Receives an honorary doctorate in literature from Utah
            State University as well as Utah State University's Centen-
            nial Award and a MacArthur Foundation Fellowship in the
            amount of $380,000. Gives each of her brothers and sisters
            a $3,000 "Swenson Fellowship" and smaller "fellowships"
            to her nephews and nieces. Swenson and Knudson travel
            to New Zealand.

1988   Named a "Literary Lion" of the New York Public Library. Knudson designs and has built a modern house in Ocean View, Delaware, for use during winters (the scene of Swenson's poem "Last Day").

1989   Afflicted with serious asthma attacks and high blood pressure. Dies of a heart attack on Saturday, December 4, in Ocean View, Delaware. Services are held in Logan, Utah, at the 18th Ward Chapel on December 9. A marble bench stands over her grave; inscribed on the seat is her poem "The Exchange," and on the pedestal are inscribed two sentences from her poem "The Wonderful Pen": "Read me. Read my mind."

Note on the Texts

This volume contains all the poems from seven collections of poetry that May Swenson published in her lifetime—*Another Animal* (1954), *A Cage of Spines* (1958), *To Mix with Time* (1963), *Half Sun Half Sleep* (1967), *Iconographs* (1970), *New & Selected Things Taking Place* (1978), and *In Other Words* (1987)—and a selection of 140 poems that Swenson published in periodicals and elsewhere but did not collect in any of her books, or that remained unpublished during her lifetime. Also included are five prose pieces about poetry, four of which she published and one that she delivered as prefatory remarks to a reading.

Swenson regularly included poems from earlier collections in later ones, and she sometimes revised poems after publication; as a result, a significant number of her poems exist in multiple versions. Swenson kept a master file of all her poems and made handwritten emendations on many of those file copies. In some cases she was able to incorporate these changes in print; in others, these revisions exist only on the file copy. In the present volume the text of each poem follows its latest version. For the most part the changes involve word choice, line breaks, and punctuation; although occasionally the shape of the entire poem is altered; some of the more significant textual variants are included in the Notes.

Each poem is printed only once in this volume (even though it may have been included in more than one collection) and is placed in the position it occupied in the collection where it first appeared, as follows.

Another Animal marked May Swenson's first appearance in book form. This group of fifty poems is included in the volume *Poets of Today* (New York: Charles Scribner's Sons, 1954), which also includes collections of poems by Harry Duncan and Murray Noss and a critical introduction by John Hall Wheelock.

A Cage of Spines (New York: Rinehart & Company, 1958) includes fifty-five new poems by Swenson as well as two poems from the previous collection.

To Mix with Time (New York: Charles Scribner's Sons, 1963) includes forty-nine new poems along with seventy-five poems from the previous collections.

Half Sun Half Sleep (New York: Charles Scribner's Sons, 1967), described as "new poems," contains sixty-one previously uncollected poems as well as two poems from earlier collections. The poems are arranged alphabetically by title. In addition the volume includes Swenson's translations of eleven poems by six Swedish poets, which are not included in the present volume.

The shaped poems of *Iconographs* (New York: Charles Scribner's Sons, 1970) were originally published in a typewriter font preferred by May Swenson, and the layout of the poems required an unusually large trim size; neither the trim size nor the font of the original edition is reproduced here. In her next collection, *New & Selected Things Taking Place*, Swenson included conventionally formatted versions of twelve of the poems from *Iconographs*. All of the poems from *Iconographs* in the present volume preserve the shaped versions of the first edition with the exceptions noted below.

New & Selected Things Taking Place (Boston: Little, Brown and Company, 1978), containing sixty-three new poems as well as ample selections from her previous collections, is the closest May Swenson came to creating a "collected poems."

In Other Words (New York: Alfred A. Knopf, 1987), Swenson's final collection, contains forty-six new poems.

When the texts of poems in the present volume differ from the versions that initially appeared in the editions cited above, the sources are noted below.

Another Animal: "Shadow-Maker" (titled "The Shadow-Maker" in *Another Animal*): *A Cage of Spines*. "The Garden at St. John's," "The Playhouse": *To Mix with Time*. "Feel Like a Bird," "Horse and Swan Feeding," "Lion," "Sun," "Horses in Central Park," "Evolution," "The Greater Whiteness," "Rusty Autumn," "An Opening": *New & Selected Things Taking Place*. "Why We Die": *Another Animal* with emendation. "Wingfolk": Later typescript.

A Cage of Spines: "To the Statue": *To Mix with Time*. "Seven Natural Songs": *More Poems to Solve*. "A Lake Scene," "Waiting for It," "Death, Great Smoothener," "An Extremity," "Frontispiece," "R. F. at Bread Loaf / His Hand against a Tree," "Deciding," "Two-Part Pease Able," "Looking Uptown," "Working on Wall Street," "Water Picture," "Executions": *New & Selected Things Taking Place*. "Fountain Piece I" (titled "Fountain Piece" in *A Cage of Spines*): *New & Selected Things Taking Place*. "Cause & Effect": *New & Selected Things Taking Place* with emendations. "The Wave the Flame the Cloud and the Leopard Speak to the Mind," "The Properties," "Am I Becoming?" "Parade of Painters," "A Haunted House": Emendations.

To Mix with Time: "Night Practice": *To Mix with Time* (revised edition, 1964). "A Boy Looking at Big David": Emendation. "The Wish to Escape into Inner Space," "Death Invited," "Instead of the Camargue," "Fountains of Aix," "Above the Arno," "Pigeon Woman," "The Woods at Night," "Trinity Church, Spring" (titled "Trinity Church, Spring 1961" in *To Mix with Time*): *New & Selected Things Taking Place*. "How to Be Old": *New & Selected Things Taking Place* with emendation. "The Universe": Later typescript.

Half Sun Half Sleep: "After the Flight of Ranger VII," "At First, At Last," "A Bird's Life," "His Suicide," "In a Museum Cabinet," "In the Hair of the Night," "The Kite," "October Textures," "On Handling Some Small Shells from the Windward Islands," "Rain at Wildwood," "Spectrum Analysis," "The Wave and the Dune": Handwritten emendations. "August 19, Pad 19," "Gods | Children," "The Lightning," "Motherhood," "Naked in Borneo," "Out of the Sea, Early," "The People Wall," "Swimmers," "A City Garden in April," "To Make a Play": *New & Selected Things Taking Place*. "The Pregnant Dream," "The Watch": *More Poems to Solve*. "Of Rounds": *More Poems to Solve* with emendations. "Seated in a Plane" (titled "While Seated in a Plane" in *Half Sun Half Sleep*); "Ocean, Whale-Shaped" (originally titled "Ocean Whale-Shaped"); "Models of the Universe" (originally titled "3 Models of the Universe"): Emendation.

Iconographs: "Earth Will Not Let Go," "The DNA Molecule," "The James Bond Movie," "Feel Me," "The Lowering," "Catbird in Redbud," "Wednesday at the Waldorf," "Year of the Double Spring" (titled "The Year of the Double Spring" in *Iconographs*), "Seeing Jupiter," "The Sunbird Settles to Its Nest," "Rocky Point," "A Subject of the Waves" (originally titled "A Subject of the Waves: 1 / The Boat Stave"): *New & Selected Things Taking Place*. (To provide an indication of the original effect, this volume includes in an appendix photographic reproductions, in a reduced size, of these twelve poems as originally published in *Iconographs*.) "The Blue Bottle" (titled "A Subject of the Waves: 2 / The Blue Bottle" in *Iconographs*) and "The Stick" (titled "A Subject of the Waves: 3 / The Stick," "Five Horses" in *Iconographs*): Emendations.

New & Selected Things Taking Place: "Speed," "The North Rim," "Bronco Busting, Event #1," "October," "On Its Way": Emendations.

In Other Words: "Three White Vases," "A Day Like Rousseau's Dream," "Saguaros above Tucson," "Ahnighito," "Angels, Eagles": Emendations.

The uncollected and posthumously published poems by May Swenson included in this volume span her career. Some of these poems Swenson submitted to periodicals; others were submitted after her death by her literary executors. Swenson chose not to include any of them in her seven collections of poetry; some were included in the posthumous collections *The Love Poems* (Houghton Mifflin Company, 1991), *The Complete Poems to Solve* (Macmillan Publishing Company, 1993), *Nature: Poems Old and New* (Houghton Mifflin Company, 1994), *May Out West* (Utah State University Press, 1996), *Dear Elizabeth: Five Poems and Three Letters to Elizabeth Bishop* (Utah State University Press, 2001), and *The Complete Love Poems* (Houghton Mifflin Company, 2003); several previously unpublished poems also appeared in the collection of critical essays *Body My House: May Swenson's Work and Life* (Utah State University Press, 2006). In the following list, the poems are arranged by approximate order of composition, as determined by the research of R. R. Knudson, and each poem is followed by the source of the text used in the present volume.

Creation: *Utah Sings* (Utah Academy of Sciences, Arts and Letters, 1934). The Vain Dust: *New Orlando Poetry Anthology* (New Orlando Publishing Company, 1968). First Star: *Utah Sings* (Utah Academy of Sciences, Arts and Letters, 1934). January This Year: *New Orlando Poetry Anthology* (New Orlando Publishing Company, 1968). Goodnight: *Saturday Review of Literature* (January 21, 1958). Oblong Afternoons: *Body My House* (2006). Down to Earth: *Village Voice* (November 28, 1956). Earth Your Dancing Place: *New Orlando Poetry Anthology* (New Orlando Publishing Company, 1968). Subconscious Sea: *Nature* (1994). Who Are You I Saw Running: *New Orlando Poetry Anthology* (New Orlando Publishing Company, 1968). White Mood: *May Out West* (1996). To D. H. Lawrence: *Body My House* (2006). Like Thee, Falcon: *Rocky Mountain Review* (February 1938). The Maiden in the Grass: *Body My House* (2006). Haymaking: *Rocky Mountain Review* (Winter 1938–39). At the Ballet: *Contemporary Poetry* (1952). In Spoonfuls: *Worcester Review* 21 (2000). Jupiter Street: *Yankee* (October 1952), with later emendations. To F.: *Love Poems* (1991). Wild Water: *Love Poems* (1991). Nightly Vision: *Raven Anthology* (1945). Trinity Place: *Seventeen and One* (1943).

Asleep: *Pegasus* (Winter 1952), as "Sleep." This Is What My Love Is Thinking: *Complete Love Poems* (2003). The Sea: *Poetry* (November 1993). War Summer: *Survival* (Autumn 1950). Sunnymead: *Pegasus* (Winter 1952). Dreams and Ashes: *Love Poems* (1991). The Indivisible Incompatibles: *Love Poems* (1991). In Love Made Visible: *Ms. Magazine* (January 1991). Two Shadows Touch: *Pegasus* (Spring 1952). Stone or Flame: *Love Poems* (1991). We Arise from the Pit of Night: *Complete Love Poems* (2003). Symmetrical Companion: *Love Poems* (1991). Close-up of a Couple on a Couch: *Gulf Coast* 13 (2001). Our Forward Shadows: *Love Poems* (1991). Say You Love: *Complete Love Poems* (2003). To a Dark Girl: *Complete Love Poems* (2003).

Equilibrist: *Dallas Times Herald* (July 1, 1951). Love Sleeping: *Nature* (1994).

Standing Torso: *Kenyon Review* (Summer 1994). He: *Body My House* (2006). What I Did on a Rainy Day: *Atlantic* (November 1993). Laocoön Dream Recorded in Diary Dated 1953: Typescript (1989). Incantation: *Nature* (1994). Night before the Journey: *Love Poems* (1991). The Time Came: *Nation* (September 21, 1957), with later emendations. Alternate Hosts: *Nature* (1994). Under the Best of Circumstances: *Poetry* (November 1993). Oh, to Be a Tigress!: *The*

Wonderful Pen of May Swenson (Macmillan Publishing Company, 1993). Once Upon: *Worcester Review* 21 (2000). From a Letter to Elizabeth Bishop: *Light* (January 25, 1954), as "Child No One Knows." The Kiss: *American Poetry Review* (September/October 1994). Something Goes By: *American Poetry Review* (September 1994). Facing: *Love Poems* (1991). Her Management II: *Body My House* (2006). Logs in the Grate: *Yale Review* (January 1993). East River, February: *Saturday Review of Literature* (July 5, 1958). As Long Ago As Far Away: *Lynx* 4 (1963). Thursday Thoughts of a Poet: *Quarterly West* (Fall 1998). My Farm: *Poetry Northwest* (Winter 1960). Annual: *Love Poems* (1991). Feeling Sorry: *Princeton University Library Chronicle* 55.3 (1994). Lying and Looking: *Nature* (1994). Listening to Strauss and Stroking an Autumn-Colored Cat: *American Voice* 45 (1998). Coda to J.: *Complete Love Poems* (2003). Not the Dress: *Nation* (February 1998). Walking with Louis: *Body My House* (2006).

The Winepress: *Yale Review* (July 1998). The Many Christs: *Weber Studies* (Spring 1991). The Truth Is Forced: *Nature* (1994). Cabala: *New York Times* (June 23, 1963). Somebody Who's Somebody: *Dear Elizabeth* (2001). My Poems: *Nation* (January 15, 1993). I Look at an Old Photo of Myself with Love: *The Face of Poetry* (1979). The Seed of My Father: *May Out West* (1996). The Pouch-Flower: *Worcester Review* 21 (2000). That One: *Ms. Magazine* (January 1991). On Lighting the Fire: *New York Times Book of Verse* (1970). Daffodildo: *Nature* (1994). Yes, the Mystery: *Nature* (1994). Weather: *Nation* (January 15, 1993). You Start Out Across: *Worcester Review* 21 (2000). The Lone Pedestrian: *American Voice* 42 (1997). LBJ on TV: *Light* 21 (Summer 1998). Horse: *Nation* (January 15, 1993). Tell Me: *American Poetry Review* (July/August 2007). Stripping and Putting On: *New Yorker* (October 22, 1990). Picasso: "Dream." Oil. 1932: *Chelsea* (1972). Overview: *May Out West* (1996). Skopus: *Nature* (1994). You Are: *Love Poems* (1991).

The Waves Are Making Waves: *Body My House* (2006). Part and Whole: *Alpha* 1.4 (1970). This Is That: *Worcester Review* 21 (2000). Celebration: Bookmark for American Library Association (November 1971). Evening Wind: *Measure* (1973). The Animals of the Ark: *Worcester Review* 21 (2000). Staring at the Sea on the Day of the Death of Another: *New Yorker* (November 12, 1990). Found in Diary Dated May 29, 1973: *Worcester Review* 21 (2000). In Progress: *Poetry* (November 1993). Walking in the Village after Many Years: *Buffalo News* (November 2, 1980). Once There Were Glaciers: *Nation* (April 4, 1994). Like a Lady: *Light* 17 (1996). Manyone Flying: *Nature* (1994). Because I Don't Know: *Love Poems* (1991). Assuming the Lotus: *American Poetry Review* (September/October 1994). Who Had the First Word?: *Worcester Review* 21 (2000). Moisture, Warmth and Light: *Worcester Review* 21 (2000). In Iowa: A Primitive Painting:

Body My House (2006). The Fortune Cookie: *Worcester Review* 2 (2000).

The Most Important: *Poetry* (November 1993). The Rest of My Life: *Poetry* (February 1988; poems include Sleeping Alone, A Spring Morning, Unable to Write It, What Matters, The Rest of My Life, I'm One Cat and I: *Worcester Review* 21 (2000). Mickey's Pillow: *Light* (1985. The Fluffy Stuff: *Nation* (April 25, 1994). Mind: *Worcester Review* 2 (2000). Third Floor Walk-Up: *Poetry* (October 1987). Last Day: *New Yorker* (December 31, 1990). A Tree in Spring: *Beloit Poetry Journal* (Summer 1990). My Name Was Called: *New Yorker* (June 13, 1988. The Hole Seen: *Light* (1987–88). Kiwi: *Weber Studies* (Spring 1991. Good Things Come from Thee: *Love Poems* (1991; poems include On the Cliff and By the Canal). Beginning Ended: *Poetry* (November 1993). Look Closer: *New Yorker* (December 12, 1988). The Snowy: *Atlantic* (February 1990). Memory of the Future? Prophecy of the Past?: *New Yorker* (April 1, 1991). A Rescue: *Ploughshares* 15.4 (1990. Guilty: *Nation* (January 24, 1993). Night Visits with the Family II *Parnassus* (Summer 1990). Dear John: *A Garland for John Hollander* (1989). Woman in a Garden: *Parnassus* (Summer 1990). A Clear Night on Mt. Hopkins: *Parnassus* (Summer 1990).

This volume concludes with a brief selection of Swenson's prose writings about poetry: "A Poem Happens to Me": Written mid-1950s. May Swenson Papers at the Washington University Libraries. Printed with the permission of the Literary Estate of May Swenson. "Poet's Choice": Introductory remarks to a reading of her poetry given at The New School for Social Research in Manhattan, March 9, 1960. Typescript provided by the Literary Estate of May Swenson. "The Poet as Antispecialist": *Saturday Review of Literature*, January 30, 1965; reprinted with the permission of the Literary Estate of May Swenson. "A Clue or Two": Preface to *Poems to Solve* (1966). "A Note about *Iconographs*": Afterword to *Iconographs* (1970).

This volume presents the texts of the original printings of May Swenson's poems chosen for inclusion here except for later emendations made by the author. In all cases the author's final version of a poem serves as the copy-text. The author herself corrected typographical errors on the master file copies of her poems. These changes and others are noted above. The texts are presented here without further changes. Spelling, punctuation, and capitalization are often expressive features and have not been altered, even when inconsistent or irregular. The following is a list of typographical errors corrected, cited by page and line number: 12.31, tatooed; 30.23, ecstacies; 43.14, forego 44.29, whitness; 51.1, irridescent; 51.31, it's chimney; 56.20, sibilent 82.21, curse?; 109.26, Roualt; 111.28, Vuilliard; 165.9, cemetary; 199.20

axiel; 253.19, phragmitie; 275.11, its; 305.28, lavendar; 338.6, Guiness; 343.1, its; 346.17, symdrom; 397.30, peddling; 460.9, wheeels; 512.12, Banyon; 516.5, foreword; 516.27, dessicated; 521.27, dustbull; 538.9, lingerlingly; 579.8, births; 615.17, halucinogenic; 666.14, Manhattanhite; 673.5, at very; 674.37, give.

Notes

Before she died in 1989, May Swenson had begun to send some of her manuscripts and correspondence to the Olin Library at Washington University in St. Louis, Missouri. However, the bulk of her correspondence with publishers, drafts of her poems, and letters to friends and associates still lay in stacks and file cabinets in the New York home she shared with her partner of over twenty years, the novelist R. R. Knudson. It remained for Knudson, Swenson's first literary executor, to expertly organize the papers, bring attention to the unpublished poems, and help define the character and describe the development of this twentieth-century American poet. A private person, Swenson rarely spoke publicly of her upbringing, her struggle for recognition, and her intense loves and great disappointments, and as a result there is little detailed information published about her life. Knudson's intimate pictorial biography, *May Swenson: A Poet's Life in Photos*, is the primary source for the Chronology and the biographical information in the Notes in this volume.

In the notes below, the reference numbers denote page and line of this volume (the line count includes titles and headings). No note is made for material included in standard desk-reference books such as Webster's *Collegiate*, *Biographical*, and *Geographical* dictionaries. For further background and writing by and about the author, see the biographical essays by R. R. Knudson, *The Wonderful Pen of May Swenson* (New York: Macmillan, 1993), and R. R. Knudson and Suzanne Bigelow, with a foreword by Richard Wilbur, *May Swenson: A Poet's Life in Photos* (Logan: Utah State University Press, 1996); the collection of May Swenson's fiction and prose, *Made With Words*, ed. Gardner McFall (Ann Arbor: University of Michigan Press, 1998); May Swenson, *Dear Elizabeth: Five Poems and Three Letters*, afterword by Kirstin Hotelling Zona (Logan: Utah State University Press, 2000); and the chronology, bibliography, and biographical and critical essays in *Body My House: May Swenson's Work and Life*, eds. Paul Crumbley and Patricia Gantt (Logan: Utah State University Press, 2006).

ANOTHER ANIMAL

12.1   *Spring in the Square*] Washington Square Park, New York City.

13.24   *The Garden at St. John's*] St. John's Episcopal Church, 224 Waverly Place, New York City. The terrace at the back of Swenson's apartment at 23 Perry Street in Greenwich Village overlooked the garden of this church.

22.2   Isis] Ancient Egyptian goddess associated with nature and magic; the mother of Horus, god of war; and, symbolically, mother of the Pharaoh.

29.16   the pranks of Zeus] Disguised as a swan, Zeus raped Leda, and as a bull, he raped Europa.

A CAGE OF SPINES

67.21   Einstein] Albert Einstein (1879–1955), German-born theoretical physicist. Poem written shortly after Einstein's death.

96.24   Daniel bared] Cf. Daniel 6.

99.1   *Am I Becoming?*] Swenson, herself an artist, was a model for a number
of New York painters, including Hans Bohler in the 1930s and Hyde Solomon,
Bernard Rosenquit, and Beauford Delaney in the 1950s, who were her friends.

102.19   *Frontispiece*] A frontispiece portrait of the novelist and woman of letters Virginia Woolf ("your chaste-fierce name"). Incorporates multiple references to Woolf's life and work: "that water-haunted house" is Talland House
in St. Ives, Cornwall, where Woolf spent summers in childhood; "the layered
light / your socket lips and nostrils drank / before they sank" refers to Woolf's
suicide by drowning in 1941; and additional phrases recall the titles of novels
by Woolf: *The Voyage Out* (1915), *To the Lighthouse* (1927), *Orlando* (1928), *The
Waves* (1931), *The Years* (1937), and *Between the Acts* (1941).

103.16   *R. F. at Bread Loaf His Hand Against a Tree*] Swenson met Robert
Frost when, as the Robert Frost Fellow, she attended the Bread Loaf Writers'
Conference in Middlebury, Vermont, in summer 1957. Incorporates references
to Frost's person and his poems, including in the last line ("g lad as the c limb
of youth"), an allusion to Frost's poem "Birches."

118.19   *To the Statue*] The Statue of Liberty in New York Harbor.

120.17   *At East River*] The East River separates Manhattan from Queens and
Brooklyn.

125.17   *The Tide at Long Point*] Long Point is a peninsula at the far end of Cape
Cod, Massachusetts, that curves to create Provincetown Harbor.

TO MIX WITH TIME

148.6   Palomar] The Palomar Observatory at the California Institute of Technology in the mountains west of San Diego.

158.27   *Instead of the Camargue*] Delta and wetland, a prime habitat for birds
including flamingos, which is formed when the Rhône divides into two arms
that flow into the Mediterranean Sea.

158.31   Fos-sur-Mer] Ancient town to the east of the Camargue, on the Mediterranean, with a tenth-century Romanesque church, Saint Sauveur. Although
today a major industrial site, Fos-sur-Mer was a fishing village when Swenson
visited.

160.30   *"Ici repose Maman . . . Dieu"*] French: "Here Mother rests in the
arms of God."

161.17   *"A Notre Fils . . . A Notre Fille"*] French: "To our son: He is gone like
a cloud, like a rapid stream in its course, and our hearts keep his image always."

"To our daughter: You who departed like a cloud carrying to heaven our love, our hearts will keep your image always."

162.30–32 *"Ici Repose Le Gendarme Pierre . . . 1752"*] French: "Here rests the policeman Pierre Pecot, Killed by a Poacher, 1752."

163.16 Etang de Berre] Lagoon near Fos-sur-Mer, to the east of the Camargue.

163.17 mistral] Strong cold and dry wind that sweeps the region of the Camargue from the northwest.

163.18–19 an environ of Van Gogh] Vincent van Gogh lived in Arles (1888–1889), a few miles north of Fos-sur-Mer, and painted in the region; sunflowers and wheat fields, mentioned by Swenson, were among his subjects. In 1889–90 van Gogh was a patient in the asylum at Saint-Rémy-de-Provence outside of Arles.

163.29 nearing Aix] Aix-en-Provence, also to the east of the Camargue, Roman colony, Provençal cultural capital, and home of the painter Paul Cézanne.

164.7 Cézanne's mountain, Saint-Victoire] Montagne Saint-Victoire was a frequent subject of Cézanne, particularly in his late work.

164.19–20 *"Au lieu de se tasser . . . l'air ample."*] French: "Rather than settle down, immense and wild, she breathes in the blue of the ample air."

164.29 Cours Mirabeau] Cézanne was born at 55 Cours Mirabeau in Aix-en-Provence.

164.32 *taureaux*] French: bulls.

165.13 *Fountains of Aix*] In a region where water is scarce, Aix-en-Provence was settled near natural springs, and is known for its many fountains built in public squares, some of which date from as early as the seventeenth century.

166.10 *The Alyscamps at Arles*] Burial ground at Arles established in the Roman era; subject of paintings by Paul Gauguin, Paul Cézanne, and Vincent van Gogh.

168.1 *Above the Arno*] The River Arno divides the city of Florence in Tuscany, Italy.

168.24–25 PERICOLO! . . . BAGNARSI.] Italian: Danger: Swimming Prohibited.

169.6 Giotto's Tower] The artist and architect Giotto designed and began the building of the bell tower of Santa Maria del Fiore, the Duomo, in Florence in 1334.

169.7 Brunelleschi's Dome] In the mid-fifteenth century, Filippo Brunelleschi designed and built the dome of Santa Maria del Fiore, the largest structure of its kind built since antiquity.

169.9 Palazzo Vecchio] Town hall of Florence, built in the early fourteenth century.

169.10   the Apennines] Mountain range running north-south in the center of the Italian peninsula.

170.16   della Robbia blue] Andrea della Robbia (1435–1525), Florentine sculptor known for his ceramic reliefs with blue background glaze.

170.24   Botticelli's Venus] Sandro Botticelli's painting *The Birth of Venus* (1486).

170.27   *Big David*] Michelangelo's marble sculpture of David (1501–4) in the Accademia Gallery in Florence.

171.25   Piazza San Marco] The main public square in Venice, Italy, outside St. Mark's Basilica. This poem refers to several sculptures on the square. On the porch of the Basilica are four bronze horses from Greek antiquity, taken from the Hippodrome at Constantinople when that city was sacked in 1204. On top of a column at the open end of the piazza is a bronze winged lion, symbol of St. Mark and Venice. On another column stands a statue of St. Theodore, patron saint of Venice prior to St. Mark.

173.21   *The Pantheon, Rome*] The Roman temple of the gods, dedicated by consul Marcus Agrippa in 27 B.C., rebuilt by Emperor Hadrian in A.D. 126, and converted to a Christian church by Pope Boniface IV in the seventh century. Raphael, the Renaissance Italian painter, is buried there.

175.2   Lombardy, Tuscany, Umbria, Calabria] Four of the twenty regions of Italy, named in order running north to south.

175.14   *the Tuileries*] Public garden in central Paris.

183.18   I thought of Rilke] The German poet Rainer Maria Rilke (1875–1926) wrote the letter quoted here on July 4, 1911, after seeing Vaslav Nijinsky dance in *Le Spectre de la Rose*, a dance based on a poem by Théophile Gautier.

186.25   *A Fixture*] Poem written after shopping at Bloomingdale's in Manhattan.

187.25   *Riding the "A"*] The "A" is one of the subway lines on the west side of Manhattan.

188.34   *Public Library*] New York Public Library on Fifth Avenue between 40th and 42nd streets.

191.1   *De Chirico*] Giorgio de Chirico (1888–1978), Italian painter.

194.19   *Southbound on the Freeway*] Written in heavy traffic on the Garden State Parkway, New Jersey.

197.22   *Trinity Churchyard*] Episcopal church and burial ground at the intersection of Broadway and Wall Street in Lower Manhattan, established in 1697.

198.21   *The Totem*] The Empire State Building on Fifth Avenue in Manhattan.

203.1 *Jamaica Bay*] Estuary located near the southwestern tip of Long Island in Brooklyn and Queens. Jamaica Bay Wildlife Refuge is a prime bird-watching location.

205.16 amnion] Membrane that encloses the fetus of a mammal, bird, or reptile.

HALF SUN HALF SLEEP

214.1 *For J.*] Swenson's companion, Pearl Schwartz.

215.18 *Ranger VII*] U.S. spacecraft that transmitted images of the surface of the moon in July 1964.

216.19 Tycho Copernicus Kepler] Three astronomers: Tycho Brahe (1546–1601), Nicolaus Copernicus (1473–1543), and Johannes Kepler (1571–1630).

219.10 *At Truro*] Town near the tip of Cape Cod, Massachusetts, site of Cape Cod National Seashore.

226.12 if you are Alice] In Lewis Carroll's *Through the Looking-Glass, and What Alice Found There* (1871).

228.26 scotomata] Area of diminished vision within normal vision.

229.13 iridium] Second densest chemical element, a hard, silvery metal.

229.15 *Dear Elizabeth*] Bishop described these birds to Swenson in letters from Rio de Janeiro dated August 27, 1963, and October 12, 1963. Swenson wrote to Bishop on June 30, 1965, to ask for her permission to use quotations from her letters in the poem before publishing it in the *New Yorker*. Swenson added the note explaining that the poem replies to Bishop, with Bishop's permission, at the suggestion of Howard Moss, poetry editor of the *New Yorker*.

231.33 demijohn] Large wine bottle or jug, glass or earthenware, with a narrow neck.

251.2 *(From a painting by Tobias)*] Tobias Schneebaum (1922–2005), American artist and anthropologist.

256.27 A gift from N.B. and D.E.] Nell Blaine, American painter, and Dilys Evans, British children's book author and illustrator.

262.23 *Wildwood*] Wildwood State Park on the north shore of Long Island.

265.5 *Provincetown*] Town and artists' colony on the northern tip of Cape Cod.

274.16 *The Tall Figures of Giacometti*] Alberto Giacometti (1901–1966), Swiss sculptor, known for his upright and dramatically elongated bronze figures.

276.8 the mess down South] Reference to racial discrimination and the Civil Rights movement in the United States.

296.5 Icarus] In Greek myth, flew too close to the sun on wings made b his father Daedalus, causing the wax in the wings to melt and Icarus to fall t his death.

296.6 The Wright Aeroplane of 1903] Orville and Wilbur Wright, America inventors, built and flew the first successful airplane in 1903.

296.20 the Cabin of the Spirit] Charles Lindbergh (1902–1974) flew th *Spirit of St. Louis* across the Atlantic Ocean in 1927.

297.2 John Glenn] First U.S. astronaut to orbit Earth aboard *Friendship* in 1962.

297.19 The Nude Descending] "Nude Descending a Staircase, No. 2," o painting (1912) by Marcel Duchamp (1887–1968).

299.11 noösphere] The sphere of human thought that succeeds the geospher and biosphere in an evolutionary process, according to theories elaborated b Vladimir Vernadsky and Teilhard de Chardin. From the Greek *nous* or mind with a pun in this context on the French title of Marcel Duchamp's painting (*Nu descendant un escalier*).

304.9 The Mobile is by Jose de Rivera] "Infinity" (1967), rotating abstrac sculpture by American sculptor Jose de Rivera (1904–1985), mounted outsid the National Museum of American History.

304.11 *the Turbojet* Electra] Lockheed-built commercial American aircraft Fatal crashes of the earlier turboprop model in 1959 and 1960 led to desig modifications.

304.27–28 St. Louis and the Gateway / to the West] The Gateway Arch in St Louis, tallest monument in the United States, completed in 1965.

307.2 "Feel me to do right"] Last words of Dan Arthur Swenson, the poet' father, spoken to her sister Margaret.

311.25 Was St. Peter buried] On June 26, 1958, Pope Paul VI declared tha the relics of St. Peter had been identified by archaeologists investigating a sit beneath St. Peter's Basilica in Rome.

316.24–25 For Martin Luther King / April 4, 1968] Dr. Martin Luther King African American civil rights leader, was assassinated on April 4, 1968, in Mem phis, Tennessee.

317.1 *The Lowering*] Senator Robert F. Kennedy was assassinated on June 6 1968, and buried two days later in Arlington National Cemetery in Virginia.

320.2 *Paul Goodman's poem*] Goodman published "For a Young Widow" in the *New York Review of Books* (September 14, 1967).

332.34 two raffish child-angels] This familiar image by Raphael (1483–1520) is a detail from the Sistine Madonna (1513–14).

334.1   *A Trellis for R.*] R. R. Knudson, the poet's partner.

335.1   *the Waldorf*] Waldorf-Astoria, luxury hotel in New York City.

335.27–28   Pan Am / roof] The Pan Am Building, now the MetLife Building, is located on Park Avenue in New York City. When it opened in 1963, it was the largest commercial office tower in the world, with helicopter service to New York airports.

335.31–32   "There's / a kind of hush world."] Hit song for the band Herman's Hermits in 1967.

336.10   L.I.R.R.'s four cars] Long Island Rail Road.

337.25–26   *When Something's Wrong / With My Baby*] "When Something's Wrong with My Baby," song (1967) recorded by Sam and Dave.

337.29   It's Accabonac now] Accabonac Harbor in East Hampton on Long Island is a tidal marsh region known to bird-watchers.

337.30   Tippecanoe] Tippecanoe River, Indiana.

338.6   *The Maidstone*] Maidstone Inn, East Hampton, Long Island.

348.1–5   *Fire Island*] Barrier island on the south shore of Long Island.

351.24   *Rocky Point*] Town on the north shore of Long Island.

354.2   *R. R. K.*] R. R. Knudson.

358.23   *The North Rim*] Of the Grand Canyon.

360.20   *Madera Canyon*] Near Tucson, Arizona, a prime bird-watching spot.

361.23   rebozo] Scarf or shawl worn by women in Mexico.

362.19   *St. Augustine-by-the-Sea*] St. Augustine, city on the Atlantic coast of Florida.

364.10   *Long Pine*] Long Pine Key, Florida.

364.22   *Sea Cliff*] Sea Cliff, on Long Island's north shore, Swenson's home.

366.13   *Shu Swamp*] Nature preserve near Oyster Bay, on the north shore of Long Island.

367.10   my house] At 73 The Boulevard, Sea Cliff.

370.2   the Library Lions] Bronze lions standing on either side of the entrance to the New York Public Library.

370.24   *Ed's Place*] American poet Edward Field (b. 1924), longtime resident of Greenwich Village and author of the memoir *The Man Who Would Marry Susan Sontag, and Other Intimate Literary Portraits of the Bohemian Era* (2006), which mentions Swenson.

371.17   Sea—of Tranquility] Region on the moon.

372.20   *the Whitney*] The Whitney Museum of American Art on Madison Avenue in New York City.

372.36   by Arp] Jean Arp (1886–1966), French-German painter and sculptor.

375.16   yoni] Sanskrit word for the vagina.

376.11   symphysis] Cartilaginous fusion of bones.

378.19   *The Naked Ape*] Subtitled *A Zoologist's Study of the Human Animal* by Desmond Morris (1967).

383.1   *Watching the Jets Lose to Buffalo at Shea*] The New York Jets and the Buffalo Bills in the National Football League playing at Shea Stadium in Queens, New York.

385.5   *Addy Road*] 13 Addy Road, Bethany Beach, Delaware, address of home owned by the Knudson family.

393.10   *Bear Lake*] In Utah where Swenson camped with Edith Welch.

397.1   *Night Visits with the Family I*] Mentions Swenson's brothers Paul, Roy, and Dan, Paul's wife Sharon, and Swenson's sisters Margaret and Grace.

399.17   rugous] Wrinkled, creased.

415.2   *(For E.W.)*] Edith Welch, close friend of Swenson during school.

420.15   crashed LMs] Lunar landing modules.

425.23   *Nanook*] *Nanook of the North* (1922), a documentary film by Robert Flaherty follows the life of an Inuit man and his family in the Canadian Arctic.

439.2   *Ventriloquist*] Edgar Bergen (1903–1978), an American entertainer and ventriloquist, was the son of Swedish immigrants. Bergen operated a wooden dummy named Charlie McCarthy.

441.20   Teddy Himself] Theodore Roosevelt (1858–1919), U.S. president, known for leading cavalry, his "Rough Riders," into battle in the Spanish-American War, for whom the popular stuffed animal was named. Sagamore Hill, Roosevelt's home, is close to Sea Cliff, Swenson's home.

449.27   this rough little cabin] At Dorland Mountain Colony, a writers' and artists' retreat, in Temecula, California, where the author was in residence in 1980.

452.1   *Point Dume*] Promontory on the Pacific coast in Malibu, California.

453.4   *Rousseau's* Dream] *The Dream*, a painting (1910) by Henri Rousseau.

458.1   *Shuttles*] The U.S. Space Shuttle program, 1981–2011, reused spacecraft for manned space exploration, launched from Cape Canaveral in Florida.

458.5   Dan Rather] *CBS News* anchorman (b. 1931).

463.1   *Indian Key*] Uninhabited island in the Florida Keys.

463.4   Halley's Comet] Comet visible from Earth every 75–76 years. A "Dirty Snowball," it consists of dust and other materials—water, carbon dioxide, ammonia—in frozen and gaseous states.

463.18–19   Aldebaran / and Betelgeuse] Red giant star in the constellation of Taurus, and a star in the constellation of Orion, two of the brightest stars.

463.24   *Ahnighito*] Inuit name, meaning "The Tent," for a massive fragment of the Cape York iron meteorite, now on exhibit in the American Museum of Natural History in New York City.

464.17–18   Remus and / Romulus] Twin sons of Mars, suckled by a wolf; after killing Remus, Romulus founded Rome.

469.12   *For Elizabeth Bishop (1911–1979)*] Bishop died suddenly at home in Boston, of an aneurysm in the brain, on October 6, 1979. Swenson and Bishop had been close friends since meeting in 1950 but they rarely saw each other over that period and maintained their friendship through correspondence.

471.1   *Her Early Work*] Elizabeth Bishop's, including her poem "A Word with You" (1933).

471.31   Jacob hugs his angel] Cf. Genesis 32.

473.15   *Leonard Baskin*] American sculptor and printmaker (1922–2000), known particularly for his images of birds of prey and other winged creatures.

473.16   *The Elect*] American Academy of Arts and Letters, founded in 1904, on West 155th Street in New York City. Swenson was inducted into the National Institute of Arts and Letters, part of the American Academy, in 1970.

478.16   *The Wildcat*] *The Daily Wildcat*, student newspaper of the University of Arizona.

479.16   Rincons] The Rincon Mountains, east of Tucson, Arizona.

480.1   St. Louis] Washington University in St. Louis.

482.1–2   Manhattan's / Grungy downtown campus] New York University.

482.28   *The Bruin*] UCLA student newspaper.

482.32   *Howl*] Allen Ginsberg's poem (1956).

482.33   *Hair*] Musical (1967).

482.38   MOLE PEOPLE] People living in abandoned urban public spaces underground.

483.15   Gandhi in his dhoti] Mohandas K. Gandhi (1869–1948), nonviolent leader of Indian independence, commonly wore a traditional garment for an Indian man, a rectangular cloth wrapped around the legs and knotted at the waist.

483.22   Like Billy Budd] Hero of Herman Melville's novella *Billy Budd* (1888–91), a sailor of great innocence and natural charm who is persecuted by his superior, John Claggart; when Claggart makes false charges against him, Billy strikes him dead.

483.31   Majority Morals] The Moral Majority was a political organization on the Christian Right that was prominent in the 1980s.

499.1   *Banyan*] Species of fig tree, the national tree of India. A massive banyan tree is a feature of Coconut Grove, Florida, and the largest banyan tree in the United States is in Fort Myers, Florida; Swenson and Knudson visited both places.

499.2   *When "Beestes and briddes . . . and synge"*] From Geoffrey Chaucer, "The Nun's Priest's Tale," *The Canterbury Tales.*

505.38–506.1   "Let us go now, you and I!"] See "Let us go then, you and I," the first line of "The Love Song of J. Alfred Prufrock," T. S. Eliot's poem (1917).

506.20   "Whether thou choose Cervantes' . . . easy chair"] Alexander Pope, *The Dunciad* (1728), Book I, line 19.

507.4–5   "The fruit of . . . mortal taste"] John Milton, *Paradise Lost* (1667), Book I, lines 1–2.

511.12–14   "Why / or which . . . of Swat?"] Edward Lear, "The Akond of Swat" (1871).

511.18–20   "There's a porpoise . . . my tail."] Lewis Carroll, *Alice's Adventures in Wonderland* (1865).

513.21–22   "All things counter . . . freckled"] Gerard Manley Hopkins, "Pied Beauty" (1877).

514.3   "Who lives everywhere . . . nowhere,"] Martial, Epigrams, VII.73 (c. A.D. 80–104).

514.4   "My purpose holds . . . the sunset,"] Alfred Lord Tennyson, "Ulysses," lines 60–61 (1842).

514.18–19   "Learn of the green world . . . place."] Ezra Pound, *Canto LXXXI*, lines 145–46 (1948).

514.22–24   "The true way . . . ground."] Franz Kafka, *The Fürau Aphorisms* (1917–18).

534.20   *To D. H. Lawrence*] English novelist, poet, and man of letters (1885–1930), an influence on Swenson.

541.1   *To F.*] Anca Vrbovska.

541.6–7   Your bus will stop . . . Square] Christopher Street and Abingdon Square are in Greenwich Village, New York City.

542.23   *Trinity Place*] Street running from north to south in Lower Manhattan, past Trinity Church and its burial ground.

564.26   *Laocoön*] Trojan priest of Poseidon who warned Troy not to accept the wooden horse given to the city by the Greeks, and was strangled by sea serpents sent by Athena as a result. Swenson wrote a first draft of this poem in 1943. She went back to work on it not long before her death in 1989.

572.18–19   *From a Letter to Elizabeth Bishop*] A letter from Swenson to Bishop, January 25, 1954.

574.15   My dad made it] Dan Arthur Swenson, the poet's father, a skilled woodworker who made toys and furniture for his family and built their house at 669 East 500 North Street, Logan, Utah.

585.11   *Listening to Strauss*] German composer Richard Strauss (1864–1949).

585.26   *Coda to J.*] Pearl Schwartz.

587.1   *Walking with Louis*] Louis Untermeyer (1885–1977), American poet and popular anthologist, known for his wit and wordplay; his anthology, *A Treasury of Great Poems* (1942; rev. ed. 1955), included Swenson's work.

590.1   *The Many Christs*] Swenson began work on this poem after her trip to Europe in 1961 and completed it in 1986.

590.4   El Greco's Christ] El Greco (1541–1614), Greek-born painter of the Spanish Renaissance.

590.10   Michelangelo's Christ] The Pietà (1498–99) by the Italian artist Michelangelo (1475–1564).

590.14   Cocteau's Christ] Jean Cocteau (1889–1963), French writer, film-maker, and artist, decorated a Romanesque church, La Chapelle St. Pierre in Villefranche-sur-Mer, in 1956–57.

590.18   Matisse made Christ] French artist Henri Matisse (1869–1954) super-vised the decoration of La Chapelle du Rosaire de Vence, including a wall representing the Stations of the Cross.

590.32   Black Christ of Barcelona] The Cristo de Lepanto, from a ship that fought against the Ottomans in the Battle of Lepanto (1571), in the Cathedral of the Holy Cross and St. Eulalia.

591.19–20   The carver, Ordonez] Bartolomé Ordóñez (c. 1480–1520), *St Eula-lia on the Bonfire*, carved relief in the choir, Barcelona cathedral (1519).

595.7   Elizabeth's liver] Reference to Elizabeth Bishop's alcoholism. Swenson met Bishop in 1950 at Yaddo, which, like the racetrack mentioned in this poem, is in Saratoga Springs, New York.

602.11   Emily's lot] The poet Emily Dickinson (1830–1886) is buried in West Cemetery, Amherst, Massachusetts, near her family home. Her gravestone is inscribed with the phrase "Called Back," a quotation from perhaps Dickinson's last letter, addressed to her cousins Louise and Frances Norcross.

603.3–5 "I'm / nobody! . . . you?"] "I'm Nobody! Who are you?" Poem 260 in *The Poems of Emily Dickinson*, Ralph W. Franklin, ed. (Cambridge, Mass.: The Belknap Press of Harvard University Press, 1998).

604.2 "An awe came on the trinket,"] "A Clock stopped," Poem 259, *Poems of Emily Dickinson* (1998).

604.11–14 "I dwell in Possibility . . . Prose."] "I dwell in Possibility - ," Poem 466, *Poems of Emily Dickinson* (1998).

604.23–27 "A word is dead . . . that day."] "A word is dead, when it is said," Poem 278, *Poems of Emily Dickinson* (1998).

605.19–26 "Disdaining men . . . my stem."] "Of Bronze - and Blaze - ," Poem 319, *Poems of Emily Dickinson* (1998).

608.16 Lafayette] Lafayette, Indiana, on the Wabash River.

608.28–29 The Smothers / Brothers] Tom and Dick Smothers, American singers and comedians. *The Smothers Brothers Comedy Hour* ran on CBS television (1967–69).

613.21 *LBJ on TV*] Lyndon Baines Johnson (1908–1973), U.S. president (1963–69).

614.1 DeGaulle] Charles de Gaulle (1890–1970), French general and president (1959–69).

625.26–27 Letters . . . World] See "This is my letter to the World," Poem 519, *Poems of Emily Dickinson* (1998).

626.14 *Laurence Stapleton*] Professor of English at Bryn Mawr College, author of *Marianne Moore: The Poet's Advance* (1978).

626.15 "Still falls the rain"] Poem by Edith Sitwell about the German bombing of London in 1940.

653.11 Zabar's] Gourmet food and kosher deli on the Upper West Side in New York City.

666.10 *Dear John*] John Hollander (b. 1929), American poet, scholar, critic, and editor. His many books include a collection of shape poems, *Types of Shape* (1969), and *Rhyme's Reason: A Guide to English Verse* (1981).

666.32 full Bloom] Harold Bloom (b. 1930), American critic.

666.34 Knopf's new Ford] Harry Ford (1919–1999), American editor.

667.23 De Kooning] Willem de Kooning (1904–1997), Dutch-born American abstract expressionist painter.

668.9 *Mt. Hopkins*] Whipple Observatory on Mt. Hopkins in the Santa Rita Mountains, Arizona.

POET'S CHOICE

677.16–17   "As the starved maelstrom . . ."] "As the Starved Maelstrom laps the Navies," Poem 1064, *Poems of Emily Dickinson* (1998).

THE POET AS ANTISPECIALIST

678.17–21   "the thinking of the body"] From Yeats's essay, "The Thinking of the Body" (1907).

683.17–18   "All space . . . those kernels."] Rilke, "The Domes of the Caliphs' Tombs" (1907).

682.39   "doors of perception"] William Blake, *The Marriage of Heaven and Hell* (1790–93): "If the doors of perception were cleansed everything would appear to man as it is, infinite."

683.37–40   "The world is poetical . . . of its existence."] From *Literature and Science* (1963) by Aldous Huxley, English writer with interests in parapsychology and mysticism.

684.33–685–5   shows us . . . himself.] Werner Heisenberg (1901–1976) in *Reality and Its Order* (1942).

685.13–28   "Infinity, when all things . . . did doe."] "Preface" from *God's Determinations and Preparatory Meditations* (c. 1680).

686.16   Huizinga] Johan Huizinga (1872–1945), Dutch cultural historian, who wrote *Homo Ludens: A Study of the Play-Element in Culture* (1938).

687.12–18   We might come to believe . . . make it *move*] Ezra Pound, "The Serious Artist" (1913).

687.20–37   The whole thing is . . . faculties.] Ezra Pound, "The Serious Artist" (1913).

Index of Titles and First Lines

THE LIBRARY OF AMERICA SERIES

THE LIBRARY OF AMERICA, a nonprofit publisher, is dedicated to publishing, and keeping in print, authoritative editions of America's best and most significant writing. Each year the Library adds new volumes to its collection of essential works by America's foremost novelists, poets, essayists, journalists, and statesmen.

If you would like to request a free catalog and find out more about The Library of America, please visit www.loa.org/catalog or send us an e-mail at lists@loa.org with your name and address. Include your e-mail address if you would like to receive our occasional newsletter with items of interest to readers of classic American literature and exclusive interviews with Library of America authors and editors (we will never share your e-mail address).

To subscribe to the series or to order individual copies, please visit www.loa.org or call (800) 964.5778.

*This book is set in 10 point ITC Galliard Pro, a
face designed for digital composition by Matthew Carter
and based on the sixteenth-century face Granjon. The paper
is acid-free lightweight opaque and meets the requirements for
permanence of the American National Standards Institute.
The binding material is Brillianta, a woven rayon cloth
made by Van Heek–Scholco Textielfabrieken, Holland.
Composition by David Bullen Design. Printing and
binding by Edwards Brothers Malloy, Ann Arbor.
Designed by Bruce Campbell.*